Rickover Uncensored

Edited by

Claude Berube, PhD

Samuel Limneos, MA

Library of Congress Cataloging-in-Publication Data
Berube, Claude, 1966- and Limneos, Samuel, 1989-

ISBN (Hardback): 979-8-9860857-3-9
ISBN (Paperback): 979-8-9860857-4-6
ISBN (eBook): 979-8-9860857-5-3

1. Rickover, Hyman George. 2. Admirals – United States – Biography. 3 United States Navy – Biography.

Printed in the United States of America.

Cover and back cover photos: From the Rickover Collection, with permission from the U.S. Naval Academy Museum

In memory of Captain Robert Denbigh, USN

Contents

Introduction.. 1

Notes about the Collection.. 11

1930s.. 21

1940s.. 173

1950s.. 203

1960s.. 243

1970s.. 289

1980s.. 385

Editor Biographies 501

Acknowledgements.. 503

Introduction

By Claude Berube, PhD

No admiral cast a longer shadow on the U.S. Navy and national security than Hyman G. Rickover. Even as this is written, nearly four decades after his death, most naval officers will know his name and the legacy he left on the nuclear-powered Navy. Unlike most other Navy admirals whose names have faded from the public consciousness, the name Rickover is still remembered. Although he never served as the commander of a carrier strike group, as a combatant commander, or as the Chief of Naval Operations, in his more than sixty-year career, he amassed and wielded unprecedented power and more influence than any of his contemporaries. Rickover transcended the Navy; otherwise, he never could have created the nuclear submarine force, which helped win a Cold War in deterring a great power and which continues to play a prominent role in the uncertainties of the 21st century. Arguably, no one else could have built the force so quickly or as safely as Rickover. Upon his retirement, three former presidents attended a dinner held in his honor.

This book is not a biography of Admiral Hyman G. Rickover. This book is Rickover. This work can be read as the primary source that it is and allow the reader to draw their own conclusions or seek out more information about the man, his Navy, or congressional and presidential history.

1

Several biographies of Rickover have been written and ought to be read for their assessments and sources. Instead, this volume seeks to capture Rickover's ideas, his connections, and his life by letting him tell it in a way that has never been done. Perhaps the volume that most closely matches some of the material is Dr. Francis Duncan's since he worked closely with Rickover, had the opportunity to interview him almost on a daily or nightly basis, and was contracted by the admiral to write his official biography. Duncan was the first and only historian to see the papers that make up more than 200 archival boxes of records until Mrs. Eleanore Rickover bequeathed them to the US Naval Academy Museum upon her passing. Consequently, some of Duncan's personal notes are included in this work. The Rickover boxes include daily love letters to his first wife Ruth Masters[1] and his observations and travels as an officer in the 1930s. They include memoranda for the record and transcripts of telephone recordings of his meetings with admirals, journalists, members of congress, and presidents. They also contain his voluminous speeches—hundreds that he wrote himself and delivered in the course of his career. Nevertheless, Duncan was contractually limited in what he could deliver in a work. In addition, there was simply far more material than Duncan, or anyone, could likely employ in a work.

The letters to Ruth Masters Rickover in the 1930s are transcribed from typed copies of the original letters, the latter of which Admiral Rickover destroyed. Consequently, he sanitized some of the names he refers to in them. In some cases of the 1970s and 1980s material, I have eliminated the names of some of those individuals who may still be living, particularly with the applicants to the nuclear program and who endured Rickover's famous interviews, in order to maintain discretion. But they are available to researchers. In

---

1 Ruth Masters was born Olga Hau (1903–1972), the daughter of the German lawyer Carl Hau (1881–1926) whose trial led in 1907 to one of the largest riots in Berlin. In his letters to Ruth, Rickover's language alludes to the possibility that he was protecting her background from public knowledge.

addition, I have included some correspondence from key figures such as presidents.

Barbara Tuchman once said that she only used primary sources because "secondary sources are helpful, but pernicious...the facts in a secondary source have already been pre-selected so that in using them one misses the opportunity of selecting one's own." The collection could have filled dozens of transcribed volumes. I have, instead, attempted to focus on those documents that were most representative of the topics Rickover addressed. In the case of some individual documents, I abbreviated them to what I believed were the most salient words or ideas. In addition, I have retained most grammatical or structural inaccuracies made by Rickover; some editorial corrections have been made to enhance readability and accessibility. I trust that this will be a humble start to the work and provide readers with a different view of Rickover who retains a unique demi-god status in Navy lore and mythology. Perhaps, in the future, a full transcription of his papers will be made available.

Historians would be hard-pressed to find such a collection from any other admiral in American history. The public will get a glimpse of the political maneuverings and intellectual depth of, arguably, the most successful peacetime flag officer. That is why that collection and, hopefully, this volume of selected material, will shed light on him. It will validate many recollections through myth or storytelling about Rickover's legendary temper, his harsh nature, his insults and belittling everyone from midshipmen being interviewed for the nuclear program to journalists, to some others in the public.

The collection, however, also reveals a Rickover few people are aware of—the man who stopped to give coins from his pocket to the destitute of Shanghai, who shared humor with his staff (who remained loyal to him for decades), who wrote notes to friends and colleagues whose family were in hospitals, or empathizing with and offering kindly advice to a young boy struggling in school with a shared first name. All the money he made from speeches, articles, and books was donated to charities such as orphanages, disabled children societies, the United National International Children's Emergency Fund, and CARE.

According to Captain James Dunford, "…at the Academy, he was ostracized as one of those who did not fit in. He was reading while others were playing golf." Rickover himself admitted having no understanding of social graces as a junior officer. Yet, as he grew, even as he retained the acerbic trait for which he was famous, he could also find ways to show his softer side to those who seemed to need it most. As Susan Clough, President Carter's secretary, wrote to him in 1979, "I did not realize until today, and yesterday, was/is your ability to sense unspoken, perhaps even unknown, needs—even if for words of comfort, or inspiration, or 'job well done.'" In his letters to Ruth, he demonstrates deep compassion for those he encounters around the world, especially the poor, perhaps reminding himself of his own childhood in Poland.

There was a duality to Rickover, clearly evidenced in his daily letters to Ruth. He could be coldly logical and analytical in one paragraph and then soft and tender in the next. He could be curt, rude, and abusive to officer candidates for the nuclear power program, to the point where the Chief of Naval Operations gently asked him to reconsider his methods. On the other hand, he could engender such loyalty from his technical and administrative staff that many stayed with him throughout his tenure as he fathered the nuclear Navy for three decades.

From the 1950s, when he successfully built and launched the first nuclear-powered submarine, to his final active duty battles with Secretary of the Navy John Lehman in the 1980s, Rickover was the subject of constant press coverage, and the media was constantly trying to interview him. He knew them all—Howard K. Smith, Edward R. Murrow, Bill Moyers, Face the Nation, Washington Post, The Atlantic, CBS, etc.

He galvanized the American public's imagination. He received thousands of fan mail letters from home and from abroad. He was as likely to get a note of thanks from a teacher in Chicago, a student in San Francisco, or a young adult in Ghana, as he would from a member of the Senate Armed Services Committee or president of a major corporation. He was recognizable—he was one of the few Navy admirals to grace the cover of *Time* magazine after the second world war.

No factor contributed more to enabling Rickover's successful career than Congress. A student of history, he realized that the Royal Navy's Admiral Sir Jackie Fisher made political connections as a young officer and, consequently, it was easier for him to make reforms. He knew how to cultivate support among members—by giving them the information they asked for and having a reputation for efficiency. He was idolized and befriended by members of Congress. Over the course of four decades, he testified before congressional committees more than two hundred times—a record that has yet to be surpassed by any military officer or civilian. Rickover spoke to them in hearings, and in personal conversations, in ways no other military officer could or would dare. He was honest, direct, and, yes, he could entertain them with his sharp wit even in a hearing, which would never occur in the 21st century. They loved him for it. They respected his technical expertise, but they also respected and valued his candor. For some, he became their friend "Rick." Rickover notes attending DC plays with Senator Scoop Jackson and their wives or dining at the home of House Appropriations Chairman Clarence Cannon, who played the piano for him.

Rickover's influence, reputation, and relationships with senior congressional leaders was such that he would be called to answer off the record questions or when some members needed help. In one case, Congressman Charles Price wanted to see House Appropriations Chairman Cannon, who was not seeing anyone. Price appealed to Rickover to intervene. Cannon, upon Rickover's request, acceded and met with Price.

In his early years as an admiral, the Navy and a Secretary of Defense tried to temper Rickover's influence with Congress, to no avail. As one admiral noted after a conference of flag officers on the

Rickover problem, "There isn't a damn thing we can do to him or about him, because he's got the Congress on his side, and we'd just better live with it."

Rickover succeeded by his intellect—or at least he was driven out of curiosity and learning what he did not know. He was a voracious reader even on his early ships and submarines, trying to understand the world around him. Among those works were Michael Ossorgin's, *Quiet Street*; Maurice Hindus', *Humanity Uprooted*; Captain Robert Scott's letters on his voyage of discovery to the South Pole; Boris Pilnyak's, *The Volga Falls to the Caspian Sea*; Karl Marx's, *Das Capital*; and Adolph Hitler's, *Mein Kampf*. Readers may be surprised that Rickover, a Polish-Jewish immigrant, would read this notorious work; however, the answer may lie in the fact that Rickover read articles and books not to agree with them but to understand the ideas shaping the world both negatively and positively. Another factor may have been understanding Ruth's country of origin better and communicating with her intellectually and culturally.

Rickover, never one to do anything by halves, taught himself German in order to translate a book on U-Boat tactics. Ruth, who earned her doctorate in international law, had been born Olga Hau, the daughter of the subject of the Hau Riot of 1907, one of Germany's largest street protests.

He faced personal challenges. He was self-aware enough as a junior officer that he could admit to his young wife Ruth his sudden fits of depression and despair and being tormented by the "slough of despond." He later admitted to his official biographer that he suffered from an inferiority complex. Perhaps these were simply part of what drove him to succeed and surpass his peers.

Rickover held integrity as one of the highest character traits. He could not be compromised. During a meeting with the British Lord Mountbatten, Rickover was offered a knighthood in exchange for an agreement on submarine information, resulting in Rickover returning to the dining room his face "pale with anger." On their way home, he told Eleanore the story and concluded with, "Can you believe he didn't know me any better than this—that I would fall for a knighthood?" He challenged elitism everywhere—the Navy, large defense contractors, economic classes—not only because he was egalitarian, but because he had risen from an immigrant child in spite of elitism. His early letters to Ruth clearly show his belief in the equality of women.

He was acutely aware of his role and his destiny in the Navy, not simply as Hyman Rickover, but as someone who had arrived in the United States with nothing and whose religious background might have been an impediment at the time. As he told his official biographer, "My job, as I saw it, was to struggle through to the greatest accomplishment of which I was capable, ignoring, as far as possible, my Jewishness. This is not to say that I denied it. What I denied was the power it had to limit self-development, to force me to act humbly, rather than arrogantly, to suffer."

His first known speech was in 1931 on the topic of the World Court to the Portsmouth, New Hampshire Kiwanis Club. Later that decade, he spoke to technical organizations. His speech to a wider audience, "The Importance of Education in the Advancement of our National Resources," occurred in 1953. Soon after, he was constantly asked to speak to a variety of organizations. Rickover's speeches were a breadth of practical, philosophical, and governmental issues: "Thoughts on Man's Purpose in Life," "Competency Based Education," "The Decline of the Individual," "An Effective National Defense," "The Meaning of a University," "Liberty, Science & the Law," and "A Humanistic Technology" are just a few. On average, he gave at least one speech per month both domestically and internationally in Switzerland, England, and elsewhere. Education would be his obsession—in addition to the nuclear navy, which he saw as inextricably intertwined.

His reputation as a tyrant was cemented by the famed "interviews" of midshipmen applying—or in many cases told to apply—to the nuclear reactor program. Rickover insulted them, put them in uncomfortable situations, and required them to have their parents or fiancées write letters on their behalf, understanding why the midshipman would have to sacrifice time away from them. Perhaps it was because the Navy had refused Rickover's own request as a junior officer for a specific billet to accommodate Ruth in her career.

At his fingertips was his rolodex with the names and personal and/or office numbers of key figures in Washington: Senators like Henry Byrd, Scoop Jackson, Strom Thurmond; Congressmen Sid Yates and Jack Brooks; Governors; Presidents Nixon, Ford, and Carter; Chief Justice Warren Burger; Secretaries of the Navy; journalists such as Bill Moyers, Jack Anderson, James Fallows, and *Washington Post* Publisher Katharine Graham; presidents of universities and college presidents; Attorneys General; Foreign Embassies; Economists Milton Friedman and John Kenneth Galbraith; Civil Rights advocate Jesse Jackson; Ross Perot; numerous admirals; and others.

This was not the standard rolodex for any Navy admiral; likely no Navy officer in history had direct access to this range of thought-leaders and policymakers. Nevertheless, the rolodex did little good, as the people with whom he had cultivated relationships for decades had retired, passed, or been defeated. After the election of 1980, a new President, a new Secretary of the Navy, and the retirement or passing of old supporters on Capitol Hill meant that Rickover had no one left to secure the position he had held for more than thirty years. There was no one left to protect him.

Most Navy admirals retire by the age of sixty. Rickover was eighty-two when his career was concluded for him. We get a sense from his speeches why he held on so long and fought so hard against the Navy and administrations from Johnson to Reagan to retain his position and never retire. Rickover believed an individual should know the "why of his own life." As he related to his official biographer, "Man's work begins with his job—his profession. Having a vocation is something of a miracle, like falling in love…it means guarding against banality, ineptitude, incompetence, and mediocrity."

In other speeches, he expressed that some positions affected "the fate of the world." As the man who heralded in nuclear power to the Navy and fundamentally changed it and national security in the twentieth century, the organization known as Naval Reactors was his purpose, and he knew that without it, his life would have little meaning, little impact, and little influence. The man who averaged less than five days per year of vacation throughout his service, now had more time than he wanted.

Perhaps Rickover's legacy would not have been tainted had he retired at the end of the Carter administration, given that he had once been the superior officer of a young Lieutenant Carter.

Rickover almost always tried to live according to his principles, including those he used at Naval Reactors, and readers will see these reflected in his correspondence, memos, interviews, speeches, and actions:

- Find out what the job is and sweep away as much as you can any of the intervening details.
- Hold people responsible for doing their work, and you see that they do it. People seem to feel stimulated and challenged.
- Have continuity.
- If you give a man a job, you must make sure that he has the right conditions to work.
- If a man sees a problem, it is his moral responsibility to act.
- Keep in contact with the real world, and don't remove yourself from it.

In 1983, a columnist from *The Washington Post* asked Rickover to write a biography of the admiral (one of many suggestions or requests from authors he had received for decades). The admiral explained that he had already compiled volumes of his thoughts and reflections on various subjects over the years and that he did not want to condense them into a book, but perhaps someone else may decide to do that someday.

That someday is now, with this volume. But this is only one volume that captures elements. Given the immensity of the collection, there are several other books waiting to be written by historians. We hope this simply marks the beginning.

Notes about the Collection

By Samuel Limneos, M.A.

On Wednesday, June 29, 2022, one of the many delivery trucks gracing the grounds of the United States Naval Academy ambled its way down the seawall along College Creek before turning down a small, unnamed service road and parking lot between Alumni Hall and the Nimitz Library. Almost exactly one-hundred years prior, a twenty-two-year-old Midshipman Hyman G. Rickover took his seat as one of the 539 members of the Class of 1922 approximately 600 meters to the southeast in Dahlgren Hall. On that June 2, 1922 morning, Assistant Secretary of the Navy Theodore Roosevelt Jr. delivered a commencement address to the graduates. Unlike the various classes that graduated during his father's presidency between 1901 and 1909, six of which graduated early to fill vacancies in the rapidly expanding and optimistic fleet, Roosevelt Jr. presided over a much more subdued ceremony. As a result of the recently ratified Washington Naval Conference tonnage displacement restrictions effectively ending the construction of new battleship fleets, 117 of Rickover's midshipman colleagues arranged to submit their resignations shortly after graduation. Only 414 ultimately commissioned into the Navy and Marine Corps from what the members termed the "Disarmament Class" of 1922.

"There was merriment to be sure," wrote one local newspaper editor covering the proceedings, "but there was something, a nameless something, that seemed to be lacking…the thought that was in many minds, that henceforth the navy is to be a preserver of the world peace, not so much a militant as a pacific force." More than any other, Hyman G. Rickover's career and legacy exemplified the mood and strategic forewarning palpable in the air that June 1922 morning.

Normally an empty avenue used as a transit highway for midshipmen heading across the school's wooden footbridge for afternoon recreation on Forest Sherman Field, a parking lot for early-arriving staff, loading dock for Nimitz and Alumni deliveries, and communal dumpster storage area, this service road assumed a busy air in June 2022. A brisk, never-ending inundation of uniformed and Naval Academy Business Service Division civilian personnel hastily traversed the road into the back loading door of Alumni Hall, which the following day would serve as the in-processing center for the nearly 1,100 midshipmen of the future class of 2026's induction day.

After turning into this space, the unassuming delivery truck weaved between the scene of fluttering activity and pulled up to the elevated loading dock outside of the Nimitz Library's service doors to drop off a special delivery of materials. A squad of dolly and pallet cart-bearing civilian librarians and archivists stood ready to receive the truck's cargo: 116 file cartons—their often-failing brown cardboard sides stitched together with masking tape betraying their age—complementing eight large, clear plastic tubs filled with a range of materials quickly went into the hands of staff for a short transportation to one of the library's ground deck archival storage rooms. In the delivery of these boxes that hot summer afternoon, the spirit and legacy of Admiral Hyman G. Rickover returned to the physical origin of its human agent's naval genesis—the United States Naval Academy.

There was a strange irony that Rickover's collection of personal papers successfully made it to Annapolis. Rickover, after all, had often been critical of his alma mater during his lengthy career. On a visit to weld his initials into the landward side of the new engineering complex named after him in April 1974, Rickover, who made a rare appearance that morning in his dress uniform, questioned the midshipman brigade commander. "What good officer in the Navy would want duty at the Naval Academy? Obviously, none." Rickover blasted Annapolis's meddling in collegiate athletics, recommended destroying the recently implemented academic majors' program and a return to a core science and engineering curriculum, praised NROTC and OCS graduates for their contrasting knowledge of the Navy, and chided the academic dean's office as a self-aggrandizing bureaucracy singularly obsessed with boosting its own ranks of faculty. "Basically, I didn't say much of anything," wrote the brigade commander of the experience. "Didn't have much of a chance. He kind of talks non-stop."[2]

Even before they made it off the cart, my curiosity got the better of me as I opened one of the new collection's many brown records cartons in the library's ground deck storage area. The very first document that met my eyes, a letter to former Secretary of the Navy John F. Lehman, Jr., written by a "Very angry reader who wasted money on your stupid book," confirmed my assumptions about what abrasive-ridden treasures the admiral's collection contained. Authored in January 1989, three years after Rickover's death, the angry writer eviscerated Lehman's recently published book, *Command of the Seas*, as a vindictive and "blatant attempt to destroy the integrity of the Submarine Force Nuclear Power Program,"—trash, good for nothing but a fire starter and to, "immortalize you as an asinine, arrogant, contemptible, biased fool." The author saw fit to conclude their missive by invoking, "the integrity of Admiral Hyman Rickover, Admiral Carlisle Trost, and Admiral Bruce DeMars is by no means destructible by a bitter has-been!"

---

2 "Rickover on USNA," *Log of the U.S. Naval Academy* 60, no. 17 (April 26, 1974), 10–11, RG 405, Special Collections and Archives, Nimitz Library, United States Naval Academy.

This polarizing rendition of John F. Lehman struck a personal chord. As a young archivist working for the National Archives at Philadelphia in 2017 to 2018, I assisted Mr. Lehman in cataloging his personal library and packaging his collection of video tapes for delivery to the Ronald Reagan Presidential Library, tasks that I completed with reverence and admiration for the soft-spoken and kind former Secretary of the Navy, who took time to invite me into his home for coffee on more than one occasion.

In processing the materials, I started with the voluminous collection of personal correspondence, the earliest of which comprised Lieutenant Rickover's personal letters to and from his first wife, Ruth D. Masters Rickover, between 1929 and 1946. The tone, nature, and content of these letters were antithetical to the preconceived and justifiable antagonistic presuppositions many have maintained about Admiral Rickover. While his salty side occasionally appeared in notes expressing his frustration about policy and personalities, these letters, which comprised typescripts emplaced in countless industrial three-ringed black binders, brimmed with heartfelt emotion and mutual affection between two authentically enraptured partners replete with equal philosophical interests and intellectual capacity.

Only a portion of Ruth's letters to Rickover appeared in the volumes. In his grief, Rickover burned many of them when she died in May 1972. In a 1984 interview with American television broadcast journalist Diane Sawyer for a CBS *60 Minutes* program, Rickover, seated in his Washington Navy Yard office chair, read a sample closure of one letter to Ruth. "Goodnight, I shall fall asleep with thoughts of you as my lullaby," Rickover read, before turning to a smiling Sawyer and asking, "Is that a good quote?"

Rickover's confidant and biographer, the late Francis Duncan, likely created the typed transcripts of the letters, which he considered "the heart" of his 1990 and 2001 biographies of the admiral for their quality in evidencing "his sensitivity to things that people normally didn't realize he had." After hearing this in a 1982 phone call with Duncan, Rickover retorted that his letters were better than those of Admiral of the Fleet John Rushworth Jellicoe, 1st Sea Lord during World War I, and the various writings of nineteenth century poet and novelist William Gilmore Simms. Rickover then swore that no one else had published copies of these important letters, and that he would happily sue anyone that happened to do so.

That quick reversion to defiance characterized Rickover's fierce resistance toward biographers, editors, and even admirers seeking mementos from the admiral, evidence of which ubiquitously appears throughout his correspondence. Evidencing his powerful intellect, guarded personality, and desire for control over messaging, Rickover's numerous private memoranda documenting conversations with and angry letters to biographers and publishers speak eloquently to these elements of the admiral's personality. Ranging from simple declinations to permission to quote letters to correspondence dripping with abject hatred hastily penned to biographers represented by publishers, Rickover's obsession over controlling the public narrative over his legacy emanated from almost every portion of the collection.

For example, the collection's voluminous legal files largely comprised all the correspondence and court documents relating to the admiral's lawsuit against Maurice B. Schnapper, editor of Public Affairs Associates, Inc., whom Rickover refused permission to publish copies of his numerous speeches on education in 1959. Rickover fiercely defended what he considered his right to refuse the publisher's desire to make money off his public speeches, in a lawsuit that dragged on for eleven years and involved investigation into his proclivity to mix personal academic interests with official Navy time and resources. At the same time, Rickover also starkly refused to send personal autographs to all, ranging from high-ranking friends to the humblest well-wisher or elementary school admirer. In later years, when the admiral's public duties precluded answering his voluminous incoming correspondence, Rickover's secretary took to typing boiler plate declinations refusing autographs "as a matter of longstanding habit."

This defiance complemented Rickover's mastery over information through written communication, organization, and order in his overarching quest for control. To that end, newspaper clippings containing practically every public mention of the admiral's naval career and activities between 1952 and 1983, many with annotations and comments scribbled in the margins, came to the archives in their original neat arrangement in meticulously preserved binders and folders. Normally the later work of archivists who must discern, reconstitute, and describe an individual's office files hastily and posthumously assembled by others, Rickover's records demonstrated exceptional organization, arrangement, and heavily documented reference use. Rickover saw fit to paste meticulous American Psychological Association-compliant bibliographies on the covers of the oversize legal banker's folders containing every single major magazine, journal, or other major professional or commercial publication article authored between 1935 and 1981 featuring himself and often addressing complex subjects such as the nuclear navy, propulsion program, and American education.

In addition to his newspaper clippings and publications, Rickover oversaw the printing, binding, and preservation of his public speeches. Addressing varied topics ranging from nuclear deterrence, to engineering, public education, and the philosophical and epistemological foundation of man's search for meaning, Rickover's speeches, which numbered more than 250 between 1953 and 1983, came out of their original boxes in neatly stapled typescripts. While numerous copies of individual dialogues appear in various other parts of the collection, Rickover annexed meticulous numerical and subject indices to his numerous standalone speeches for easy reference. At the same time, the admiral also attached both numerical and subject indices to transcripts documenting his testimony before congressional committees between 1950 and 1979.

Rickover also applied this organization to his official and personal correspondence. The admiral maintained his exhaustive assemblage of letters, memoranda, orders, and other correspondence in near perfect chronological order, requiring only minor segregation to safely house the collection's voluminous physical size into mountains of archival-compliant, acid-free folders and boxes. In the final years of his naval career, the size of Rickover's personal correspondence dramatically increased, and the admiral started neatly arranging incoming and outgoing letters into folders arranged into chronological and alphabetical order by correspondent surname, likely for quick reference use.

Rickover's defiance and emphasis on organization, order, and control complements his ubiquitous propensity to document everything. Francis Duncan himself, who worked closely with Admiral Rickover for many years, saw the physical execution of this documentation. In hotel restaurants, in cafes, at bus stations, and in airport hangers, Duncan observed the tedious and circumspect Admiral nearly always reading and scribbling notes on newspapers, journals, trade magazines, reading files, memoranda, and papers from his briefcase, or tirelessly typing up official and personal documents with his portable typewriter. Rickover's tireless energy and proclivity to document saturates the collection.

Practically every folder containing personal, office, legal or other files, correspondence, and various other records comprising the collection includes circumspect and legal-like memoranda for the record. Rickover documented most of his conversations, especially those with high-ranking naval and other military officers, congressmen, senators, political appointees such as the Navy and defense secretaries, and even presidents in formally written, first-person tensed and occasionally bullet- or number-pointed memoranda. Documenting the location, date and time, and medium of the conversation, these memoranda provide a veritable wealth of interpersonal commentary that evidences Rickover's frank appraisal of high profile individuals; the psychological and social dynamics of the admiral's intentions, goals, and objectives; and unique exposition of important naval, economic, political, and geopolitical issues overarchingly important to the grand narrative of Cold War history, as well as naval nuclear propulsion and civilian nuclear power.

The folder titles of his research notes, selected from a plethora of typescript prose elucidating a veritable matrix of complex ideas and interconnected themes, reveal a nuanced understanding of the essence of western freedom. "US vs. USSR—Preservation of freedom through education and development of potential," reads one folder selection of notes. Rickover's skepticism and outright disdain for what he considered gimmicks appear in his notation-resplendent evaluation of educational programs, the financially wasteful self-aggrandizing and occupational-sustaining egoistic adventurism of collegiate academic administrations, the myth of American educational and intellectual superiority, and the base fraudulence of supporting metrics and processes such as intelligence tests. Rickover's intellectual summation of such "gimmicks" appear in witfully truncated folder titles rendered in such gleefully upper tier, conspiracy-theory-like annotations as "IQ Tests—Criticism / Intermarriage of High IQ Individuals—Race of Geniuses / Raising IQ Through Brain Surgery."

Rickover's coherent pedagogical ethos or framework emerges, stressing individual autonomy, maintained through education and professional competence as the wellspring of American liberty, egalitarianism, and freedom. "U.S. Western World Concept: Individual Autonomy in Society Depends on Quality People—Education Essential," reads one annotated folder heading. Rickover urged average citizens to reassess their way of life, and, considering their deadly struggle with communist totalitarianism, rediscover the survival impetus that guided a generation of American ingenuity and innovation at home, as well as mercantile and military dominance abroad.

This thoughtful sheen of Rickover's drive for mastery and excellence complements the playfulness and quick wit edified by the modest assortment of Naval Reactor's office humor included in the collection's final sections. Therein, the ubiquitous appearance of Naval Reactors' office secretaries as objects of both fun, admiration, and esteem highlight their likely unrecognized role and influence in both Rickover's management style and ability to apply his meticulous documentation and organization to the rest of his records. Rickover's veritable army of civilian female secretaries, some of whom worked for him for decades, feature in fun photographs and a host of self-deprecating office humor-oriented ephemera that bely a surprising degree of the admiral's self-awareness of his own legacy for abrasiveness and tough love.

In one collection of photographs from the late 1970s and early 1980s, Naval Reactors secretaries, mouths slightly ajar with oversize cigars, fiercely pose at their typewriters behind desks and stacks of papers bedecked with facetious stickers and posters. A host of witty phrase cards color the otherwise silent collection of office humor photographs. "NR Girls," reads one small, pocket-sized phrase card about Rickover's Naval Reactors' secretaries, "Quality, Service, Reliability, and above all…Beauty!" Other cards emphasize Rickover's more popularly viewed trait of excessive candor. "Good morning, what a beautiful day!" proclaims another card. "Just watch some bastard louse it up." Regarding employee work performance recognition, Rickover printed another card, "Doing a good job here is like wetting your pants in a dark suit. It gives you a warm feeling, but *Nobody Cares*."

In still another wallet-sized fourth-revision, February 1979-classified card entitled "Current Popularity Rating for Naval Reactors Excuses," Rickover outlined a numerical scheme of justifications and apologies for his staff to choose from, including, "I didn't know you were in a hurry for it," and "Why bother, the admiral won't buy it."

Together, these and like collections present a holistic archival record ripe for study and appraisal of Admiral Rickover's personality, leadership style, and impact on the civilian nuclear power industry, the geopolitical context of the Cold War, and the twentieth century inception of the American nuclear Navy. First, the collection provides future biographers, historians, and interested scholars pursuing ancillary topics the primary sources for a targeted appraisal of more than simply the admiral's famed leadership style and storied abrasiveness, but also Rickover the man's personality, character, and development as a professional officer and academic educator.

To the latter point, the assemblage of neatly gilded and leather-bound ship and boat keel laying, commissioning, and launching books nested at the end of the collection represent the ubiquitous engineering and management presence of Rickover in nearly all the major naval platforms that today project American power abroad, safeguard maritime interests, and maintain geopolitical stability in tense waters.

Rickover received invitations to or attended ceremonies for practically every single nuclear-propelled Navy ship or submarine laid, commissioned, or launched during his lifetime, including the events for numerous vessels still in active service—such as the USS *Ohio* (SSBN-726) and the nuclear carrier USS *Dwight D. Eisenhower* (CVN-69). Stored just half a mile from where young Midshipman Rickover listened to Theodore Roosevelt Jr. present commencement remarks about the Navy's future role as a securer of world peace one hundred years ago in 1922 rests the archival collection evidencing Admiral Rickover's contentious and brilliant naval career and showcasing his implementation of a singular vision to establish nuclear deterrence and maintain global stability.

1930s

20 June 1929, US Naval Hospital, Brooklyn, NY

In the next room, a young officer is dying. His bride of six months has just arrived from California. I can see their brief period of happiness—now about to become nothing but a sad, sweet memory. How terrible it is! What bright hopes are being shattered, what poignant sorrow there is.

The sky has become overcast with dull clouds, and the wind is changing from a gentle breeze to a brisk gale. There is lightning, thunder, and rain, and trees are swaying to and fro.

A sheltering portico extends outside my window. Many birds have left their nests to avoid the rain and are under the portico. They are singing.

And above the sound of the rains, the song of the birds, and the rustling of the trees can be heard the steady roar and throb of the city—grinding of steel cars, rolling of wagon wheels, blowing of whistles.

What a strange mixture all of this makes.

Here in one little corner, I am experiencing what is most worthwhile in life, and but a breath away another is suffering mental anguish. And to the wind and the rain and the birds and the city neither of the two strong emotions is of any consequence.

26 June 1929, Brooklyn, NY

Saturday, I ceased being an invalid. Of course, I had made detailed plans for spending the day, including a trip downtown. So when I slid down from the bed and started to walk away, much to my disgust and surprise I could make no headway and was glad to have a chair to lean on. The nurse and the hospital corpsman stood by and laughed, asking how soon I was going downtown.

By practicing, I did manage to walk slowly but found myself lurching sideways every once in a while. After two or three round trips about the corridor, I was glad to get back to bed and decided that I didn't want to leave the hospital that day, anyway.

Now I can hike like a trooper. I can even go up and down the stairs without stopping on each step or holding on to the banister.

Despite my earnest request to be discharged from the hospital, the doctor merely smiled and insisted that I convalesce. Whereupon I conceived a brilliant idea:

About a mile from here is a school where naval electricians are given a course in the theory and operations of the gyroscopic compass. This is a complicated electrical device, which points to the Earth's true poles instead of to the magnetic poles, as is the case with the magnetic compass. Why could I not convalesce at the gyro school as well as at the hospital?

So, I waylaid the doctor and by dint of lucid reasoning and abundant promises not to exert myself, he reluctantly consented to what he termed a "crazy idea."

Although the course of instruction ordinarily lasts two months, I think I can complete it in a week. I am at the school from eight in the morning to four in the afternoon and study all evening. It does tire me a little because I must stand all day—working on the compass. But I have the supreme satisfaction of knowing that I am not wasting my time and that I am accomplishing a useful purpose. And it was so good to be busy again.

Since you urged me to tell you what I have been doing, here is more: I have finished the first volume of Hyde's book, having studied it rather carefully, including all of the footnotes. It has clarified many points for me and has removed a few misconceptions. Incidentally, I came across three distinct references, which may prove to be of interest. No doubt you are thoroughly familiar with Hyde; anyway, I have made note of them and will let you know upon your return.

I am grateful to you for "Gosta Berling,"[3] and hereafter accept you unqualifiedly as my literary mentor. I enjoyed the book greatly. For Gorta, I have no respect—not because he is carefree and does nothing, but because he betrays those who place trust in him. He barters for drink the food entrusted him by a hungry child; he betrays old Ulinka Dillner by so acting as to take away the only thing left [in] her life—a decent burial; he drives out the major's wife—the woman who saved him from death; he would take advantage of a half crazy girl to marry her in order to gratify his pride; he deserts the post of duty on the breaking dam and permits the valley to be flooded. Yes, he is capable of love, but it is a surface love, which, except in rare occasions, centers about himself and not around others.

The major's wife and the young countess are powerful characters. I admire the resolute old woman, outwardly hard, but tender within. And the young countess puts me in mind of you. She leavens the dourness of life with her heavenly nature. She is the form of purity and happiness for bleak Varnmland.[4]

5 July 1929, Brooklyn

Last year at Annapolis I lived with a Naval Aviator, Lieutenant George Seitz[5] (German by the way). George and I had been on the same ship for two years and had been strongly attracted to each

---

3 An 1891 novel *Gösta Berling's Saga* by Selma Lagerlöf.
4 A province in western Sweden.
5 George Seitz (1897–1947).

other. He is as fine a man as I have ever met. Frequently we went ashore together, in Los Angeles, San Francisco, and other places. When we learned that we were both to go to Annapolis for graduate study,[6] George suggested that we live together.

During the entire year, there never was anything but the finest relationship between us because we respected each other and did not mind each other's business. He never asked me about my affairs, and I never questioned him about his. What we each did was our own concern. Of course, I don't mean to imply that we knew nothing about what the other was doing, but I do mean to say that each of us knew only that which the other told freely.

The reason I have told you about George Seitz is so that you will know that what you and I have decided, about the best way to get along, is not merely an academic question as far as I am concerned, but that I have seen the necessity for that respect, not only in the mistakes of others, but also in my own experience.

The young officer I wrote you about is dead. Day and night his wife was at the hospital. It was pitiful to see her walking up and down the corridor and rushing to his room every time she heard the slightest sound. She didn't know a soul in New York; the wives of my officer friends took turns staying with her all the time. They had never known her before, but in the Navy, we consider it one big family under such circumstances.

16 July 1929

The work at the General Electric Company promises to be interesting. Schoolwork during the morning; during the afternoons, we are at liberty to visit any of the 230 buildings, which constitute the plant. This afternoon I spent at the machine shop, the largest in the world (truly). A large number of turbines were being manufactured there. You will, perhaps, obtain some idea of the vastness of the

---

6 The Naval Post-Graduate School was established in 1909 in Annapolis. It moved to Monterey in 1951.

work being carried on when I say that the machines in process of manufacture in that one shop this afternoon represent more electrical power than exists in all of France. The scene there was more typical of industrial America than anything I have ever seen.

Another building I visited was the place where the electric refrigerating machines are made. Many of the workers are women. Since they do piece work, you may imagine that no one is slow. I thought of the first shop where so much powerful machinery was being built and instead of its being used to better life, it meant that every member of the family, including the young girls, now had to work. Certain phases of the manufacturing process in this building require particular atmosphere conditions. So, at times during the summer, it is necessary to shoot steam into the atmosphere so that the work may not be delayed. Ideal conditions for working!

I have been keeping up with my study of German, but I seem to be making little progress, probably because I insist on memorizing every word I come across so that I can build up a vocabulary.

3 September 1929, Wilkinsburg, PA

I realize that I must finish my grammar by the end of September, for after then there will be no time for that concentrated study, which is so essential for the economical study of a language. After joining my ship, I can keep up by a few minutes daily reading... Soon I shall write you in German, and then you must answer similarly.

4 September 1929

I have so much to write and so little time—on account of your blessed German. I must cover a letter a day to be finished in time—which means five hours work on weekdays and much more on weekends... In one or two days, I will mail you Hyde's Int. Law. So don't buy a set.

8 September 1929

I realize that success in this world is in great measure due to "self-advertising," etc.—still my nature is such that aside from what you think of me, I value my own self-approval far more than I do the approval of others. I cannot create false impressions, my character with the consequence that my individuality would be submerged. These many years I have refused to conform, combating continually the natural tendency to become engulfed in the ordinary.

24 September 1929

I feel as if I were of a different generation than the war generation. I have something else to tie my life to, the war did not disconnect my processes of thought. Probably if I had been actively engaged in the struggle, it might have made me that way. We in the United States went through no such trials. That is why war and its horrors is an academic question here—one to be read about and discussed at literary meetings of women's clubs but one which is not felt by the mass of people.

The war, in this country, is connected with a great industrial movement, a movement which has led to higher wages and greater ability to purchase automobiles and radios and silk stockings.

Even in France, and Germany, and England, when the war generation is gone, who will there be to stop the hand, which would resort to armed strife? This question of the abolition of war is much deeper than even the intelligent people of the world realize. What popular organizations do exist are attacking the matter purely from a standpoint of armaments and belittling everything military. I believe they are on the wrong track. They should devote their efforts to forcing this country to set up agencies such as courts, leagues, etc., which will be capable of settling disputes which would otherwise involve war. Then there must also be a moral disarmament. Even in countries where the law is firmly established and agencies exist for its execution, matters sometimes get beyond the control of the authorities—e.g., lynchings in the South—etc. When people are once convinced that modern war does not pay and they are willing to be disarmed morally—physical disarmament will become a minor matter, easily achieved.

26 September 1929

I met an interesting officer [at the country club near Westinghouse], Captain McEntee. We talked for quite a while about world affairs. He recommended that I read "Das Kapital." One statement he made was surprising: that the man on *The N.Y. Times* staff who writes the naval editorials is a retired British naval officer. If you could verify this, it would be a fine point to make in one of your seminars.

I find that I am always very much at ease in conversing with older officers because they generally talk about international affairs and cultural subjects. The younger ones are not that way; they talk more of petty matters and various technical details. Captain McEntee[7] quoted Eddington[8], the physicist, as saying that man has his mind but half open who believes that only those things are true which he can actually see and hear—that there is a great deal more, which must be accepted on faith.

27 September 1929

Another matter—there never has been a college professor who did not believe that his subject was the most important one taught, and, even though there did exist other courses where credit of equal amount was given, still this was due to the magnanimity of the university authorities. One can only be guided by his own judgment, which is, at least, disinterested.

---

7 Captain William McEntee, U.S. Naval Academy Class of 1900.
8 Sir Arthur Stanley Eddington (1882–1944).

I should appreciate receiving the book and pamphlets you mentioned as soon as possible. Can you mail them as soon as you receive this?

I also thought that the review of "All Quiet [on the Western Front]" was insipid and that the reviews had missed the theme of the book. You would be exceedingly surprised did you know how closely allied our thoughts are on the subject of war. On the surface it appears that our attitudes are opposite because of our divergent occupations. In reality, there is harmony. I wish that not so very far in the future we may tackle a problem together. I believe that the combination of our two methods of approach would be ideal. What we wrote could not be termed "Militaristic" because of your well known stance, nor could it be called "pacifist" because of my work. Often I have the desire to be working along with you. My pet theory is "moral disarmament" and the use of scientific and rational methods instead of all of this emotional "crying to heaven" of the churches and women's organizations. Appeals to the heart in matters such as abolition of war have but a temporary effect; what is needed is more of an appeal to the mind.

28 September 1929

Now that my period of schooling is about over, I attempt to analyze it. True, I have picked up a few engineering principles here and there; no doubt I shall be better qualified to handle material. But what are these compared to mental concepts?

Last night I read "All Quiet" and could not stop until I had finished the book, at two this morning.

There is not one word of hate in the book. That is why it commands attention and respect. The part that impressed me most was the roll-call after coming out of the trenches, when thirty some men were left of a company of one hundred fifty.

There can be no doubt that it is the story of any soldier, no matter what his nationality. When a man must spend more days under conditions where life is a gamble and a hell, the artificial instinct of nationality and patriotism must very soon give way to the simple desire of self-preservation. The many patriotic poems, full of fervor, which clutter up literature, were not written by men who were ever required to suffer for their patriotism, as is the common soldier—no, by poets who dreamed and stayed at home. With them, patriotism was an abstract conception to be given form by inspiring words. Sir Walter Scott's "Breathes there a man with soul so dead, who never to himself has said. This is my own, my native land. —If such there be, go, hang him high, etc." Imagine the soldier in the front line trenches being fortified and inspired by sentiments such as this! Yet, we were taught that during the first years in grammar school.

To be sure, I am not writing in this manner because of "All Quiet." Very fortunately I have always tried to reason matters such as this for myself and have been able to differentiate between basic ideas and word-rubbish.

I have one criticism to make. Remarque should not have been quite so artistic. He should not have felt the necessity for introducing inconsequential matters such as Himmeltoss,[9] saluting, etc., in order to strike a balance between the terrible and the ridiculous. The book is an epic; its underlying thought needs no conventional artistic treatment. Shorn of this excess, I believe the effect would be as arresting as a [thunder clap.] A crude subject should be treated in a crude and direct manner.

The inspired literary critic of the "Army-Navy Register" was too busy checking up on the details, especially the unimportant ones, and so the only significance of the work to him is that with so many references to matters which are ordinarily not spoken of in drawing-rooms that it has escaped the well-known vigilance of the Boston police.

30 September 1929, Philadelphia PA

Your energetic way of living worries me. Become a little selfish and don't give so much of yourself to relatively unimportant affairs,

---

9 A corporal in charge of training in the book *All Quiet on the Western Front.*

such as floor parties. You have a definite mission to perform—that is what you have set your heart on—don't become distracted by too many trivial details. There are many who have no object in particular; let them run these affairs.

1 October 1929

This evening, I had dinner with Commander Hale, a very good friend of mine, who is a naval doctor. He is the type of officer I would have you meet, for I know you would enjoy him greatly. He is well read, intelligent, and has a fine character. Although he is a much older man than I, we always were great friends on board ship. At present, he is living with his widowed sister who has five children—three going to college. Gordon Hale has sacrificed himself for his sister and the children and is supporting and educating them. That, in itself, shows what sort of man he is.

I was embarrassed at first because he had been telling his sister what an exceptional person I was; after I talked with her for a short while, and she learned the truth, we got along much better.

It is with officers such as Doc Hale that I am intimate; with the drinking and sporting type I care very little to associate.

3 October 1929

All day today we walked through factory after factory. These people have the best system for getting the most work out of people. Needless to say, they pay by the piece in order to speed up production. In many of the departments, there are always acid fumes and danger from lead poisoning. In one section, the men must wear a gas mask all day long during their work. I saw one poor chap working as fast as an automatic machine over hot ladles of molten lead, who looked as if he had not very much longer to live.

Our civilization is becoming even more selective than that of the ancient Greeks. Every day there is a greater proportion of the people who perform merely automatic work, which has a deadening effect. This particular company employs much Filipino labor because it is cheap. Of course, they are not considering the effect on the future welfare of this country by introducing these people into the U.S. I could go on writing about these things I have seen for hours.

Also, I am becoming a pacifist. This afternoon at lunch with some of the officials of the company (they now have a $200,000 contract for Navy storage batteries), we were discussing disarmament. I said that the Navies of the large maritime nations were too large and could be reduced. Whereupon everyone said how England had duped us in 1921. I then remarked that there were many people in England who believed that they had been fooled in 1921; I also made the point that considering the poor financial situation of this country in 1921, would Congress have gone ahead with the vast naval building program of 1916? I have come to the conclusion that nearly all people have closed minds and resent having to listen to anything, which disturbs their normal trend of thought.

12 October 1929, New London, Conn

After lunch, one of the officers, Prime,[10] produced a book and commenced reading aloud. You couldn't guess in a million years what it was—*Cyrano de Bergerac* by Rostand. And he read the part where Cyrano is taking the place of the good-looking lover and making love to Roxana, who is leaning over the balcony. What a strange thing it was—to welcome me on board, so to speak, with Cyrano. This is the second time I have found a home through Cyrano—the first one is my spiritual haven—and now my physical home.

---

10 Rear Admiral Nathaniel Scudder Prime (1904–1961), U.S. Naval Academy Class of 1926.

13 October 1929, New London, Conn

This has been an unusual day—trying to become accustomed to the new life. One goes to sleep to the blatant sound of a radio with its volume of inharmonious jazz music and one wakes to a similar tune.

This is the only home most of the men have, and the officers cannot rightly object to their amusing themselves, even if it does mean grating on ears and nerves. Sometimes it is impossible to hear one another talk on account of this d__n radio. We shall never, never have a radio in our home....

...This afternoon, I glanced through a popular magazine; there was an article on "love." It treated it as a game between man and woman, with the clever woman continually attempting to outwit the man. Why cannot people have faith and trust? Why are they always looking for selfish and improper motives?

14 October 1929, New London, Conn

This life is so very much different from the one I led while I lived at International House. Here, no one has time to meditate or to let his mind wander away. One cannot engage in delightful philosophical arguments about various subjects, such as "nationalism," "peace," etc. When the ship is underway, one's mind must be constantly on what he is doing—the danger is too great otherwise. There are many other ships in the vicinity, and their movements must be watched carefully to avoid collision... From what I have read of submarine warfare in the post-war and from the little I have already learned of present submarine tactics and development, there is no doubt that in any future war, this type of ship will be a weapon far more formidable than people can realize.

18 October 1929, New London

I am sorry that my description of some of the features of submarine duty make you unhappy. If I believed that this will always be the case, I would stop writing about the various incidents and conditions. The German officers who served on submarines in the North Sea underwent far more of discomfort than I shall ever be called upon for.

I am too cheerful a person, and I have too high an ideal to give undue weight to these trivial details. That I tell you about them is for the reason I think you are interested in my work. I always enjoy reading about your studies; of course you are engaged in academic work, and consequently you must not assume that all work in this world can be performed under conditions as ideal as those at school.

Last year when I used to discuss matters with people at International House,[11] there always was that atmosphere of the academic; they were perfect in their theory—their points were always formulated in the quiet of a study room. They were never called upon to make responsible decisions; they knew all about the details of life's hardships—but they never experienced them....

Many times I have told and warned you that you overestimate me mentally—nearly everyone you meet in your classes probably can excel me that way. In truth, at Columbia I was like a fish out of the water. But can these people meet me in a field where the ability to work with men in trying and adverse conditions counts? I am very proud of some of the requirements of a Naval officer and the high standard of performance and devotion to duty required. When one errs at Columbia, his mark is lowered; here, there can be no mistakes. The constant realization that duty must be performed exactly develops a sense of responsibility and ability to make decisions quickly, which is, in many cases, lacking in those who shine

---

11 Graduate housing at Columbia University where Rickover met Ruth Masters while both were students.

academically. I am not detracting from scholars; I am showing that my development has been in a different direction…

…What you write about your friends and their faulty steps into the stream of life causes me to see more clearly the elements which are a prerequisite. We have never approached matters except with faith, and consideration, and with the firm conviction that we possessed characters so fine and sensitive that anything we did would be ideally right. Such a manner of thinking leads, naturally, to control. Control once attempted, and found to work, shows the true path, which one should follow.

How can people but become disillusioned and dissatisfied when they adopt a sudden businesslike resolve to taste of that which they believe to be the ultimate in life—and find disappointment instead.

27 October 1929, New London

I am refreshed. I slept late, went for a long walk in the afternoon, and spent part of the evening in reading "The New Germany" by Dr. Ernst Jacklyn, and "Deer susse Brei" by Grimm.

Since last week, a great change has taken place in the woods. The leaves are no longer full of life and color; they are withered and brown, hanging limply from the branches. The barren limbs of the trees extend upward like scepters, awaiting their months of snow. Only by much effort was I able to capture a few leaves, which still possessed life and color and maintained their saucy appearance.

30 October 1929, New London

There will never be any such question as my becoming jealous of your work or what you do, and this is why I approve so much of your career. Furthermore, I know that you are going to make a great contribution to mankind and that you will be instrumental in doing away with war. I must talk with you concerning this matter; I have much to say.

At this minute, a prize-fight is coming in over the radio, with a loud, high-pitched tone which actually hurts my eardrums. And I must listen to all of this trash and be practically surrounded by people while I try to send you my thoughts. This is why my thoughts lack connection and why I cannot write nice letters.

31 October 1929, New London

Recently I had dinner at the home of a friend. The girl is from the South. During our conversation, I brought up the Negro question, thinking she naturally would be interested, asking her about political and educational conditions in her state, Florida. Although she is a college graduate, she knew nothing about the methods adopted in the South to disenfranchise the Negro; in fact, she knew very little about the entire question. Not only this, but I am afraid she really resented discussing the matter! So, I gradually shifted the conversation to another subject. It is surprising how narrow-minded these people are—that they are even unwilling to hear the problem discussed. And, of course, they think that the people in the South are the only ones who know anything at all about the Negro question.

I am very much interested in your Code—"Responsibility of States." You will have to tell me all about it when we meet. I will depend on you to help keep me in touch with international affairs. In the November *Current History*, there is a good article on the Palestine Question. The Arab side does not appear as convincing as the Jewish side. The article on "Did the Kaiser Plan the War" is also very unconvincing. How ridiculous the picture appears of all the leaders, military, civil, and financial sitting in a room and the Kaiser asking each in turn, "Are you ready for war?" And the whole article is based on hearsay evidence of one man—who certainly must have had more sense than to discuss a conference of that nature with any and everybody.

Then there is another article in "Anglo-American Agreement in Naval Disarmament" where the author claims that it costs $500 per minute to operate a battleship. This is about $300,000,000 a year per battleship. Of course, many people reading this will never question the facts as stated.

23 November 1929 (at sea)

This evening, I looked up all the data that could be found in the "Naval War College International Law Documents" about the legal aspect of submarine use. My idea for an article on the subject is to call it, "The Status of the Submarine."[12] Briefly, here are some of the points I have:

1. In war time, neutrals prohibit the entrance of belligerent subs to their territorial waters on pain of being fired at without warning.
2. The U.S. was asked to do this by the Allied governments in 1916 but refused, stating that it would accord subs the same privileges as other men-of-war.
3. In the Spanish decree, explaining their stand, they say, "It is acknowledged in the preamble of the Hague Conventions that each nation has the power to modify the precepts contained therein in case actual experience should reveal the necessity to do so in order to safeguard its rights."
4. According to the minutes of the Washington Conference, the sub cannot be used against a merchantman, neutral or enemy, even when the sub is part of a blockade force.
5. France ....
6. The crew of a sub, even when carrying out the orders of their government, can be tried for piracy by any country, should they attack a merchantman.

---

12 The article would be retitled, "International Law and the Submarine" and later published in Naval Institute *Proceedings*, September 1935.

What I should like to do is dig up everything that has ever come up in connection with the sub from a legal standpoint.

Last night I read and completed, "The Crisis of the Naval War" by Admiral Jellicoe. The book concerns itself nearly altogether with the sub menace. One statement amused me. "There is no doubt whatever that had the Germany craft engaged in the unrestricted submarine warfare manned by British officers and men, adopting German methods, there would have been but few Allied or neutral merchant ships left afloat by the end of 1917."

[In this letter, he asks if he can send his outline of "Offensive and Defensive Qualities of the Submarine."]

1 December 1929

Read Von Tirpitz's[13] and Bernstorff's[14] memoirs today for points about submarines and came across the following...

The more I read on this subject, the more I agree with Von Tirpitz that Germany lost the war because of lack of a definite policy with regard to the submarine war and because of the general stupidity and lack of vision of the Kaiser's minister.

5 December 1929

Your own ideas of submarines are very good and show a remarkable knowledge of the subject. I am afraid, however, that, for some reason you are inclined to underestimate the defensive character of the submarine, and so your thoughts are accordingly colored. There is no doubt that the submarine is primarily an offensive weapon, but it has many good points for the defense also—especially the

---

13 Grand Admiral Alfred von Tirpitz (1849–1930).
14 Johann von Bernstorff (1862–1939), German Ambassador to the United States, 1908–1917.

protection of coasts. Here, the French are backed by the U.S., Italy, and Japan—all except England.

On one of my walks, in thinking over the question, I decided that the only possible solution of the problem at present (since the treaty for not attacking merchantmen has not been ratified) was to require non-arming of merchantmen and prohibit the use of false flags. I arrived at this conclusion independently, and later I saw it mentioned by two other writers—which was rather gratifying. Such a plan would give the submarine exactly the same status as any other ship of war. I do not agree with you that provisions of this type would necessarily be violated in wartime. Certainly naval officers would not sink vessels if they were instructed to the contrary, and the arming of merchantmen is a government and not a private matter. The surest deterrent to arming merchantmen would be the knowledge that this would lead to legal unrestricted attack. As far as the misuse of flags is concerned—this is not so serious a matter if the ship is not armed.

I had intended to write rather broadly on the subject, but now I shall limit myself more or less to the "offensive" and "defensive."

You seem quite surprised that battleships attack coasts. The German battle cruisers did that quite often to the English coast in the last war. Why do you think Helgoland was so well fortified, and why are there a series of fortifications all along the Atlantic and Pacific coasts as well as at Panama and Hawaii?

This is where the submarine would shine—and there is no question about it at all—despite what the British say. If you conceive of the submarine as being a cruiser of large radius and capable of submerging (which the modern sub is), perhaps your conception of it will be clarified and you will realize that it may even be used for protecting convoys of troopships—for surface vessels would be wary about going near areas where subs might be. And again, despite what the British say, it was this fear of subs that led to decisions at the Battle of Jutland, which prevented the annihilation of the German fleet.

Even if the sub did not sink a single vessel during a war, the great extra effort required to combat it would use up a very great portion of the enemy's energy. England claims that there were never more than 10–15 German subs operating at one time, and yet 3,000 surface craft were always actively engaged in anti-sub warfare!! (These are figures given by the British themselves.) Perhaps the little I have said has changed your ideas somewhat. I am not influenced at all because I am in submarines. That is why I can see their limitations also. Why, I am a pessimist compared to what most sub officers believe—and often they are not far from wrong. You must remember that during the war, the sub was used for one purpose only—commerce destruction. It was never given the opportunity to carry on in its other roles—that is why it is easy for Englishmen to prove that it is of no value otherwise.

8 December 1929

You say that we are both hopelessly European. Call it what you will. It is simply an understanding that what is inside of us counts most and not that which we appear. And despite the many petty things we are constrained to do by reason of our environment and custom, our true feelings are immutable. We know that we can place absolute dependance upon each other and that the trust we repose is sacred. We each possess a deep appreciation of the finer thoughts of life and our way is lighted by the fires of purity and nobility. With our outlook—is there any happiness to which we cannot achieve?

3 January 1930

I believe that before your year in Paris is over, you will have a more tolerant attitude toward the French. To arrive at a true understanding of the people and the country one must adopt a sympathetic attitude—or understanding will never come. One must see things with their eyes, feel as they do.

From the little opportunity I had at International House of judging between the French and the German students, I should say that I like the French better. They were more "human," less inclined to be "settled" and dogmatic. You have some French characteristics! A true German could not be as liberal and willing to change, to give up deep-rooted convictions as you do. Of course, you combine the good points that are to be found in all nations, so it is really superfluous to say what I have said.

Then again, I don't believe you can make a fair estimate when you compare an international metropolis like Paris with a place like Freiburg. The conditions are entirely different.

Before understanding comes, there must be sympathy. It is the same in love as in the knowledge of people. Can't you ever get over your early nationalistic training? Your reason leads you one way, but every once in a while, this gives way to feeling.

I must confess, that I like to take the other point of view. With we two, we can do that safely because we are able to discuss "incidental" matters impersonally. And it is good, too. Because we are then able to see both sides.

I have great admiration for Germany and Germans. Nevertheless, I cannot but remember that the French are largely responsible for whatever of freedom exists in Europe today. The Germans were influenced—many, even forced by the French to adopt liberal ideas. Freedom is a greater loss to people such as you and me than plumbing.

I agree with you that there is no reason why we cannot have both freedom of thought and plumbing, but between the two, I prefer the former.

4 January 1930, New London

Even though you have become quite adept at guessing my unspoken thoughts, I am sure you cannot guess what was the first thing I did upon reaching "home." (I say "home"; the only home

I shall ever have is that place, near or far, where you are.) To allay your breathless suspense—I place the picture where I can see it always and where, at night, when I am in bed, I shall see it because the moon will shine on it with its silvery light. Your smile will greet me whenever I wake up during the night as well as at dawn.

This is your November likeness; it is a counterfeit presentment. You are ten times as happy and as pretty now. No picture can do you justice—no picture can imprison within its fastness your fleeting spirit. Could that be, there would be preserved the essence of art, of poetry, of love. Men have endeavored for thousands of years to describe in sculpture, in music, in words, that which you represent; success has never attended their efforts, for it is an ethereal and not an earthly spirit, which is yours.

Being away from you is like waking from a soft, beautiful dream. Alone—I find that I am again in and of the world. But there are some memories, which can never fade, which remain eternally green—such is our fairy tale.

You have not only fulfilled all of the ideals I cherished for so long, but you have even created new ones for me. I understand now that in you there is more than I can ever fathom, more than my limited senses can perceive, more than I can ever deserve.

If I do not take our love placidly and for granted, and if I appear to doubt, it is not because you have not given me of your deepest affection, of your generous trust; it is simply because I value and esteem your love as highly as I do. You are more than life for me—can I be blamed, therefore, for taking you seriously?

Need I tell you of my newfound world of happiness? That was more than evident. In the brief space of a week, you have undone the harshness of twenty years and have carried me back to my childhood days. For the first time in my life, I have been myself; for the first time the veil of restraint was removed, and I found it possible to smile, and to laugh, and to act ingenuously. A little effort on your part, and the impossible is accomplished.

What a genuine being you are! What a wealth of personality resides in you! What youthful exuberance is yours! Can I ever forget the charm and grace of your motions as you glided to and fro in that aery, fairylike way? Then you were like the rarest of flowers—a black tulip. The exotic fragrance of my delicately poised flower made me drunk with love; enchanted, I could do nothing but tremulously admire. I trembled as I followed your gentle, harmonious movements, which blended harmoniously with the shadowy background. Each action was a touch of beauty, for you are Beauty's self.

I would not mind falling asleep for all time—what more can life have in its store? I have had a glimpse of Heaven and have been left unblinded.

For even during my life, I shall try to so think, to so do, and to so be that you will be proud of me—if I merit your approval, I become worthy. You have given me a new sense of my value—if you believe in me, then there must be some good in me; I feel like tackling the impossible and know that I shall not fail.

5 January 1930, New London

I awoke this morning with the sunlight streaming into the room; there was also sunshine in my head. Never before have I experienced real joy of living as I did this morning. For a while, I lay in bed and smiled at your picture in the manner you wish me to smile; I like to smile this way because you like it…

There is more genuine kindness in this world than I ever believed possible. Wherever you have been, there you have created the desire to be kindly and considerate and tender. This kindness and love, which is being showered upon me, moves me as nothing has ever moved me before. Here I am writing one or two words and then raising my eyes to your picture. My smile has become a habit, and when you read this, you will know that countless smiles are greeting you….

...Next, I telephoned you—and you laughed at me!! However, you sounded so happy, and your laugh had such a happy ringing tone that its contagious character spread to me. I like to hear that musical "yes" when you answer the telephone. It is so soft, so delicate.

7 January 1930

I have been soaring on air ever since leaving you. I miss you every minute, but in a dear, sweet sort of way. For instance, at mealtime, I think how utterly enjoyable it would be if you and I could dine together, where the act of eating could be forgotten through mere knowing that you were so close and feeling the radiance of your charming spirit. I don't know of any time in my life when I have felt so carefree, so rested, and in such bubbling spirits...

...If anything, my reverence has grown to a greater extent than my love, and that is why our love has never and can never become static. I see and feel in you the source of all that is worthwhile, noble, fine, and beautiful, a source fed by ever-flowing springs. Each time I am with you, my reverence discovers new wonders in you. This is one reason why I shall never be satisfied with past ideals, for I know that within you resides the gems of newer, higher ones.

8 January 1830

I have commenced my study of German, and plan to spend an hour or more on that subject each day. I also learned that it has been discovered that I am supposed to be an "electrical expert"—which I tried to keep quiet. As a result, the officer who instructs the submarine student officers in electricity has asked me to aid him in revising the course at the school instead of my receiving instruction in electricity.

Also, I must find time to rewrite the submarine article. Probably I shall be able to do no work on this except during weekends. All of the above, combined with the reading I wish to do about international affairs, promises to keep me fully occupied…

You do know this in me, don't you, that I shall never fight for your love? That whatever I do for you is for the reason that I love you, and it is in the nature of worship of character and beauty? I could not bear the thought of having engaged in any contest for you and having won you; you are not an object to be won. Despite the greatness of our love, it is a very frail matter. We both expect so very much from our affection, that even a minor incident might become a terrible disappointment. We must bear this in mind constantly and not jeopardize that which we have been searching for all our lives and have at last discovered.

9 January 1930

This evening, in obedience to your admonishment, I walked into the country. I had been diving all day and did not return until after five, but I wished to get away from the machine-like characteristic of the submarine and be able to commune with you in the solitude of the country roads. It was after sunset; the moon and stars were out, forming shadows which mellowed into the trees—the scene was appropriate for dear thoughts of you…

I have never been entirely at ease about our love, and I suppose I shall never be. I am becoming obsessed, more and more, with the thought that I in no way measure up to what you will eventually require and expect…I need your help in this. The greater our love has grown, the more has this doubt been gnawing within me; knowing myself as well as I do, I am afraid that someday, I shall do something rash. Perhaps this viewpoint of mine is distorted. I could never be convinced that I am in any way equal to you. That is a question of fact that I am not committing a crime against you by permitting you to love me, matters would become easier—but I don't know how I will ever agree to this.

13 January 1930

This has been a busy day, and it is now midnight. For the last, however, I have had a visitor who was discussing politics, philosophy, etc., with me. Very tiring. If there is anyone who can be boring, it is a conservative naval officer. And of course I took great delight in disputing everything he said. I try to avoid these discussions when possible because these people have preconceived ideas and will never change.

14 January 1930

I am trying to learn as much as I can during these six months, for I realize that later on, no such opportunity will be present. A submarine is the most complete mass of valves, pipes, gauges, and instruments which can be imagined; to be a submarine officer one must be able to find and operate them blindfolded—this in the event of detonations from depth charges, causing all lights to fail...

Do you mind my editing of the newspaper clippings by underlining various parts? I do this not because you are incapable of finding these yourself, but to save you time in case you do not desire to read the entire article.

15 January 1930

Don't you know that all my life I have been waiting for this time—the fulfillment of my dreams and hopes—when there might exist someone for whom I could do small things.

20 January 1930

This is a greeting for that day, which is of deeper significance to me than any other; the day the world was enriched by one destined to combine delicate beauty, lofty intellect, and fine character, and to blend these with the grace of ancient Greece.

And though you fulfilled the prophecies of those who have dreamed and sung for countless ages, you are as modest as you are beautiful, as warm-hearted as you are fine. You weave a spell of enchantment about all who come near, and leave them wondering, admiring.

Well do I remember the very first time it was my fortune to behold you; I saw not a human form but a lovely tulip, a flower to be admired from a distance and not to be approached. Since then, I have been burned by your spirit, purified by your love.

21 January 1930

Yesterday, for the first time, I had charge of the boat as diving officer, and gave all of the necessary orders for submerging the submarine, keeping her at the proper level, and bringing her back to the surface.

Your comment on the divorce case in Chicago amuses me; it is so typical of you. Judge Sabath,[15] as you know, is considered the foremost American authority on divorce cases (he is a brother of the congressman who appointed me to the Naval Academy).[16] He has a reputation for persuading as many people to live together as for divorcing them. Now, in this particular case, the couple were over 60 years old and had lived together for 48 years. Surely there can be no valid reason for them to separate, and if they have a chance to think the matter over, they will probably see how foolish it all is. Therefore, I think it was a wise decision. You are interested in the legal side only. Better than any form of reasoning is the result, for reasoning is only a means to an end, so if the result was sensible, the reasoning must have been good. Of course, you will retort by

15 Judge Joseph Sabath (1870–1956).
16 Congressman Adolph Sabath (1866–1952) served in the U.S. House of Representatives from 1907 to 1952.

saying that you are considering the matter legally only. I know, and this is where I differ from you. Justice which is not tempered with mercy and judgment is not justice. The very training you get tends too much toward the "serenely judicial." These problems become abstract to you. A treaty is impersonal, but in its effect, it touches many individuals quite personally. The student of international law who can envision the personal bonds of a treaty or a law understands that law or treaty much better than one to whom these are mere words to be interpreted exactly. This is not a criticism. What I am saying is quite generally true of scholarly people who are out of the currents of everyday life and never see the results achieved by the execution of their ideas.

My own experience has taught me that if I had always been judged according to the strict interpretation of the law, or the Naval Regulations, I would have been court-martialed more times than I can count. Therefore, I have learned to be tolerant of the transgressions of those about me and to treat my subordinates as leniently and decently as I myself have been treated.

25 January 1930

I hereby scold you for sending me two more packages! You mustn't do that. I need nothing but your love and letters to make me extremely happy, and here you go, trying to spoil me!

I do not like to have people do things for me—it always makes me uncomfortable. I suppose this is so because I am not accustomed to it. The U.S. Navy is run pretty much on a war basis in peace time, the routine now being the same as during war. Going to war would make practically no difference in the lives of naval crews.

Talking about the Navy, I have some comments to make on Disarmament. The enclosed clipping contains some of my views. Dallas' read of the weakness of the Japs is ridiculous. Advise him to read, "The Military Side of Japanese Life" by Kennedy,[17] if I remem-

---

17 Captain Malcolm Kennedy.

ber correctly, and he will learn that the Jap is a hardy soldier. The formula for the weight of a shell....

The real reason the U.S., Japan, and France desire 8" guns is because the Washington Conference permitted merchant vessels to be armed with 6" guns, and provided that the mounts installed in peace time shall not be of a size greater than for this. Furthermore, an 8" gun is twice as effective as a 6". Its shell weighs 256 lbs, can be fired at a longer range, and contains more explosive, about 4 times as much as a 6" gun shell.

Regarding the relative value of a merchantman armed with 6" guns and a cruiser with the same caliber guns, the cruiser is, on the whole, more effective. It has the advantage of greater speed, greater maneuverability, a larger target, an organization better qualified for attack, and greater protection, both in strength of hull and in duplication of essential machinery.

The merchantman, assuming one similar to the Leviathan, has practically no protection. It has the advantage, the only one, of having a higher and more steady gun platform. However, the better training of the crew on the cruiser would more than counterbalance this. In a time of war, Mr. Dallas can choose his Leviathan; I prefer the cruiser.

The German view of the London Conference is that it is an attempt by England to prevent the U.S. from becoming the dominant naval power, which she ultimately would if matters ran their course.

With respect to the battleship question, it is necessary to understand that naval strength consists of three factors:

(a) Number and type of war vessels
(b) Merchant Marine
(c) Strength of bases (this includes manufacturing resources and raw materials)

Now, England is vastly superior to the U.S. in (b), while the U.S. is, at present, about equal to England in (c). One might think the

U.S. superior in (c), but you must remember the many naval bases Great Britain has.

Therefore, if all of (a) were to be abolished today, England would become the predominant naval power. Parity can only be achieved by striking a balance between all three factors. The present conference is the first one in history where (b) and (c) are being considered relative to (a).

The reason the U.S. is sticking up for battleships is not so much that we are convinced of their usefulness, but rather to maintain a condition more near parity. Ostensibly, the greater (a) is in tonnage, or in numbers, the lesser importance does (b) have.

You may have noted that the U.S. now ranks third in shipbuilding and that the prospects for our merchant marine are brighter than they have been since 1865. This is largely because of the White-Jones Act, which authorizes the Shipping Board to advance up to 75% of the cost of new vessels at a nominal rate of interest—3%. This means that we shall eventually approach England in (b). When that time comes, there will automatically be a greater degree of naval disarmament.

Also, there is a great deal of talk about reducing the number of battleships to 15. This is already provided for in the Washington Conference and is to be effective by 1936.

One must realize that the general public in no country of the world is prepared for drastic disarmament; the statement in the opening talks, which I sent you, stress the point that it must be a gradual matter. I believe we shall have a series of recurring conferences at short periods, each of which will result in further reductions until a reasonable level is reached. The next step must come on the part of France and the Little Entente. Will they be willing, or will Italy be willing to cut its armed land forces before they are sure there will be no trouble from the peoples absorbed after the war?

26 January 1930

What is your idea of our anniversary? Is it Cyrano or May? I think of still another anniversary, or rather two, and perhaps you can determine the dates. I first saw and admired you at the initial meeting of the Foreign Relations Group when the subject of discussion was "Tariffs." Can you find out this date? That first time you were outstanding, but of course I never had the temerity to speak to you—I could only marvel from a distance.

The next anniversary was my formal introduction—my excuse for "teaching" you military law. That occurred at about 9:30 a.m. on the first Monday of the mid-term holiday. You were sitting on the sofa next to the Information desk, and, no sooner had the introduction been completed when you commenced threatening me—presaging the future. Ever since I have been the object of threats and abuse! I hope you can determine the dates because both memories are priceless.

29 January 1930

This is just a last word to greet you Saturday morning and tell you that I am longing to be with you and that I love you more than it is possible to say.

I am so thrilled at the thought that two days from now I shall be able to admire you—the soul of beauty.

We are very much in need of each other now, and I know that we shall be the better for this day of communion.

I find it difficult to write you, but I shall make up for this a few hours after this letter reaches you. I have never had such a great deal of tenderness stored up. You may have a legitimate complaint in that I may starve you. So, heed your own advice and enjoy a hearty ration before entrusting yourself to my mercies…

On the train, I was haunted by your condition—so apparent in the cab—and that more than any other thing brought home to me how terribly inconsiderate I have been, and I am too self-centered in considering the two of us. You must have the patience of an angel to bear with me—and I don't understand why you do.

What happened last night has resulted in making me see, as never before, that I have been taking too much upon myself in the way I have been going about making sudden decisions; that you also must be considered, and I assure you that henceforth I shall have more faith in the permanence of our love. I hold you so highly and think of you as being so far above me that the possibility of your loving me in the manner I adore you and being as necessary to you are oft-repeated attempts to show me wherein I erred and where I was undermining the beauty of our love. I know that I have been foolish.

As matters are now, I have brought about a state of affairs where you will hesitate ever to tell me of my shortcomings, or of actions which are not conducive to our complete and future happiness. If this letter serves no other purpose, I hope and I pray that it leads you to see that I have been shocked into realizing the danger and lack of reason for such a spirit on my part. It is clear to me now that I have been draining the store of our love and bringing about situations unbearably trying to you and always placing you in the position of maintaining our relationship—preventing it from being broken. Only your bigness and lack of resentment has preserved our love.

I am extremely unhappy and miserable—not because of what you said, but because of myself. There is one thing you could do to make me feel still worse—and that is to attempt to apologize. I don't mean in the manner I spoke of yesterday, but to try to appease me and to make matters easier by assuming part of the blame yourself. None of it attaches to you—it is all my own.

4 February 1930

Your letter has caused me to see, more than ever before, what an infinitely dear person you are and how blessed I am to have your love. You don't know how affected I was when I read "I need you with all your fineness and tenderness and protection—I need your love both in its sweet and quiet and in all its manifestations." My eyes are moist. I promise you that all my life I shall strive to be what you imagine of me, and I hope I may never trespass again.

I need your love for its honesty, its completeness, its tenderness, its idealism. I need you for your beauty, your compassionate understanding, and for your forgiveness. Love is such a mysterious phenomenon—I don't know how to take it. How sublimely elastic it is. I stretched it to the breaking point, but you held it tightly together. We are creating a common destiny for the two of us, and we are being subjected to the pains of creation. But it has led to a deeper understanding of each other and of our love, and for this reason, we should be thankful that what happened did happen...

7 February 1930

In a clipping I mailed today is a statement of the American requirements for naval strength. You will notice that we shall have to build even more cruisers than are now appropriated for. Of course, the ultra-pacifists, not seeing the big accomplishment of the Conference, will complain.

The acceptance by the British of this American plan for parity marks the greatest diplomatic defeat England has ever suffered. This is really the beginnings of the eclipse of Great Britain as a great world power. The U.S., considering the possible needs which she may have for her Navy, has a far superior force than has England. Just think, England must protect numerous trade routes extending all over the world—Australia, India, etc.—and yet for all of this she has a Navy only as great as the U.S.! In 1914, 40 cruisers were engaged in searching for the Emden. In 1931, England will have a total force of 50 cruisers!

The recent action of Great Britain in adhering to the Optional Clause of the World Court is in line with her recognition of naval inferiority. She realizes that to ally herself with Japan or France would at once result in the building by the U.S. of a naval force large enough to overcome both her and the ally. (Do you remember the indignation in this country when the Anglo-French Project for the Limitation of Arms was being discussed in 1928?) Therefore, her only hope lies in building up the strength of the League and trusting that this will afford her a measure of protection.

My opinion is that Viscount Grey[18] lacked vision when he declared war upon Germany. From past experience, especially the Napoleonic wars, he should have known that Germany could never seriously menace England as long as the latter maintained control of the seas. Assuming Germany was victorious, and the dominant Continental power (England not having entered the war), this would at once have resulted in an alliance between England and the U.S. to checkmate Germany and would have served to maintain the strength of the Empire. Now, Great Britain is a crumbling Empire—the Dominions independent and seeking to separate themselves even more; India about to rebel, Australia aware that for maintenance of a "white Australia" policy she will have to depend upon her own resources and strength.

That what I say about an alliance with England is not as far-fetched as may appear will be evident if you consider that probably the chief reason the great naval building program of 1916 was adopted in this country was the possibility of a victorious Germany. Such a fleet was not necessary, had we thought it might be necessary to make a war on England. We should only have had to stop exports to England to bring about her defeat by Germany.

9 February 1930

One thing you do for me makes me very grateful—your underlining of passages in the books you give me. These indicate your processes of thought, and they also point out courses of action to me.

---

18 Sir Edward Grey (1862–1933), British Secretary of State for Foreign Affairs (1905–1916) and British Ambassador to the United States (1919–1920).

10 February 1930

This afternoon, I walked out into the country. It was snowing; but I was oblivious to the falling flakes of white and thought only of the problem mentioned in your letter. And I evolved a new definition for "equality." Last year, when we first discussed our mutual relations, we agreed that equality was an essential. However, the conception of equality we had at that time was one more mathematical than one actually suited for "us."

The equality you and I desire strive for must take into consideration the fact that you and I require different manifestations of love for our happiness. True equality will exist when we both act as we wish—without premeditation. For instance, if I enjoy preparing breakfast for you and if you like to lie in bed and have me serve you—there is equality—with no trace of a shadow or worry on your mind, while I do all the planning—therein lies equality. On the other hand, if you wish to go absolutely and independently about your work and I about mine—equality also exists.

In other words, we cannot judge this sort of equality by means of a pair of scales. A stranger, however, could only judge objectively— he lacks the understanding you and I have without the necessity of saying a single word...

In love, as in any other phase of human activity, one must exert a corresponding effort for each benefit derived. For two beings to get along is more of an art and a science and more difficult than the study of submarines or of international law. Once we recognize this, we shall have obviated much of the cause for minor differences. I admit I have been lax in the recognition of this fundamental fact, but I am sure that in the future I shall take our love more as an object to be jealously and carefully tended.

Love endures only when both lovers have many interests in common and fully understand, welcome, support, and assist each other.

11 February 1930

Tomorrow morning, I am going to practice coming up from a depth of water using the new submarine escape apparatus. This was invented since the S-4[19] was sunk. By means of this "lung," which is charged with oxygen, one is supposed to be able to leave a submarine at a depth of up to 150 feet and come to the surface. It will be interesting to see how it works.

An experiment was carried on here the other day of supplying air and liquid food to a sunken submarine. The sub was submerged in the river; divers went down and fastened high-pressure air pipes to special valves installed on the superstructure (these are fitted on all subs now). A rescue vessel pumped air into the boat through one line. Through the other, there was poured a bucket of boiling hot coffee. I hope no one was standing under the valve when the hot coffee came pouring into the submarine. Finally, another air line was secured to one of the main ballast tanks and by means of compressed air, the sea water was blown out of the tank, and the submarine came to the surface. As I rise through the water with my new-fangled "lung," I shall think of you...

You will observe that I am not sending you very much about the Naval Conference. This is because 90% of the news is repetition. However, I am keeping you informed of all the real developments, such as the official statements...

The American attitude at the Conference seems to be like that of a big, overgrown boy who knows he can get whatever he insists upon. I am referring now to the proposal to build a new battleship in order to make the British and American fleets exactly equal in strength. This proposal indicates lack of vision because the naval advisors should be able to see that a great hue and cry will be raised in this country, and this one ship may become an issue, which will do the Navy more harm (in the way of curtailment) than good.

---

19 S-4 was sunk in 1927 after a collision with the Coast Guard ship *Paulding*.

Wherever we go, we breathe the spirit of peace—the Kellogg Pact, etc., etc., but you will observe that we still follow Roosevelt's dictum—"Trust in God and keep your powder dry."

The English are naturally aroused over this new battleship question, and I find it hard to blame them. Their weakness is being forced down their throat by the moralistic Americans.

When the Conference is over, there will be published an imposing list of ships that are to be scrapped—and the public will rejoice. But how many people will know that this imposing list will consist of old ships, which are out of commission and useless? For instance, the U.S. is credited with having 122 subs—and we will probably scrap about 60. But the 60 we shall scrap have been laid up for years and are unserviceable. The same applies to about 100 destroyers we shall have scrapped. Also, three old battleships are to be scrapped and at least 18 new, 10,000-ton cruisers are to go into commission!

Another interesting point: The British are making it appear that we are the only country responsible for the impossibility of abolishing the battleship, and France culpable for retaining the sub. But who is responsible for retaining the cruiser? The British appear to be hurt because other nations will not give up the particular weapons they (the British) consider no longer useful—at the same time, causing all of the others to increase their strength in cruisers.

15 February 1930

There is a growing movement in all parts of the world to restrict immigration. This induces a strong nationalistic spirit in the country having the restrictive laws, for they are excluding "inferiors," and also leads to a feeling of nationalism in the people excluded. For instance, I have no doubt that our exclusion laws have tended toward greater nationalism in Japan, and the exclusion of Jews from South Africa will have a similar result. The trouble is that this particular brand of nationalism is not the one which is conducive to international harmony and cooperation. Instead, it leads to resentment and ill-feeling.

At present, there is no international law on the subject, but it seems to me that eventually this whole question of immigration will be brought before the League and some beginnings made to consider immigration in its effect upon the world as a whole and not with reference to one particular nation.

17 February 1930

Much of the studying I am doing here is so elementary that I feel I am wasting my time—yet it must be done, and I never feel right unless I know a lesson thoroughly. I study in the morning every day now.

There is some strange spirit in me. All the other people at the school seem to be satisfied to "get by" and do not work very much. As for me, if there is one question I cannot answer perfectly I feel guilty...

...I see that you are coming around to my way of thinking about the Philippines, India, etc. Their political speakers insult our intelligence with their emotional talk, talk. I was very much surprised last year at the enthusiastic reception Mme Naidu[20] received by the members of International House, and this caused me to doubt that many of those there could differentiate reason from emotion.

Take the case of Japan—she labored under as many difficulties as China, yet she said nothing. Instead, she developed a good system of courts and then, having demonstrated her ability to administer justice, successfully asked for the abolition of extrality privileges. China, on the other hand, where piracy and brigandage is rife, and where there is no stable government, devotes much of her time to denouncing foreigners instead of remedying internal conditions.

---

20 Sarojini Naidu (1879–1949), civil rights activist and poet from India who visited the United States in 1928. She joined Gandhi for the 1930 Salt March.

In considering the possibility of an uprising in India, there is always one point that must be remembered—that all of the firearms are under the control of the British. Also, a revolution will entail the breakdown of the transportation system with resultant starvation for great masses of people. The Indians have been given a great deal of self-government—enough to enable them to better conditions, but they treat government as if it were a religio-philosophical subject, where contemplation alone is necessary. Ghandi's philosophy of non-resistance is typical. Such a method may win a desired point, but there is nothing constructive about it—it can never lead to progress.

Poor England! Her industry is in a bad shape, and she simply cannot lose India as a market at the present time. I believe it would be a good abject lesson to give the Filipinos their independence—absolute independence, and see how quickly these politicians would make a mess of things. At present, there is not one sovereign tropical country which is decently governed...

I believe there has never been a period in the history of the world so fraught with possibilities as this one—Capitalism vs. Socialism; League of Nations; Abolition of War; Rise of Subject Peoples; Development of Communication and Transportation. Can all these forces come into play without clashing?

18 February 1930

Walking is the best way to go over problems and clarify them...

I believe that our marriage could never be successful if you had no interests of your own. I have never had the desire to be married to a woman who would look after the home to the exclusion of anything else. I admire independence and dislike to have anyone devoting herself to me—except spiritually. For people of our mental caliber and with our outlook, the only sort of marriage which can work out is the one we are contemplating. However, we must also remember that not all people could find happiness in a scheme like ours. Ignorant people consider these "modern" marriages as matters of convenience—schemes to divest one's self of responsibility and inconvenience. Yet these marriages are far more difficult to maintain and require infinitely more constant attention and consideration than the stereotyped unions.

23 February 1930

You have never been more lovely. Friday evening you were a gay little fairy queen, radiant, happy, and beautiful beyond words. At the theatre when I glanced at you, I was struck by the clearness and symmetry of your features. It was no coincidence that you had been given the center seats; they were your due—the whole world revolves around you.

Saturday and today, you bloomed like a flower. A dainty shade of red appeared in your cheeks—you are gorgeous. And how dear and tender you are to me, no one can deserve that much love.

How happy I am that you were not tired this time! Dear, it will be more than heavenly when we have our own little cozy home furnished according to your perfect taste, when we can make love to each other "midst proper surroundings."

2 March 1930

I have read part of Civil Aeronautics. On first thought, I am inclined to favor the view that the air above and a certain height should be considered as international—the same as the high seas. The two cases are not analogous, however. A vessel on the high seas is ordinarily incapable of harming a nation bordering on the sea, and, if it becomes disabled, etc., the harm done is only to itself. On the other hand, an aeroplane flying in "international" or "high" air is capable of dropping bombs on the land beneath, and, if it suffers disablement, may do damage to property beneath.

I might say that the accident that air happens to be of a lighter density than water has jurists to decide that a nation's sovereignty extends, without limits, to their air above…

…You have had a remarkable effect in the development of my character. I am so moved when you say I come up to your girlhood ideals. I know I do not, but I shall try, and in trying I may approach that high level. The more you expect of me, the more will it be possible to give, for we naturally tend to come up to that expected of us.

4 March 1930

Russell's book came today… It may be of interest to you to know that despite the obligations Russell mentions as those of a husband when there are children in the family, he himself divorced his first wife and married the governess.

Also, in general, it is not good policy to formulate decisions on sex questions immediately after reading a book on sex, for our emotions are always somewhat aroused by such reading. I think you will agree with me when I say that books of this sort are, for most people, an excuse to give in to their feelings…

The theme of this letter is this: Should or should we not wait? I don't know. The two reasons you mention are not the major ones, which have influenced me so far.

The outstanding reason is one of idealism—it is the expression of the romantic side of my love—I do wish a legal tie beforehand. True, the code of morals we, you and I, will always follow, will be one of our making, though it has no sanction, besides our approval; it is nevertheless, just as binding on us as if it were law…

I have gone for so many years hoping that I should find true love, exquisite love, love of the heart and soul, and I have found it. In my calmer moments, I know I would rather suffer and suffer than give up the least bit of my idealism… In matters so profound as our love, I can bear the hardship of waiting, the torment, if it will strengthen and perpetuate this priceless affection we have found.

6 March 1930

You will observe in the newspapers that the U.S., Japan, Great Britain, etc., all moved by altruistic spirits, will probably limit all future submarines to 2,000 tons displacement. Doesn't this clearly demonstrate an earnest desire for limitation, disarmament, etc.? But—how many people know that subs over 2,000 tons have been found to be impractical and not as valuable as those of about 1,500 tons. Nearly all subs being built now are about 1,500 tons. Some of the things connected with disarmament are amusing. It is the same with aircraft carriers. The large ones have been found to be not as valuable as the smaller ones—so you will doubtless see a further limitation in their size—and this will be pointed out as another of the great accomplishments of the Conference.

10 March 1930

On my walk this afternoon, I thought of a perfectly good reason for not marrying you—but alas, I can't remember it now! This will show you in what a light manner I consider you! However, I know an excellent reason for divorcing you (after we are married). This actually happened: A lieutenant commander in the Navy married a girl of German nationality in 1918. Now, in 1930, he has brought suit for divorce, his reason being that she is unpatriotic! As proof, he cites that in 1918, she refused to sing the Star-Spangled Banner—even though he not only urged her, but even insisted! The court did not grant the divorce. Of course, there must have been some other reason for the divorce action, but can you imagine bringing this patriotism even as a reason for the divorce?

Consequently, you are hereby ordered and directed to practice singing the Star-Spangled Banner for ten minutes at sunrise and sunset. Whatever you may be doing at the time is of secondary importance. The following procedure will be observed: At the first ray of sunrise or the last ray of the evening sun, you will rise, stand at attention (the toes at a 45-degree angle and the right hand over the heart), and you will sing the Anthem in a moderate tone. A report of progress shall be submitted weekly. A board of inspection consisting of one officer of the rank of lieutenant will visit you at rare intervals to conduct an examination in your proficiency in this (and in other subjects). Marks in this (and other subjects) will be assigned.

I am laughing now as I think of you standing at attention in the manner ordered, and in the uniform you like to wear when you are alone, and singing in a moderate tone!

…I have read "Rasputin, the Holy Devil"[21]—most of the officers living here have read it and recommend it highly. I was asked my opinion of the book, and I said it did not ring true. The author's purpose is to show that Rasputin exercised a great control over Russian politics by means of his unsavory influence with the Czarina and the Czar.

I tried to discuss Russian history with them and show how they were mistaken, but no, they were convinced that conditions in Russia were exactly as depicted in this, what seems to me, to be a cheap sensational book. This book, the same as Russell's, was thumbed in the places dealing with Rasputin's relations with women.

On my walk today, I thought and thought and finally I arrived at what I think to be the real reason for Rasputin's influence. He was a peasant who had practically no book education but had amassed a great fund of common sense through contact with men and women in all walks of life. He must have been like the peasant in "Red Rust."

Now, all of the Czar's advisors were as far away from the peasants (99% of the people) as they could possibly be. Their education, their social attitude, their environment all tended toward a complete lack of understanding of the Russian people. Here, on the contrary, was a man who could feel "the pulse of the people" and give judgments not based on self-interest. I think that this is the reason for

---

21 *Rasputin: The Holy Devil* by Rene Fulop-Miller (Viking Press, 1928).

his influence and not the supposed relations with the Czarina and all the other lies.

I am becoming more tolerant of these men who have no book education; they are more likely to make decisions and can see matters clearly—I mean intelligent men, of course.

The thing that shocks me is that all of these officers, who represent the younger generation, already have closed minds. Aside from purely professional subjects, they are dead, mentally. Certainly there is something woefully wrong with our system of education, which brings about a condition such as this.

11 March 1930

It seems to me that the many people who are strong in their belief and desire for another world cannot be entirely happy in this one, and they are looking to the dim future to offer them recompense for what they somehow sense they have missed here.

I have tried to analyze my faith—and I find that my faith is in you. When I write and say that I worship you, it is more than a figure of speech. I do conceive of you as surpassing human limitations and existing as a being apart from the rest of us.

13 March 1930

I fully agree with Shotwell that the only way reduction of armaments can be achieved at this time is by some sort of mutual guarantee—but—the political leaders in Washington know that such a guarantee would never be approved by Congress. Out national pride demands a Navy as large as England's even though we do not need one so large. The fact that we are willing to cut down shows this. The Geneva Conference in 1927 was criticized for too little preparation. This Conference has had too much preparation. It also shows that the new method of diplomacy, as Shotwell terms it, may not be so much better than the old one. Nowadays too much pressure is brought to bear on delegates—Shotwell and people of his type being responsible—to permit them to work freely. It seems to me that if Shotwell were a one-man delegation to a Conference, he would greatly resent attempts by anyone to influence his views— and yet he does not see that he owes the same obligation to others. He has never been clothed with power by the people of the U.S. to state their views—and yet he assumes this privilege. A moralist and prophet must not urge—he should only indicate the proper path.

17 March 1930

On my walk today, I meditated about the philosophical questions you brought out in your letter... There is one thing which seems evident to me. You have developed the habit of arriving at certain conclusions and then, by a process of reasoning, justifying the conclusions you have already formed.

Several years ago, when I was studying Strategy and Tactics, this point was forcibly pointed out to me by a captain whom I had asked to criticize a solution of mine to a War Problem. He read my solution and said—"You are playing bad baseball. You are merely justifying the decisions you have already made. You should reason first and then as a result of your reasoning come to a decision."

To be sure, I knew at the time that such was the logical consequence, but I was not aware that I was making the mistake...

In formulating a philosophy of life, we should not think too hastily. There is plenty of time. It was Tagore[22] who said that men and women should spend fifteen minutes or so daily in deep meditation. He is right. The philosophy of life is a slow, continuous process and does not come about by quick mutations...

The people who are really happy in this world are those who have the courage to develop according to their own personalities and who discard the undue influence of the world about them. They develop personality—for they are real persons.

---

22 Possible Bengali poet and writer Rabindranath Tagore (1861–1941).

1 May 1930

Thank you for your additional views on the Lusitania. It is true that International Law, with respect to maritime matters, has been unduly influenced by the strong naval powers. In this respect, however, International Law is no different than any other form of law, for custom and usage have had profound effect in all other forms of law, and many provisions of law are still maintained because of custom. For instance, in the recent Supreme Court decision about Chicago and the Great Lakes, there was involved an interpretation of riparian rights—rights which had grown up by custom and are no longer suited to present-day needs.

So, you must not blame England too much because she happened to be in the position where her own interested views could be given the status of International Law. Germany, or any other nation, would have done likewise.

4 May 1930

I was so happy to be able to speak with you again. Your voice is so very soft and music-like and always thrills me. I need you a great deal, and to wait a whole week seems a long time.

There are times when love for you creates in me a calm sort of happiness, and the need to be with you is not so great. At other times, however, such as the present, the desire to be with you is very strong.

6 May 1930

Could we not devote part of Saturday toward revisiting the scene of that memorable day when our hearts first beat in unison? There is nothing I should like better than to be in the open with you, in the pale silvery rays of the moon. Of late we have, unfortunately, been compelled to forego this part of our love—the part which requires nature for its setting. Now that young Spring has returned, let us seek her and repledge our love, as we sit on the rocks, and the "spirit" softly comes over us.

14 May 1930

One of the officers talked with the Detail Officer at Washington by long distance telephone and obtained the details for the whole class. And my detail was the "V-4," a submarine based at San Diego! Can you imagine how I felt? I was ready to write and tell you that we must break off and not become married because this would interfere with all your hopes.

Then I decided to talk with the Detail Officer myself and, if possible, persuade him to change my orders. Can you guess how I felt when he informed me that I was going to "Div. 4," which means Submarine Division 4 instead of V-4? A mistake had been made originally by telephone!

15 May 1930

Today was a very interesting one. Early this morning I rode over to Fisher's Island, where an army post, Fort Wright, is situated. They are conducting experiments with sub-aqueous sound apparatus for detecting the presence of warships trying to attack the coast. The army officers there were very kind to me and explained everything. I was glad that the little electrical knowledge I have prevented me from appearing entirely ignorant. This whole field interests me, and I think I shall do some studying along this line.

A research expert from the Navy Experimental Station was here Tuesday, and I spoke several hours with him on this same subject. He has promised to send me a good deal of information. It was through him that I was enabled to get away from school today and go to Fort Wright.

I am interested in the subject more from the standpoint of detecting surface ships from a submarine than from any other. The field is broad and interesting to me, and hardly anyone in the Navy seems to know very much about it.

22 May 1930

I have been reading Walter Lippman's book "A Preface to Morals," and I must tell you my reactions.

He starts off with the assumption that religion, which was once a unifying force, no longer is such for modern thinking man, and, as a result man is like a lost soul, with nothing to tie himself to—with no philosophy of life. The purpose of the book is to indicate a code of morals for those who can no longer fall back on religion.

One essential, according to Lippmann, is asceticism—the conscious denying to one's self of things he may wish—for in this way we grow up, departing from carefree childhood and bringing ourselves face to face with reality.

Now, all of this sort of philosophy leaves me cold. Certainly, I come under the classification of those for whom religion no longer is a unifying force—but I am perfectly happy, and life does not appear so complicated to me as the author states. I believe that only those who have no deep interest in life are forever tormented and are seeking a code to guide them.

Neither of us permits our desires to dominate us—we are just naturally that way, and we are not conscious of practicing any form of asceticism. In fact, we are governed by the wish to do that which the other likes—and we find an additional source of happiness thereby.

It may be that my mind and outlook are not philosophical, but somehow, I can never become worked up over these matters of moral codes. There must be something lacking in those who are forever seeking a better way of living. Don't you agree with me?

It has been well said that the greatest truths are very simple. I think that the happiest life is also very simple and that those who seek complications and codes and rules are attempting thereby to fill that part of their life, which is vacant, in an artificial manner.

27 May 1930

This is all that we may ever hope for—to find another understanding soul. How much of sentiment, of high-mindedness, of devotion we have aroused in each other. How dull and commonplace the life lacking these forces and urges. When I see others who are incapable or unable to experience a love such as ours, I think of little blind kittens—they live a half-life only. These things which once were of importance are now no longer so. True love is the great emancipation, freeing us from the bondage of unimportant matters.

You cannot understand the various "problem" books. To me there no longer seem to be any problems—except how to being happiness to you…

Walter Lippmann disagrees with Bertrand Russell in that the lover and the husband should not necessarily be the same person. His argument is what we already know, that when ideal love exists, the two wish to be united in every possible way…

My philosophy of love is that you are everything to me and that it is my great privilege to be the gentlest, the tenderest, the most sympathetic, and understanding of lovers. In return, my thoughts are ennobled, my life is joyous and happy, and I can breathe of her divine spirit and admire her loveliness.

30 May 1930

I have been reading "The Docker Looks at Literature" by Joseph Collins. It is a series of psychological studies on life and letters and has opened up for me a new vista of literature. I did not realize that there was a group of modern writers who had contributed so much to the study of abnormal life. Among the writers considered are: James Joyce, Dostoievsky, Marcel Proust, Dorothy Richardson, Henri-Frederic Amiel, and D.H. Lawrence.

All are brilliant creative people, and their works are the stories of their inner lives. But all are profoundly unhappy. They are obsessed by sex; one has homosexual tendencies, another sees only the physical in sex, still another is too idealistic, and so on. In reading the essays, I could not help but be thankful that we are entirely normal in our relations, and that we do not over-emphasize any characteristics...

...I like your thought that by physical contact we can express completely all we feel. And, in no other way can fine shades of feeling be expressed. To abuse this wonderful instrument is to disregard and be contemptuous of the greatest treasure we have. Men spend their lives and their health in the quest for riches and glory, neglecting to develop their own natures. They seek the roundabout, the more difficult, and longer road to happiness. An exquisite feature of true love is that although it contains a beautiful promise for the future, one is stirred by it during the present. It is the denial of reason—of mathematics. One sips of the cup, and the cup remains full to the brim. It is limitless. It increases and grows with time...

...Despite all that has and is being written about the "new freedom," birth control, modern married life, etc., etc., I do not believe that people will be any happier in the future than they have been in the past. All writers confine themselves to the consideration of external matters, of environment, of customs, of social and economic conditions. They neglect the development of character, the desire for beauty, innate consideration, the willingness to give. These are what count; these contain the seeds and the elements of married bliss. And so the world goes on, men continually developing methods and means to eliminate the symptoms, instead of lending their energies to the development of the inner self... Any man worthy of a woman's love will never try to dominate her in any way, for he can only love a woman who is vastly superior to him; if he is aware of this superiority, he acts truly neither to himself nor to her, when he attempts to impose his own inferior views upon her.

22 June 1930

What a great deal we have to be thankful for. Here am I, midst all of this mass of pipes, valves, motors, wires, machines—and yet I am happy and pleasant—all because of you. I am sure that I can get along better with people because of you. You have taught me by your example, patience, bigness, forgiveness.

More than you realize, you have influenced me. This is so different from last October. I can concentrate on my work, knowing all the time, within me, of the certainty of your great love. The storm and the strife are over, peace reigns within me—and my most earnest wish is that you, too, can live at ease in the bigness of our love.

24 June 1930

Tonight, I was studying descriptions of our engines. They are exact duplicates of those on the U-117, a German World War I submarine. In fact, the illustrations and photographs are actually from the U-117! So, if you makes you feel any more patriotic (German), you may consider me as being the Engineer Officer of a German submarine. In copying these engines, we even copied the mistakes the German designers had made! Japan is supposed to be an imitative nation; the U.S. is supposed to lead in ingenuity, inventiveness, and originality!

28 June 1930

You ask for my opinion of the Simon Report.[23] I have not considered it much because I know that the nationalists in India will not accept it while it will be accepted as gospel in Britain.

---

23 Also known as the Indian Statutory Commission, the Simon Commission under Sir John Simon (1873–1954) studied constitutional reform in India.

Isn't it strange that a people, the Indians, who have developed the best philosophy, should be so overcome by a modern, non-philosophical conception—Nationalism. When one speaks of the growth of Internationalism, he closes his eyes to what is going on in the world. Probably, during no period of the world's history, has there been so great a growth of Nationalism as there has been during the last 12 years. Everywhere—South America, Mexico, Central America, the West Indies, the Balkans, Central Europe, Russia, Asia Minor, China, India, Africa—there are evidences of Nationalism. You and I live in a little world which desires international cooperation, and so we become blind to what is really going on, and we become prejudiced in our views. We think the world is as we would wish it to be.

With the Indians, as with the Chinese, I have no sympathy. Both waste too much energy in belaboring the foreigners. Nothing foreign is good—except Nationalism. The "subject" races are willing to give up railroads, electricity—everything modern, if they can but have Nationalism. In one respect, they are right. Who is to say that the white man's way is best? May not divine authority consider the marriage of an 8-year old girl to a grown man as proper? You and I say "No" because it is abhorrent to us—but—are our ideas necessarily the true ones.

The cry of India is the old cry of "Leave us alone." But the inexorable world goes on, and none can stand still.

The officers on this boat appear to know little of international affairs, and so I have said not a word in this direction. The captain is quite an authority on mushrooms and baseball—subjects, which, unfortunately do not excite me in the least bit. It is surprising that a man who has so much time should remain ignorant of world events...

...The McLeod case you mention is quite familiar. It is generally quoted in history books as an example of the difficulties the U.S. may get into because it has no control over an individual state.

The U.S. was perfectly willing to free McLeod, but N.Y. was not. Fortunately, he was released.

I agree with you that an individual, a member of an authorized expedition, should be treated as a prisoner of war. I speak now as a soldier—I am merely obeying orders; I have no alternative. Therefore, the wrath of the offended government should be vented on the authority which ordered me on the expedition—my government. I would make no distinction between an expedition justified or not justified by International Law. The individual soldier cannot decide the justice of the expedition. He has not the training in law to do so; nor is he allowed to disobey an order. The Hague rules with respect to distinctive uniform should, of course, be observed.

It seems to me that single individuals, acting to blow up ammunition depots, etc., should be treated as spies, as you suggest. The extreme punishment attached to the spy is not on account of the depravity of his acts, but that on account of the secrecy and fraud connected therewith, it may readily expose a military or naval force, or a military objective, without warning, to the greatest disaster. A spy knows full well the risk he is taking and is not required to act thusly. His action must, necessarily, be voluntary. The uniformed soldier, however, acts under orders. The spy himself, has willed to do his deed; therefore, he is punished. The soldier is obeying the will of his government; therefore, the government should be punished.

I am certain that the military men of all nations would agree with me on this.

30 June 1930, USS S-48

Earlier this evening, I attended a concert in the Control Room. The electricians were working away, lying on the battery tops, wiping off sulfuric acid, when two other engineers decided to play for them. An Irishman named Clancey and an Italian, Cozza, played together, the former employing a mouth organ and the latter a banjo. They were very good. Upon urging, Cozza lost his bashfulness and sang Italian songs. He has a good voice. It is surprising to think of him working on diesel engines. The officer I relieved told me Cozza was "no good," but I can see nothing bad in him. A man who sings and plays must have good points. In the scheme of middle-class efficiency, music has no place.

I asked Cozza where he learned the songs. He answered, "My father used to sing in a choir. At home he used to play Italian songs on the phonograph, and I had to learn them."

I like the men in my gang very much. They are an excellent group and fairly hardworking. It is a pleasure to work with people such as they. However, I am not so vain as to think it is all my doing that things are going along as pleasantly as they do. I am permeated with love for you, and it affects me every minute of the day.

1 July 1930, USS S-48

This will be just a short note. I haven't had any sleep in two days, and I am very tired. We finished charging batteries at seven this morning. At that time, it was too late to turn in, so I have been going about half-tired all day. The worst of it was the battery gas. Our battery is old and evolves excessive hydrogen. This causes one to become dopy. The air was so bad early this morning that at one time I almost lost consciousness. The men who were sleeping coughed during the night.

2 July 1930, USS S-48

Even though I do not accomplish much on board, still I spend a great deal of time on the boat. It is difficult to overcome being enveloped by the routine work and maintain one's interest in outside affairs. Intellectually, this ship, I mean its people, is dead. I do wish there were someone on board with whom I might talk intelligently—but there is no one, and I must therefore redouble my efforts at self-study in order to prevent stagnation.

This noon, the wife of the executive officer and a friend dined on board. It became as plain to me as a thing could possibly be that if being married meant to live with such uninteresting women, I could never become married.

These middle-class people are lacking in something—it may be undefinable, but it is evident. I think that civilization has taught them a certain amount of repression, but they have neglected to make use of intellect in order to overcome the deficiency caused by repression. This is why it is possible for intellectual people to live happily—their repression is compensated for by their intellect. But these people must lead such dull lives—lives devoid of fullness.

All of this makes me understand what an extraordinary and unusual person you are—how you combine all that anyone might wish.

5 July 1930, USS S-48

I must tell you something concerning my reactions to the Italian singer. You guessed correctly. He is not such a good engineer. However, I thank God that I have a little of the milk of human kindness in me, where I cannot treat any of my men as mere instruments. And so, the Italian can be sure he need have no fear about getting along on the ship. I cannot be harsh to men under me, as some men are. They are human beings, too, and I know each man has some good in him. Several days ago, one of my men was placed on the report for being quite untidy in dress. He had been warned several times, and the captain had determined to punish him this time. I interceded for the man promising the captain I could straighten him out if he gave me the chance. Reluctantly, he agreed. I spoke to the man in a nice way, explained matters to him, and I am certain he will be neat in the future. I prefer to deal with my men in this manner.

6 July 1930, USS S-48

In a clipping I mailed you yesterday, there is a statement of Japanese policy, about Japan having a Monroe Doctrine for Asia. I believe this enunciation of policy, together with its acceptance by the United States, is one of the most important declarations since the war. No doubt it will have a great influence on international relations, especially insofar as China is concerned. The world seems gradually to be dividing itself into three distinct political entities—(1) Europe and the African colonies, (2) The Western Hemisphere, and (3) China, India, etc., under the leadership of Japan. Russia, of course, is outside.

Japan's policy under her liberal leadership has been friendliness toward China. This means that soon we may have some sort of league in Asia, just as we have now in Europe under the League of Nations and in the Pan American idea, strengthened by the Monroe Doctrine. This crystallization of political thought into large divisions is a natural consequence of the development of economics. The Pan-Europe idea, the U.S. Tariff, Commonwealth Preferential Tariff—all are leading to this new grouping of states.

Although the "Monroe Doctrine" for Japan is of great importance, I have seen no article which dwells upon its significance.

I agree with you that to invoke the Monroe Doctrine for claiming the South Pole is far-fetched—and this will not be taken seriously by anyone. As a matter of fact, the U.S. has recently "backed down" somewhat on the Doctrine, and it is not likely that it will be used for the acquisition of territory…

…You asked about how to keep shoes from squeaking and about Zim City. The answer to the former I have been unable to find out—but why don't you buy a new pair of shoes? Zim City is a religious colony near Chicago under the leadership of a man named Voliva.[24]

---

24 Wilbur Glenn Voliva (1870–1952) was a flat earth evangelist who led the religious community of Zion, Illinois. Rickover's referring to it as "Zim City" may have been a colloquial Chicago term for Zion, or it may have been an error when Rickover had the original letters transcribed. Articles from the *Chicago Tribune* in that era refer to it only as "Zion City."

Since all people of Zim City are of the same faith, the local ordinances are really religious ordinances. Among the things which will effectively commit one to Hell are smoking and chewing gum. To be sure, there are many more rules and regulations for the guidance of the faithful, such as proper length of skirts and sleeves, etc., etc.

8 July 1930, USS S-48

We steamed out past the lighthouse. Then the chief machinist's mate in charge of the Engine Room came up and reported that a stem on one of the exhaust valves of the diesel engine was cracked, and that at least an hour would be required for repairs. Well—there was nothing to be done but stop once more. Finally, when we were chugging away again, and I had begun to lose my dour expression and long face, the word came up that the new valve stem was heating up. So, we stopped once more.

By this time, I was completely downhearted. For so many things to happen in a short time! We started off once more and increased our speed to that required for full power, and I was about to inform the captain that I was ready to commence the run when three of the port engine cylinder jackets developed leaks. This meant that there was a possibility of getting salt water into the lubricating oil system—which is dangerous. This casualty was a result of a poor feature of design in the original German engines, and the fault had been copied by the American designers.

I made a quick decision: Probably the captain would become disgusted if I kept on reporting casualty after casualty, so I decided to take a chance and run with the leaky cylinder jackets. I really didn't expect the engines to hold out the 20 hours required, and I knew that if anything serious should happen there would be a Board of Investigation, and I would be held responsible for not having informed the captain of the state of affairs... Never in all my experience in the Navy have I had such a multitude of ill-starred events befall me. I am surprised that I am acting like an ordinary human being and not overwhelmed by all of this.

17 July 1930, En route Boston, New London

Across the dock from where we were moored was the Coast Guard Cutter "Tampa" of about 3,000 tons. There I sojourned and took the first bath in four days.

The "Tampa" is the flagship of all Coast Guard activities in the Atlantic from the straits of Florida to Nova Scotia. They have a roving commission, staying out at sea for 6 or 7 days at a time, and steaming whenever they think rum runners may be found.

The Coast Guard appears to have an efficient secret service, which notifies them of any vessels suspected of evading the liquor laws. So that whenever they see a boat, large or small, they approach, note the name, and check up on it in their catalogue of suspects. They also note if it appears suspicious. If within the 12-mile limit they encounter a suspicious vessel, they trail it, at the same time notifying shore headquarters by radio. Immediately a small vessel is sent out to trail the suspected ship, while the "Tampa" goes on her way.

The rum runners easily find out what speed the Coast Guard boats can make; they then build ships for the illicit trade, two or three knots faster, and are thus easily able to evade the patrol.

The officer I spoke with seemed to have no definite idea when "hot pursuit" could be used. I tried to find out what their latest instructions were in this respect. He was unaware of Hyde's statement, that hot pursuit was justifiable only when there was actual danger present to the U.S.

20 July 1930, USS S-48

It has been too hot all day even to go hiking. Consequently, I have done nothing but rest, study a little in "Diesel Engines," and reread, carefully, Jessup's "Neutrality."[25] The first time I read the book was over a year ago, when my foundation on International Affairs was not as solid as it is now. I find it very instructive, and it helps me in crystallizing the whole problem of neutrality, freedom of the seas, etc., in my mind.

With this letter, I am sending you several interesting clippings. One describes the German system of government; another is a Federal Court decision relative to whether a war terminates or merely suspends a treaty. In addition, there is an excellent article on the Pan-Europe plan.

I have read Briand's proposal rather carefully, as I have, also, the replies to it. It strikes me he must have known that the submission of his plan would bring into relief the fact that there can be no European federation so long as France dominates Europe. In addition, I think he also saw that as long as this condition exists, there can be no disarmament.

All along, Briand has been far-sighted; in their initial state, his policies have never had the backing of his countrymen; ultimately, they have agreed with him. My theory is that he purposely proposed the plan to show France there can be no real basis of peace in Europe unless and until she is willing to set the example in disarming and renouncing her domination of European politics. France rules Europe by might, and Brian knows that eventually there may arise others mightier than is France.

Also, nothing has happened in the last 10 years which has added so much to the prestige of the League as the fact that all other European nations are against any project which might tend to weaken the League.

Not only is the time now ripe to face squarely the issues which must be met to eliminate all the hard feelings engendered by the war—but the Pan-Europe proposal will also tend to emphasize and accentuate the League's work along the lines of peace. No doubt

---

25 Phillip C. Jessup, "Neutrality: Its History, Economics, and Law" (Columbia University Press, 1935).

the League conferences on health, tariffs, etc., will henceforth be regarded more attentively, and the results of the conferences will probably be translated into definite action.

2 August 1930, USS S-48

I have the duty on board tonight. As usual, we are working. Ever since I have been on board there has never been an end to this incessant working—machinery constantly breaking down and the men working day and night to repair it so that we may carry out our schedule.

In *The New York Times* today there was a report of a meeting at the Williamstown Institute where there was discussed the danger of the machine predominating over man. This is more than a danger on board a ship of this type. As far as the men are concerned—they are already conquered. Living as I do, day by day, in a small space crowded with machines, and where my constant preoccupation is keeping them in operating condition—I feel this danger for me, too.

There is no one here with whom I can speak of abstract matters—of philosophy, of history, etc. You cannot imagine how dull such surroundings become at times. I do like one thing, however, the wholehearted way in which my men work.

There are times when it is disadvantageous to have a fine and sensitive nature. When I see the men on here treated harshly, unnecessarily, it hurts me as much as it does them. I shall never be able to understand why officers cannot treat enlisted men as they would be treated themselves—why they must be petty and abuse the privileges of their rank. It is all so needless. The men on this ship are of a very good type, and more enthusiasm and work could be gotten out of them if some little considerations had been shown them. I do not speak as a theorist. I have never seen a ship where there was as little spirit left in the men as there is on here. Initiative is discouraged.

6 August 1930, USS S-48, Boston, Mass.

We are in drydock now, and I have been able to see what we look like out of the water. We look like a big fish. The reason for going into drydock was to inspect all sea-valves and also to remove the growth of marine parasites, which always collect on the underwater portions of a ship's bottom. Most of these are small, white-shelled barnacles about three-eighths-inch in diameter. One can watch them as they die—for they are unable to live outside of the water. The organism pulsates to and fro—reaching for water—but none is there. Soon the ship's side is completely dry, and they have ceased their futile efforts. Then the navy yard workmen come along with scrapers and remove the barnacles, which have been living on the side of the ship all their lives.

I suppose one could philosophize about this. One sees so much in nature which merits deep thought.

14 August 1930, USS S-48, New London, Conn.

There is one factor of submarine warfare which is never taken into account in all the discussions—and that is the increased effectiveness of the submarine in material condition and especially in skill of personnel. Here we are, day after day, operating as we would in war time, firing torpedoes. Not even the best German commanders were as good as our submarine captains are now. This is no reflection on the Germans, but rather a tribute to the result of constant practice.

For instance, today, we fired at a zigzagging target, making over 20 knots speed, at a distance of over 2 miles, and we hit! No submarine commander during the war would ever have dreamed of firing from such a long range. They generally never fired from a distance greater than 500 yards—where no skill was necessary. And since the war, the large navies have all built up a reserve of trained submarine officers, so that if a new war ever broke out the submarine, relatively, would be as deadly a weapon as it was in 1917.

1 September 1930

In all of these sea-port towns there are large numbers of women who prey on sailors—women who have no sense of decency, but who desire merely to get as much money, or clothing, as they can. And when one of their "lovers" is at sea, they immediately procure another from a ship that is in port. This degeneration of love to the purely physical is a terrible thing. Its worst effect is upon the characters of the people concerned! In reality, they are devil beings.

1 October 1930

In reading about your having children, etc., I find, as I have mentioned before, that at present, I am totally uninterested in the matter. I need and want you alone. You can realize the extent my conceptions of love have changed when I tell you that previous to knowing you, I was certain one must have children for happiness in marriage. Now I instinctively feel that no one, nothing, is necessary for my complete happiness but you. Which reminds me that I am becoming thoroughly diplomatic. The captain (about to be married) stated that it was sinful to marry without having a flock of children (one every year, I suppose, for he is Catholic, and his brother is a priest) and that the great evil of the modern age was birth control.

22 October 1930, Newport, Rhode Island

Tonight, I went ashore to Newport for a walk. This, as you know, is a social center for the extremely wealthy during the summer. One's grandfather (the one who made the money) must be dead before one can be accepted into this exclusive circle. There is a long street of the most beautiful estates—all deserted for the winter.

Perhaps I am too soft hearted, but when, in the business district, I noticed old men out of work, in ragged clothes, I became quite sad. I wish matters were so adjusted that there would be enough food and clothing for everyone. Sights such as this make me feel as though I were receiving my pay without properly earning it. I wish to see everyone happy.

16 November 1930, New London

Your description of France, the customs, people, etc., is very interesting. Even though there is much misgovernment in the country, still the opportunities are greater, and there is more real democracy. Whether this condition will continue in the U.S. is problematical. Up to now, there has been a frontier—people dissatisfied with their conditions of life could go west and take up a homestead. Now it is beginning to be different. Opportunities are diminishing, and the beginnings of a class system are in evidence.

For instance, last week several of the railroads have introduced lower rates for certain classes of travel, corresponding to the second- and third-class travel of European countries. Time was, when an action such as this would have aroused widespread criticism as being undemocratic. Yet, I didn't see a single comment in any newspaper.

Times are very hard. There is genuine distress among the working classes… Unemployment is increasing, and there are more bread lines than ever before.

This generation learned a significant lesson—that it is perhaps not so desirable to have children. There is the lesson of the war—and now unemployment. No wonder birth rates are falling. Parents do not desire to expose children to the uncertainties of this ultra-scientific and technical age.

There is enough food, shelter, and clothing in this country for everyone. We have the spectacle of wheat being cheaper and more abundant than at any time in the last 35 years, and yet large numbers of people are unable to buy bread. Unless those who have the wealth act sensibly in times such as this, there is great danger that they will be forced to share their means with those who are not so fortunate.

17 December 1930, Portsmouth NH

The current attitude of men towards women tends to create an inequality against the woman; and she is made to feel her weakness. When that is so, I consider the man to be a scoundrel, for he has taken more from love than he has given. And to take from one whom he professes to adore is rank hypocrisy. I simply do not comprehend such natures.

Equal rights, woman's suffrage, etc. are merely evidences and symptoms of an unequal condition. They cannot remedy matters. For the remedy lies not in law, but in the heart and mind of the man and woman concerned. The law cannot regulate personal relationships or dictate thoughts.

8 January 1931, Portsmouth NH

I didn't "talk" to you last night because I was busy preparing a speech on "The World Court," which I delivered tonight at Portsmouth. Apparently it was a success because no one hissed, and the people kept on asking questions for about a half-hour, which, fortunately, I was able to answer. Even Jessup couldn't have stumped me tonight.

I have gotten to be great friends with Captain Boyd—the officer I mentioned once before. I always seem to get along better with elderly naval officers—those who have had experience and are broadened. We have many discussions on various matters—these are always interesting. Tonight, he explained his philosophy of life to me. He believes a great deal in things of the spirit—the same as we two.

You asked what I have been reading—the usual things. However, I have studied "Introduction to Political Science" by Garner,[26] which I found highly instructive. For the first time I understand the origin of constitutions, legislatures, the state, etc. It is a deep subject and shows me how little I really know. It is appalling to be so ignorant. Yet, all I ever do is to skim the surface.

19 January 1931, Portsmouth NH

I am becoming a second Babbitt. The Kiwanis Club of Portsmouth wrote me, saying: "The news of your splendid address has spread" etc. etc., and so they want me to speak to them at a dinner on the World Court! Imagine me talking to these businessmen on the World Court!

27 January 1931, Portsmouth NH

I must tell you of the Kiwanis… As I looked at that self-satisfied, cultureless group of businessmen, I felt boiling mad inside of me that I was to speak to them on the World Court. They didn't have the faintest conception of what is worthwhile in life. They listened attentively and asked questions, so my talk must have been all right, but I was glad to leave.

I don't think I'll do any more talking before such organizations. It is a waste of time.

9 February 1931, Portsmouth NH

In one of Tagore's essays, I found the reason for the practice of early marriage in India. Their conception of marriage is that the individual exists for the sake of the household—the household being the medium for developing the race and civilization. Realizing

---

26 James W. Garner, "Introduction to Political Science" (American Book Company, 1910).

that the feeling of love is very strong in many individuals, and that this feeling might overcome their desire to marry for the benefit of the household, the marriage age was set so low that by the time the man and woman arrived at the age where passion takes hold, they would have been married a long time and the passion would be a relatively unimportant feature in their lives.

It is a sort of Fascism, isn't it? Always, always, the tendency to force the individual to give his life and happiness to an abstract principle. I believe that it is why those who are subnormal in some respect can fit into such a scheme. Even you and I accept our new freedom somewhat hesitantly and still have a twinge of conscience over our "selfishness" in forgetting the world and losing ourselves in our own feelings. The force of tradition and environment does have a strong hold.

Tagore continues: —Those who have found the answer in love are like a silent object, which can be seen, but not heard. He means that when two people are deeply in love, it can be seen by everyone, even though the two are inclined to say very little in public. "They remain silent, which the rest of the world continues with its shouting and its clamor."

One is of the world only until he finds his destiny. Then he withdraws.

22 February 1931, At Sea

I believe the sea has a certain effect in building fine character. One gets away from the multitude, and there is time on the lonely night watches to think, to evaluate matters of life. What more fitting surroundings could there be than the stars, the sea, and the wind for lofty thoughts, for thoughts are the expressions of a long sought for ideal.

28 March 1931, Coco Solo, Canal Zone

It may be that my philosophy of life is entirely wrong. Perhaps one is intended to find happiness in whatever he does—and not think too much of the past or the future. But I cannot attune myself to such conditions. I am like a lonely wayfarer. In dreaming there is never fulfillment. Imaginings are but empty shells—and occasionally one must have substance to reward his thoughts.

3 April 1931

I have just returned from a walk to Panama City. I have not been there since 1927. The place looks just the same, except perhaps that it has become a little more Americanized. This is typical of all the places with no culture of their own—they soon become slaves of American advertising and customs.

6 April 1931, Balboa, Canal Zone

Nearly all the popular literature that has been written about Panama and the Zone has been by tourists—people who pass through here in a steamer, staying perhaps two or three days. To them, this is an unusually interesting place...

Climate is not all—there are the people. The Panamanians are by nature and environment an unprogressive race. They must not be blamed too much for this characteristic; the climate is largely responsible. Early in the morning, when it is still cool, one starts out with excellent resolutions as to what he will accomplish that day. By nine or so, the heat has become intolerably intense, and it is very difficult to drive one's self to work. The afternoons are impossible for work. The evenings are again cool. One can sleep here for hours, and not mind it.

The Panamanians—they exist as an ancillary to the canal. The only reason Panama has ever amounted to anything at all is because of outside influence. In the 1850s, the Panama Railroad was built to take care of the great increase in freight... Of their own initiative and efforts, the Panamanians have created nothing. They have merely been the recipients of what good fortune has thrown in their laps. Like all peoples placed in a similar position, they constantly rave and rant about American imperialism. Wait until you come here; some of your contra-nationalistic ideas may undergo a change.

The great mass of the people are utterly ignorant, and are the cats-paws of the few who rule. Recently the Arosimena crowd[27] was thrown out of office (you remember two of the girls at International House) and a new one took their place so as to divide the loot more equitably...

The people live in crowded, smelly houses, worse than anything you have probably seen. Only so much of hygiene is evident, as is made compulsory. Did I tell you that on Good Friday, when I was in the Cathedral for a few minutes, mothers were bringing their children to kiss a certain spot on a statue of Christ—the same spot thousands had kissed that day. I shudder when I think of it. And the perfumed smell of the unwashed throng! Some may see beauty and "picturesqueness" in such a scene. I cannot. Increasingly there has come to me the truth that for real beauty to exist, it must start from the inside—that what is outside will not be at variance with that within. A poet, or an author on the search for a romantic scene, could have become rapturous over what I saw Friday; I saw only superstition, ignorance, and filth.

9 April 1931, At sea off Tobago Island

One should, no doubt, let reason reign, and understand that what is impossible cannot be. However, one [would be] ess than human to push aside longings by force of logic.

---

27 Likely referring to Florencio Harmodio Arosemena Guillén (1872–1945) deposed in a coup d'etat in 1931.

11 April 1931, Balboa, Canal Zone

Despite what you have often told me—that one should bend where standing straight will be too great a strain—I believe you are the same way. I believe you will stick just as strongly for your ideals as I do for mine. You accuse me of being an obstinate character. You are, too, and I admire you for it, for your obstinacy is directed toward attainment of ideals. You impel me to be so, even in my thought, as I imagine you would want me to be. Can one have a greater influence than that?

22 April 1931, Anchored off Pedro Gonzales

Together with a boat load of men, I went to visit the King of Pedro Gonzales Island… The settlement, consisting of our huts, lies back in the hills about one half hour's walk along a rocky beach… An event such as this naturally sets one to thinking. Here are these people, living a calm, placid life, untroubled by nationalism, capitalism, etc. They have no wants which they cannot satisfy on the island—there is a sufficiency of coconuts, pineapples, bananas, iguanas for meat, and fish can be caught. Furthermore, the island is not useful for any known purpose, so no one will ever disturb them.

On the other hand, they must be incapable of any great emotions. I believe this can only come with civilization, and the greater the extent of civilization, the greater emotion is it possible to have.

29 April 1931, At sea off Malpelo Island

One interesting experience was the school of porpoises we passed through. I sighted a white turbulent patch of water about two miles ahead—evidently thousands of fish jumping to the surface. When we came close to the commotion, it proved to be a mass of countless dark porpoises, somersaulting slowly. Several of the men on deck had rifles, which they used against these large fish. It was saddening to see a wounded porpoise jump twenty or thirty feet out of the water, cavorting wildly, and then fall back into the sea.

Why people delight in taking life needlessly I cannot understand. It is the same way with birds. They sit upon deck shooting at them. Every once in a while, a bird is shot through the wing, falls into the water, tries to fly again—but his feeble efforts are not sufficient. So he is doomed to the water—his wings soon become waterlogged, and he becomes a prey to large fish or to starvation.

On the other hand, there is the kindness of the men toward young birds which, because of their inability to fly, sink exhausted to the sea. When these float by the ship, the sailors will crawl over the side and get them on board. Here they feed them and give them water. The poor things valiantly flap their wings, trying to dry them. The next day, when we must get underway for diving operations, one of the men will take the bird to a high part of the ship and cast him loose. He generally flies for a moment or so—when he falls back into the sea. His wings are not strong enough to bear him up. Such is the way of nature.

30 April 1931, At the Equator, Long 81 degrees—30' W

This evening, we crossed the Equator... In accordance with the ancient custom of the seas, early this morning Davey Jones, King Neptune's right-hand man, appeared from the sea and issued subpoenas to all the [pollywogs] on board. (A pollywog is one who has never entered the royal domain—crossed the equator)... I, being the senior pollywog, was the first one to be blindfolded and brought before his Serene Highness to answer various charges referred against me...[continued 1 May 1931]

...I was ordered to get on my stomach and crawl like a jellyfish—a rather difficult thing to do for me, not well versed in the physiological habits of that creature. However, I must have succeeded tolerably well, for, by way of appreciation the royal barber invited me to be seated at his chair—a stool rigged up so that one would be constantly shocked by an electric current. Being an officer, I was only given a shampoo of thick engine grease and fuel oil. As I rose from this unusual experience, a hose of sea water was plied on me, and I was then ordered to walk the gangplank—into the ocean—which I did. And then swam back to the ship's side—thus completing my initiation and earning the cognomen of "shellback."

Some of the men did not fare so well. I neglected to mention that there was a royal doctor, too. He forced a vile concoction down each of the men's throats by means of a hydrometer used on the storage battery. I am afraid not all of the sulfuric acid had been washed from it. The barber treated them royally, too, cutting their hair in a delightfully haphazard way with a pair of tin snips. Then, after being beaten quite well with the clubs of the police, they were afforded the privilege of kissing King Neptune's dimpled knee (a fat machinist's mate), the Queen's hand, and the baby's face, the baby being a Filipino.

7 May 1931, Coco Solo, Canal Zone

I have just read one of your "objective" evaluations of me—wherein you state that after two years study of me, you have come to the conclusion I am "perfect." And to make matters worse, you add that you are not blind as am I.

I am afraid there are other people who judge me without the aid of romantic glass, and to date none of these has ever informed me that in me abides perfection.

15 May 1931, Coco Solo, Canal Zone

Mail service has improved considerably since you left France, and now it only takes a little more than two weeks. I agree with you: The French are abominable!

24 May 1931, Coco Solo, Canal Zone

All that I see in the lives of others confirms me as to the difficulty of retaining what we have, of warding off the commonplace. This continues to make me think seriously of our future life together. There is so very much of disillusion in couples living together for no valid reason, that I become sad. Last night I visited, for dinner, a lieutenant from the ship and his wife. She pretends to be a "countess." She imagines that she is very intellectual and subtle. In fact, she is neither. She goes about a good deal in the company of young officers and has a rather unsavory reputation among the Navy people here.

The first time I met her was in New London. She sat down next to me on a couch and moved very close—I was a stranger then. I don't believe I have ever met a woman who repels me as much as does she. In my mind, I think of her as a temperamental bitch. Of course, one cannot refuse invitations always, especially when she is the wife of an officer on the ship.

We discussed marriage last night. She said—"But what is one to do when there is no more in marriage?" and I answered—"Do not let marriage reach that point. Look for happiness in yourselves instead of from the outside." There she was, untidy, and she was wondering why there was no more in marriage.

I only mention all this to show you once more that I am greatly concerned with that same problem. I am so very serious about this. I know that, at the present moment, we have what very few people in the world possess, a true, deep, beautiful love. I also know that no matter what happens, we shall always remain great friends and companions.

28 May 1931, Coco Solo, Canal Zone

Last night I acted as the host for a farewell party given in honor of a lieutenant who was today detached from the ship. The captain's wife was sick; therefore, he could not attend and requested me to take his place.

There was dinner at the Washington Hotel, then we all went to the Atlantic Café—a typical Panamanian Café. I dreaded the event, because I had been there before and once is enough for a lifetime. Besides, one of the couples invited were openly quarreling—this depressed me to start off with. Then, after she had had several drinks, the lieutenant's wife began acting like the very ordinary girl she is and making certain half-way suggestive remarks, which caused all the others (they are all married) to laugh. And I thought, "Must I forever be party to social affairs which I utterly detest and simulate liking for people I care nothing about?" And it seems that this cannot keep up forever. I cherish my self-respect and my ideals. And when people become gross, I am deeply offended.

I have determined to accept no more invitations for affairs which will involve this form of entertainment. I prefer to be alone if necessary.

28 June 1931, Coco Solo, Canal Zone

What has gratified me exceedingly is the growing realization on the part of the world that Germany is in dire straits—that she is not being treated fairly. The French, nor anyone else, can no longer point the finger of war guilt at Germany. In the U.S. and England, there has grown up a distinct feeling of friendliness toward Germany. I notice it in the press and in remarks people make. And—France is slowly emerging as the champion of militarism and reaction. Her recent refusal to accept, without quibbling, the American proposal for a moratorium, shows her in her true light. Your descriptions of the German people have affected me profoundly—and I believe I know their difficulties. If only the extremists do not gain control and alleviate the good feeling that twelve years of "playing the game" by Stressman and Bruening[28] have engendered. It is very plain to me

---

28 Gustav Stresemann (1878–1929), German Foreign Minister, 1923–1929; Heinrich Bruning (1885–1970), German Chancellor, 1930–1932.

that the proposed moratorium is the last step in the force of war debts. That is why France is against it. And—the end of war debts is the beginning of a real demand by Germany and Austria for revision of Versailles. It is inevitable.

Amusing—the stories we read of the hard-heartedness of Germany after the war of 1870! Compare it with the French treatment of Germany.

3 July 1931, Coco Solo, Canal Zone

You will never be able to imagine what I have gone through this last year with the captain. He leaves Monday morning. That is why I am writing of it now. The new captain is a real officer and a man. To have someone over you, finding fault every minute of the day, treating one like a servant (he treated all the officers and men that way) and not to be able to say anything in return. How many times this year have I been boiling and raging inside of me to think that I, who have a sensitive nature, should have to appear calm and be the recipient of constant insults from one so lacking in the qualities of leadership and decency.

A submarine is an unnatural place to spend one's life under the best of circumstances. When, on top of this one is forced to undergo extreme mental cruelty—well—it is bad.

Graf, the other officer—I have seen crying after a particularly bad case. Can you imagine what a relief it is to emerge from an intolerable condition such as this.

All year I have refrained from writing of this, for it would only have worried you. Had I not had to consider you, I should have taken some drastic step by now—probably made an official report. This would have, probably, done me great harm, but it would have been worth the price to make known the unofficer-like type of man he is. These are not my sentiments alone. Every officer who has ever served in the S-48 has made statements as strong—even stronger. Thank God it is over.

I used to dread going to sea with him—the constant nagging and fault-finding for no reason at all.

I am so glad now! In a week I shall be the Executive Officer, which means that I shall really have charge of the ship's organization and the other officers.

19 August 1931, Coco Solo, Canal Zone

There is one thing which does not please me as much as you imagine—your cooking. I am not joking, either. You may have thought I was from my previous letters, but I was not.

Please do not go in extensively for cooking. You will spoil something for me. If there is to be any mild form of drudgery, we'll both do it—and I'd much rather do it myself... Your cooking does not lend itself to romance. We'll manage the first month, somehow. And after that there will always be a maid.

20 August 1931, Coco Solo, Canal Zone

This entire year I have been unsettled mentally and physically. I need reorientation, and I know I shall obtain this from you. There is this vague feeling of void and emptiness in me, which prevents me from working as well as I should and from enjoying real happiness. In a few more weeks, this will be remedied.

I am so grateful that my life was so ordained that I met you. By what a narrow margin I missed going along in complete oblivion of what a dear person you were.

27 August 1931

I am not a very pleasant person anymore. I become irritated readily, and I can't for the life of me concentrate on anything. Never before was I this way, and I don't know what to do about it. I do hope that you will have the proper healing influence.

3 February 1932, USS S-48 at sea

You have been ever so dear and fine to me—and you have made me regard you in a higher, nobler way than ever before. Our companionship has grown apace, and now you are so close to me, that it no longer seems we are individual persons.

I was miserable and wretched Sunday after I left you. The world does not seem a proper place when I cannot be with you. You are absolutely the sweetest and loveliest and most charming little thing there ever was, despite what you may modestly say to the contrary. And everything about you is the same. Your hair is the nicest and most fragrant there ever was; your dear little fingers are simply exquisite; your shining eyes are brighter than the stars I look for; your lips are the softest things on earth; and your pretty cheeks are rosier than any sunrise.

7 February 1932, USS S-48, Guantanamo Bay, Cuba

This afternoon we shall finally leave on the first leg of the cruise, 1,000 miles, and end up at Key West, Florida. The members of the expedition have had a little trouble in getting their apparatus working properly. This accounts for the delay until today.

Guantanamo Bay is an unusual place. There are about twenty naval families on the station—and so you can imagine what type of social life they have here. A friend, Dr.___, and his wife live here; I went there for dinner… The surrounding country is barren, and the soil is of a hard clayey nature, so that it is difficult to cultivate plants. Even water must be brought in barges from a distance…

It was rather pathetic to see how little people have to interest them here.

10 February 1932, USS S-48, off Jamaica

We had a great deal of trouble with certain valves, which are of great importance when diving—and shortly after passing the eastern-most point of Jamaica, when we dived they commenced giving trouble once more. So, we lay to at sea for five hours while we made temporary repairs... The captain has had very little sleep, and was on edge. He was all for sending a dispatch to the Navy Department that the S-48 could not complete this cruise. Two of the other officers agreed with him, but I succeeded in dissuading him from such an unwise action. It would have been very bad for him and for the ship. The way I feel about it is that if we are assigned a duty to perform, it is up to us to accomplish it, no matter how much extra effort, lack of sleep, etc. it may involve.

12 February 1932, At sea, about 50 miles SW of Key West, Florida

All the fresh food has run out, and now we are subsisting on canned goods. There is no more bread either, and the biscuits the cook bakes are like lead balls. However, I am, in a measure, enjoying the cruise. For us to finish it completely, will be in the nature of a real accomplishment, and I had much rather be doing this, than be tied up alongside a dock doing useless and foolish tasks...

Doctor Meinesz[29] is a rather intelligent person aside from his scientific bent. We were discussing the lack of moral strength in intellectuals where war was concerned, and he told me of the meeting at Stockholm in 1930 of the Geophysical Society—an international scientific organization. The president, a Frenchman, absolutely refused to invite a leading German geophysicist; only when the other members forced him to, did he do so...

My own confidence in my views seems to grow. I am aware I have not yet fully developed some of them to myself; there are opinions not yet fully known to me. These must be fully brought out and considered; also, inconsistencies to be set right—but on the whole I seem to have a grasp of a comprehensive system.

---

29 Dr. A. Vening Meinesz (1887-1966), a Dutch geophysicist aboard the submarine to conduct a gravimetric survey along with scientists from Princeton and Brown.

13 February 1932, U.S.S. S-48, Key West, Florida
[West India Gravity Expedition][30]

This afternoon we all had to go to the commandant's home for tea. He was ill—so the commandant's wife took charge and didn't give the guests a chance to say a single word. It was an interesting study—to see this obese woman with red fingernails, huge gold bracelets, talk and talk away and smile mechanically at the right time—and say nothing. She said, "Oh, I think scientists are so interesting (this at the doctor!). How unreal it all is. Why should such ignorant and commonplace people be put in positions of social leadership. It all seems wrong. This evening, the doctor and I went for a walk into Key West. We discussed this question, and we agreed that a civilization without idealism is the same as clogging the circulation of the world's life. It is the same as at Panama—people being placed in a position entirely above the one they should occupy. This doctor complained that during the entire tea, he had tried to say one sentence and was not successful because she took his words away from him and managed to cover a field of conversation as broad as from rain, bootleggers, earthquakes, to Rome and Japan and Guantanamo...she made a shift to the subject of mosquitoes, which reminded me that I was itching to get away, and that her dark red fingernails and bracelets made her look like an African savage, and that among some aboriginal tribes people of that sort are disposed of in one or two unique ways: (a) "Roasting" method, or (b) "Drowning in river" method. Perhaps I am too tired to appreciate such social amenities right now.

1 January 1933, USS S-48, Coco Solo, Canal Zone

I must write you again. There is nothing else I wish or care to do—but to write you, to attain the feeling of closeness which this affords me...

---

30 For more information see "The Navy-Princeton Gravity Expedition to the West Indies in 1932" (Government Printing Office, 1933).

Not all selfishness has been driven out for me. When I desire your happiness, I still wish to be the agent whereby it is given you. I am not strong enough yet to dissociate myself from this, which should be an abstract affair—the eminence of our love...

No matter what you may write, it does not matter. Things have become much clearer for me. The misery and the contemplation of the past months are gone. In their place I have this calm view of your unearthly love and of heavenly you. I feel that my affection for you and my care for our love has soared to nobler heights.

8 January 1933, Anchored off Flamenso Island

This has been a very busy day. We left the Submarine Base at 0530 and spent all day until 4 p.m. transiting the Canal. The locks on the Pacific side are being overhauled, so traffic is much slower than usual.

Then we steamed to sea and made a trim dive to get ready for the inspection by the admiral tomorrow morning. This will be my last inspection on the S-48, and I am very glad.

It hardly seems possible that in four months I'll be able to leave this ship and cast from my mind the many unpleasantnesses I have encountered on board. I don't take matters very seriously anymore—although I still become aggravated at the constant, ever constant fault finding by ____ —I think the man is mentally ill; I am sorry for the other officers who will be on board with him another year after I leave.

There is a great deal of renewed hope in me, and I am determined to do everything I can so that our life together may be a happy one... I don't know yet where I am going for shore duty, I hope it is Washington, of course. I have done all I could to get Washington duty, and only last week I submitted another request, which I was assured would receive a favorable endorsement by the commander of the Submarine Force (Admiral ___). This does not ensure that I'll get what I ask for, but it may help.

11 January 1933, USS S-48, Coco Solo, Canal Zone

Today was a very busy one. I was President of a Court Martial, which tried two men for theft. They plead "not guilty" and had a civilian lawyer to defend them. When the prosecution brought in two lottery tickets as evidence, the defense counsel objected to their introduction stating since it was contrary to the laws of the United States to conduct lotteries, it was not permissible to introduce lottery tickets as evidence!!! I don't pretend to be much of a lawyer, but I was not convinced, and I overruled his objection.

Well—the case dragged along, and it seemed as though there were not enough evidence to convict the defendants, when, lo and behold, the civilian lawyer, wishing to show his clients that he was really working hard for them, put them on the stand to testify in their own behalf (a sailor is impressed by such a thing). Since this gave the prosecution and the court a chance to cross examine the defendants, we brought out certain damaging facts and inconsistencies of testimony, which resulted in a finding of guilty for the two men, and a sentence of dishonorable discharge from the Navy.

I felt very sorry to have had the duty of punishing the men in this way, but it can't be helped. This is an unpleasant phase of naval duty.

About a month ago, one of our men became affected with venereal disease for the sixth time in two years. Consequently, we recommended him for discharge from the Navy. Last week there came a letter from his mother stating she had heard from her son he was to be discharged, and asking us to inform her of the reason. Try to conceive how you would go about answering such a letter...

I read in the newspaper this morning where it was proposed in one of the Senate committees to make Army and Navy tours of duty in outlying places, such as the Canal Zone, last for a period of four years! Well—I will not even begin to entertain the possibility of such an event. It would be just too much. These people can have no conception of what it means to have to stay in a tropical country for that length of time. They come down here for one or two weeks, and it is a welcome change for them—there are plenty of drinks and everything looks luxuriant and romantic. I certainly hope I get my orders for shore duty before such a calamity is enacted in a congressional bill.

17 January 1933, USS S-48, En route Kingston, Jamaica

This trip is just as rough as the one last year—when we were both in the Caribbean at the same time, and when I wished I could have been with you to comfort you.

As soon as we got outside the Canal Breakwater, we had to close all hatches; there has been no opportunity to open them yet, so the air is foul inside the ship. We are rolling heavily, and the seas are constantly coming over the bow.

I have a hard time when I climb up on the "A-frame" to get sight of the stars and the sun. One of the men has to hold me so that I may be free to work the sextant and not fall overboard at the same time.

...as I look up into the skies searching for stars, tears almost come into my eyes, for it is you I am really searching for.

20 January 1933, USS S-48, Kingston, Jamaica

We are anchored off the Myrtle Bank Hotel, a short distance away. This is good because we are not bothered by visitors. All day long, however, small boats with natives came alongside, either to sell fruits or to solicit washing.

Each boat generally contains one or two women and a man to row. Sometimes the women row, and the men are the passengers. The women have a great deal of personality, while the men appear stolid. This morning, one came alongside and said, in the typically broad native dialect, "Good morning, Mr. Smith and Mr. Johnson, and all my other namesakes. God bless you—let me wash your skivvies (drawers)." And she kept up an animated conversation with the men, her eyes flashing and all her white teeth exposed. It is really a pleasure to watch these natural people—although as an officer, in the presence of the men, one is not supposed to display too great an interest. I always delight in seeing natural people (you are the most natural person I have ever known!)—it is so different than what one ordinarily sees.

_____ has a stock answer to all solicitations for laundry—"We have a Chinese laundry on board—he washes all our clothes every day." One of the engineers always says—"We never have dirty clothes—we throw them away after we use them." They are always surprised at this answer, and they reply—"Oh, this cannot be true—it is too good to be true." There is a great deal more to their expressions and their manner of answering than there is to the words they employ.

Even the local "girls" come out in the small boats and solicit trade by placing their cards on the end of an oar and reaching it to the sailors. This is the first time I have ever seen this seagoing form of advertising. This afternoon, a boat with four mulatto girls rowed by, close aboard. The girls lifted their dresses (they had some flimsy underthings on) and urged the men to come visit them!

It was an instructive though sad sight. It shows what "love" means to a great many people. Just the mere use of a woman's body, without her own desire, or without any thought by the man for the need of the woman.

2 February 1933, USS S-48, Coco Solo, Canal Zone

Yesterday morning, I was informed that one of our men was locked up in the Colon jail. I went there to help him. It seemed he had been living with a Columbian woman for the past four months. Recently her old lover returned, so she and the latter determined to get rid of the man (of the S-48). So, she hid her 28 dresses and her "jewelry" and went to the police and accused him of stealing the dresses and the jewelry. _____ was arrested while he was in a saloon in Colon. Later, the first lover came to see him and offered to withdraw all charges for $500. ___ hired a Panamanian lawyer who is a good friend of the judge before whom the case is to be tried.

The whole matter is disgusting. This particular woman has done the same stunt four times previously against sailors. Even so, ___ has already had to pay the lawyer $100 for his fee; otherwise, he would not have been released without bail by the judge, and once bail is given in a Panamanian Court—well... I saw the woman when she came to see the chief of police. She wore gold bracelets around her ankles! Probably the charges will eventually be dropped. One of ___'s friends went to the woman's apartment, for which he had been paying the rent, and found the 28 dresses hidden away behind the dishes in the cupboard.

There are so many of these sordid affairs. To be sure, some sailors may not know any better and there is some excuse for them, but even people who have had the benefit of education and good family often give in to every whim, thinking thereby to find pleasure and happiness. As you said recently, restraint is a wonderful thing; without it, one loses that which he strives to gain.

7 February 1933, Anchored off Pedro Gonzales Island

Today I started reading Volume I of Marx.[31]

25 February 1933, Coco Solo, Canal Zone

Letter from Rickover to the Navy detailer

I have been informed by Lieutenant ___ of the Bureau of Engineering that I am to be ordered as an assistant Transportation of Naval Material at Philadelphia, Pa.

I am writing to ask you whether it is possible that I be assigned to duty at Washington, D.C.

---

31 Karl Marx, 3 Volume work "Das Kapital."

My wife is a Doctor of Philosophy in International Law and is actively engaged in that profession. Recently, her book "International Law in National Courts" was published. At the present time she holds a research fellowship at Columbia University. Ever since our marriage in 1931, we have been away from each other most of the time because my duty has been at a place where she is unable to engage in her work.

I had hoped to obtain duty in Washington and have named such duty consistently on my fitness reports for the last two years, because there is a possibility my wife may obtain a position at the State Department; if this does not materialize, she will be able to continue with her research work in Washington because of the excellent facilities available in that city. In the event I am ordered to Philadelphia, it means that my wife and I will again be unable to establish a home, because I feel I have no right to ask her to give up her profession—insomuch as she is accomplishing a worthwhile object, and her work is as important to her as my profession is to me.

I should be satisfied with assignment to any duty in Washington, although I, of course, prefer duty in connection with Engineering.

I realize that in making assignments of officers, the interests of the Navy must be considered first, but I hope that in view of the reasons I have stated consideration will be given to my request for duty in Washington.

28 February 1933, USS S-48, Coco Solo, Canal Zone

It is too bad the news of Philadelphia duty reached you at a time when you were otherwise dispirited. I didn't wish to wire you, because I knew that you would be disappointed—yet I felt honor bound to do so.

...as to your plans—I need not state, once more, that no matter what my personal feelings may be—that I shall never urge you to do anything you believe to be injurious to your profession, or otherwise. I look at it this way: That I might have been assigned duty in some inland city, or in the South, or on the West Coast—which would have been tremendously worse. Let us not rebel too much at Fate. If the letter I have written bears no fruit, I am not going to lose myself in vain regrets; instead, I shall do the best I can in my new duty. At any rate, I shall be free of the S-48, and of the transfers, and I'll be my own boss.

3 March 1933, USS S-48, Coco Solo, Canal Zone

It is late at night; all day the captain and I have been working away on a lecture on submarine tactics, which will be delivered next week. I have been engaged in its preparation for the last two weeks, and today we put it into final form. Tell me what you think of it. Today, he was really very pleasant, and I managed to lose my antagonistic attitude. I thought how different it could have been if he had been this way for the last two years—if he had tried to be friendly, instead of superior. But I am afraid it is only a flash in the pan with him. He is too self-centered.

8 March 1933, USS S-48, Coco Solo, Canal Zone

Do not worry about the duty in Philadelphia. Probably this week I shall receive an answer to the letter I wrote the Detail Officer. I only hope that as a result of my request I do not fare worse than I do now. The duty I was assigned to at Philadelphia was about the best job available there—absolutely my own boss, free to come and go as I chose, and with short working hours. But I knew you preferred Washington, so I wrote that letter. Let us forget all that now. I have a certain philosophy in life—that when one does the best he can, and matters then do not turn out as he desires, one should not worry over them. What else is to be done? For the present our affairs are in the laps of the Gods. I pray that we do not get worse than we already have.

Really, if we look at this from a broad standpoint, it is all so relatively unimportant. The main thing that counts is whether we love and have each other. The rest will take care of itself. I shall become a Simon Legree[32] and force you, with a whip, if necessary, to keep yourself occupied. And if you attempt to become a model housewife, I'll desert you for good! I didn't marry you because I expected you to cook; it would have been cheaper to hire a nice Swedish girl for that. Besides, anyone can cook!

9 March 1933

I have a certain philosophy of life, which includes a great deal of tolerance for others, their beliefs, actions, etc. But I nevertheless appreciate the fact that in the world, as it is constituted, my theories, though they may be ideal, are not entirely workable.

14 March 1933, USS S-48, Pinas Bay, [Republic of Panama]

After transiting the Canal yesterday, we went straight out to sea, and we were underway all last night until early this morning when we commenced making torpedo practice runs...

I am enclosing a miniature chart which shows Pinas Bay and Galeu Island—the lovely place of which I once wrote to you—and where I should like to go with you sometime. I have also indicated where the Panamanian prison colony is. The reason we have chosen Pinas Bay as the scene of our operations for the next two weeks is because the sea bottom is of a harder texture near that place, than anywhere else within easy sailing distance of the Canal. We are engaged in firing torpedoes by sound; i.e., we listen for the target by our sound equipment and plot her course and speed, without looking at her through the periscope, and fire torpedoes at her. If the bottom is soft, the sound emitted by the propellers of the target

---

32 A character in Harriet Beecher Stowe's "Uncle Tom's Cabin."

ship is absorbed in the mud, and this is very difficult to pick up. A hard bottom, on the contrary, reflects the sound.

According to the chart, which was constructed from soundings taken in 1931, there were but seven huts in the village at the bend of the bay; today there are thirteen! This is probably owing to the depression, which has caused many city families to give up the fight and move to these out-of-the-way places where, if they haven't all the advantages of a modern civilized community like Panama, they at least have a place to live, and food obtainable without too much exertion—and no danger of starvation.

The more I see of this primitive mode of life, the more do I realize that it has certain great advantages. The waters hereabouts teem with all manner of fishes; one has merely to throw a line into the water to obtain a bite. The natives paddle by in their canoes, made by themselves from a log. They paddle gracefully and easily.

The Bay has a mouth about a mile wide; it is easy to enter, and it is surrounded on both sides by high hills, which make it a sheltered spot, because the wind is deflected.

16 March 1933, Pinas Bay, R.P.

We are already on friendly terms with the natives. Right now, we have several bunches of green bananas hanging in the motor room; these we obtained for a bar of saltwater soap. As the bananas ripen, the men eat them. Isn't it peculiar how different classes and sorts of people can get along friendly and peaceably as long as both know there is fair dealing on each side. From what I have seen of "natives," they are always courteous and pleasant, and will harm no one if not interfered with unduly.

Sometimes it occurs to me that it will be a blessing for the world when the existing supplies of cheap and abundant fuel are used up. This will necessarily bring about a slowing of the present industrial system—because, in the end, it is based on the ability to obtain fuel with little effort. You will note that the sudden jump in industrialism coincides with the introduction of oil as a fuel. When these fuels dwindle, perhaps mankind will be forced to go back to a sane life. To offset the possible decline in the available supplies of fuel, scientists are attempting to obtain sub-atomic energy. I sincerely hope they fail in this. It reminds me of Pandora's Box; where a great deal of misery was let loose by learning too much.

The news from Germany is not very pleasant; I am sorry that so much hatred has to be generated in order to obtain modification of the Versailles Treaty and eliminate the Republic. The Italian fascists were much more dignified and sensible. Isn't it strange that one should say that of the Italians, as compared with the Germans? I do hope that what is left of the Junker class is able to seize power and rule the country. I imagine you must be a great deal upset by the course of events in Germany.

16 March 1933, Pinus Bay, R.P.

I have been reading "The Martial Spirit" by Walter Millis, published by the Literary Guild in 1931. Although it is primarily a study of the Spanish-American War, it nevertheless shows how unnecessary that war was—and the manner in which we were dragged into it. The book is written along the same lines as Moon's "Imperialism." One could almost imagine that Moon had written it himself. At any rate the author has been influenced by Moon—or by his approach. The book has shortcomings in that it is absolutely one-sided, but, in general, it does show that we entered into a war for no reason at all.

You may find it interesting reading—despite its under mass of detail. It seems to me that nations must be insane to go to war; certainly the people would never wish it—if they understood all the implications. One thing I liked about Dunn's book was his discussion of what is meant by the expression "Japan wants Manchuria" etc., etc. In other words, we are inclined to attribute the desire for Manchuria to every inhabitant of Japan, wherein such desire is common probably to a few of the higher officials.

I believe that many of our troubles, national as well international, are caused by the selfishness of individuals who are trying to gain material advantages in a measure beyond what they deserve. One is amazed at the stupidity of nations and people, and yet the fight appears hopeless. The more I learn about the conduct of our affairs, national and foreign, the more am I inclined to wash my hands of them and concentrate on personal matters. At the present time, despite all the prevalent misery and the recent memory of war and inflation, we are again on the verge of more wars.

22 March 1933, S-48, Anchored off Pedro Gonzales Island

I am very sorry to have to tell you that I received a reply to the letter I wrote the Detail Officer, and that it is definite that I shall go to Philadelphia for duty. I know how much store you set on your career, and the place it occupies in your life, and I am very sorry that I am instrumental in preventing you from doing what you wish. I will only reaffirm what I have said previously—that you must not give too much consideration to me when you decide what to do. I would not want you to do that. All I know is that we are both fighting valiantly for our love and that we are determined to do all in our power to make it shine forth...

This morning, the S-48 acted as a "lost" submarine. We submerged in a region unknown to anyone else, and the other ships of the Division were required to search for us. All they knew was that we were somewhere in an area of 25 square miles.

We sank slowly to the bottom and lay there in 110 feet of water for four hours. Men were stationed fore and aft tapping on the hull so that the sound emitted might be picked up by oscillators. Also, at regular intervals, we discharged oil to make an oil slick on the surface.

Although we could pick up with our own oscillator the noise of propellers, we, ourselves, were never discovered. Finally, we released our marker buoys. These are structures which are watertight and contain telephones and signal lights; they rise to the surface when released, provided the submarine is in water of depth no greater than 400 feet. Shortly after this we established telephone communication with one of the searching vessels.

Even though we were on the bottom at a depth greater than 100 feet, there was sufficient light to see what was going on outside, through the conning tower ports. The effect of the sea waves was also felt. All during the four hours we were rocked gently from one side to the other. The movement of the sea water, to and fro, could be observed through the ports.

Many jellyfish could be seen, contracting and expanding. The water at the bottom was full of minute suspended matter, and the jellyfish were absorbing it by their movements. I never realized that they lived so far down. I thought they were a surface species. Later, when we surfaced, and came up with a rush, one of them was too slow to get clear of the ship, and I found him expiring on deck.

25 March 1933, Balboa, Canal Zone

Do not be too worried about Germany. I believe that the weight and the responsibility of power will chasten the Nazi leaders, and they will not be as extreme as people imagine. The parallel occurred in Italy prior to the March on Rome. Class hatred was being preached by the Fascists, but in a short time, when the leaders felt surer of themselves, they restrained the unruly elements.

It is disheartening, of course, the possibility of another general European war. The young Nazis are no different than the young Peruvians, Bolivians, Paraguayans, or Columbians. War is a glorious adventure when one does not know what it means. But let there come an actual war, and they will soon lose their enthusiasm. I, for the life of me, cannot understand why any sane human being should desire war. How can men and women be so lacking in sense and discernment?

You must not permit yourself to become incensed against the French or the Poles...I believe I am beyond the effect of any nationalist propaganda. Ordinary human beings who are forced to engage in war reap no benefits, and never really know why they are fighting. The reasons for waging war have become so complex that even those responsible for permitting it to occur do not know why. Who of the 1914 statesmen now living knows why he led his country towards war—or whether he was right in so doing.

I am sorry that Germany must be led by the great mass, instead of by the chosen few. This is not so remarkable, however. The levelling of classes resulting from the deflation, and the Republican government, would tend to diminish the prestige of the higher classes. In this, Germany is no different than any other modern democracy. The others, however, either through greater capacity, experience, or astuteness in democratic forms of government, are able to sway the masses to the will of the leaders. In Germany, at present, the reverse seems to be the case. Briefly, it might be said that the world expected greater things of Germany—that she is capable of more than she is doing.

The Hitlerites have adopted an old expedient in fomenting against the Jews; such a method leads to internal solidarity. The Bolsheviks did exactly the same with respect to the Russian middle class.

The above are my personal reflections about the German situation. I believe that much of the agitation will soon stop. I also believe that if war should break out, Germany would be crushed...and that this time the French would not rely upon treaties to prevent the rearming of her enemy. Within a few hours after the declaration of war, air raids would commence on Germany. Modern bombing planes could easily fly to Berlin and return to the French border. It is a fiction that commercial planes can easily be converted to military use...

It is all dreadful. I hope that we do not have another war to end war!!

30 March 1933, S-48, Off Saboga Island

This week I read Zola's "Lourdes" and liked it a great deal. Except for the ending—yet for a novel some sort of compromise is necessary, I suppose, to finish the book smoothly. One can lay blame upon the Catholic church for tolerating magic springs, etc., yet they do give rise to faith, and they do fill a certain need. How tenaciously people cling to life! I agree with you in that I am not afraid of death, nor would I care to live blind or as a cripple, except if you needed me. Often when we are submerged, I think—what if I should lose control of the ship and she should start down too rapidly to stop. And I find that I don't care much, except for you.

25 April 1933, USS S-48, Coco Solo, Canal Zone

Tomorrow morning, I am to deliver a lecture on "The Care and Operations of Submarine Electrical Machinery." It will be delivered extemporaneously. I have just finished making the outline. If times were better, I believe I could earn some money on shore duty delivering speeches. It is surprising what small knowledge most audiences have—and it is not very difficult to prepare a talk for them. I remember that ___ used to speak in most general terms—and yet received as much as fifty or seventy-five dollars at a time.

This evening, I read the letters written by Captain Scott, the Englishmen, on his voyage of discovery to the South Pole. He reached the pole only to find that Amundsen had been there two months before. It is one of the great epics of loyalty between a group of men that has ever been written. What interested me most was the letter to his wife—particularly the last one—addressed to "My widow" and written while he was starving to death and suffering from frost.

Even here he could not unbend, but remained a dignified husband. He goes so far as to say—"You have meant very much to me." I cannot understand this…I love you dearly and must keep on telling you so. I have often thought of what my reactions would be if I were placed in a hopeless condition in a submarine. I know that my thoughts would be of you alone—and that I should spend my last efforts in writing you of my love, and in telling you what a dear precious person you are.

27 April 1933, USS S-48, Coco Solo, Canal Zone

You must never believe that I remain unaffected by the Depression or by events in Germany, etc. Inside of me I become worked up as much as do you—but I don't permit them to affect me outwardly as much as they do you. Today I saw a picture in the paper of a group of Nazis in uniform forcing the Jewish population of a city in Saxony to clean the streets and whitewash walls. The men were dressed respectably—evidently of the middle class. My feelings are very bitter, too—that a mediocre section of the population should impose their moronic views on an entire people. I have great faith in the German people—that the intelligent ones do not approve. But it would be the same in this country...if a lower section of the population should secure control—the thinking class would be able to do nothing.

Hitler wishes to bring Germany back several hundred years—whereas the Russians are advancing—and therefore ordering their lives in accordance with realism. During the last 100 years, a great deal has been won in the way of freedom of speech, liberation of women, etc. Now the pendulum is swinging the other way.

Yet, despite all of my deep feelings about these matters, I do not permit them to affect me too greatly. What is one to do when he sees an unemployed person or one who is extremely underpaid? Is he at once to give the man money? This isn't the answer, either. Both you and I recognize that the system is wrong whereby so many people, intelligent and otherwise, must literally beg for the chance to earn their bread. We'll talk a great deal of these matters when we meet, but do not for an instant think that I lack human sympathy, or that I am not affected.

2 May 1933, USS S-48, Submerged

There is only one more hour to go, and we shall surface (7:05 p.m.). All the men and officers are going about with a minimum of clothes. It would be unbearable otherwise. I begin to question whether I should like to be in a submarine in wartime, where this extreme physical unpleasantness would be the order of the day. Last night I managed to get a little water from the evaporators. When the evaporators are first started, the water made is salty, and unfit for drinking. But it is excellent for bathing. It was really a great treat to wash in fresh water! And I felt fine—my first real bath in four days—and living in compartments where the temperature is constantly over 100 degrees F. I am afraid many of our men will develop itch and other skin irritations.

This morning when we dived, there were inexperienced men on the bow and stern planes—and the ship started down with a steep angle. Soon we were at 150 feet. We blew tanks and eventually came into the control room and announced: "2500 fathoms" (3 miles deep). He is required to obtain the depth of the sea at regular intervals, and he chose this instant to inform us how deep the ocean was!

30 May 1933, USS S-48, Baltimore, Maryland

Today I read "The Volga Falls to the Caspian Sea" by Boris Pilnyok—a translation from the Russian by Charles Malamuth. The main point of the book is the new place of women under the soviet system; it shows the weaknesses and dangers of the new code of "morals" as well as the advantages. It is really a plea for complete equal rights for women. It portrays the status of women just about as Hindu depicted it in "Humanity Uprooted." Russian novels are tiresome reading, particularly since it is obvious they are pure propaganda, ennobling the true communist and casting slurs on all others. What is not generally realized by those who acclaim the social "advances" made in Russia, is that only a small portion of the population have the intelligence and character to carry on the new social ideals—and that in other western countries there is probably a far greater proportion of men and women who live lives as free, even freer, than in Russia.

In a short time, when women will have equal legal rights with men in England and in the United States, their position will be more advantageous than that of their sisters in Russia. Probably it is my romantic instinct—but I am willing to give women not only equal rights, but a great deal of additional respect and courtesy. There is a definite place for chivalry; it has always existed, and a certain fineness in the relationship between the sexes vanishes when chivalry is discarded.

12 July 1933, Office of Inspector of Naval Material—Gimbel Bldg, Philadelphia, PA

I felt particularly happy and carefree today. Of course, the fact that there was a letter from you had something to do with it. The morning was spent at the office looking over old files and thereby becoming acquainted with the various particulars of my duties. In the afternoon, I was at the Exide plant discussing problems with them.

Having been under ___ for so long, my style insofar as initiative is concerned had become somewhat cramped. On the S-48, no one was ever allowed to make his own decisions. Here, on the contrary, no one has said one word to me since I have been in Philadelphia on what I shall or must do.

26 January 1935, USS New Mexico, San Pedro, California

Last night I went to Los Angeles with a friend and saw the Monte Carlo Russian Ballet. I admired their grace. Every moment was adept and graceful. It is remarkable what complete control they have over themselves.

On our return to San Pedro, about midnight, as we parked the car near the Navy landing, we were accosted by two girls who asked us to help look for their friend, another girl, who was missing somewhere along the dock. They seemed worried, so we searched. I elicited the story that the missing girl was "engaged" to a sailor in one of the ships in the harbor; that afternoon, she had learned the sailor was also "engaged" to a girl back East—that as a result, she was very despondent. So, I searched all up and down the long pier, glancing into the dark water below, expecting at any instant to see the floating corpse of a girl whom love had driven to suicide. After ten minutes of this, there was a yell from the end of the dock; the missing girl (very drunk) had been found inside the admiral's barge. I then remembered: last week there had been a feature story in the magazine section of the Sunday *Los Angeles Times* which told how human Admirals really were. To illustrate, the account was given how a poor, hungry, homeless girl had slipped into the admiral's barge one night as it lay along the pier; of how, at 2 a.m., when the admiral came down to the dock and entered his boat, and saw the girl sleeping peacefully on the sea, a tear came to his eye, and, instead of throwing her out, he left $5 and went to a hotel that night, so that the poor, tired, hungry, homeless girl would not be disturbed. Evidently the girl had read this story. But this time it ended differently. The shore patrol dragged her out and then I heard—"You drunken tart, get the hell away from here or I'll have you thrown in jail." The last I saw of her, the two sailors were literally throwing her into the rumble seat of an auto.

13 April 1935, USS New Mexico, San Pedro, Calif

At last I am on board ship. This was a good day to report, because there were very few people on board; also, the chief engineer had the duty—and he appears to be a very fine and friendly officer. From all I can gather, the New Mexico is a very happy ship…

There was a check for $--- from the Naval Institute in payment for the "International Law and the Submarine" article. This will come in handy. I am enclosing a copy of the article, which won the prize. I haven't been able to make heads or tails out of it. What do you think of it? (Please don't return it, as I believe I'll be able to struggle along without it.) Apparently, the fact that he advocates the U.S. retaining a Navy of five as compared to Japan's three is what caused the prize to go to him. Therefore, my formula, or title for a prize-winning essay: "Why the U.S. Navy Should be Equal to the Sum of ALL other Navies."

18 April 1935, USS New Mexico, San Pedro, Calif

At last, all of the excitement of this week is over. From one standpoint, I arrived here at an unfortunate time—the annual inspection. All week everyone on board has been running in circles and waving and shouting. In addition, my relief is leaving tomorrow, so I had to learn enough about the job to be able to take it over. And besides—we are getting ready for the coming cruise. Any one of the three situations would normally be enough of unusualness for one person at a time.

This morning, I was in the engine room from 7 a.m. until 2 p.m.; part of the time learning the installation and the rest of the time during the underway conditions incident to the inspection. For an hour and a half, all hands on the ship (including the Engineer Force) wore gas protection clothes and gas masks. The clothes consist of a cover-all, which covers all parts of the body and makes one look like an arctic explorer. The material is of specially treated cloth, which is resistant to poison gas. In addition, the wearing of a gas mask is necessary. Tear gases were actually used throughout the ship, and a number of men whose masks did not fit properly had a hard time of it. It was quite uncomfortable, and I was glad when the signal was sounded to "secure."

The men on watch in the engine and fire rooms looked like weird phantoms, with their white, hooded clothes and gas masks.

What a contrast: To be operating highly intricate machinery in such clothing. And yet, modern naval war is such that poison gas may be introduced either by bombs from aircraft or released from special shells when they explode after hitting the ship.

21 April 1935, USS New Mexico, San Pedro, Calif

There is so much for me to learn. I hardly know where to begin. I am reluctant to be in charge of so much machinery without being familiar with the details. To give you some idea—we carry more than 1,500,000 gallons of oil. I'll feel much more comfortable when I know more about the ship.

...The House passed the bill providing for seven years additional service, and it has been reported favorably by the Senate Naval Affairs Committee; so the chances are it will soon be law. The Navy Department estimates that (if the bill is passed) 69% of my class will be selected! This is a fairly good percentage. However, I really don't concern myself very much more about it—in view of the 21-year retirement features.

25 April 1935, USS New Mexico, San Pedro, Calif

It is strange how far away one can get from great events when he is living on board ship. I receive *The New York Times* every day and read it very hurriedly—but I can't maintain the same interest in world affairs—Germany, for example, as I did when we were together in Philadelphia. Of course, it is probably due to the fact that I do not have you to talk with. I am sort of tongue-tied in these matters when I speak with other people. You often deplored the fact that I keep thoughts to myself—but compared with the way I am now, I was like unto a flowing founding of garrulity.

We receive all of the Los Angeles, Long Beach, and San Pedro papers on board and copies are in the Wardroom. Foreign news is not their strong point, and details of events in Germany are never included. If there are officers on board who are interested in foreign affairs, they, at any rate, never speak their minds. And as you know, I do not intend opening any discussions on the subject.

Today, one of the lieutenants was reading in the news that a man on relief had been sent to prison for six months because he had become drunk on relief money. He said it was a well-deserved punishment. I mildly remonstrated, pointing out that there was really no reason why a man on relief, who through no fault of his own could not obtain work, should be punished more severely for getting drunk than anyone else. He saw the light—because his brother is an unemployed engineer who has been on relief jobs on various occasions.

2 May 1935, USS New Mexico, San Francisco, Calif

This afternoon I went ashore for a long walk, and just as I was near the boat dock on my return, I ran into F__ S___, of all people. It was very good to see him because we are very good friends...

When we were in Panama together, he introduced me to a Dr. N___, who recently arrived from Germany and was rather successful in practicing medicine. The doctor, who was an intelligent and likeable chap, is married to an Italian (European) girl. He and I used to like to talk whenever I visited F___. Now, F___ informs me, this doctor is head of the Panamanian Nazi group. All of the Germans in Panama are in this group. They hold meetings, discipline members, etc., etc. and everybody belongs! I asked F___ if the knowledge that N___ and I were friendly at one time might not hinder N___ if the news were bruited about. How strange it all is! I remember the day when Einstein stopped at Colon and N___ was designated to act as interpreter.

How proud he was, how full of admiration, and how happy that Einstein had presented him with a sheet of scratch paper upon which he had been making some notes at the dinner table. Here he is, married to an Italian woman, and in Panama, the leader of the Nazis.

It is all like a vast espionage system. I suppose that if a German resident in Panama is a lukewarm Nazi or doesn't contribute as much as is expected to campaign funds, etc., he is boycotted and ostracized by all the other Germans and that the information is duly transmitted to Germany so that his relatives may be watched. Isn't it an insidious organization!...

The routine on board ship is pretty much the same every day. In view of the fact that I do not even go to quarters in the morning, there is no particular time I must get up. However, I am up about 7:30. Then I spend some time in the Engineer Office taking care of paperwork, etc. In the afternoon, I usually roam about parts of the Engineering Plan trying to learn. In the evening, at sunset, we darken the ship, so that no prowling submarine will see us. I confess, it is much more comfortable to be steaming about in peacetime than in wartime, because a theoretical torpedo hit in peacetime doesn't bother anyone. There are two aircraft carriers along with us. Their planes are continually scouting the areas through which the ships pass during daytime and in the evening; they fly far enough in advance of the Fleet to pick up any submarines which might possibly reach the Fleet during the night.

This morning, we had a rather interesting incident. Our old destroyers do not have a very great cruising radius, so it is necessary to fuel them at sea. We had one alongside the New Mexico and gave her a large quantity of oil. We shall be doing this a number of times before the cruise is over.

8 May 1935, Above letter continued

I was up at 5 this morning—because we had to fuel another destroyer. We go along at about ten knots, the destroyer comes alongside and keeps up with us at this speed. Meanwhile, we run an oil hose over to her. Today we broke all records—supplying oil to the destroyer at the rate of over 70,000 gallons per hour! It is a pretty sight to see a number of battleships steaming along—each fueling a destroyer. Planes are constantly in the air.

We carry three planes on the New Mexico, and at regular intervals we fire them off the catapult. Everyone is kept pretty busy while we are at sea.

10 May 1935, USS New Mexico, En route Long Beach, California to Hawaii

Tonight, we received some bad news. One of the aviators from the aircraft carrier Lexington crashed while conducting scouting operations to detect for submarines.[33] I was in the Wardroom when the communication officer came in and spilled the news. Two of our aviators were also there—playing cards—and I observed them carefully to see how they would take the news. But everyone appeared to take it as a normal event. After a moment's conversation, the matter was dismissed.

Then later in the night, two destroyers collided. One had her bow pretty well damaged, and the other was hit in the stern. Very fortunately, only one man was killed. Such things are bound to happen with large numbers of ships steaming close together in the dark with no lights on. However, on a battleship, there is nothing ever to worry about; it's the safest place in the world—with no chance for any excitement.

13 May 1935, USS New Mexico, Pearl Harbor

Yesterday we finished the first leg of the cruise—and we are now docked at a pier in Pearl Harbor. The harbor is almost completely landlocked, so that it is an ideal place to assemble a large Fleet. During the last few years, large sums of money have been spent dredging

---

33 This incident occurred during Fleet Problem XVI, one of a series of pre-war naval exercises.

and otherwise improving the harbor, so that now it is capable of accommodating the entire U.S. Fleet.

There is a large Navy Yard, a Submarine Base, an Air Station, and numerous storage tanks containing fuel oil. The Army maintains more than 30,000 men on the Island, in addition.

We are tied up alongside the Maryland at a concrete mole. To get to Honolulu, it is necessary to take a ship's boat to the other side of the harbor; then a bus for 18 miles to the city. I went ashore yesterday afternoon with three other officers. One of them was an Elk in good standing, so he took us to the local Elk's Club where we drank beer (I had 2 glasses!). Later, we went to the aquarium where there is an unusually fine collection of native fish. (Being in the Navy has its advantage here—because we didn't have to pay the customary charge of 25 cents.) By this time, we were ready for dinner, so we went to Lay Yee Charis—the famous chop suey house.

This place reminds me almost exactly of Panama—the color of the vegetation, the clouds, the blue sky, and the sunsets. I am sure I'd not like to live here for any length of time. As you know, many of the people are Chinese, Japanese, Korean, Filipino, etc. It is quite common to see Chinese women in their national costumes...

Today I was invited for lunch by my good friend B___, who is captain of the destroyer ___. He and I were shipmates together twelve years ago.

He is a very fine chap... His family has been in the Navy for over 100 years. His great-grandfather was an officer during the 1812 war; his grandfather was a Commodore in the Civil War, his father an Admiral—and I think he will be one, too.

25 May 1935, En route Midway Island to Pearl Harbor

Ever since we left San Francisco, we have been sighted by one merchantman—and that was West of Honolulu. He must have been surprised to cross a large formation of warships.

There was another sad incident last night. A squadron of bombing planes flew from Midway Island to attack the Fleet—which was about 150 miles away at the time. They came just before dark, and we could see them in the sky, just out of range of our anti-aircraft guns. I was surprised at the time that they were flying so far from their base during twilight, and I asked our aviator if it was safe. He replied that it was. A short time later, we heard that one of the planes had crashed—with the loss of two officers and four men. The next morning, a bit of wreckage was picked up—all that was left of the plane.

10 June 1935, USS New Mexico, At sea

The chief engineer practically lets me run the whole show and, of course, I am trying to do my best. I see a number of things which should be done; eventually, I'll get around to them.

I do feel that I have had a beneficial effect on a number of the younger officers in the Engineering Department. They are working like the devil trying to learn, and to such an extent that all the rest of the ensigns on the ship are razzing them for working so much. Nevertheless, all the others are trying to get into the Engineer Department because they realize that instead of treating them like schoolboys (as they are frequently treated elsewhere on the ship), I give them responsible duties to perform. You know my old system of getting other people to do the work!! By making them feel that the work is very important. I get great pleasure out of seeing these youngsters suddenly becoming interested in their work. Each of them has told me that this is the first time since they were commissioned that they were treated like me.

19 June 1935, San Diego, California

I, of course, remained a staunch Democrat, defending President Roosevelt, etc.

22 June 1935, USS New Mexico, San Diego, California

Your accounts of conditions in Germany are very interesting, but here on the West Coast it all seems very far away. The newspapers are the worst I have ever seen. They typify Southern California—being full of scandal, murders, the love-life of the "luxuriant Hollywood creatures," etc. Of foreign news, they say practically nothing; if it weren't for *The New York Times*, I'd be entirely out of the swim.

28 June 1935, USS New Mexico, San Pedro, California

Things certainly appear to be happening in the United States. The Wagner Labor Bill has passed both Houses; the Banking Bill will probably pass; the Utilities Hold Company Bill has passed the Senate and will pass the House in a few days. The president has asked Congress to increase income taxes for high incomes; legislate higher inheritance taxes, and tax corporations in accordance with their size. The proposed tax on incomes is 80% above $2,000,000! I hope the Depression keeps up a little longer. We shall have a fine country, if it does…

Do you remember the political philosophy you finally arrived at after thinking the matter over for two years and discussing it with me? Well, I have also come to the same conclusion—although it took me longer. It all seems clear to me now.

3 July 1935, Santa Barbara

A young chap, about 27, was also at the Club as a guest of his uncle. He told me he had just been married and had, the week before, bought a 1600-acre ranch outside Santa Barbara for $35,000… I asked him whether he had earned this money himself. After hesitating for a moment, he said "no"—it had been given to him.

An incident such as this brings home more closely than any amount of academic discussion the inequalities which exist. Here is this chap who probably has never done a stroke of work in his life—all set to live off the world. Well—I felt great pride and joy swelling in my bosom at the thought of our Connecticut "estate." It is only ten acres, but it was bought with the proceeds of the "honest sweat of our brows"…

Yesterday our orders were changed suddenly. Instead of returning to San Pedro on July 5th, we go to San Francisco for three days to celebrate "Commodore John Barry Day." This is nothing but a big racket to get several naval vessels to San Francisco so that the men can spend their money there. John Barry was a naval officer in the War of 1812, and so had nothing to do with San Francisco. This is the first time I ever heard of such a stunt. If this is carried to its logical conclusion, soon every day of the year will be named after someone or other, and the Navy will do nothing but go from one port to another—maintaining a constant celebration.

7 July 1935

By the way, we have at last learned what we are here to celebrate. It is the 150th anniversary of Commodore Barry's retirement from the Navy. Now—isn't that a wonderful excuse for dragging a number of warships all the way to San Francisco? For I understand he was about to be court-martialed, so he conveniently retired.

9 July 1935, USS New Mexico, San Francisco, Calif

As I wrote recently, events are happening quickly in the United States. It appears that the president has at last reached a definite philosophy of government, and that he realizes "big business" will not "play ball" with him. All of his recent actions have been uniform in direction and follow, what I believe to be, the proper line between that radicalism which entails too great a loss of personal liberty and that conservatism which binds most of the people in economic slavery.

For part of this, Huey Long[34] and Father Coughlin[35] must be given credit; had they not urged their points of view so vociferously, it is doubtful the administration would have gone as far as it did. The Hearst papers are almost calling Roosevelt Communistic, and the press, as a whole, is decidedly against him, but they dare not say so too openly, because they know they do not represent popular opinion. *The New York Times* appears to have become liberalized in its news sections, although it is just as conservative in its editorial section.

There is general condemnation of Mussolini for deliberately provoking a war; people are beginning to realize the implications of the Italian form of government, and I am sure they will have none of it here. About two weeks ago, an American Ethiopian defeated Carnera, the Italian heavyweight boxing champion! And Harlem went wild with joy!

4 August 1935, USS New Mexico, San Pedro, California

England has just announced a new naval building program. Ours is going full blast, and the Japs are beginning to build up their naval forces. So, it looks as though navies will be in the increase for some time to come. Do you remember how, in 1929, disarmament seemed imminent? The new formula is "equality of security" not "equality of ships, categories, etc." And it is to be left to each nation to decide how many ships of each type she requires to give her "equal security" with other states. There is also talk of the U.S. fortifying some of the Aleutian Islands and strengthening the fortification on

---

34 Huey Long (1893–1935), a Louisiana Governor and U.S. Senator who was assassinated a month after Rickover wrote this letter.
35 Father Charles Coughlin (1891–1979), a Catholic priest who was widely heard on radio in the 1930s.

those Pacific Islands where strengthening has been prohibited by the Washington Treaty.

9 August 1935, USS New Mexico, San Pedro, California

My opinion of Roosevelt is changing all the time—I admire him more and more. I believe that he is gradually attaining his objectives—attaining them so slowly that the opposition cannot crystallize against him and yet much more rapidly than many would have believed possible. I hope he is reelected for another four years so that he can continue the good work. The trouble is that a temporary setting in of "prosperity" may halt many of his social objectives. The social security bill, by the way, passed both houses today and will be law in a few days.

18 August 1935, San Francisco, California

On my walk (in the Italian neighborhood), I heard a bell pealing Mendelsohn's "Wedding March," followed by "Oh, Promise Me." It came from a large Catholic church...

My next adventure was with four soldiers (I was in civilian clothes). Evidently, a transport had just arrived from the Philippines, Canal Zone, or some other place, for I saw numerous small groups of soldiers. One group approached me; one of the men asked, "Where is the nearest whorehouse?" I replied that I was sorry I didn't know, but that I had heard that the "women" in San Francisco were all afflicted with disease and that he would probably carry some lasting reminder away with him if he persisted in his endeavors. He assured me that he would be well protected, but I had cast a doubt in his mind. I am sure my warning did no good.

26 August 1935, USS New Mexico, Bremerton, Washington

The other day, Will Rogers died. That day, the first six pages (literally) of the West Coast newspapers were full of the account—which was particularly amazing in that few details were known of his death in an airplane crash in Alaska. By the third day, the papers were down to 4 pages. It still keeps up! What heroes we must have! Yet I suppose it is far better that we heroize men of that type than certain others. Here, the mediocre and ordinary are lionized—yet people do live happier in the U.S.

3 January 1936, USS New Mexico, San Pedro, California

I am sending you "Mein Kempf" together with a little notebook you may possibly be able to use.

5 January 1936, USS New Mexico, San Pedro, California

The other day you mentioned "Oil for the Lamps of China" Commander Huey, the executive officer, when he was on duty in China knew the two principal characters personally, and he says the story is entirely true. Probably you are aware that the book was filmed, and because of objection by the Standard Oil Co.—the ending was changed to show what a fine Company it was and that in the end justice prevailed, and the man was given a swell job.

It is amusing—one of the officers is reading "The Robber Barons," and he said—"Gee, I never heard of such things—I have lost faith in some of these people." They believe every word they see in print—so from now on it will, no doubt, be impossible for him to understand that under the circumstances, the railroads could have been built in some other way. Books that make all economic, scientific, and social phenomena beautifully simple are the most popular ones; people detest debatable issues, nor do they want unpalatable truths.

16 February 1936, San Pedro, California

I am very glad you like your new work. I also feel that most historical philosophy is propaganda. Even today, when numerous source materials are available, nearly all history is written from a prejudiced point of view. How is it then, when one writes of past events—only sketchy materials are available? And then, so many who write on learned matters have such little practical foundation for their writings. I think your visit to Panama was a valuable experience in that it demonstrated how one-sided one could become if he didn't have first-hand information about his subject.

1 March 1936, USS New Mexico, San Pedro, California

I also am getting a little fed up with some of the extreme radical movements. I think their psychology and their approach is quite poor. Every week or so, a few Communists try to spread mimeographed propaganda bulletins on the naval vessels in port. The sailors resent this very much and generally beat up the Communists. It all shows such a lack of judgment—to tell the sailors that they are being insufficiently paid, that they are being starved, and that their officers are mistreating them—when it is so evident that the contrary is the case. It seems as though they were copying the pamphlets used to stir up the Russian military force before the Revolution.

I am reading Parson Weem's "Washington" and find it silly and dull. It appears to me more an exercise in the use of noble words and phrases than anything else. Yet it shows that many current conceptions are based on no proof at all. One eventually reaches the point where he doesn't know what he can believe, and is then forced to view all events from the basis of his own ideas...

Wednesday I was invited to see a preview of "The Country Doctor," a picture about the Dionne quintuplets. A preview is for the purpose of learning the reactions of an audience before the picture is finally released. In order to make the picture of the babies of sufficient length (in time), a plot has to be improved. And of all the vulgarity, this picture takes the prize. And yet the next morning, one of the Los Angeles papers rated it as "the most stupendous production ever emanating from Hollywood." It is a fine commentary on the picture industry. The audience, however, seemed to enjoy the crude and vulgar parts enormously, so I suppose the picture people know what they are about.

Good night, dear. With much love and a kiss.

3 March 1936, USS New Mexico, San Pedro, California

The mail orderly distributed the mail after we left the harbor. We have been underway since then. Last night, the fog was so thick that we could barely make out the 1,000,000 candle-power searchlights of the ship 500 yards ahead of us in column. We will probably return to San Pedro tonight, to get underway once more Wednesday morning. An airplane bombing practice (with real bombs) is to take place—and it will be interesting to witness it from the New Mexico. Being flagship, we shall be directly astern of the target. I hope the aviators are accurate in setting their bomb sights!

...I should like to see "Mulatto"[36]—but I am afraid this will, of course, be impossible. However, I am convinced that no amount of sympathy gained in the North will help the Negroes in the South. Tolerance and understanding are necessary, and people who are uncultured and in economic straits usually lack these attributes. The other day I was speaking with a newspaper writer who was unaware I was Jewish. Among other things, he said that the Jews, as opposed to other minorities, such as the Irish, were international from a racial standpoint. I thought this over a great deal later on, because on the face of it this appears to be true, and under present conditions is a just criticism. But—I do believe that if the Irish were placed in the same position as the Jews, or if any other people were—they would become equally international racially. There is very little to distinguish the Irishman from other people where he generally settles—whereas the average Jew does appear differently.

---

36 "Mulatto: A Tragedy of the Deep South" was a play written by Langston Hughes and performed on Broadway.

The American or English Jew feels a great responsibility towards the German or Polish Jew because he knows that debilities imposed on the German or Polish Jew can easily be emulated in other countries. Thus, he helps the unfortunate for (largely) a selfish reason.

12 March 1936, USS New Mexico,
Anchored off San Clemente Island

Today, we anchored early in the afternoon off San Clemente, and since I learned that a motor whaleboat was to go into the beach with a party of men, I decided to go along, so as to be able to take a walk. Being the senior officer in the boat, and therefore responsible for its safety and that of its occupants, I studied the chart of the island to learn where we could land. San Clemente is uninhabited—so no one on board knew anything that could help me. The chart showed many outlying rocks, but finally I discovered one place marked "Boat Landing." So, I sat up in the bow looking intently for rocks.

Finally, we came to the place where the supposed "boat landing" was, but it appeared very rocky, so we moved the boat in very cautiously so as to permit the men (20) to get ashore. But there was really no place to land, and, despite my caution, the side of the boat touched the rocks along the beach, so I ordered all the men to jump out of the boat—and we backed off to a safe place where I cast our anchor. In order that the men might enjoy themselves, I permitted them to walk about for an hour, while I remained on board with the coxswain and engineer and tended the anchor.

Although they all got completely wet, clothes and all, they were a very cheerful group on the way back. A short time after our return to the ship, two of the men, delegated by the rest, came to my room and thanked me for the fine time they had! At the time I was reading "Romanoff" by Leonid Soboleff—a description of life on board a Russian man-of-war in 1914—and the way the men were mistreated by their officers—and I felt proud to be in the U.S. Navy where officers do feel a personal responsibility towards their men and help them all they can.

15 March 1936

I have been selected for Lieutenant Commander... Somehow, I had no feeling of elation when my telephone rang and a friend on watch in the radio receiving room informed me that I had been selected. I was thinking of C___, M___, and another officer on board who were passed over. That took all the joy away. It is all a horrible mess, and I think the Navy is making a big mistake. The number of appointments to the Naval Academy have just been increased, and, in a few years, another hump will be created and some drastic action will have to be taken. I am afraid the people at the top are not aware of the human suffering they are causing. As a rather interesting point, I noted that the three Jews in my class who were among those considered—were all selected. This is encouraging also in that it shows that only merit counted.

29 April 1936, USS New Mexico, At sea enroute to Panama

This morning I went up in one of our planes—being catapulted from the high catapult on top of one of the turrets. Taking off from the catapult caused a funny feeling in my stomach because the plane accelerates from zero to 60 miles an hour in about two seconds. The flight itself was pleasant. The weather was misty, so we did not go up to any considerable altitude. After being up for about an hour, the plane landed on the sea, alongside the ship, and we were hoisted on board.

14 October 1936, USS New Mexico, San Pedro, California

I have finished "Gone with the Wind." It is exceedingly well written—easy to read, but I do not think it is outstanding. The first part is the better one and gives a fairly accurate picture of life in the South. But the character delineations of Scarlett, Rhett, and some of the others is poor and far-fetched. It is not a book which will last, although it is interesting to read. If you are interested in the Reconstruction period, you should pick up "Bricks Without Straw" by Mary Johnson. I read it several years ago and thought it good.

3 January 1937

I have been reading "The Coming American Revolution" by George Soule and find it exceedingly interesting. His ideas concerning the nature of revolution and the manner in which revolution comes about are novel to me, yet they appear to be true—despite that they are contrary to the currently accepted concepts of revolutions.

25 January 1937, USS New Mexico, Bremerton, Washington

I have been very busy these last few days as a member of a board to determine cruising radii of the battleships in this Division. Since I was a junior member, the work of figuring the data and writing the report naturally fell to me. The report had to be in today; so last night I and seven ensigns (my assistants), worked from 8 p.m. until seven this morning. Late this afternoon, I turned in for a few hours and now (near midnight), I am wide awake! At any rate, the report is completed and signed.

The senior member of the board was one of the type who are meticulous about whether the word should be "the" or "an," etc., etc. and kept on changing his mind to and fro by the hour—each change in mind requiring the rewriting of several pages. My two yeomen are ready to run away. You know how impatient I can become with such piddling, inconsequential details.

28 January 1937, USS New Mexico, Bremerton, Washington

Thank you very much for your sweet letter, which arrived on my birthday. We shall have a combined celebration when you arrive. You are a very dear person, and I am more than proud of you. To think that one can combine so much dearness and loveliness, and nevertheless be one of the prize contributors to the Carnegie Endowment! But you are the only one who could fulfill these conditions. I am very happy and glad that all of the intensive work you have been doing on the International Organization will not have been wasted. If you succeed in having them publish two or three more articles, it will then be easy to assemble them in book form and publish them.

The results of the selection board have been announced. Mr. C___ and Mr. S___ both made commander, while the chief engineer was passed over again—which means he must retire in June. Of course, one is sorry to see anyone passed over, but he certainly did not deserve what he expected. For the last two weeks, he has paid absolutely no attention to the Engineering Department and no doubt, there is less chance he will do so from now on.

The executive officer left tonight for the East Coast—he will also retire in June. The wardroom officers gave him a party—and it was rather sad. I suppose it is hard for anyone who has been in the Navy nearly 30 years to leave.

29 April 1937 USS New Mexico, Dutch Harbor, Unalaska

We had rough weather all the way here, and two nights had to slow down to a very slow speed. The cruisers and destroyers had a pretty bad time of it.

Dutch Harbor is a small place. Gales came up on a moment's notice, so we have to keep steam up all the time to avoid going aground. It has been snowing or hailing ever since we have been here.

The hills of the surrounding country are bare and desolate, and covered with snow. It is a dismal place where the sun rarely seems to come out.

A number of the natives came on board yesterday. They are very peculiar-looking people, short and squat—they are a mixture of Russian and Aleutian—who were originally of Chinese extraction. M___ would have had a marvelous time seeing them...

Tomorrow morning, we sail for the Fleet Problem.[37] We should be in Honolulu about the 13th or 14th.

9 May 1937, USS New Mexico, Pearl Harbor, T.H.

The "war" ended sooner than expected, and we are now safely berthed inside Pearl Harbor. Outwardly it appears the same as last year—the green water, the lovely distant hills, and the beautiful sky at dusk, but since you are not here, it doesn't mean anywhere near as much...

The New Mexico, unfortunately, never did get into the "war." By the time we had reached the vicinity of Hawaiian waters, the rest of our Fleet had been sunk, so the captain wisely decided not to engage the entire enemy Fleet, but to make the best of his way to the homeland. The enemy, however, despite our superb valor and skill, succeeded, by dint of overwhelming superiority, in thwarting our purpose. Were it not that this was a war game, I should be lying with my companions in a watery grave, instead of sitting comfortably in a wicker chair in my neat and tidy room writing to you.

War demands sacrifices and privations. We ran out of milk a week ago, and there were no movies for two nights since we left Seattle!

---

37 Fleet Problem XVIII in May 1937 focused on amphibious operations.

19 August 1937, USS Finch,38 Tsingtao, China

We had to stop over in Tsingtao to await the arrival of the USS PECOS. She was enroute from Singapore to Chefoo via Shanghai carrying stores for the AUGUSTA and other naval vessels. On account of the trouble in Shanghai, she was directed to omit that port and go direct to Tsingtao....

There are ten Japanese passenger ships in Tsingtao to evacuate all of the excess Japanese population, which has been streaming in from the interior. Two Japanese shore patrol were shot here a few days ago, and liberty for naval personnel has been restricted. The city is quiet, however, and probably nothing at all will happen here.

Everybody here agrees there is nothing to be concerned about and that Americans are particularly safe.[39]

22 August 1937, Shanghai, China

Yesterday was one of the most unusual, if not the most unusual day I have ever spent, and I am going to put as much of it on paper as I can remember.

We left Tsingtao Thursday night, carrying anti-aircraft ammunitions and medical stores for the AUGUSTA and general stores for the Island. In addition, there was a deck load of 1500 gallons of gasoline in 5-gallon tins, because we had received a dispatch stating that there was a shortage of gasoline in Shanghai, and I thought this would be highly welcome. However, the presence of this gasoline (which is really liquid dynamite) on deck was disconcerting, especially since firing was reported to be going on in the Yangtze and Woosung Rivers, and a stray bullet might explode it, with disastrous results.

---

38 USS Finch was a Lapwing-class minesweeper commissioned in 1918. It was sunk in 1942.

39 The Second Sino-Japanese War had started six weeks before this letter was written with the Marco Polo Bridge Incident.

Enroute to Shanghai, we prepared our two, 3-inch guns for firing and held some training in machine gun fire, in the event it should be necessary to return any fire deliberately directed at us.

The weather was excellent, with perfect visibility at night because of the full moon; at midnight Friday the lights, about 60 miles off Shanghai, were picked up and we headed for the entrance to the Yangtze channel. At 0100, we sighted two Japanese aircraft carriers accompanied by four destroyers and a large supply vessel 50 miles East of Shanghai. All navigational lights were out on these vessels, and they apparently were anchored. We attempted to exchange calls with them, but they would not reply. Although they were about a mile and a half distant, the full moon showed them so plainly in silhouette that I was able not only to identify them, but could even count eight planes on deck of one of the carriers ready to take off. Considerable activity was going on inside the hulls of the supply vessel, as could be seen from the glow of cargo lights, which showed up from inside the ship. The next morning, Nanking was bombed by sea planes, which must have been the ones we saw. The two carriers are remaining in this area from which they are conducting bombing operations against Shanghai and other places.

About 0500, we stopped off the entrance to the Yangtze and picked up a pilot from the pilot ship, and then proceeded up the Yangtze. The pilot informed me that the smoke we saw towards Shanghai was the result of a large oil fire—which had been started the previous evening as a result of bombing by the Japs. He also said that the five Japanese pilots of the pilot's association had been impressed by the Japs and were being used exclusively by the Japanese men-of-war as they moved up and down the river. Two days previously, a Jap destroyer had come alongside the pilot vessel and had removed their radio installation. (The pilot vessel flies the British flag.) Vigorous representations were made by the British Consul and the radio equipment was returned—accompanied by the apology of the Japanese naval Commander-in-Chief.

There appears to be a good deal of hasty action on the part of subordinates, and the Jap Commander-in-Chief is kept busy apologizing.

(At this moment, bombs are being dropped about one-half mile away from here on the Pootung side. I will tell you more about this later.)

At 0600, we passed a Chinese river boat accompanied by a Japanese destroyer. The river boat, with approval of the Japs, was to be used for evacuating some of the many thousands of excess Chinese refugees who had found their way into the International Settlement before the gates had been barred.

At 0630, we passed two cruisers, a seaplane tender, and a division of Jap destroyers. A seaplane had just taken to the air and was headed towards Shanghai. Six other planes were on the deck of the tender. (About two hours later, a seaplane was forced down by the Chinese. It must have been one of the planes we saw.)

At 0700, we passed a Japanese cruiser with catapult trained out ready to catapult its planes. She was steaming about for a favorable position to do this, and the planes could be seen fueling. I have a list of all the Japanese ships we saw and gave it to the commander-in-chief later on. It is a complete list of Japanese ships in Shanghai waters; the staff was glad to get it because it contained later information than any they had. It was almost like passing a naval review to see the many warships in the Yangtze and the Woosung rivers.

At 0730, we entered the Woosung river channel and proceeded toward Shanghai. Although the Yangtze is one of the busiest rivers in the world, it appeared deserted, except for men-of-war. The sections of the city on either side of the Woosung seemed unpopulated, all the people having left. At this time, we could hear bombing explosions farther up the river.

Many of the buildings along the river had been shelled, as could be seen by sections of the walls knocked out. The river wall showed the effects of shell fire also, sections of that being tumbled about.

Except for the fact that the streets on either side of the river were completely deserted, the river had a holiday appearance because all the buildings were flying huge flags to show that they were British, French, American, etc.; in this way hoping to escape damage.

The numerous Japanese destroyers and other men-of-war we passed had their crews at gun stations. All of the decks were lined with sandbags, and the guns were trained to repel aircraft. (I have pictures of a number of them.)

Upon reaching the Texas Oil Co. dock, we stopped to pick up stores and mail for the AUGUSTA. At this time the BARKER, a destroyer from Chefoo, had just arrived via Tsingtao, and she also gave us mail for the AUGUSTA. The USS PAROTT was moored to a dock at the Texas Oil Co., and she signaled that a Jap seaplane had just sunk alongside of her. (This is the one I mentioned previously.) The plane had been forced down by the Chinese. A Jap gunboat was there attempting to raise the plane by means of a wire hawser, but the tide was so strong, this appeared an impossible accomplishment. I signaled to the PAROTT asking if the aviators had been killed, and the reply was that they had not.

We then proceeded up the river again. The huge cloud of black smoke we had seen several hours previously was a burning oil tank at the Asia Petroleum Co. In addition, there were other fires burning, notably at the docks of the Japanese D.K.K. Line.

We passed men-of-war constantly, and our crew was kept busy standing at attention. By 1130, we had reached the Customs Jetty, near which the AUGUSTA is anchored. (This is opposite to where the Dollar Line[40] tender took us.) The AUGUSTA had been notified by radio that we had stores for them and knew that we were supposed to come alongside, but no preparations had been made by her. The boat bows were still swung out, etc. So, as we turned the bend of the river, figuring we could go alongside, we noticed that she was not ready to receive us. Just at this moment two ships, one

---

40 The Dollar Steamship Company (aka the Dollar Line after founder Robert Dollar) was renamed American President Lines in 1938 after financial struggles.

a French cruiser, were coming down the river. It looked very serious because the channel is narrow at this point, and furthermore many junks and barges were extending out into the river. We dropped our anchor and fortunately managed to avoid hitting another ship. It was the toughest spot I have ever been in on a ship. Soon the AUGUSTA cleared her side, and we went alongside.

I saw the admiral and told him that the senior naval officer in Tsingtao had requested me to inform him that officers on the AUGUSTA were writing disquieting letters to their wives in Tsing-tao—this was undoing the efforts of the naval and consular authorities to quiet the people there.

At 1300, we commenced discharging the stores, ammunition, and gasoline. The day previous, as you probably know by this time, one man had been killed and eighteen wounded by fragments of an anti-aircraft shell, which had landed amidship on the AUGUSTA and exploded on contact with the deck. Hallett Abend,[41] *The New York Times* man, was on board with the chief-of-staff, and I imagine he was trying to obtain the official version, since it was a headline affair in the U.S.

It was probably a Japanese shell fired at one of the Chinese planes, which had been making unsuccessful attempts for several days to bomb the Japanese cruiser IDZUMO (their flagship), which is anchored about 1,000 yards away from the AUGUSTA. The IDZUMO apparently bears a charmed life. Day after day the Chinese have been bombing her, but unsuccessfully.

The night before, the Chinese made an attempt to torpedo her. They had a fast, foreign-built, large motorboat, equipped with two torpedoes. The boat, without any lights, ran towards the IDZUMO, and when about 100 yards away, fired her two torpedoes. She then headed for Nanking, jetting along the Bund, and the crew deserted the ship after opening the sea valves. The skill of the Chinese was poor, and the torpedoes missed even though the distance was but

---

41 Hallett Abend (1884–1955) was an American journalist who also wrote "My Time in China, 1926–1941" (Harcourt, Brace & Co; New York, 1943).

100 yards. Mind you, all of this goes on right near the Customs House on the Bund in the midst of much shipping.

A board was meeting on the AUGUSTA to determine officially whether the shell was Japanese or Chinese. The members of the board, accompanied by a marine officer from the Shanghai U.S. Marine Detachment, was up on deck re-enacting the event.

While we were alongside the AUGUSTA, eight Jap planes were bombing the Chinese section of Shanghai, and at irregular intervals one could see the planes swoop and drop their bombs. By watching carefully, it was possible to follow the bombs as they left the bomb racks. Thus there were constant explosions, followed by the breaking out of fires. One of these fires, not very far away, reached tremendous proportions, and even at half past two this morning it was burning fiercely, lighting up a large section of the city.

The Japs are attempting (and apparently succeeding) in laying waste all of the Chapei region so that there would remain no cover for the Chinese troops. The Chinese were replying by attacking the Jap planes with fire from one or more anti-aircraft guns. I could see the white puffs of smoke as the shrapnel burst in air. No planes were hit. At this time the AUGUSTA blew her whistle, which was a signal for all hands to take cover. Two fragments of shell had fallen about 50 yards off her bow, and the lookout (which is constantly maintained in her foretop) had given the alarm. In about ten minutes, we all came out again and the work of unloading went on.

At four-thirty, our work alongside the AUGUSTA was completed, and we got underway and steamed about four hundred yards farther up the Whangpoo River, mooring alongside the ISABEL and the SACRAMENTO at one of the naval buoys. Our anchorage is opposite to the French Concession—just about where they had the electrical display on July 14 when we were in Shanghai.

Three hundred yards farther up from here the river is blocked. A few days ago, the Chinese sank six Japanese merchantmen and several junks here to prevent passage of Jap men-of-war to their arsenal and navy yard located two miles up the river. Shortly after

140

we moored, one of the junks worked loose and commenced floating down the river in the strong tide, the junk lying on its side, its masts pointing toward the FINCH (I have a picture of it).

On tying up to the ISABEL, the captain took great pleasure in pointing out a Chinese Customs Service ship moored toward the other bank of the river about 50 yards away from us. The Haps boarded her and smashed her engines so she could not be used. Then, night before last, she was hit by two shells, which the Haps fired from one of their warships in the river at Pootung. Two shells, instead of landing at Pootung, hit the ship. It is very easy to see the holes, one at the water line and one about five feet higher.

For the rest of the evening, while there was still light, the Japs bombarded Pootung with bombing planes, some of the bombs falling not more than one thousand yards from where we are. The planes swoop down at a terrific rate of speed and as they start up once more, release their bombs. Soon, a cloud of debris or black smoke rises, and shortly after the explosion is heard, dull if it is any distance away, and sharp if nearer. They are not as loud as one would expect, but resemble more the noise a falling roof or wall of a house would make. I believe that most of the bombs the Japs are using are 100 pounds.

The reason Pootung is being shelled and bombed is because there are concentrations of Chinese troops there and because the Chinese are assembling artillery to fire at the Jap men-of-war in the river. (Shells are being fired now.) Some of the bombs resulted in houses being set on fire.

All the men-of-war (foreign) are flying large flags, and even have extra flags painted on their topsides so that all airmen can identify them!

Just at the border of the French concessions is a building flying a British flag. The flag has a hole shot through showing where an accidental shell passed.

There were movies on the quarter-deck of the SACRAMENTO last night, "Trans-atlantic Merrygoround," I believe. Well—here was a tremendous fire raging in Chapei with the sky red, and two or three other fires visible in Pootung, and yet life goes on as usual, including classical music over the radio.

I hadn't had much sleep, so I turned in early on a cot on the upper bridge and quickly fell asleep. At two-thirty, I was awakened by shell fire. Jap men-of-war were firing at Pootung in our direction. They were using tracer shells. (These are shells which can be followed in flight by means of a chemical which is emitted.) The shells looked like large, green balls of fire; and they were being fired on a line which passed about 50 to 100 yards ahead of the FINCH. Of course, they landed before reaching us, but it gave one a weird feeling to see them coming directly towards him...

No liberty in Shanghai is permitted for enlisted men, but officers may go ashore from 1 to 7 p.m., in uniform, in the International Settlement. I went ashore this afternoon for two hours or so. Our boat landed at the Customs Jetty, and I went through the same customs house where we landed July 14.

The place was deserted and locked, but was opened for me because of my official status. The Bund was almost completely deserted. Soldiers and marines stood guard at the corners where the streets intersected the Bund. Sandbank emplacements were located at each corner. The Chinese are not permitted within two blocks of the Bund in the International Settlement. All of the places of business were closed, their windows shuttered with pine boards...

As I walked along a little farther, the Japs again began bombing Chapei, the Chinese retaliating vainly with their anti-aircraft fire. Crowds of Chinese were craning their necks watching the goings-on. All over there are posters showing how to wear gas masks (although there are none in Shanghai), and how to act in the event the city is bombed or gassed. Crowds of Chinese stand idly, studying the posters. Newsboys by the hundreds run about yelling the latest news and selling the one-sheet extras. In the side streets, families with all their household effects, evidently refugees, are sitting resignedly.

In the French concession, I took a picture of the place where another of the bombs dropped by the Chinese planes did considerable damage. This bomb made a hole in the street about 250 feet square and did considerable damage to a nearby building. Since it is at a busy street intersection, many people must have been killed. (Another explosion just now.)

24 August 1937

We have had a little excitement not directly connected with the hostilities going on. I have mentioned that numerous vessels are moored near us in order to be as far away from the active part of the river as possible. About 9 p.m. last night, one of these, used ordinarily to capture Chinese pirates, broke away from her moorings and commenced drifting down upon us in the strong tide. Our small boat was out at the boom. We rushed men into the boat and got it clear, and the boom in. About this time the ship dropped her anchor and just managed to clear us.

A few minutes after this, we saw what looked like lighted cigarette butts falling downward from the sky. At the time, one or more planes were in the air and anti-aircraft fire was in progress, so it must have been fragments of shrapnel heated "red hot" by friction of the air. One of the pieces fell about 15 yards from the ship. The SACRAMENTO, which is alongside us, picked up several pieces of shrapnel, and a bullet passed through one of their boats...

At 2 p.m. I went ashore and intended, among other things, to visit a Chinese department store which I had passed by yesterday. When I reached within two blocks of the place, I realized that the streets had been cleaned. The policeman informed me that a shell or bomb had landed at 1 p.m. and had killed about 200 people.

My uniform permitted me to go anywhere. So I had an excellent opportunity to witness the damage. The Fire Department was cleaning away the debris... Many places on the sidewalk and street were still smeared with blood, which the Fire Department was quickly scrubbing away. The insides of the two large stores were a horrible mess.

I inspected pieces of the shell which had been picked up, but could not tell whether or not it was a bomb. I believe what happened was this: at about 1 p.m., a Jap seaplane carrying two bombs was being pursued by a Chinese plane. In order to get away more quickly, the Jap dropped his bombs. The other bomb fell through the U.S. Navy storehouse, which is about two blocks from the Navy Purchasing Office. Fortunately, the bomb did not explode. However, it passed through the three floors of the building. A Board of Investigation has been appointed to determine its origin. By the way, a *New York Times* correspondent was one of those injured when the first bomb fell.

There has been considerable firing all day, and also much aircraft activity. At the moment, the heated shelling is going on since we have been here. Shots are being fired regularly by the Japs. Another large fire has broken out. But on the ship next to us, "Broadway Gondoliers," a musical comedy, is being shown to the echo of the heavy gunfire!

26 August 1937

This was another eventful and extremely interesting day. As you are aware, the current in the Whangpoo River is very strong, being about four miles an hour, so that it is very difficult to get underway or come to anchor except at slack water (when the tide is changing). In addition, the river is crowded with men-of-war and other vessels seeking refuge, and since the harbor master is no longer functioning, everyone does as he pleases.

We had to get underway at 10 a.m. when the tide was going full force and, since the FINCH was headed up the river instead of down river, she had to be swung in a very narrow space. Chalk up a few more gray hairs. Passing the IDZUMO, I noted they had blocked the right-hand side of the channel with torpedo nets—since the recent Chinese attempts to torpedo her. This contributes toward making navigation even more difficult.

Today we had official photographers from the AUGUSTA along—also LT Phelan,[42] intelligence officer on the AUGUSTA, and LT Krulak,[43] intelligence officer of the 4th Shanghai marines. We were to proceed to an area where the Japs were operating and where no other naval vessels go, so it was an excellent opportunity to check up on what the true state of affairs was.

The newspapers are completely unreliable (as we learned from today's trip). I imagine any of the newsreel services would have given thousands of dollars to be able to have gone on the FINCH today and taken pictures. But none of them are allowed to go.

There were the usual larger numbers of Japanese destroyers, gunboats, and an occasional cruiser in the river. The real activity began, however, when we reached Woosung. Japanese troops (soldiers) were spread along the waterfront firing towards the Chinese. The fact that they were so close to the river indicates that at this particular section, they have not been able to drive the Chinese inland. Several destroyers, heavily sandbagged about their decks, were lying close to the positions held by the troops, with their guns trained out, ready to support the soldiers.

All the buildings along the river were completely destroyed. It is a humble thing to see how a populous Chinese city of more than a million people has been demolished. As we left the Whangpoo and entered the Yangtze, there were a number of destroyers, and the same seaplane tender we saw nearly a week ago. Formations of planes, probably from the aircraft carriers farther out to sea, were flying towards Shanghai.

About this time, four Japanese transports passed us inward bound. Each carried about six fast boats for use in landing troops. Not a single soldier was in sight; we estimated, however, that the

---

42 Rear Admiral George R. Phelan (1902–1975), U.S. Naval Academy Class of 1925.
43 General Victor H. "Brute" Krulak (1913–2008), U.S. Naval Academy Class of 1934 and later 31st Commandant of the U.S. Marine Corps.

four ships must have been carrying about 8,000 troops. As the ships passed us, they were joined by a number of destroyers, and then all went up the Yangtze, toward Pootung City, evidently to land the troops and commence an encircling movement to drive the Chinese out of Shanghai. This information is available to no one else but the naval authorities.

Since the GOLD STAR[44] had not yet arrived off Block House buoy, our meeting place, I anchored. At 1 p.m., she anchored close by, and I went alongside her. The captain told me that he had seen one of the four transports go aground, because one of the lightships near the entrance of the Yangtze was three miles out of position. The other, very foolishly, followed, and they also nearly went aground. The first one managed to get off because the sea bottom is soft mud.

The GOLD STAR was bringing 104 marines from Manila, together with stores and ammunition. The marines, under command of Major R___, together with all their personal effects were soon on board. The executive officer wanted me to take ammunition to Shanghai, but I politely informed him that I had no suitable stowage below decks and would have to carry it on deck, which was too dangerous...

All the marines being on board, we shoved off from the GOLD STAR and again anchored until 3 p.m., so that the current would be favorable upon our return to Shanghai...

On nearing the Woosung River, we both heard gunfire from the naval vessels, and could even see the flash of the guns plainly. A cruiser was heading toward us, her turrets trained out, firing at the Chinese.

Our pilot was quite nervous and urged me to be sure to go on the opposite side of a division of destroyers, which were firing. I told him I would try to, but if the waters were not sufficiently deep, I would have to go inside the line of fire of the destroyers. I told him not to worry; the Japs would not fire at an American man-of-war,

---

44 USS GOLD STAR (AK-12), a Navy cargo ship commissioned in 1922 and decommissioned in 1946.

and that, furthermore, I would sound attention as we passed each of the Jap ships, and they would stop firing until we passed. The Japs were firing at a point about 200 yards from the shore, evidently to dislodge snipers and to destroy their hiding places. It was a pretty realistic war.

Sure enough, as we passed each ship, we sounded attention, our men stood at the salute, and the Japs ceased firing and did the same! What was really bothersome, though, was the sniping. Occasionally a rifle bullet would whiz past, and I was glad when we passed this region. Our new marines were well trained. Every time I yelled "Take cover," they all dodged in two seconds max! Our men have gotten to be careless, and don't dodge so quickly. For example, at 2 a.m., again anti-aircraft shrapnel, fired by the Japs, burst all about us and woke me up; but it is extremely difficult to make the men take cover....

This afternoon I went in our motorboat and explored the section of the Whangpoo a short distance above us, which is blocked by sunken ships. It is a sad sight to see all these ships under water, with nothing but their masts or stacks remaining above water. I have pictures of the scene. Nearby a British ship was just leaving with Chinese refugees. It is impossible to imagine that so many people could be jammed into a ship. Even the holds are tightly packed with this human cargo...

Late in the afternoon, four Chinese planes encountered four Jap planes, and a great deal of fast maneuvering commenced at quite a high altitude. Eventually the two groups separated with no planes shot down.

The destruction by fire and by shelling is appalling, and to my mind show the Japs to be utter barbarians. They have nothing to gain by destroying a large city such as Shanghai and ruining the entire countryside—yet they are doing this in a methodical manner. Of course, they are not meeting any real opposition in a naval or aerial way, and so they have things all their own way. As far as I can see, all that they have succeeded in doing is to demonstrate that they are capable of destroying—provided there is no hindrance.

A few jingoistic army officers start a war, and the result is untold misery for millions of people. It is sickening to see the patient poor people sitting in the alleyways all day long with their possessions—driving from their homes and their farms.

Last night the ship alongside had a war picture with lots of shooting, etc., but the shooting in the picture was louder and more frequent than it is in this actual war. Also, it was probably more romantic. There is nothing romantic in the huge fire, which is still creeping along the waterfront of Pootung, or in the homeless thousands on the streets of Shanghai, or in the herds crowded into the holds of ships. And one can find no one in Shanghai who considers the present warfare to be romantic.

Yesterday when the Japanese transports passed us and we were discussing the number of troops each carried, I was sorely tempted to send one of them a signal: "How many soldiers do you have on board?" I firmly believe that in his surprise at such an unexpected question, I would have received the correct answer. But we all agreed it might lead to an unpleasant incident in which the Japanese admiral would lodge an official complaint with our commander-in-chief—so I refrained.

30 August 1937

The Japs have a hospital ship tied up alongside the IDZUMO, and they are indignantly protesting that the Chinese snipers are shooting at it!!

Already the hero stories are being manufactured—similar to the "3 human bombs of Chapei." It seems that recently when a Jap seaplane was hit by the Chinese, the pilot, realizing his plane would soon be wrecked, drove it into another Chinese plane, wiping out not only himself but also the Chinese plane.

This is being given prominence in the Jap newspapers to inspire the people. Although I find it hard to understand how a damaged plane could outmaneuver an undamaged one. Another Jap aviator, whose plane was struck, directed it at a Chinese gun, destroying both himself and the gun. This sounds like another fairy story. However, when one knows a little of the Japs, he realizes that every death must necessarily have been an exceedingly brave one!...

Tonight, a very serious affair occurred. Just before dinner we intercepted a message from the large Dollar Liner, PRESIDENT HOOVER, that she had been hit by a bomb about 50 miles East of Shanghai, and that several of the crew were injured. Two destroyers, the PAROTT and the EDSALL, were immediately sent to her. The HOOVER requested medical attention. Fortunately, H.M.S. CUMBERLAND,[45] the one that was in Tsingtao when we were there, was nearby and came to the HOOVER's assistance.

I was on the AUGUSTA about one half hour after these reports came in, and they seem to think the bombing was done by Chinese planes. I hope not. Possibly the Chinese thought she was another Jap transport coming up the river. A few minutes ago, we intercepted another message stating that the HOOVER would not come to Shanghai, but was at once heading for Japan instead—and that the destroyers had been recalled.

Wednesday morning, the FINCH is again going out beyond the Woosung forts to contact the Dollar Liner, McKINLEY. We are to take a large quantify of stores from her and deliver some to the GOLD STAR for further transshipment to Tsingtao and Chefoo, and bring the rest to Shanghai. There are also a large number of gas masks for the naval vessels here.

Today when I was ashore at the Navy Purchasing Office making arrangements for the trip, I heard something which pleased me greatly. The Japs had asked whether they could fuel their vessels at the Standard Oil Company or at the Texaco Co., and our admiral informed them he was sorry, but the oil was required for the

---

45 HMS Cumberland was a County-class heavy cruiser commissioned in 1928.

American naval vessels; but that as soon as the Japs would open up the river to shipping and permit tankers to discharge their cargo, the Japs could have oil!

31 August 1937

Much of what I have written in this letter is information which I have come across in my official capacity, so please do not mention it to any Navy people—that is those parts which obviously are official.

Any letters you or M___ desire to mail to the U.S. or to Europe should be mailed on one of the American naval vessels in Chefoo, using U.S. stamps. This will ensure delivery. Do not use Chinese stamps.

2 September 1937

The USS GOLD STAR is to leave tomorrow morning for Chefoo, arriving there on September 7. So, I am taking advantage of this opportunity to write again.

The area of fighting has moved away from here during the last few days. Continued fighting is going on near Woosung, where the Japs have landed more than 25,000 troops and where the Chinese are stubbornly resisting. The Japs have not made much gain despite their control of the air, the help they receive from the warship guns, and the fact that the Chinese have practically no artillery…

A young American who represents an American aviation sales company was on board the ISABEL the other night. He is quite familiar with the Chinese aviation situation. He says that man for man, the Chinese is a better aviator than the Jap, but that as soon as the Chinaman gets his wings, he believes he knows everything and will no longer listen to his foreign tutors. Also, when any piece of machinery or equipment goes wrong, they always blame the machinery and are incapable of understanding that improper operation was the real cause of the trouble.

Whenever an airplane salesman comes around, he is always asked, "Can you sell us planes which are capable of bombing Tokyo?" No other city in Japan will do; it must be Tokyo. Incidentally, they have offered some American pilots $25,000 (gold) each if they will bomb Tokyo, but the Americans are reputed to have held out for $50,000. It is only about 650 miles from Shanghai to Tokyo, so that a bombing expedition is entirely feasible.

The Chinese never quibble about the cost of a plane, but they are unwilling to spend one dollar on spare parts. So that when the least thing happens to a plane, it is out of commission for good.

I believe our admiral committed a serious error in judgment when he ordered Dollar Liners not to call any longer at Shanghai—because he is setting a precedent which the Japs will quickly take advantage of. No war has been declared. Nevertheless, the Japs have declared a "peaceful" blockage against Chinese ships, and they are now talking of extending it to neutrals carrying war supplies.

Furthermore, they announced this morning that foreign men-of-war must keep out of their way! They do not want to declare war because they are afraid the U.S. will invoke the Neutrality Act and thereby interfere with their raw material supply, and that England will follow suit. Really, the only language they know or respect is "force," and I believe our authorities are beginning to realize it...

Shanghai is becoming somewhat more normal since the firing in the immediate vicinity of the International Settlement has stopped. Every day large trucks go about picking up refugees from the streets and sending them either to refugee camps, or away from Shanghai. But these poor, patient people are so pitiful! They sit for days and nights on the sidewalks, with their two or three bundles, uncomplaining.

The pictures I am sending with this letter, many of which were taken yesterday, show this clearly. This is the horrible part of war. It is not that many soldiers are killed, but that so many innocent families are uprooted and cast about. I believe pictures such as some I took would make better propaganda for peace than some of those showing soldiers being wounded or killed. Incidentally, I can appreciate better what the bombing of Madrid means, and what a horrible thing the Nationalists are doing in bombing their own people.

P.S. Please do not tell anyone the contents of this letter.

4 September 1937

The Japanese spokesman in Shanghai stated this morning that they could have done much better with their attack on Pootung yesterday had the foreign men-of-war not been in the way, and hinted that they should get out!

...Incidentally, there have been no prisoners taken on either side so far. This will give you an inkling of the kind of war this is turning out to be.

Yesterday I read the account of our naval attaché who was with the Italians in Ethiopia 1935–36. He states that the Italian people are completely behind Mussolini, and that the Army and Navy officers are desirous of war with England. The Italians, through their propaganda ministry, are beginning to circulate books and pamphlets mollifying England, thus creating a feeling toward her such as is being created in Germany towards Russia. The Italian's aim is sovereignty over Egypt and of all the rest of northeast Africa, and the British are aware of it.

In light of what he writes, the Italian action in Spain seems quite consistent, and I wouldn't at all be surprised that the recent extensive sinkings of merchantmen and the torpedoing of a British destroyer in the Mediterranean is a deliberate warning by Italy to England to get out of that sea—which is to become an Italian lake.

8 September 1937

Two days ago, the body of a Japanese soldier with a large bullet hole in his back floated alongside and got stuck in our gangway; we had to shove it off with a boat hook. Many bodies float by nowadays, as well as huge pieces of timber from burned ships or warehouses.

Sunday I went out to Jessefield Park, which is the largest park in the International Settlement. It is a reasonably sized park, and well kept. It was a pleasant surprise to see green grass and a few trees again—after the crowded streets and alleys of Shanghai. There is an admission charge of 20 cents, so that only "desirable" people will enter. It is in the vicinity of this park that the better residential district of Shanghai resides.

All of Sunday, bombing of the region adjoining Jessefield was going on, and so while I was walking on the peaceful paths of the park, planes were flying overhead, and the boom of guns could be heard.

At present, I am engaged in reading the history of China. I have read the book I sent to Chefoo, and am reading a more detailed volume. I have a large map of China before me as I read. Also, my reading is punctuated by gunfire, and I must say that what I read has a deeper meaning, and I am sure I will never forget what I am learning now...

As I was waiting at the Customs Jetty for our boat this afternoon, I noticed a typical event. As you know, a large number of sampans are tied up nearby. The water was particularly filthy because the tide was slack. A dead animal, decomposing, was nearby, and one of the men in a sampan was urinating into the river. But in the next sampan, a man had just finished his supper and wished to clean his teeth. So, he bent down and filled his mouth with the river water and gargled with it. Then he dipped his towel into the water and wiped his teeth with it. Well, it's beyond me that they don't die like fleas. All of Shanghai's sewage flows into this river!...

Another sight that is common is the swastika flag. I wondered at first why this emblem was so common in Shanghai and thought that the Germans certainly were going out of their way to please the Chinese. Finally, I realized that the emblem of the Chinese Red Cross is the real swastika!!

Yesterday I stopped at the Metropole Hotel for an hour or so and had a drink with Captain F___, the pilot who brought the FINCH into Shanghai when we first came here. He introduced me to a number of American businessmen, and were they disgusted! They had just read President Roosevelt's statement that any American who remained in China did so at his own risk. These businessmen are content that they have devoted their lives to building up an outlet for American goods in China, and that, after all, the welfare of the U.S. is affected by our trade with China. When one sees how trade works out practically, he is not so sure that unrestricted use of the Neutrality Act is entirely wise. If we voluntarily give up our trade rights in the growing market of China, someone else will grab it.

The businessmen held a meeting that afternoon and cabled their protests to our government. I really believe the U.S. and England should adopt a stiffer attitude toward the Japs, but I suppose that is out of the question for England at present, in view of the European situation.

9 September 1937

At eight, the FINCH got underway for a reconnaissance trip. This time we took no pilot, so I was very busy on the ship and hardly had time to see what was going on. Commander D___ of the admiral's staff and a number of other officers accompanied us.

There were at least thirty transports in the vicinity of Woosung; in addition, there were numerous destroyers, two cruisers, a seaplane tender, and two hospital ships. The line of Japanese vessels extends for about 10 miles, from 5 miles above Woosung on the Yangtze River, to 5 miles below Woosung. These ships are in addition to the IDZUMO, and a number of destroyers and gunboats in the Whangpoo River.

We estimated that there are about 100,000 Japanese troops in the vicinity...near the Baptist College, about halfway between Woosung and the International Settlement, the Japs now have a landing field, and numerous Army planes were in the air...

The Japs have a new type of landing boat about 35 feet long, constructed of heavy timbers, and with a ramp in the bow for landing horses or field pieces. Each of these boats have a machine gun and a light armor shield for protecting the gun crew. There is an anchor and an anchor engine in the stern...

It appears that the present hostilities will last some time. Commander D___ said the Japanese flag lieutenant hinted they expected the "China Incident" would last about a year. It is certain that the Japs are not having an easy time of it, because it is evident they have been unable to advance their positions very far during the last two weeks. But they have certainly visited destruction all about. Yesterday they again bombed a train carrying refugees away from Shanghai, and killed several hundred of them.

I don't believe there has ever been a time in modern warfare when destruction has been visited on a people with such callous and wanton disregard as the Japs are doing at Shanghai. It is militarianism at its worst. Yet the rest of the world is so preoccupied with other major problems that the Japs will probably have a free hand again—just as in 1931. From the tremendous effort they are exerting here, there is no doubt in my mind that the whole of Japan is being mobilized for a major war and that hostilities will continue until China is defeated or until Japan is exhausted.

17 September 1937

You should see what happens at morning colors! In accordance with naval etiquette, each ship having a band must play the national anthem of all the naval vessels present, and everybody on deck must stand at attention until it is all finished.

Thus, the LAMOTTE-PICQUET[46] commences by playing the French National Anthem, followed by the Chinese (because this is Chinese territory), followed by the British, Japanese, Italian, and Netherlands—in order of seniority of the naval officers present.

---

46 A French cruiser commissioned in 1927 and sunk in 1945.

The MONTECOCEOLA[47] starts with the Italian anthem, followed by the Chinese, American, British, French, Japanese, and Netherlands, while the IDZUMO starts with the Jap, followed by the Chinese, etc., etc., and then the British flagship also does her part. So there is this confused medley of the different anthems all being played at the same time. It lasts 10 minutes, and we try to avoid being caught on deck during this time. I finish my breakfast before the last anthem is played!

21 September 1937

When the Italian cruiser MONTECOCEOLA arrived last Thursday with troops from Abyssinia, an unusual event occurred: Owing to the large number of men-of-war present in the upper section of the Whangpoo (men-of-war ordinarily moor at the buoys three miles below the Bund), no space was available for her. The Japanese have a space between two buoys, just upriver from the FINCH. The Jap admiral permitted the Italians to use their buoys. This is the first time that a ship of another nationality than their own has been permitted to use these buoys, and it is significant, as it indicates the extremely friendly feeling between the two governments.

If, by any chance, hostilities were to break out in Europe, an extremely serious situation would result here. Men-of-war of nearly all the leading powers are moored in close proximity, and there is no doubt that attempts would be made to damage or sink enemy vessels. With the modern system of undeclared wars, this is more than a possibility.

23 September 1937

In the past 5 or 6 years, the Japs have been building numerous cotton mills and factories at Shanghai. A number of these mills are located so as almost to surround the Power Company. At present,

---

47 An Italian Condottieri light cruiser commissioned in 1935.

these mills are being used by the Japs as ammunition depots, store-houses for military supplies, etc. The roofs of these mills are of thick concrete, much thicker than ordinarily necessary, but very desirable during bombing attacks.

The above illustrates how carefully what is going on now was planned and how industry in Japan is completely tied up with national defense. The Japs figure that the presence of a valuable American property will deter the Chinese from making an attack in the vicinity (two of the mills are directly across the street from the Power Co.) for fear of anti-Chinese feeling in the U.S., and apparently, they are correct. Thus, military activity is being carried out by the Japs under protection of American interests.

2 October 1937

I saw a very sad sight in the "Chinese City," south of the French Concession. A man was lying on the sidewalk. His body was so thin and his ribs so evident that he must have been starving. So, I approached to give him a few cents. As I came close, I noted that flies were all over his body. Although his eyes were still partly open, and he was still breathing, he was unable even to move his arms to take the money. This was the first time I have ever seen a dying person. Yet, people were going by unconcerned—paying no attention to him. The Chinese are a very practical people and probably feel that there is no use wasting time on dying human beings when there are so very, very many live ones. One feels so helpless at such a time. There is nothing he can do. It is very degrading.

6 October 1937

Yesterday I was relieved of command of the FINCH by a classmate of mine, Lt. Evans.[48] I will have practically nothing to do until the arrival of the CANOPUS, somewhere about the 20th of the month.

---

48 Rear Admiral Donald Sidley Evans (1901–1965).

27 March 1938

I am reading Zinsser's book, "Rats, Lice, and History" and find it very interesting—particularly his theory that all diseases are vanishing and new ones arising. I am also intrigued by what he says about mankind developing immunity to diseases and that the more effective (but also more cruel way) is to let nature take its course. This causes an interesting thought in me—about insanity (which we once discussed), whether we would not be much better off to let insane people alone (I mean not emasculate them as Germany does)—or else we may never get rid of insanity.

7 June 1939, Peiping, China, Temple of the Sleeping Buddha

I feel like a monk of medieval times, sitting in my cell and writing on parchment by kerosene lamp. After much gesticulating and announcing my wishes in what I thought they should sound like in Chinese, the boy finally brought several small sheets of paper which, sad to say, were meant for other purposes....

On the MARBLEHEAD,[49] I was treated royally. I inspected the engineering plant and was listened to with great reverence and deference by all concerned as I pronounced pontifically whether each item of machinery was or was not in good condition. Simon Lake is the navigator, and with the modern selection system, he never once got off the bridge while the ship was underway.

They told me about the recent happenings in connection with the Int. Settlement at Amoy. As you know, the Japs made certain demands on the foreign consuls, which practically amounted to complete Jap control. The Marblehead, with Captain Staples (So. China Patrol) as Senior Officer on Board, was sent to Amoy...

By now the situation is again deteriorating because the J. have probably found out that the "allies" are just bluffing—as they always have...

---

49 An Omaha-class light cruiser commissioned in 1924.

We reached Chiniangtu Sunday aft. I tried to make arrangements to visit the Great Wall that afternoon, but as usual the local U.S. Marine people and the civilians at Chin. had never heard about such a thing and, by the time I managed to get all the inf., it was already too late for that day.

So I left China that night for Tientsin (on a sleeper)... I walked thought he streets of T. for about 3 hours. The only interesting thing I saw was the quantities of J. manufactured goods being transported along the river on barges... I have seen everything you indicated and have even gone out to Marco Polo Bridge to look. A nice Jap took me around and showed me THE spot where the China incident started (I have a picture)...

I visited a Chinese primary school for about an hour—to the great distress of my guide. I heard singing and went in to investigate. The guide acts like you do in such matters! The children are the most serious I have ever seen in any school. In one room, the male teacher was playing tunes on a small piano and the children were singing pretty songs (Western style) to the tunes. Sometimes one half of the room would sing, sometimes all, and sometimes just one boy or girl. Whenever one boy or girl sang and finished, the rest all clapped hands enthusiastically. It was much more machine-like than any class of singing in a Western school.

Typical scene: Japanese soldiers visiting the marble boat, which was built by [the Dowager Empress] with money intended for the Navy. The Chinese have the marble boat and the J. have China. The J. civilians go about all the temples and palaces as very proud owners.

10 June 1939, En route Mukden-Keijo

I left Peking at 2000 and arrived at Shanahwan [sp] 06230. I took a rickshaw out into the country and then climbed up to the Great Wall about 12–15 ft. high at this point. And I even managed to get back to the station one hour before 11:15 when the train left. It was good exercise...

At Shen. there was a young J. passport inspector who was very suspicious of me. He even rode with me for 2 hours asking questions. What mystified him greatly was my birth in [Russia]. Finally, I told him that Dad and Mother were the Am. Ambassador & Ambassadoress to R. respectively; hence my birthplace. This stopped him for a while and gave me much face. It was so amusing to hear his unsubtle questions and to answer them casually…

At another station (after this chap had left), one of the railway guards, who wore a sword, saw me taking snapshots on the station, so he came inside the car. Lo and behold, I had open a large map of Man., which I had gotten from the J.T.B. Was he suspicious! He wanted to confiscate it. I, of course, made off it was precious, so he became the more so suspicious. Finally, I pointed out to him the symbol of the South Manchurian Railway Co. and he stopped…

At Antung, the passport & customs inspectors were quite lenient, and I had no trouble at all. But, after midnight, sometime after leaving Antung and after I had managed to fall asleep, another (Korean) customs inspector woke me, and the same process began. I find that the Landing Permit, although it is valid for N. China, only does the trick each time because it is attested to by the sacred Shanghai J. Navy and all of the local officials probably take the attitude that if the J. Navy approves my travel, it certainly must be okay. He asked me where and how long I was going to stay in Korea & Japan. I told him it all depended on where I was courteously treated, etc.…

…On the ships…shortly after I fell asleep, I was awakened by another passport man. He was very nice and sympathetic when I explained that my occupation had become the submitting to various forms of inspection. I now had to fill out an extensive form. For "religion" I noted "Mohammedan." This stumped him until I explained that it was becoming quite the fad for up-to-date Americans, particularly Army & Navy officers, to become Mohammedans, and that I was intending to visit Mecca on my way home…

At 7 a.m. after a very short night, there was again only about 20 minutes to catch the connecting ferry to Moji—and now came the most stupid inspector of all. A new batch of officials took charge. I had to be checked by three individuals, individually. Meanwhile, the time was getting shorter. Finally, in desperation, I showed him the J. Navy Landing Permit and informed him that if it was okay for the J. Navy that I travel it should certainly be okay for the local outfit. They discussed this for a while and stamped the passport. I had to run to catch the ferry and just made it. As you said, somehow or other, baggage never gets lost in Japan. And when I landed in Moji, my baggage was at the station. I had been concerned over it because I hadn't seen it leave the ship…

Moji and later Nagasaki—which are typical small-sized J. cities (125,000 & 250,000)—certainly showed no signs of food or clothing shortage. Large quantities of food & clothing were obtainable everywhere. The people did not appear shabby, and if I had just descended from Mars I should by no means have known that a war was in progress.

16 June 1939, S.S. Mingsang, En route Shanghai–Hong Kong

After a very cursory customs examination by Jap customs officials at the NYK wharf at Shanghai, which has a sign stating, "NYK Welcomes You," I dashed into Shanghai to make the quickest arrangements possible for getting to Hong Kong. The Mingsang was leaving the next morning—but was completely booked. I went around to the Jardine-Matheson office and told them how important it was for me to get to H.K. at once. Finally, the passenger agent hesitatingly said, "If you do not object to sharing a cabin with a Hindu, it can be arranged. The Company cannot, of course, suggest such a thing." I assured him that it was okay by me. So, I have a very nice cabin on the upper deck…

My roommate is a Hindu merchant from Swatow. He is a U.S. citizen, was born in N.Y., fought in the U.S. Army in France for 2 years, and speaks English without a flaw. He carries Hills' Bros.

coffee with him and has the boy make his own brand for meals, instead of using the ship's coffee...

I didn't tell you in my last letter about my picture-taking experience in Keijo because I wrote the last letter while I was still under J. surveillance and didn't want to have self-incriminating evidence on me... In Keijo, when I went up to the top of the hill where there is a shrine and from whence a good view of the city can be obtained (Chosen Jinga I believe), my auto driver motioned "no pictures" because no one is allowed to photograph from an elevation. Very foolishly and out of devilment, I did take a picture of the city. A guard saw me, and I was taken to the temple police headquarters. Fortunately, it was the last film of the roll, and I managed to roll it up inside the camera so that when looking through the red window it appeared there was no film in the camera. Several police questioned me, and of course I made off like I didn't understand. They didn't know how my camera opened and wanted me to open it to see if there was film inside. I didn't understand. They even opened one of their cameras to show their meaning, but I still didn't understand. A brilliant thought struck me. I had an extra new roll of film in my pocket. I showed them this, indicated that there was no film in my camera, but that I was intending to load the camera with the new film. They took my name and hotel.

19 June 1939, M.S. Yochow, En route Swatow–Hong Kong

We arrived at Swatow on the Mingsang [means Increasing Glory] at 0800. The entrance to the harbor is very beautiful, with hills on either side for some distance. I was in hopes we would be stopped by the Japanese destroyer, which we met about 5 miles outside, but nothing untoward happened. In view of the fact that we were carrying 1,400 tons of cargo, and it is unloaded entirely by coolies, it soon became evident that we would not leave on the same day, as scheduled. So, by dint of much running around, I was able to change over to the Butterfield & Squire ship Yochow, leaving that same afternoon for Hong Kong.

Swatow is a large city with wide, well-paved streets and substantial houses—of the apartment type. Before the war, there were about 180,000 people here. There are now about 30–40 thousand. I believe Swatow is one of the original Treaty Ports listed in the Treaty of 1842. Earlier in this letter, I mentioned why the Japs had not taken this place, although they could easily at any time. The local residents say also that the J. Navy has wanted to take the place, but the Army does not wish to because it will mean the use of more troops, which they do not care to do at present, and also another center of guerilla warfare with attendant losses. However, the rumor is that within a few days, the J. are going to take the city. All women of under 30 have been ordered evacuated so as to prevent rape by the J.

Tank traps are being constructed on many of the streets. These consist of mounds of earth piled across the street and a ditch in front of the mound. There are about 15,000 Chinese troops in the vicinity, and they are said to be fairly good. Two weeks ago, the J. attempted to land on a small island about 5 miles from the city but were repulsed by the Chinese. People and businesses are constantly being evacuated, and the Chinese plan to blow up all the important buildings if the Japs are successful in coming in. There are 2 J. destroyers, a small transport, and 6 trawlers in front of the harbor. There is also 1 British and 1 U.S. destroyer inside the harbor. Capt. Sprigg's ship, the Pillsbury,[50] is the U.S. ship.

The foreign colony consists of about 200, of whom 40 are U.S. citizens. Swatow is the major Chinese place for the export of embroidered handkerchiefs and other hand embroideries to the U.S.—the exports amounting to about 3–4 million gold annually. About 90% is in the hands of U.S. citizens... [describes visiting factory]

The industry was started about 25 years ago by a Mr. & Mrs. Haskins. Mrs. Haskins is on this ship, and I have been talking at length to her. They have been all over the world and in many enterprises. I

---

50 A Clemson-class destroyer commissioned in 1920.

gather they were in the itinerant theatrical business about 30 years ago, and had a stock company in Cuba. Then, somehow, they came here. She saw the cheap labor possibilities combined with the native skill. She purchased a few Swiss hand-embroidered handkerchiefs (they retailed for as much as $100 in the U.S. then) and started. The Haskins have also been engaged in the jade business in Burma; i.e., buying the raw stone. She is an expert on jade and told me a few things about it. They have been living at Canton and had considerable property there—but they expect that will all be lost now…

There are no anti-aircraft guns here, and besides the orders are not to resist any aerial bombardment because this might lead to an intensification of effort by the J. On one raid a year ago, the planes came very low and machine-gunned people in the streets, particularly along the waterfront and in sampans. Six hundred were killed that day…

All strangers, including Chinese, are watched. Two weeks ago, a Chinese girl arrived from Amoy and was found to be a J. spy who had been paid $100. She was liquidated…

The Yochow is an old ship of about 2,500 gross tons, built in 1901 and torpedoed in 1918—as the plaque over the clock states. We were supposed to sail at 1500 but were delayed because the Chinese customs, while inspecting the ship, found 11,000 silver dollars stowed away in a fuel oil tank. They were trying to locate the guy or guys who were implicated, but we finally left at 1700 without their being able to lay hands on the guilty parties…

At dinner last night, the captain was going full blast on the subject of women's clothes & hats, etc. I agree with him. He said that in Bali, the prostitutes keep their breasts covered. He also told an amusing story of the new governor who came to Bali and who was supposed to be rather moral. Since this was his first visit to the island, and the head-men wished to make a good impression, all the girls were instructed to cover their breasts as the governor passed. They did so—by pulling up their sarongs!

We will be in Hong Kong about noon. I am going over to the U.S. Consulate the very first thing to find out how you are and what you intend to do. My plans will then be made.

21 June 1939, SS Canton, En route Hong Kong to Haiphong

There is a Belgian who is a representative of a life insurance company. He says that 55% of the white people in Fr. Indo China are opium addicts—he knows this because they will not insure such persons. At parties in Fr. Indo China, opium pipes are provided for those who wish them. Even at H.K., where the sale of opium is a Govt. monopoly, Chinese, when they give parties, often provide pipes. Opium, as a rule, does not do much harm, if not used to excess, but now heroin tablets are being introduced, and they have a bad effect in seven years; the Japs are introducing the heroin…

Through my insurance friend, I met a Mr. Brelli, an ex French Army officer who served several years in Syria. He is the manager of the "China Gazomotive Company," which engages in the import, assembly, loading, and shipment of auto trucks to China. I believe they are the largest organization of this type in Haiphong. Here is a summary of what he told me. (a) 30,000 tons of material are arriving per month at Haiphong. (b) 18,000 leave Haiphong for China… Trucks last about 3 months, after which 1 good truck can be built from the remains of 3 damaged ones. There are not enough spare parts, or repair facilities, or trained personnel to permit adequate repair; hence, great wastage. Also, not enough gasoline to operate all trucks…

Apropos of China—I don't believe I told you of my meeting one of their financial agents on the PRES. CLEVELAND when I was returning from Hong Kong last April. This official was evidently on a financial mission to the Philippines and was important from the character of the delegation that met him at Manila. Another officer and myself were discussing casualties with him, and we asked him what steps the Chinese were taking to train new officers to replace those killed. He smiled and said that not many officers were killed—they knew how to take care of themselves, and it was the coolies who could be easily replaced who were killed…

I asked why there was an auto road direct from Haiphong to Chungking—the many auto trucks now at Haiphong did not get on their way. It seems that one of the Soong is head of the China Southwest Transportation Co., which has the monopoly for all of S.W. China, including the new military road to Burma; and since Soong makes a handsome profit in his business, he impedes the assembly and shipment of these trucks, which would reduce his business. Such trucks are sent to Haiphong—Soong charges high freight rates for the transport of government war supplies in the Govt. trucks.

Some time ago, an American banking syndicate had offered the Chinese Govt. a loan of $10 million gold through this same Soong. The deal fell through because Soong wanted 1 million for his commission!

Lt. Brandt, who has been stationed at Chungking for over a year and who is now on the PECOS,[51] told me the expression in Chungking is, "The Chinese will fight till the last drop of coolie blood."

23 June 1939

At the China Travel [in Hanoi], they assured me the Michelin leaving today, Friday, was all filled and there was no possibility of getting on board. So I showed them my special letter from the Chinese Consul at Manila in which it is stated that I am to be allowed to go anywhere I wish in China and for all officials to assist me—that this sort of hinted I was the official representative of the U.S. to investigate various conditions in China and that upon the results of my investigations, various important developments would depend. So, the manager of the China Travel at once stopped all work and went with me to see the station master. He also said all spaces were

---

51 A Kanawha-class replenishment oiler.

taken. So, they called some big shot by telephone and apprised him of my importance and of the necessity of getting me on the train. He said okay, and some other poor passenger was arbitrarily kicked off the train—and his reservation given to me...

The manager of the China Travel, realizing that the ultimate fate of China might depend on me, took great pains to tell me that he had been in Nanking at the time of the Jap occupation & of all the atrocities there. He was particularly anxious that I report that he had seen a Jap soldier hold a U.S. flag upside down & then trample on it. I had no little difficulty in restricting his words to the more useful project of getting me the R.R. ticket. This I did with my usual diplomatic manner...

The more I see of Hanoi, the more am I amazed, but there certainly is a difference between the modern city and the conditions of the ordinary people. Considerable residential building activity is going on—the houses being built appear to be quite substantial and well laid out.

The paper-making process was very interesting, and I marvel that the individual sheets do not become one mass as they are pressed together. I took the liberty of going inside one of the houses where the bark is prepared and the paper finally dried and sorted. Quite a few women work inside the houses stripping the bark. And later, on Silk Street in Hanoi, I saw a woman carrying two bales of paper bargaining with a shopkeeper for a piece of cloth to exchange for her paper.

25 June 1939, Yunnanfu

There is a project for constructing a pipeline to carry gasoline from Burma to Yunnanfu. The pipeline is to parallel the road and is to be capable of delivering 300 tons of gasoline per day. At the present time, about 30% of the railroad freight (for government use) is gasoline. A pipeline would reduce the load on the railroad by that amount. I met, by appointment, the man who is pushing this project—Mr. P.H. Cheng—a graduate of Michigan and a PhD from Cornell in 1917. He previously was in charge of building one of the railroads in North China. I advised him to have a pipeline expert from the United States survey the route and see whether the project is technically feasible. He wants me to talk to the president of the local big bank and tell him the same thing. What they are actually trying to do is obtain a loan from the U.S. Government for the construction of the line. From a long-range standpoint, the pipeline is a good idea because there is bound to be considerable development of motor transport in Southwest China, and the obtaining of sufficient quantities of motor fuel will always be a problem.

26 June 1939

I learned on good authority that the relations between the Central Government and the Szechwan Government are none too friendly. A month ago, a break was imminent, and the Central Government actually had two divisions of troops ready to overthrow the local organization. This province has been practically independent for many years, and its support of the Central Government has been rather half-hearted. Some troops, not well-trained, have been furnished to the Central Government, but the best troops, consisting of the warlike Meos and Laos, are kept within the province to defend the local organization should the need arise. It is said that one reason the Japs are not now conducting air raids on Kunming is because they do not wish to do anything which might crystallize local sentiment towards cooperation with Chiang Kai-shek.

The Central Government is aware of the extensive graft and great inefficiency of the local officials but is hesitant to take drastic steps for fear that an open break might occur, which would be bad at this time. The feeling among foreigners is, however, that when the war is over, there will be a grand clean-up here and that it will be accomplished by the "Communists."

From personal observations, I must admit that the Chinese officials here are incompetent and shoulder no responsibility. The high officials work few hours per day, and it is hard to find them—and, mind you, a war is going on…

…Houses of Prostitution. Certain streets are designated for this purpose. There is a gate at one entrance of the street, and the other end of the street is blocked off so that entrance can be had only through the gate. The admission charge (like a cover charge) is 50 cents. A Mr. Briety took me there this evening. We were accompanied by the Chinese hotel manager so he could ask questions for us. I am enclosing the ticket purchased at the gate, together with the translation.

There are courts on each side of the street. Each court has about eight large rooms to a side—four on the ground floor and four on the upper floor The establishment is run by the government. If a man decides to stay with a girl, he must pay seven dollars—five for the government and two for the "Mother" or sponsor (guardian) of the girl. The girl gets nothing except such tips as satisfied customers give her. Nearly all of the rooms have opium pipes, and both the girls and their admirers generally smoke. Tea is also served—and the official name of the place is "Tea House."

We talked with several of the girls. One was 17, and her mother and two sisters were all in the same house. Several had babies or younger sisters living with them. The walls of the rooms were generally covered with lithographs of pretty Chinese girls.

At 11 p.m., the police make a careful check of each room to see whether an admirer is present and whether the necessary seven dollars has been paid. Cases of holding out on money or of giving one's self for free are severely dealt with.

Girls caught practicing prostitution outside the government sanctuaries are sentenced to be placed in a "Tea House" without any remuneration to the "Mother."

The place we were in is apparently for the middle class. There is a similar place also for coolies, where the charge is two dollars.

27 June 1939

If you think Kunming is a medieval Chinese city, you should see Tsio Hiong! Kunming doesn't hold a candle to it. It is exactly as it must have been 100 years ago. I had heard of the practice of using dogs to clean the babies after they had performed their No. 2—but here I actually saw it being done. The fond mother was holding the back of the baby to a friendly dog who, after disposing of the more lucrative droppings, set to work on the baby itself...

There is another school here. I counted 21 fighting planes lined up on the field. I also saw a group of student pilots; their appearance was excellent.

30 June 1939

They woke me at 4:50 instead of 4:30, as I had requested. My Army officer friend, however, was really afraid I would leave at 5 sharp without him, and was actually in the truck at that time. So, when I showed up at 5:05, he pointedly showed me his watch and made many cutting remarks in Chinese about me to the driver and the interpreter. My face fell considerably! Shortly after we got underway, we passed an old monument on the road. The interpreter explained that this was in honor of General Kunming, after whom the city is named. The general lived about 1,000 years ago in the Han Dynasty and was in the Chinese army. He was sent to this part of the country to subdue a war lord who had a large army loyal to him. He succeeded in capturing the war lord, but released him. This he did seven times. Finally, the war lord surrendered and became a loyal subject of the emperor, sending him yearly tributes.

I remarked that in America, we would have executed him the first time he was caught and not permitted him to go free six more times. Furthermore, on the day of execution, he would have been awakened at 4:30 sharp and the job finished exactly at the stroke of 5.

This caused everyone to laugh—even the Army officer, and my face rose a little. We finally became good friends.

1 July 1939, Pao Shan

During the meal [Major General Fang and I] talked at length about the war. He feels that the Chinese do not have a chance and that the Japs can end this war at any time they wish by sending a large number of troops to China. He says all the higher-up Chinese know this—but speak differently in public in order to keep up the courage of the people. He knows—and the others know—that there is no danger of an economic breakdown of Japan. Furthermore, about half the ammunition the Japs are using is now being made in China by the Chinese. You will remember that the Mukden arsenal is now the largest one in the Jap empire. The Chinese soldiers are good at defense and at minor guerilla tactics, but are not too good at offense. They can never see the Jap soldiers and are afraid of them…

…We reached Lung Ling at 7 p.m. The accommodations were of the most primitive sort—just three boards set up in the office. The man in charge was able to borrow a Chinese quilt for me, which I used as a mattress. I have never seen a more muddy or wretched place than Lung Ling. We walked a half mile to the local inn to have supper. The inn had an earth floor, which was muddy, and the "kitchen" was in an earthen depression in back of the inn. It was the "prize" kitchen compared to any I had ever seen. I insisted on having a kettle full of boiling water for cleaning my dish and cup, and I watched the rice being fried in pig fat to be sure it was hot enough. My companions think I am queer to make such a fuss over this matter. In order to save me time and trouble, they tell me that they have seen the dishes washed in boiling water—and I don't need to trouble myself about it. But I insist on doing the job personally.

3 July 1939, USS Marblehead, En route Lashio Burma to Mandalay

I frequently feel that China's cause is hopeless when I see so many Chinese who should know better. In peacetime it may be all right—but right now they are at war—and they must use precision if they are to win. Believe me—to carry out a schedule in China—as I have insisted this past week—is a major job and requires overcoming endless difficulties.

...Each train has a "guard" who is in charge and gives the signal to start the train. The one on this train is a man named Jackson, who was born in England but went with his parents to Michigan when he was two. At 18, he left to visit his uncle in England, had an affair with a girl, and enlisted in the British Army. He was sent to Burma, where he served for seven years. Then in 1927, he obtained this job with the railroad... He invited me into his little cubicle, and I stayed there for two stations... He said that about 85% of the ammunition which comes to Lashio from Rangoon is of Russian origin; this confirms what the general at Pao Shan told me. It is shipped to England from Russia and transshipped on a British ship to Rangoon. An average of 52 freight cars comes to Lashio every three days. Each car carries ten tons.

1940s

[Editor's note: There is a significant gap in the Rickover collection with very few documents from 1941–1944, most of which time he was serving in Pearl Harbor on ship repairs. The letters to Ruth continue as he is en route to his assignment in command of a ship repair facility in Okinawa.]

2 April 1945, San Francisco, California

The weather was unusual, and so I spent most of the morning walking in the sun with an Army officer, a Colonel Theis, who is going out to be on Admiral Nimitz's staff in Guam. He has been engaged in the planning for the North Africa and Normandy campaigns, and has recently been working on the post-war organization of the Armed Forces for the Joint Chiefs of Staff. I was happy to learn that the recommendations are in line with what I have been thinking of. The high-ranking people on duty in the War and Navy Departments are against any of the new ideas—but Eisenhower, Nimitz, MacArthur, Halsey, etc.—all of the high-ranking people who have actually been doing the fighting are all for it.

12 April 1945, Honolulu, T.H.

I will be glad when I am finally on Okinawa—actually watching the buildings go up and getting into the swing of things. This preparatory planning stage, although it is essential, is not very gratifying. I have a great deal of leeway in making the layout for the Navy yard, in picking additional equipment, and so on.

I was shocked to learn of the president's death. I believe it is a far more serious event than people will generally realize. I am reminded that when the Germans made their breakthrough in France, people in many places simply went on with their usual daily work. So it was here today. Upon receipt of the news by radio, the flag in front of the C-in-C's headquarters was half-masted; then someone remembered that the news had not yet been received officially—so the flag was two-blocked.

2 May 1945

At home one thinks of the front area as being difficult, warlike, etc. It really is not. Aside from the relatively few people at the front, the rest might be described as a large-scale outing expedition. People live in tents, but water is available, good food is present, etc. Even the sound of guns going off a few miles away creates no particular impression. And near the island, large numbers of vessels of all kinds are anchored. A few of them are firing constantly into every position on the Southern part of the island. At nighttime, the flashes become routine.

The Japs are unable to obtain any reinforcements or supplies, so it is only a question of time until they will be liquidated. To see the large number of our vessels at anchor, so close to Japan, is pretty good evidence that Japan has very little seapower left.

4 May 1945, Guam

As I look back at it now, my outstanding impression—aside from the war aspect—was the effect on the civilian population. I had the good fortune to drive through a section of the island where there had been no active military operations, and so the people were already working in the fields once more. Nearly all the workers were women because there are very few men of military age left on Okinawa. One sees young boys and then old men...

Outwardly, the people do not show any resentment. They are a sad-appearing lot—not what one would see in Japanese villages, but in poor Chinese areas. Apparently, the Japs made little attempt to bring them up to the standards of Jap life and cleanliness, but exploited them as much as possible. Many of the people look like Chinese (which they were originally), some few like Japs, and the remainder in between. They dress like Jap peasants...

I felt very sorry for them. They probably do not understand what it is all about and certainly have no responsibility for what has happened.

I was wondering what would happen if we kept the island and introduced modern hygiene and a proper school system. No doubt within ten or fifteen years there would be a tremendous change in the people. The Chamois at Guam are not better people than the Chinese—but to see the children well fed and dressed, romping around outside the schools indicate what could be done with the Okinawans. I should like to see the experiment tried.

7 May 1945, Saipan, Marianas

I am sitting in a Quonset hut on top of a hill overlooking the harbor on the west side of the island. There are more than 150 vessels of all types anchored there. The sun is just setting, and there is one of those lovely Pacific sunsets which we used to see of Marivales.

It took only one hour to fly here from Guam. On the way, we stopped at Tinian Island, which is just two miles south of Saipan. Tinian has a large air strip used by the Flying Fortresses. It also has a small boat repair outfit.

Tinian was captured by us without much difficulty, after we had Saipan, because we found on Saipan complete plans for the defense of Tinian and the exact location of all defenses. Furthermore, a few days after we landed at Saipan, a captured Japanese major, who was one of their intelligence officers, willingly gave complete information about military matters. This officer had been educated in the U.S. and realized that Japan could not win. By his action, he believed the war would end sooner, which ultimately would benefit Japan.

...Everything is quiet here now. The last air raid was in January when 40 some Jap planes raided the airfield and caused considerable damage to parked Superfortresses.[52] Thereafter, we bombed Iwo airfield regularly to prevent such attacks. Then in February, we landed on Iwo—and now the Japs have no place near enough for bombing.

I talked with the commandant of the Naval Base—a Captain War—a retired officer. He mentioned that many of the enlisted men were complaining in letters home about the better treatment officers were receiving over enlisted men in recreational facilities, and believed it would be better to put them on the same plan in that respect in forward areas. The particular point at issue is that officers can obtain hard liquor at their clubs from 4 p.m. to 9 p.m., whereas the men are only allowed beer and then until about 5:30. In view of the fact that the background of many of the men now in service is not much different from that of many of the officers, I am inclined to agree with him.

Another point is the Red Cross nurses who hand out doughnuts, coffee, etc. at the airport and other places. There are very few of them, and they usually go out with officers only. This arouses resentment among the men, and Captain War believes it would be better to have no women at all on the island than just a very few.

Last night I decided it would be a good idea to obtain information about how the Military Government functioned on Saipan. So, I arranged to visit a Lt. Com. Schattle, who is the Acting Deputy Chief Military Government Officer. Before joining the Navy, he was a Captain of Detectives in Cincinnati, Ohio.

---

52 B-29 heavy bomber.

When we invaded Saipan, the civilians had all been told that certain death was to be their doom if they were captured or even if they surrendered. The civilian population consisted of about 20,000 Japs, 1,500 Koreans, and 3,000 native Chamois.[53] Nearly all of the Japs headed for the northern end of the island, and some 2,000 actually committed suicide by jumping off a high cliff onto the rocks below. First the children were thrown over, then the women, and finally the men. We tried to stop them by sending messages via other civilians who had surrendered and who informed them that they would receive good treatment—but very few were persuaded. One Jap—the manager of the local newspaper—poisoned his children and wife and was then knocked unconscious before he could poison himself. He is now in the compound and broods over the matter.

These compounds have been established for civilians: one for the Chamois, one for the Koreans, and one for the Japs. The Chamois have been given the best housing—that which was still left standing. The Koreans are next best treated because it is assumed they will eventually be an independent people, and the official instructions are to this effect. The Japs are in a large compound, 18,000 of them. Their houses consist of shacks which have been built of salvaged galvanized iron. They have a raised wooden floor, no doors. They have water but no electric light. Several families live in one of these small shacks. In view of the number of children in one of these families, you can imagine the congestion. Nevertheless, when I visited the camp today, they all appeared happy and well fed. A baseball game attended by about 1,000 spectators (of the camp) was in progress, and there was as much cheering as at an American game...

About 107 of the Japs are from Japan. The remainder are from Okinawa. I ventured the opinion that the Okinawans did not mind coming under our flag, but Lt. Com. Schattle stated that was just wishful thinking. He believes the Okinawans are fully as patriotic as the other Japs. To illustrate he said that for months, O.W.I.[54] broad-

---

53 The Chamorro people of the Mariana Islands.
54 Office of War Information (1942–1945).

casts in Japanese had been announced to the Japs and that they paid practically no attention to them. One day, as an experiment, a Tokyo radio program with colored war news, etc. was permitted. The people perked up and listened with great attention. After a few more O.W.I. broadcasts with no results, they were stopped.

He feels that the Japs still do not believe we will not kill them. Even though they see so many evidences of our strength, it has no effect upon them. Recently he took a group of internees, who work in his office, on a trip where they were permitted to see almost everything. When they came to the harbor and saw that many big ships could now come right up to the dock at one time, they stopped talking—because the harbor had not been dredged during Jap occupation, and here in the space of a few months we had accomplished it...

There has been practically no trouble at all with the Japs. They obey properly and cooperate well. Sixty-four (64) of them have been made policemen, and they take care of all disciplinary matters. Of the 64, only 4 were previously on the police force. They wear yellow brasards[sp] to indicate their positions and authority. The police are loyal to the Military Govt. and report everything that goes on in camp.

The only serious happening was one night when a large number of them held their own court on one of their foremen. The police at once reported this to Lt. Com. Schattle, who spoke roughly to the assembled Japs and threated to stop their food supply if they even attempted to hand out justice themselves. There has been no trouble since...

The feeling among Military Govt. is that the right type of people are not selected for the leading jobs. They think it is a mistake to take ordinary line officers, give them a brief course in military government at a university—and expect them to be expert at it. The same applies to PhD's. These have not had enough practical experience in handling the problems of sanitation, food, and living to make out good on such a job. Rather, they believe the ones selected should be businessmen or city administrators, if such are available...

The quarters in which I have been living here are rather simple. There is a large, galvanized tub outside the building from which we can obtain water by means of a bucket given to each of us. Frequently the tub is filled by rainwater.

However, there is a lovely view both in the evening and in the morning. Early in the morning, when the light is just right, the spring can be seen breaking over the reef which protects the harbor. This view can be seen for about 15 minutes only. It is beautiful.

I thought the drinking water at Pearl Harbor was not too good. Then at Guam, I thought that was almost impossible. But at Saipan, it is the worst yet. The water is yellowish, probably from the coral, and it is so heavily chlorinated that it tastes very stale, and one must hold his breath to drink it. In this way this taste is eliminated. It is much easier to drink when it is cold. The taste is hidden somewhat.

Toilet facilities are the same as were used before the advent of modern plumbing. It certainly is not modern in that respect, but this cannot, of course, be helped. The accent in construction is on air fields and other military projects. Comforts necessarily must wait.

9 May 1945, Ulithi (Mackenzie) Islands

I am now on the USS BAHAM for a few days, to study the methods of organization and of conducting repairs on repair ships—as the work at an Advanced Base will be more like that on a repair ship than at a Navy yard. At a yard, with civilian employees, elaborate accounting systems must be used, both for labor and materials, but since we will be using enlisted men only—we will not have that problem, nor the one of labor relations.

I spent all day today on the USS AJAX, and will do the same on the USS JUPITER tomorrow. The repair officer on the AJAX was on a ship of the Asiatic Station when I was at Cavite.[55] He told me that all of the houses on Cavaco Road (where we lived) were burned when the Japs first attacked…

---

55 A province in the Philippines.

After leaving Saipan, I flew to Tinian… There are still numbers of Japs, about 500, on the island. They have been surrendering at the rate of 20 to 40 per week. Recently, 3 of our soldiers who went souvenir hunting in an out of the way part of the beach were seized by the Japs, dragged into a cave, and killed.

The method of inducing the soldiers to surrender is to send a civilian from the camp or a surrendered soldier back to his mates. They are permitted to stay overnight with the soldiers. This has been the most successful method. Once they persuade the soldiers they will be treated properly, they surrender. Here also only one person persuading soldiers to surrender has been killed by one of them…

In Saipan, they had an unusual case. A civilian Jap reported in and stated he wanted to look the camp over before deciding whether or not to stay. The Military Government decided to let him do so; he stayed for two days, talked with the other Japs, and then reported to the Military Government that he wished to remain. He was informed that he had to go back, but come back permanently a week later if he still decided he wished to. This was a clever move. He not only came back but was instrumental in bringing others in, too.

16 May 1945, En route Peleliu to Manus

At Ulithi anchorage, I spent several days visiting various repair ships, and by now I have a fairly complete idea of the type of repairs being conducted in the advanced Pacific areas.

Many ships are damaged these days off Okinawa—mostly by suicide planes. Some of them are repaired temporarily at Kareno Retto, a small group of islands to the west of Okinawa, where we have a number of repair ships. Others go to Guam or to Ulithi…

I visited one aircraft carrier, which had been hit by a suicide. Much of the flight deck and the hanger deck had been burned; fortunately, very few people were killed because of excellent precautions which had been taken. Another ship, a battleship, had narrowly missed being hit in the bridge structure because at the last instant one of the wings of the suicide plane was shot away. The plane missed the bridge by 4 feet and hit the superstructure instead. All of the officers on the bridge were intent on watching suicide planes on the other side of the bridge, and did not even know they had been hit until someone reported a fire burning on deck.

25 May 1945

Visiting Manus—still supposed to be a few Japs. I visited one of their last camping grounds in the jungle...even the bottles in one container differed somewhat in shape and showed the imperfections, such as bubbles in the glass, incident to hand-[crafted] work. This shows that the Japs are not benefitted by mass-production, as are we.

31 May 1945, Pearl Harbor

First let me tell you that your book came. It is really an excellent piece of work—and I am not telling you this just because it is you. I have had much experience in recent years with technical matters, and I can judge what is pseudo-technical and what is actually a good job.

I find the reading interesting; your style is excellent, and I am sure many "lawmen" if they knew about the book would read it... I am certain you will receive a great deal of praise for your work...

My work since I have been back has been largely one of planning. I have about 15 officers here working with me. We work from 8 a.m. to 10 p.m. every day of the week. There is so much to do, and so little time that we are forced to these hours. What we do not accomplish now will be impossible to accomplish later on.

You have no idea how difficult it is to get things done—the number of people we must go through, etc. Everyone tells me I have accomplished so far more than anyone else, but I am not satisfied because it is not what we get done, but how much we get done as compared with what remains to be done.

4 June 1945, Pearl Harbor

Today I accomplished a little more in connection with planning, but you have no idea of the wearisome efforts that are required—the red-tape and the doing of the same thing over and over again. No wonder most people become fed up and accept things as they are. But gradually some things are shaping up.

I am bothered that we may not learn the real lesson from this war—that it is the extension of American mass-production methods and products, which have given us such an overwhelming superiority that most any of our military leaders could win. Nevertheless, here at Pearl Harbor there is duplication upon duplication, inefficient organization, slip-shod administration. To me there does not appear to be present any sense of urgency...

I have been thinking a great deal of this slow way in which things get done, and whether is it possible to overcome it. But I am regretfully coming to the conclusion that it is impossible—except in small, isolated cases. But I cannot believe that the Germans or the Japs would be guilty of such gross delay as is encountered here. The basic fault is that wars are almost entirely of an industrial character now, and the leaders in the Army and Navy, with few exceptions, do not comprehend modern industry and its methods.

When we captured Yanton airfield in Okinawa, we found the crude apparatus—all hand tools—with which they were pulverizing coral to build air strips. They have no idea of our type of machinery. Consequently, they do not plan for, nor do they imagine, how quickly we can build airfields, bases, etc. That is why they were beaten. They are just as brave, just as resourceful as we are, but they do not have the backing of a gigantic system of factories.

But what would be the outcome were we opposed by an enemy having equally modern industry but with a more businesslike and urgent way of conducting his affairs? ...

In the U.S., there have been numerous surveys to determine whether war agencies use excessive manpower. At the Bureau of Ships, it was next to impossible to get an extra officer or additional civilians. Here, they pick as many as they wish of the best officers sent to the Pacific. The place is loaded with officers doing work which could be done by enlisted men. And since most of these officers are above the average, they naturally become discontented. I firmly believe that waste of manpower is inevitable if a job is to be done right in war time—but there comes the point of diminishing returns where the presence of too many people acts only to slow actions.

Well, I hope to set an example in my own outfit.

6 June 1945, Pearl Harbor

I note that your reaction to Roosevelt's death was about the same as my own. The press is already playing up Truman and making a hero of him. But actually, can you imagine a large corporation choosing its top man the way he was chosen? No doubt he is a good, honest man—but what is needed at this time is not only a good politician and administrator but someone who has a large grasp of international affairs and is an idealist. I don't see how he can qualify on this basis. Naturally he will be more popular with Congress and many others because he will let them alone much more than Roosevelt did...

Along political lines I am afraid we may be playing too much with Great Britain. There is no doubt that she cannot forever hold her subject peoples back—which Churchill is definitely committed to; by siding with her so much we are becoming identified with her policy, and this will lose much of the good will we have everywhere.

Russia, of course, with no color line, offers much more to Hindus, etc. than we do.

15 June 1945, Pearl Harbor

Do you remember Elliot Loughlin?[56] He was the one who married the Danish girl, when I was on the New Mexico.... He has been in submarines for some time. About 3 months ago, he was in command of a submarine and sank a Japanese hospital ship en route from Singapore to Japan. The ship had been given safe conduct by our government. There was one survivor. As a consequence of this, the Japs torpedoed one of our hospital ships—which put in for repairs at Guam when I was there. Quite a few patients and nurses were killed. The captain was given a General Court Martial; I do not know what the full sentence was—but he will not be permitted to command a ship again during the war.

It is difficult to judge the merits of the case because I do not know what the circumstances were. But you can imagine how our press would have raved under the circumstances if the Japs had done anything similar. This has never been published as far as I know.

3 August 1945, Okinawa

I am the Commanding Officer of the Naval Repair Base; this includes not only the Ship Repair area, but also the camp for about 5,000 men. We will have all sorts of things, such as laundries, bakeries, Red Cross facilities, chapels, etc. etc. In addition, I am responsible for about six or seven other activities on various parts of the island.

There were about 400,000 people on Okinawa when we came... Most of the villages were destroyed during the fighting; the rest are being destroyed by burying or flattening to make way for airfields, roads, camps, etc. Soon the place will look as though no natives had

---

56 Rear Charles Elliott Laughlin (1910–1989), U.S. Naval Academy Class of 1933.

ever been here. However, after seeing the miserable houses, I feel that in the long run the people will be better off.

They are all puny, half-fed, and diseased. The Military Govt. is doing all possible to take care of them, but with the present shortage in shipping, and the tremendous problem, not too much can be done. When I see the large number of children, poorly cared for, in rags, and living under the most primitive conditions, I think of Robert and how fortunate he is.

In connections with school for Robert,[57] I believe it would be desirable at this time to have him go to a private school because the D.D. schools are pretty bad off, as you know. With salaries as high as they are in Washington, many people who ordinarily would send children to public schools are sending them to private ones, so there is not so much difference between the two.

9 August 1945, Okinawa

We learned today of Russia's declaration of war and of the atomic bomb. We have very little news here; furthermore, we are too busy to worry too much about it.

12 August 1945, Okinawa

The night before last was a very exciting one here. The word about the Japanese offer to accept the peace terms came in over the radio, and at once everyone started shooting. The ships in the harbor were firing machine guns in all directions, the Army anti-aircraft batteries were firing tracer bullets, and various men and officers in the naval camp were firing rifles and pistols in the air.

For one hour the sky was full of live ammunition—going in all directions. I was never so scared in my life. It was the most disgraceful episode I have ever witnessed or heard of. There was no place to go for protection because we naturally are not prepared

---

57 Robert Rickover, the only son of Admiral and Ruth Rickover.

for the eventuality of being shot at deliberately by our own people. The only protection was the canvas tent of our office—so we stood outside and watched the spectacle.

Finally the air raid alarm sounded and the firing gradually stopped. During the turmoil, a Jap torpedo-plane flew into the anchorage and torpedoed one of our ships.

The next morning, we learned that a number of people had been hit, some fatally. In fact, one of my men sleeping in his tent at Baten Ko (several miles from here) had his lung penetrated by a bullet…

I believe the lesson has been learned, because last night there was practically no shooting at all. It is difficult to explain such an event. I cannot understand how the officers on board ship (where the men are easily controlled) could permit such goings on. It is criminal for people to be killed or wounded after the war is practically over.

20 August 1945, Okinawa

The job now is far more difficult than it was during the war because there has been a complete let down and all of the people want to get home. Yet the work still remains to be done, and it is tremendously important that morale be maintained. I know the drop of morale and the mutinies which occurred in 1918 and 1919, and I am doing everything in my power to have as contented a group of officers and men as possible. Unfortunately, these historic lessons are not generally understood, and trouble may result.

31 August 1945, Okinawa

An Army colonel is here on temporary duty awaiting transportation to Japan to investigate the effects of the atomic bombs. He was one of the top officials working on it. The newspaper stories are generally correct, including the vital part played by the German refugees.

The point that I had cleared up is that it is possible to make the bomb with such overall small size that it could be smuggled into a country. Furthermore, it will be impossible to manufacture it eventually without too elaborate apparatus. You can see what this means for groups such as the Nazis. In a few years, when everyone is again sympathizing with the Germans (or the Japs), they will move 100 or so of the bombs, smuggle them in, and locate them in various places. No airplanes or rocket projects will ever be necessary. The bomb is inactive and can last thousands of years. The "guts" of the ones dropped on Japan weighed 15 lbs. and was 3 inches in diameter. It was the smallest quantity which could be dropped and still detonate.

5 September 1945, Okinawa

Things are very uncertain here—that is, there is no definite decision as to the extent of the installations to be made. What with all the officers and men weary of the war and of the Navy, and desiring to go home, it is difficult to get things done, and far more work and leadership are required at this time than ever before. I remember the period after the last war, and the trying time we had. It is worse now. The reserve officers have been in the Navy long enough in this war (much longer than in the last war) to see some of the stuffed-shirters and plain incompetence, and nearly all want to get out of the Navy as fast as possible. This, of course, makes things very difficult for me, because we are losing our best officers, although the job must be done...

We are sending a Division of Marines to North China. I understand the Japs will not surrender that area to the Chinese communist who control it, but are willing to surrender to us. I think we are getting mixed up in the squabble between the two factions, and we will get no good out of it...

This evening, I talked with an officer who was in charge of a number of landing craft who were in the first group to land on Honshu. The Japs all fled to the hills—and it is only now, after more than a week, that they are beginning to return. They left in such haste that meals were left cooking in the houses.

They had all been indoctrinated that all of the women would be raped and the young children massacred by the Americans. In fact, our men did quite a bit of looting. I think this has been stopped by now as more control is being exercised.

24 September 1945, Okinawa

I was in the mess hall [in Guam] at a four-place table with another officer—when two lieutenants sat down. My friend and I were discussing the appearance of prisoners in the manner I wrote you. After a while, one of the new officers spoke up and announced that he and his companion had just come from Japan where they had been prisoners for 4 years.

We talked for about 3 hours, and I gained some vivid impressions of their experiences. One had been in Corregidor and the other in Guam. Prisoners in Guam were given little food for about 10 days. Natives risked beatings to smuggle food in to them... Contrary to general opinions, the prisoners in Corregidor were not robbed of their personal possessions. I noted that one of the officers wore a Naval Academy class ring and asked how he had managed to retain it. He said no personal possessions were ever taken; in fact, in Corregidor, shortly after the surrender, Jap soldiers had bought wrist watches, camera, etc. from American prisoners; but when the Jap officers found out they were angry and made the soldiers return the objects. These officers had with them some of their original clothing, towels, books, etc. The Japs never limited them in the quantities they could carry—the natural limit was their strength to carry it....

The treatment accorded depended pretty much on the camp commander. Some camps were relatively good—some bad. These two were at a "good" camp. It was the first one set up and was very frequently visited by all manner of Jap officials because of the initial curiosity to see American prisoners. Also, it was one of the camps Red Cross representatives were permitted to visit.

12 October 1945, Okinawa

You have probably read that we had a terrific typhoon on Okinawa and that many people have been killed.

The ship repair area is completely levelled except for one building out of 70, which still stands. All tents are ruined except one.

Fortunately, none of my people were killed—although a number
were injured. The wind was of about 150 miles velocity and simply
blew the buildings to pieces. For several hours large sheets of metal
were hurtling through the air at tremendous speeds and would have
cut in two anyone they might have hit.

Most of our people had been ordered up in the hills before the
storm and so were out of danger...

During the worst of the storm, we had men patrolling the beach
to pick up survivors from ships in the harbor. About 80 ships were
beached. It was the worst disaster of the sort any of us have ever
experienced.

24 October 1945, Okinawa

There has been considerable criticism by Congressmen to the
Navy Dept. about conditions in Okinawa by men released from
service; as far as I know, none of it has been directed at Ship Repairs.
I have certainly gone out of my way to do everything possible for the
men—and yet, have done little for myself or the officers.

I figured it was the proper thing to do—and realized it was politically the wise thing to do.

1 November 1945, Okinawa

An officer has just come in from Tsingtao. He says the city and
surrounding region is under control of the Communists and therefore we have still not disarmed about 20,000 Jap troops in the vicinity.
Meanwhile we are transporting in U.S. Naval vessels Chinese National

troops from French Indochina to Tsingtao to take over the place! I suppose we will have to keep on supplying the National troops.

I believe we are making a grave mistake. Probably it stems from our desire to keep the Russians from getting too powerful. But, in the long run, since the Communists in China are really a Populist part bound to win out, I am afraid we will incur considerable enmity and lose the good will we now have.

Reading the many clippings you send me, it appears that we are making the same mistakes this time we made at the end of the last war. For "top" people in each country leads us to make and follow policies, which do not represent the real view or real interest of our people.

For example, in my wanderings around Okinawa, I ventured into a place called KOZA run by the Military Government. About 13,000 Okinawans are settled here in a number of villages. Included in the area is an old people's compound, and one orphanage. A description of these two places is exactly what would be encountered in a German concentration camp. Children without clothes, starving, and neglected. Old people and imbeciles in a filthy, crowded native hut. I have never seen anything like this in all my life.

I informed the admiral this morning of what I had seen. He sent for the Military Governor and went to visit the place with him. This will do me no good, but my conscience would never have given me any rest had I not done my best to save the children. When I was first there 3 days ago, I offered to send food, clothing, or anything else that was needed to the Army captain in charge. He said the children would not eat it. I offered to send ice cream; he replied the M.P.'s would be angry because they also were not getting ice cream! (This regarding starving children!)

11 November 1945, Okinawa

As a result of my action relative to the orphan children—the situation has been cleared up. New quarters are being built for them, a medical officer has been assigned—and they will be taken care of hence forth.

18 November 1945, Okinawa

Of the many officers who were attached at the ship Repair Base only about 10% were really worthwhile, although nearly all came from good families and had formal college educations. In fact, the best officer was an ex-enlisted man; he was with me on the FINCH in China, and I arranged to have him come out with me… From what I have seen so far, reliability is by far the most important quality. After that comes initiative. I have found many enlisted men here whom I would like to make officers in place of those who do not come up to officer standards—but this is impossible under our system. I never realized how little opportunity an enlisted man has in our Navy until I came out here. All other countries, such as Russia and Germany, are far in advance of us in this respect.

The Navy has lost face tremendously with the men; they see officers who are incapable getting away with doing practically nothing and at high rates of pay and are protected in their positions.

On the surface we appear to have a democratic set-up in the Navy, and as you know I have always spoken up for that view. But actually, we have done away with undemocratic appearances while the undemocratic features actually remain to a large extent. This particular best officer I have is not eligible for a permanent commission in the Navy because he is a little over-age and because he has not had a formal education—and he must return to warrant officer status. While any number of incompetents are eligible and will be commissioned in the regular Navy.

This all makes me wonder of the future of the Navy and of the U.S. when we take such an easy course with our national defense. Most of the stories and articles of the great officers of the Pacific war are a lot of rot if Okinawa is any example.

26 November 1945, Okinawa

This will be my last letter from Okinawa…it's been quite an experience, and it has given me the opportunity to see how operations are conducted in the fighting areas. I am not too impressed, and I believe that if we were fighting an enemy who had equal material resources it would go hard with us.

The attitude of nearly all the men and many of the officers is like that displayed at a high school football contest.

Today an order came out that greater respect should be shown by the men to the officers. I was wondering what my reactions as an enlisted man should be under the circumstances. The admiral has had built for himself the finest quarters imaginable—huge rooms, chintz curtains, over-stuffed furniture—while some of the men are still living in tents with mud floors. Today we transferred a number of men to the Naval Operating Base (where the admiral lives). They came back in a short time and asked permission to sleep here because they were given no cots or bedding and the mud was miles deep…

Thanksgiving Day I went to the orphan camp with a crate of oranges and one of apples. They were very pleased to get them. The school children sang for us, and it was highly amusing to hear them sing one of Robert's favorites… Like young children all over the world, the young Okinawans are very cunning and likeable, and we wonder why all children cannot have a decent childhood.

28 December 1945, Terminal Island, California

The problem with putting all of these ships out of commission is a tremendous one—but unfortunately the people doing the job have had little experience in organizing or in actually doing this kind of work. Again, it is the old story of putting ranking officers in charge who have had no material duty. As a consequence, the work is not being done properly. I went into all phases of the matter and have prepared a long report outlining proposed remedies—but since my recommendations would involve hurting people's feelings, I doubt anything will come of it. So, two or three years from now the Navy will suddenly find out that the ships they have advertised as being ready for war—are not ready. I am getting rather tired of seeing this sort of thing time and again and nothing happens because everyone protects everyone else.

14 January 1946, San Francisco, California

I have been very busy working at Mare Island—where we have many ships, including submarines. Here, as at the other places, there has not been a full realization of the job to be done—and I feel that my being there for several days stirred them up a little and will probably have some beneficial effect. However, it appalls me to see the lack of understanding of organizational procedures and principles wherever I go—and that is one of the reasons for conditions being as they are.

As a result of the first 3 reports, the admiral has now requested me to conduct a study of the operation of his own staff! There is surely plenty to be corrected—but I am afraid that since he himself worked up his organization, he may not kindly respond to effecting changes. There are no written duties for his staff and no organizational chart. As a result, his officers (the list includes 7 captains, one of whom is in charge of office furniture and typewriters) really do not know what their duties are and are not allowed to assume responsibility or to sign letters (all of this is done by the admiral himself). However, I shall submit proposed organizations with full description of duties and responsibilities.

I sort of like work of this kind—but I am constantly amazed at the inability to copy industrial principles where the problem to be solved is almost entirely industrial in nature.

March 23, 1946, San Francisco, California

As a result of my campaign to reduce work on the 19th Fleet vessels, the Navy Yards are now asking for additional work to keep them going. This shows what can be done if a few business methods are applied to naval ship repairs. In attempting to find out what it costs to repair ships of various types, I learned that the yards did not even keep up-to-date records of total costs, and that it took about a week to unearth the cost for a particular ship! I could save the Navy a great deal of money—if they were really willing to operate on a modern industrial basis. I always knew that yard costs could be reduced about 20 to 25% by intelligent screening of work (this year we are spending about 700 million for repairs at yards).

April 16, 1946, Portland, Oregon

This has been an uneventful week of analyzing the local 19th Fleet activities. It is amazing how the group commanders fail to realize the basic problems confronting them and to take the necessary remedial measures. As usual, myself and my staff were coldly received—because we are inspecting them, and what we advise is taken with some skepticism. After a few days, they become aware that maybe what we told them was valid after all. Then they become angry because an outsider discovered it instead of themselves.

It is always appalling to see such large ventures entrusted to officers who are unable to grasp that the problem is not the same as commanding a battleship…. [The officers] are so sedate, and so reserved, and so authoritative; meanwhile, the job runs itself without their being aware of much that is going on.

I imagine, from their standpoint, it must be galling to be told the things I have to tell them—but there is no other way.

April 19, 1946, Astoria, Oregon

I received word from the Bureau today that I am to take one year's course in "nuclear energy" at the Massachusetts Institute of Technology, Boston, starting in June. They asked me how soon I can be detached. I talked it over with my admiral, of the 19th Fleet, and I'll probably be able to be detached early in May. I'll let you know well in advance when I'll be in Washington. After reaching Washington, I am to go to Boston to work out the details of my course, and then I'll have to be there early in June. This program should make it possible for you to do some planning for completing your book and for getting some needed rest.

4 May 1946, San Pedro, California

In a personal letter I received yesterday from the Bureau of Ships' Detail Officer, he states that the plan now is not to send me to school but to be engaged actively in some project connected with the matter, somewhere in the U.S. I don't know what that means and will not be able to find out until I reach the Bureau.

8 June 1946, Oak Ridge[58]

The Army people are very nice and friendly to me. I have been placed in an office with the man in charge of the operation of all the plants—and this is a good vantage-point from which to learn. I have been busy trying to learn as much as possible and to lessen my general ignorance of the subject.

13 June 1946, Oak Ridge

The days go fast here. There is so much to learn, and so little time to learn it, that I wish more hours were available. The people

---

58 Oak Ridge National Laboratory in Tennessee.

here are treating me as well as I could wish. All sources of information have been made available to me, and it is, of course, far more instructive to be able to look at the objects talked about than merely to read about them. My head is completely full of protons, neutrons, alpha particles, beta particles, gamma rays, etc. But somehow, most of it is beginning to fall into some form of order in my mind. I suppose I am too impatient to learn.

28 September 1946, Oak Ridge

I have been busy for the last few days writing a speech, which perhaps General Groves[59] will deliver sometime in October. The purpose of the speech is to gently "let down" the public about the peaceful applications of nuclear energy and to indicate that very much study, work, and money will be necessary before we can have atomic energy. The main point I make is that an atomic power plant is more difficult than was the atomic bomb. And since $2 billion was required for the former, much money will be required for the latter.

I don't know why they picked on me for this because they have a large publicity staff in Washington. At any rate, I have been doing practically nothing for several days.

Then yesterday I was asked to deliver a speech at Nashville, Tennessee before some Army Reserve Officer Association on "How to Stop Atomic Bombs." This is a good subject and one the answer to which many people are seeking.

28 October 1946, Oak Ridge

Navy Day was celebrated here on Friday the 25th with a dinner at Knoxville, which all of the Oak Ridge naval contingent, including

---

59 Lieutenant General Leslie Grovers (1896–1970) headed the Manhattan Project during World War 2.

myself, attended. Admiral Solberg spoke[60] [Engineering Duty Officer]—he had charge of the technical work for the Bikini Tests.

15 October 1947

To: File from Captain H.G. Rickover, USN

Subject: Dr. Zinn's account of Construction of 1st reactor at Chicago

1. Today I met with Dr. Zinn[61] at Chicago to discuss the present status of the submarine nuclear development. Subsequent to that discussion, Dr. Zinn told me about his experiences during the construction of the first reactor at Chicago, in 1942.

2. According to Dr. Zinn the following took place: Dr. Fermi was in charge of the over-all design, construction, and operation of the first graphite pile, and Dr. Zinn was his assistant. The original intent was to build the reactor at Palos Park. Dr. Zinn had been informed by General Groves that he could commence construction on 7 November 1942. In preparation for this, Dr. Zinn and his group arrived at Palos Park together with several truck loads of material for the reactor. He found that the building construction was not yet completed and that workmen were proceeding with electrical wiring, carpentry, etc. Nevertheless, Dr. Zinn and his crew commenced unloading material to build the reactor.

3. When this began, all labor personnel at the site stopped work and "struck." They were union personnel and objected because Dr. Zinn's people were non-union and were working

---

60 Rear Admiral Thorvald Solberg (1894–1964), U.S. Naval Academy Class of 1916.

61 Dr. Walter Zinn (1906–2000), a nuclear physicist who supervised the construction of the first nuclear reactor.

at the same site. The Army representative, a captain, mediated the situation and finally proposed the following to Dr. Zinn:

a. That all work on the reactor be done by union personnel.
b. That Dr. Zinn give all his orders to the Army captain, who, in turn, would transmit them to the union construction people. Thus, the situation would be that an inexperienced person, the captain, would be transmitting technical orders to inexperienced construction people. Dr. Zinn objected on these grounds and suggested that the site be vacated of all construction personnel even though the building work was not completed. He stated that he and his people could operate the site as it was and could improvise to take into account the uncompleted construction.

10 May 1948

From HGR to Captain Henry E. Eccles, USN, Naval War College

Dear Henry:

I have read with interest recent comments in the Naval Institute on your article written by Captain Hammer and by Commodore Carter; and I am very happy to see that you are taking a strong stand to the end that the contribution of shore-based units may not be overestimated by those who plan for a future war.

As you may realize, I have done quite a bit of thinking in the last few years on this subject, particularly as I was fortunate enough to be permitted to visit advanced bases in other parts of the Pacific besides the one at Okinawa; and I have come to the conclusion that it would have been far better and that much less effort, both in manpower and materials, would have been expended, had we confined ourselves more to a seagoing effort for repairs to ships, rather than to have stressed as much as we did the shore-based effort.

I think that if such were possible, an analysis of the return we got as compared with the effort expended on shore bases, would be well worthwhile, and would indicate some interesting results. One of the major troubles with the shore-based units was that the overhead in construction and maintaining the camp and its facilities was far too great. Some of this was inherent in the shore-based unit; the rest was due to lack of understanding either by those in command of the unit itself or by their superiors, as to what the real objective was. Therefore, too much effort went into the non-essential and unimportant from that standpoint.

Mannes was probably as typical a repair base as one could find; that is, it had been in existence for some time and was working on a routine basis. There, I made some effort to compute the overhead; and apparently, it would be safe to say that the overhead was at least 66%. This was not entirely due to the officer in charge of the repair unit, but was due to the limitations which were place upon him by his superiors and by the necessities and exigencies of the situation, as well as the fact that he was not trained for an effort which required a great deal of imagination and a thorough realization of the prime objective.

On Okinawa, we could not begin to build a ship repair unit because the necessary roads to deliver material to the site were not ready. The roads were not ready because much of the road building effort was concerned with building a wide road to a healthful area where the C.B. command could have its permanent location including club houses, fairly good living quarters, etc. Had the attack on Honshu taken place at the time anticipated, there would have been no semblance of a repair activity available to service the fleet. Consequently, all of the planning effort, the use of shipping space for ship material and training of personnel, their transport, etc. etc. etc. would have been completely wasted.

I realize that in the planning stage, such as you conducted at Pearl Harbor, it was assumed that the people on the spot would have as broad a view of the problem as you had. However, this is not always the case. The local commander has many other problems to consider; he may not be familiar with the importance of the project, and so the desires of the planning authorities may not necessarily be complied with.

I have not written the above for the purpose or objective of assigning blame to anyone. Considering all of these matters, after a two-year calming down interval, I realize that what happened was inevitable. However, I am writing you because I realize that in a future war, we shall not have the preponderance of material and personnel, which will permit us to be as wasteful as we were in the last war. Therefore, my opinion is that we should be very careful about setting up large shore establishments in advanced areas for the repair of ships, and so forth.

2 September 1949

Memorandum from HGR to Rear Admiral David H. Clark, USN[62]

Subj: Additional Engineering Duty Officer Personnel for Nuclear Propulsion Assignments

1. In the assignment of Engineering Duty Officers to nuclear propulsion billets, nearly all efforts to date have been devoted to obtaining younger officers. Recently, a plan was placed into effect for the education of new younger officers. An adequate input of younger officers into this important field of work is now established. However, there still remains the considerable gap in seniority between myself and the other Engineering Duty officers assigned to this field. The

---

62 Rear Admiral David Harris Clark (1899–1982), U.S. Naval Academy Class of 1921.

nuclear propulsion field is quite distinct from other aspects of atomic energy work and should be regarded separately.

2. The introduction of a new senior officer actively into the nuclear propulsion field should be done only after he has devoted a considerable period of time to familiarizing himself with the very complex technical and administrative arrangements. My own estimate, based on seeing several officers introduced into this field during the past two years, is that about two years is required before a capable officer can become a really effective agent.

3. I recommend that one senior Engineering Duty officer be assigned in the near future to nuclear propulsion work for education and familiarization in this field and then assigned as an ultimate relief for me. This officer should fulfill the following requirements:

    a. Be qualified to command submarines, as familiarity with their operation and technical characteristics is essential.

    b. Desire assignment to this type of duty and believe in the future it affords.

    c. Have a seniority in the general range of 1928–1932. A more senior officer would have less long-time availability for assignment. A more junior man would be too close to several capable officers who have already had three years' experience in this field.

    d. Be experienced in machinery design, especially in submarine machinery.

    e. Have had experience in the Bureau in a technical position.

    f. Be sufficiently mentally alive to readily learn a field that is quite new and unusual both technically and administratively.

    g. Be able to deal effectively with civilian scientists, some of whom do not have a strong liking for military men....

4...

5. The question of an officer to take my place has given me considerable concern during the past two years. I consider that the attainment of nuclear propulsion for naval vessels is of utmost, and perhaps crucial importance to the future of the Navy. For this reason, I have carefully reviewed the list of Engineering Duty officers including those senior and junior to the seniority range mentioned above. I have talked and corresponded with several likely possibilities. My considered opinion is that Captain R.L. Moore, Jr.[63] best possesses the qualifications and capabilities of doing the job. He is intelligent, far-sighted, hard-working, and has that degree of energy and persistence which is so necessary in the formative state of a venture of this sort.

---

63 Possibly Captain Royal Lester Moore, U.S. Naval Academy Class of 1922.

1950s

9 December 1952

Letter from Senator-Elect Henry M. Jackson[64] to Secretary of the Navy

As a member of the Reactor Development Subcommittee since its inception, I have followed the nuclear-propelled submarine and carrier programs with the closest attention... I therefore frankly find myself at a loss to understand why this officer was "passed over" for promotion a second time and now faces early retirement.

Although I have been a member of the House of Representatives for twelve years, I have never before made inquiries as to a decision concerning the promotion of an individual within the military.

19 December 1952

Memorandum of Conversation between RADM H.M. Wallin, RADM Leggett, RADM Sylvester, and CAPT H.G. Rickover

---

64 Henry "Scoop" Jackson (1912–1983) served as a member of Congress (1941–1953) and U.S. Senator (1953–1983). Jackson was Rickover's greatest supporter for decades on Capitol Hill.

1. On Friday, December 19, 1952, at approximately 1330, I was asked to meet with Admiral Wallin[65] to discuss the article which LIFE had submitted to the Navy. Present at the meeting were:

   Admiral Wallin [Bureau of Ships]
   Admiral Leggett
   Admiral Sylvester
   Captain Rickover

2. I asked Admiral Wallin if the present meeting was an official investigation, and he replied it was not. I then asked if he had been ordered to question me. He replied that he had been asked to do so by Public Information.

3. Admiral Wallin told me of the article and asked if I had seen it. I replied that I had just read it about an hour before when it had been shown to me by Charter Heslep [Atomic Energy Commission], Information Services, insofar as AEC matters were concerned. I advised that there were some inaccuracies in the article where AEC was concerned, and these I had pointed out to Mr. Heslep.

4. Admiral Wallin stated, in reading the article, so far as he was concerned, it was quite inaccurate, falsified matters, created wrong impressions, and was put out as a "public journalistic triumph." I told Admiral Wallin that in reading the article quickly I noted it took issue with the Navy Selection System; that I thought the Navy Selection System could be improved. Admiral Wallin also stated it attacked the Navy's Bureau of Ships, various officers, and men in the Bureau with whom I had been associated for many years and that the article would

---

65 Vice Admiral Homer Wallin (1893–1984). At this time, he was chief of the Bureau of Ships (BUSHIPS); Rear Admiral Wilson Leggett, Deputy BUSHIPS; and possibly Rear Admiral John Sylvester (1904–1990), special assistant to the chief of the Armed Forces Special Weapons Project.

do no good; in fact, it would harm everybody concerned, including myself. I advised him that I was prepared to take the hurt which would result from this article.

5. I suggested to Admiral Wallin that he call in the LIFE writer and point out to him the inaccuracies in the article. He stated that he would do so. I advised Admiral Wallin that as I had not prepared the article, it was not my place to point out to the writer the inaccuracies. Admiral Wallin wanted me to go on record that the article should not be published. Then Admiral Wallin asked if I were loyal to the Navy, and I replied that I was just as loyal as he, Admiral Leggett, or Admiral Sylvester, and many others. I also stated that Admiral Sylvester had watched me over a period of years, and I was sure he knew of my loyalty to the Navy. Admiral Wallin stated there were comments in the article taken from my fitness report. He asked if I had given them out. I replied that I had not; in fact, I had not seen my record for several years. Admiral Wallin asked where the LIFE writer obtained his information. I suggested he ask the LIFE man.

6. Admiral Wallin also stated there was an erroneous impression in the Bureau that any time I wished I could get magazines and newspapers to write articles about me. I replied, as Admiral Leggett well knew, that shortly after the meeting of the last Selection Board I had been instrumental in turning down the articles which LIFE and TIME had printed; I consistently discouraged magazines and newspapers from writing articles about me; that he must realize that atomic energy was of great interest to the Public and for this reason many writers were interested in the subject. I further advised Admiral Wallin that the recent Colliers article had been offered to me to write, but I had turned it down. Admiral Wallin expressed surprise that I had not been willing to write this article. I again stated that I had consistently refused to write such articles. Because I had stopped personnel in my

organization from so doing, I felt it was not right to do this myself.

7. Admiral Wallin stated the article implied criticism of Admiral Mills. I told him I did not think it did; that Admiral Mills had helped me in getting the project started. I also stated that I had gotten considerable help from the Bureau of Ships, particularly recently. I agreed with Admiral Wallin that he had helped me since his tenure of duty in the Bureau and, similarly, many other people had done so. However, there was a feeling among many people in the Bureau, probably engendered by loose remarks by senior people, which resulted in lack of cooperation in this project. This was important because we had to go to these people to get technical action and to get out letters. This was partially true because this was a new project, and many people did not wish to align themselves with anything new unless they felt certain it was going to be successful. Admiral Leggett stated this was a natural reaction toward any project. I told him I thought this to be true; in fact, when I took this project over several years ago, I fully realized this and ultimately what I anticipated happening did happen.

8. Admiral Wallin stressed the point that he wanted me to cooperate with him and the Bureau in having the article stopped or thoroughly corrected, and if I did not do this, I would not be cooperating with him or the Bureau. If that was what Admiral Wallin considered cooperation, I was sorry I could not agree with him and go along with his recommendations. I told him his conception of cooperation might be quite different from mine. I again stressed that Admiral Wallin should go to the author of the article to have him stop it.

9. Admiral Leggett was aware, I stated, that I had pointed out the Bureau's part in the nuclear power program. As an example, recently the AEC had released an article on the CVR. I suggested something should be included about the

Bureau's participation. Immediately something had been done about this, and the press release gave due credit to the Bureau of Ships.

10. As to my being personally responsible for all of the work that had been done in the nuclear propulsion field, I told Admiral Wallin this was completely erroneous. All of this work had been done by members of my organization; that I was fortunate enough to be in charge. I wanted it distinctly understood that I was not responsible for all of the work, and I had stated this many, many times.

11. As to the morale in my organization, to be sure the morale had fallen somewhat because people were wondering "what was going to happen." It was pointed out in the article in question that the chief technical man in my organization had stated he would leave if I left. I stated that this was Dr. J.A. Kyger and that it would be wise for Admiral Wallin to talk to Dr. Kyger about the matter. (Later in the day, Admiral Sylvester talked to Dr. Kyger and Dr. Kyger stated if I left, he would also leave.)

12. In connection with my not being indispensable, I had pointed out to do any job, either people assisted people or the job did not get done; if anyone doing a good job were detached, it would hurt the job. In my particular job, a great deal of the good that was accomplished over the years was the result of personal relationships with scientists, engineers, admirals, and others, and any new person, no matter how good, would have to establish such relationships. Much of the work was done because the persons wished to do it and not because they had to do it.

13. Admiral Wallin stated that previously he had talked with me and understood me to say that I would be willing to stay on this job as long as it was necessary. I told him that he must be somewhat mistaken; that I had advised him that I would stay on for "the time being."

14. Sylvester pointed out that the article stated that when the nuclear power program first started, I had found office space in the "ladies powder room." He said this implied that the ladies powder room was indicative of the importance of the program to the Navy. I stated it was not actually a powder room but a room assigned at the beginning to personnel working on this program, and it would be more proper to say it was a converted powder room, as all the fixtures had been removed.

15. In connection with whether or not the article was accurate, I stated that none of the people present in the room could state from their personal experience whether the facts were accurate or inaccurate; they had only been around a short time. I also stated that I had consistently opposed publicity because it interfered with work I was doing, and it took up too much of my time. I pointed out that I had frequently discouraged people from writing about me. I also pointed out that various organizations had called my home, shortly after the last Selection Board reported their selections, to find out if I had been passed over on religious grounds. I stated, in answer to these inquiries, that this definitely was not the case. I certainly did not want this stated because it would hurt my wife and my youngster.

16. Admiral Wallin then stated he had heard there was to be a congressional investigation. I stated that at any time I would be willing to bring out all of the facts.

17. I told Admiral Wallin of the letter Dr. Edward Teller, of the A-Bomb Project, wrote to Dr. L.R. Hafstad in August 1947 about me and my group of people; about how Dr. Teller recommended that I be allowed to go ahead, and contrary to my recommendations and Dr. Teller's recommendations, the group had been split up as soon as we got to Washington.

18. I reminded Admiral Sylvester that I had always talked "straight" to him and possibly this was not true with some

other people who, occasionally, told him what he would like to hear.

19. The gist of the meeting was that I refused to state that the article was inaccurate or that it should not be published. I further stated that that was up to them—not to me.

December 24, 1952. Office Memorandum

To: FILE
From: *Captain H.G. Rickover, USN*
Subject: *MY INTENTIONS RELATIVE TO RETIREMENT*

Memorandum of telephone conversation between Captain R.F. Yager, USN, Code 250, and Captain H.G. Rickover, USN, Code 490

1. Captain Yager stated that Admiral DuBose, Chief, Bureau of Naval Personnel, wanted to know what I intended to do. I replied I had been too busy to give this any thought. At such time as I had had time to think this through entirely, I would let them know; that for several months I would not be able to let them know.

2. I stated that Admiral DuBose had written a letter stating I could stay on as long as I wished. I asked Captain Yager to tell Admiral DuBose[66] that I was too busy to give this much thought at this time.

26 December 1952

Letter from Acting Secretary of the Navy H.R. Askins to Congressman Jackson

---

66 Admiral Laurence DuBose (1893–1967) who, at the time of this letter, was a Vice Admiral and Chief of Naval Personnel.

...Promotion to flag rank in the Navy has been based upon a system of "selection of the best fitted" since 1916....

For the current fiscal year, there were 28 captains, restricted to Engineering Duty Only, eligible and in the field for consideration for selection to fill two prospective vacancies in the grade of rear admiral. Captain Rickover was one of the 28. All 28 had outstanding records. It is in no way a reflection upon him personally or professionally that he was not one of the two recommended by the selection board for such promotion...

As to Captain Rickover's scheduled retirement on completing the designated years of service 30 June 1953, it is very probably that he will be requested to continue on active duty, subsequent to retirement, to meet expected requirements for captains of his specialized qualifications.

15 January 1953

Clay Blair [journalist] to General Hoyt Vandenberg extensive confidential memo

Jim Shepley has recently spoken to you about the possibility of recruiting Navy Captain Hyman George Rickover to build the Air Force's nuclear-powered aircraft... I have known Captain Rickover for the past two years, during which I have made a point of exploring fairly completely his life, career, and his personal life...

Recently I discussed with Captain Rickover the possibility of his taking over the nuclear-powered aircraft project. After a long (in fact, a five-hour) conversation, he admitted he might like to do it, albeit with many qualifications...he is a tireless man, but I don't think he relishes the idea of going through another petty fight such as he experienced with the Navy during the last seven years...

...if he takes over the aircraft program, he will do it only with complete freedom of movement. That is to say, he wants funds he does not have to fight for, he wants personnel of his own choosing, he wants rank enough to enable him to move people when they need moving...

The Navy, however, caught up in the intellectual swirl Rickover had created, could not keep up with his thinking nor the progress he was making. What ire they held for Rickover previously, was now magnified manyfold. Rickover became a hated man. Even so, many were amazed at Rick's ability to squeeze money out of Congress and the AEC.

16 February 1953

Memorandum of Telephone Conversation with Rear Admiral Lewis S. Parks, Chief of Public Information

I advised Admiral Parks that I had heard rumors which had apparently emanated from the Pentagon that there was derogatory information in my service record and that this information had been given to newspapermen.

I advised Admiral Parks that I was sure he personally had not spread any such rumors. Nevertheless, I requested him to advise his assistants to this effect so that they might be aware that I had heard such rumors, and to assure that they might not become involved in any such rumor spreading.

Admiral Parks stated that he knew no rumors which had ever been spread about my record; further, officers' records were confidential and, therefore, it was not permissible to disclose matters contained in them. I advised Admiral Parks I had no objection to the Navy publishing my entire record if they so desired.

Senator Brien McMahon, June 16, 1951, to Admiral Forrest B. Sherman, CNO in service record: "He has so much drive and determination that he rubs some people the wrong way; but if they are worthwhile people at all, it is my impression they usually wind up as his fast friends."

20 February 1953

Senator John F. Kennedy to Sen. Leverett Saltonstall, Chair Senate Armed Services Committee

Congressman Sidney Yates has written me concerning the case of Captain H.G. Rickover, USN, and the Naval selection boards. It seems as though Captain Rickover was passed over for promotion.

I am wondering if the committee is considering any action on this matter.

4 July 1953

Memorandum of informal discussion with Rear Admiral W. D. Leggett on July 3, 1953

I told Admiral Leggett I had noticed in a draft of a letter prepared by Captain Kraft, which was concerned primarily with officer personnel, a statement that a re-organization of the Nuclear Power Division was contemplated. I had questioned Captain Kraft on July 3, 1953, and he had stated that he had put this in at the specific request of Admiral Wallin. I told Admiral Leggett that I had also heard rumors that there had been discussions among Admiral Wallin and Naval Operations, and possibly others, about the organization of my Division. I stated that it was entirely within the chief's prerogative to have any organization he desired, but I did not think it proper for such discussions to go on for any length of time without my being told about it. Furthermore, this was having quite an unsettling effect on my entire organization. Admiral Leggett agreed this was not the best way to handle things, but it was something over which he had no control.

I reminded Admiral Leggett of what happened when the Navy had passed me over. I told him in view of the recent performance of the Mark I plant there was a possibility that a greater interest would be manifested if the Bureau were to effect changes in my organization which might result in hurt to the nuclear power game. Admiral Leggett said he understood this. I suggested to Admiral Leggett that he convey my sentiments to the appropriate individual.

6 July 1954

> *From Admiral Robert B. Carney, President of US [Naval Institute] to [USNI] Board of Control,*
>
> *Subj: Rear Admiral Henry Williams', USN (Ret) Review of "The Atomic Submarine and Admiral Rickover," by Clay Blair, Jr.*

1. I have read the subject review and wish to go on record to the effect that I consider it to have been unsuitable for publication in the United States Naval Institute.
2. I have been informed that Rear Admiral Rickover has submitted his resignation from the Institute and assume that Rear Admiral Rickover took this action because he took understandable offense at the Review... I consider this book review to be offensive to a distinguished officer on the active list of the Navy, and its appearance in *Proceedings* constitutes, at the minimum, a regrettable error in taste and judgement.

3 March 1953

> *Memorandum to File*
> *From: Capt H.G. Rickover*
>
> *Subj: Request to visit Senator Jackson*
> *Memorandum of Telephone Conversation between Captain H.G. Rickover and Senator Jackson on Wednesday, March 4, 1952*

Senator Jackson called me this morning and asked me to come over to his office in the United States Senate Office Building today. I stated I did not think this was the thing to do as I could not get up there and put this thing on an "I," "I," "I," basis. Senator Jackson said he understood my position and agreed with me. He then asked me if I would have some of the members of my organization come to his office. I immediately raised the question as to the reaction of Admiral Sylvester and Admiral Wallin to this. Senator Jackson said any questions relative to such visits should be referred to him.

I immediately telephoned Mr. Charles Elliott, Assistant to the Chief for Legislation and Liaison, Code 113, and advised him of the above and that I also suggested to Mr. Elliott that he might advise Admiral Wallin of the gist of this memorandum. Unless otherwise instructed, I would send a member of my staff to visit with Sen. Jackson.

6 July 1954

Letter from Robert Carney

My young son-in-law, who is Secretary-Treasurer of the U.S. Naval Institute, has informed me that you have submitted your resignation… Explanation can never excuse oversight…

July 13, 1954

Dear Admiral Carney,

It was very thoughtful and generous of you to write me about the book review in the U.S. Naval Institute *Proceedings*. I am asking Commander Taussig[67] to withdraw my resignation.

---

67 Captain Joseph Taussig, Jr. (1920–1999). U.S. Naval Academy Class of 1941. He was Admiral Carney's son-in-law and at this time serving as the Secretary-Treasurer of the U.S. Naval Institute.

I am deeply appreciative of your vision for the future of our Navy and your personal interest in nuclear power applications.

30 June 1954

Letter from William Liscum Borden [executive director of the Joint Committee on Atomic Energy from 1949–1953)

Dear Rick,

In our recent conversation I mentioned the promise that Secretary Kimball made to Senator McMahon regarding the promotion controversy involving you that extended from mid-1951 through early 1953. It occurs to me that I might just record, through this personal letter, what did happen and what I do distinctively remember. The luncheon took place probably in December 1951. The place was the secretary's small private dining room, just off his main office. Present were Senator [Brien] McMahon, the secretary, and myself. In the course of the conversation, Senator McMahon raised the question of your promotion. The senator expressed disappointment and concern over the events which had transpired to that date; and he spoke in rather strong terms. The secretary flatly promised the senator that the Navy Promotion Board would not again pass you over. The senator was given to understand, and certainly I understood, that we need feel no more concern on this score and that it could be taken as a foregone conclusion that, when your name again came before the Promotion Board, the result would be favorable to you.

I might emphasize that this conversation does stand out vividly in my mind, partly because of some of the other topics which were discussed; and I feel greater confidence than would normally be the case as to a conversation occurring more than two years ago that I have stated accurately the sense of what was said. Driving back to the Capitol from the Pentagon, the senator indicated to me that he felt relieved and pleased that, at least the second time around, the Promotion Board would do right by you.

11 March 1955

Memorandum of conversation between RADM W.D. Leggett, Jr., USN, Chief, Bureau of Ships, and RADM H.G. Rickover

1. Admiral Leggett stated that Commander L.H. Roddis, Jr., USN, my senior assistant, saw him yesterday afternoon (Thursday, March 10, 1955) in connection with the latter's impending resignation from the Navy to accept the position of Deputy Director of the Division of Reactor Development, U.S. Atomic Energy Commission. He said this matter raised the question in his mind as to who would be available to succeed me if I left. Admiral Leggett stated he wished to be assured that I would not leave my present position without adequate advance notice to the Navy, so that steps could be taken to find a suitable relief.

2. I told Admiral Leggett that there had been rather frequent rumors that I was to be ordered away; for example, the papers had recently been notified by someone at the Puget Sound Navy Yard that I was to be detached from the Bureau of Ships to become Commander of the Yard. The newspaper people had gone to Senator Henry Jackson, of Washington, in whose District the Puget Sound Yard is located, and had asked for verification. Admiral Leggett stated this rumor was untrue, and that the Navy had no plans to shift me. In fact, the Navy was very satisfied to have me stay on. I then replied that if ever the Navy wished me to leave this job, all they had to do was to say so and I would go at once.

3. On the other hand, I enjoyed this work and there was still a great deal of advanced work to be done before nuclear power could be fully realized in the Navy, and that we must be very

careful not to have immature or inexperienced people making the major decisions; that he well knew I was conservative
in watching that the Navy did not go faster than was wise in
the nuclear power program. He agreed to this.

4. Admiral Leggett also stated that as far as he was concerned,
he would like me to stay as long as I wished. He further
stated he had discussed this with Secretary Thomas, Admirals Carney, Duncan, and Good, and that all had agreed I
should stay as long as I wanted.

5. I requested that before he (Admiral Leggett) left the Bureau
of Ships he make arrangements for me to discuss the matter
with Secretary Thomas and Admiral Carney so that I could
be personally assured of the Navy's desire to have me remain in my present job; otherwise, new people coming in to
their positions, and without being familiar with all the facts,
might decide it was desirable to order me away to other
duty.

14 April 1955

Letter to Captain Edward J. Fahey, USN[68]

Thanks for your letter of 22 March 1955.

The main thing for the submarine people to understand is that if
we are to have modern submarines capable of meeting the situation
which faces us not only today but which will face us in the future, it
is up to the submarine operating people themselves to demand such
submarines and to see to it that they get them.

They must not stand on the sidelines and expect that some
supposedly omniscient person or group of persons in Naval Operations is taking care of their problem or that these people in Naval

---

68 Rear Admiral Edward Joseph Fahy (1910–1989), U.S. Naval Academy Class
of 1934. At the time of this letter, he was the Force Material Officer on the Staff of
Commander Submarine Force, Atlantic.

Operations are all-wise and all-knowing. What I am getting at is that the responsibility for the situation in which the submarine service finds itself rests squarely on the submarine service itself.

The excuse given by a senior member of the audience that "we submariners constitute only two percent of all of the officers in the Navy" is not a valid one. Practically everything that has ever been done in this world has been done by a very small number of people. Instead of bewailing their small number, let the submariners become an elite and act as one. They should realize that a small number can accomplish a great deal, particularly when they face a complacent majority.

27 February 1956

Letter from Congressman Gerald R. Ford

It is almost impossible for me to express adequately my deep appreciation for the opportunity I had to meet you and visit the Nautilus. It was a most worthwhile experience in every respect, and I for one feel most indebted to you and the others for what we heard and saw. I certainly hope and trust that other members of Congress will take subsequent visits to the Nautilus, and more specifically, I hope that you will be able to accompany such groups, for your presence and presentation are the climax…

March 2, 1956

Letter from Congressman Gerald R. Ford[69]

The two Nautilus insignia patches which you forwarded for my sons, Mike and Jack, were most enthusiastically received by them. In their typical boy-like eagerness, they demanded that the patches be immediately attached to their jackets in a very proper fashion.

---

69 38th President of the United States.

Their interest in submarines has skyrocketed, needless to say. And at the tender ages of four and six, they speak only of "nuclear-powered submarines."

March 5, 1956

> *Letter from Congressman Gerald R. Ford, Jr.*

Dear Admiral Rickover,

As I indicated in my letter of February 27th, my weekly newsletter for this week is a report to the folks at home on my trip with the Nautilus.

I hope and trust you will find it technically correct. It was my intention to be as informative as possible, giving my friends in the Fifth District a first-hand look at the Navy's revolutionized fighting ship.

Again, my sincere thanks for your wonderful help in briefing me on the Nautilus. I hope you will find the enclosed Washington Review both interesting and factually correct.

26 November 1956

> *Letter to RADM Elton W. Grenfell,[70] USN, Commander Submarine Force, United States Pacific Fleet*

Dear Joe:

From what we hear you have been doing some good missionary work on the potentials of nuclear submarines. I know you are often under the gun when you support submarines in outspoken fashion, but it must be done.

---

70 Vice Admiral Elton W. Grenfell (1905–1980), U.S. Naval Academy Class of 1926.

However, I must confess in return, like the missions to Hawaii, I have only spiritual gifts to offer. I have given careful consideration to your comments on deploying NAUTILUS to the Pacific for a demonstration cruise following core replacement.

The NAUTILUS is the only fully operational nuclear submarine until the SKATE (SSN578) goes to sea in 1958. As you know, we have had difficulties with the SEAWOLF, and this makes it doubly important that we keep the NAUTILUS operating satisfactorily and retain the maximum degree of access to her by important people in support of the current development and building programs. In my opinion, this is most important in order to get support for the new submarine Navy.

We now plan to defer the first regular NAUTILUS overhaul until 1958, but we expect to renew her core in an around-the-clock, seven days a week availability early next year. To follow up this core renewal with a cruise of some 16,000 miles to the Pacific, having deferred her regular overhaul, would be overstretching our luck at a time when we should not gamble. For these reasons I feel that NAUTILUS operations prior to the time she is joined by the SKATE should be restricted to those of the highest operational productivity and to those which are otherwise vital to the technical progress we are trying to make. A demonstration cruise to the Pacific, important and productive as it might be along certain lines, would not only interrupt our close work with the NAUTILUS but would also add many hundreds of hours of steaming to a ship that will have already been operated many months past its routine overhaul time.

I know that my position in this matter may be a disappointment to you, however, we are working hard at Mare Island on the SARGO, a ship which, I understand, will probably be assigned to you on a permanent basis.

I hope to get out to Pearl Harbor soon, and I am looking forward to visiting with you. However, please don't tell anyone this.

8 June 1957

Memorandum of a conversation between Rear Admiral Mumma,[71]
USN, Chief of the Bureau of Ships

1. Admiral Mumma asked me what my thoughts were about continuing in the field of nuclear propulsion for ships. I replied there were three things he could definitely be certain about.
   a. I did not desire to become the Chief of the Bureau of Ships.
   b. I did not desire to become the Director, Division of Reactor Development, U.S. Atomic Energy Commission.
   c. I did not desire any outside job at this time.
   I stated it was my firm intention to keep on with the Naval Nuclear Propulsion work as long as I was capable of doing so. My mission was to develop a series of prototypes and various ships of a class so that the Navy could go ahead and become converted to nuclear power.
2. I reminded Admiral Mumma that at the time his selection for Chief of the Bureau was being considered, I had been asked if I desired this job, and I had requested that my name not be considered. I also reminded him the same issue had come up about my being considered for the position of Director, Division of Reactor Development, U.S. Atomic Energy Commission. I again asked that my name not be considered because of the far more importance to me of my work....
3. ...
4. ...

---

71 Rear Admiral Albert G. Mumma (1906-1997), U.S. Naval Academy Class of 1926. His brother Rear Admiral Morton Mumma graduated in 1925. When Rickover mentions Mumma later, it is likely Albert to whom he is referring.

5. Admiral Mumma then said it had occurred to him whether I would wish to go to England to help the British develop atomic power. I told Admiral Mumma that I was sure that the British would not, in a thousand years, want an American to come over and develop atomic power for them. They were very proud of their people in atomic power and would never ask for such a thing.

6. Admiral Mumma then asked if I might be willing to go over and be an advisor to the British on developing naval plants for the British. I told Admiral Mumma any time the British approached me with such a proposition, I would immediately resign from the Navy. I told him there was no dearth of jobs in the United States. He replied this was "just a thought."

7. Admiral Mumma stated he had found out how well I got along with the British, and this was the reason he thought about this and asked me about it.

11 March 1957

Remarks for delivery at the awards banquet of the Science Talent Search for the Westinghouse Science Scholarships, Statler Hotel, Washington, DC

"The Talented Mind—An Opportunity and an Obligation"

As I look at the bright faces of the young men and women whose achievement we have come here to honor, how fortunate are these young people! Fortunate, in that God has blessed you with an endowment which is priceless. What has been given all of you—the 40 winners, as well as the 260 runners-up—is the most lasting, the most persistently satisfying, the most all-around useful of natural endowments—a really good mind.

I trust that you will not let yourselves be proud of this gift. It reflects no particular credit on you. Nor is it a guarantee of success in life. Rather does it resemble a vein of precious metal imbedded in rock—valuable only when it has been mined intelligently and laboriously. But with it, an unusual opportunity is granted you to develop yourselves into successful human beings in a field of activity where success must always be rare and difficult.

You are here tonight because you have already taken the first step towards making use of your good fortune. You have given that good mind of yours what it most needs—exercise in meeting an intellectual challenge. In doing this you have shown yourselves worthy of the endowment with which you have been blessed. You have demonstrated that you can marshal the ambition and stick-to-itiveness which a good mind demands. You have taken the first step towards success in your chosen fields, but only the first.

Like most of today's youth, you must at times have felt that you missed something exciting and important because you were born in the 20th century, at a time when almost all frontier areas of this country had disappeared and with them the adventure formerly enjoyed by many a young man and woman, of hewing out their destiny, dependent on no power on earth but their own will and ability. Today there is hardly a spot on this globe which has not been discovered and mapped. For most people, life, while doubtless more comfortable, lacks the spice of discovery and adventure so dear to young spirits.

Yet it is precisely in this respect that your good fortune manifests itself most dramatically, for you carry in your minds potentialities for adventure and discovery not shared by most of your contemporaries. You have as many opportunities for exciting living as people born a hundred or more years ago; different in kind, perhaps, but opportunities not one whit less exciting and rewarding than those which vanished at the turn of this century.

Capable and ambitious young people could once fashion their lives by their own efforts in wild and unmapped areas of the physical world; you can be pioneers today in the wild and unmapped world of science. In the short span of three centuries, since man first learned to think and experiment scientifically, enormous advances have been made. But enough remains to be discovered and mapped to guarantee excitement and adventure to more young scientists and engineers than we are likely to have for many years to come.

I recommend that you make your life an adventure of the mind. This will at times be hard, but always deeply rewarding. When you reap the fruits of your own intellectual labor, you will experience the satisfaction of having proved yourselves good cultivators of the talents given you by Providence. Over and above all this, you will know that yours is a kind of pioneering which yields not alone personal gain and satisfaction, but it also contributes significantly to the economic and hence the political strength and security of our country. This you will find the greatest reward of all.

There never has been a time in the history of our country when it so greatly needed the services of its talented youth. One hundred and eighty years ago, this nation was born on a new continent, sparsely populated by four million people. Seldom has a new nation started life under such favorable circumstances. Not the least of these was the political inheritance which enabled the founding fathers to devise a form of government marvelously suited to a vast land with fabulous natural resources which had to be developed by a small population. The Constitution ensured fullest scope for each individual's abilities. Moreover, our continuing scarcity of labor helped us to hold fast to that basic respect of the individual, which the first settlers brought with them from England, and which is the foundation of our democratic way of life...

You young people have the ability to grow into empire builders of the intellectual realm. I hope that you will be inspired to adventurous search beyond present boundaries. I hope that you will not let yourselves be deflected from pursuing this aim by accepting positions having less intrinsic importance but greater material rewards. I hope that you will firmly withstand the constant pressure by the advocates of the greatest of modern fallacies—that material possessions are the mark of the successful man. Man's acquisitive traits are not what make him great. Nor can true greatness be measured in dollars and cents. What money value can you assign a book on which the author has labored for years, and which may inspire you to actions having incalculable effects? Is it worth only its price of three or five dollars? How would you value the piece of paper on which Einstein scribbled the simple equation, which in its ultimate effects may preserve the freedom of the West by providing it with nuclear power to replace coal and oil. Is the pay you receive to be the only measure of the value of your job? No! Nothing material can ever give the intelligent man or woman such deep satisfaction as the successful solution of an intellectual problem that challenges the mind.

We are engaged in a grim duel. You are familiar with the threat to American technical supremacy, which may materialize if Russia succeeds in her ambitious program of achieving world scientific and engineering supremacy by turning out vast numbers of well-trained scientists and engineers. Democracies move slower than totalitarian dictatorships. We have let our educational problem grow much too big for comfort and safety. We are beginning to see now that we must solve it without delay. Perhaps the greatest danger has been our failure to provide adequate educational opportunities for our gifted youth and, in particular, to seek out the talented at an early age and to give them an education which challenges their minds and induces them to become trained professionals. I am particularly happy, therefore, to be here tonight because the Science Talent Search sponsored by the Westinghouse Electric Corporation is exactly the sort of device we need to discover and develop our greatest national resource—the young man and woman with a really good mind.

It is a typically American device in that it represents an effort on the part of private citizens to accept the responsibility of government. It has ever been characteristic of Americans that when faced with a community problem, we do not sit with folded hands waiting for government to solve it but pitch in ourselves. I hope more and more corporations will pitch into the problem of fostering America's wealth of young talent. And I hope that more and more talented young people will make the fullest use of their intellectual endowments. Democracy is not merely a political and social device to ensure that under a popularly elected government each citizen may enjoy complete personal freedom, bounded only by the equal rights of other citizens. It is far more than that. Democracy guarantees to the individual freedom and opportunity to develop his mind and character to his maximum potential without hindrance from external sources so that he may put them to use not only for himself but for the community as well.

Sometimes we forget that democracy is not a matter of rights alone; that it depends for its very life on acceptance of corollary duties. If democracy meant no more than freedom of each citizen to enjoy himself, provided in so doing he harmed no one else, it would be a shabby creed indeed for the people of a great country; an uninspiring banner under which to fight the enemies of freedom.

The men who established this nation and who devised the political institutions which have served us so well realized that democracy puts heavy obligations upon the citizen. It demands of all of us that we participate wisely in choosing the men to govern us, and it places on those who have special talents the obligation to develop these talents to their fullest, and to apply them in the service of the common good.

8 June 1957

To: FILE

Subj: Nuclear Propulsion Aircraft Carrier—Increased Costs of Propulsion Plant

1. I told Admiral Mumma that I had been looking into the problem of costs of the nuclear propulsion plants, and it appeared there would be an increase in costs for the plant for the aircraft carrier of about $50 million dollars. Admiral Mumma asked me whether this was an estimate or was it a firm figure. I replied that I considered it would surely be this much.

2. I then stated that he was the only one I had told about this because I did not wish to jeopardize the chances of the nuclear-powered carrier in Congress if the question of increased costs came up at this time. I then asked Admiral Mumma's advice regarding what I should do. He stated that for the time being to just keep him informed.

3. I then stated that the House Committee had approved the carrier and that the Senate Committee would surely also do this.

4. Admiral Mumma then asked why costs had increased. I stated that the cost of everything was going up normally about 7% per year, and it had been some time since the initial estimate had been made. Furthermore, many companies which were making parts for the nuclear plants had gotten into the business with the idea that they might make money. Many were losing money; many installed equipment to manufacture nuclear propulsion plant parts at their own expense and now wished to recoup. For these reasons, costs were high. I pointed out that for ships, such as submarines, the costs were coming down.

5. Admiral Mumma again asked me to keep him privately informed of developments. I replied that I would do so.

21 June 1957

Memorandum of telephone conversation with Mr. Lipsner, Washington Representative of Allied Artists

Admiral Rickover returned Mr. Lipsner's call of June 19, 1957. Mr. Lipsner said he was calling with reference to a conversation he had with Admiral Rickover in November of 1954 regarding the making of an atomic submarine picture. Admiral Rickover told him he objected to doing such a picture, in 1954 and also at the present time, for personal reasons and because he believes it would be harmful to the atomic propulsion program. Mr. Lipsner said he wanted to discuss the matter again at this time because he had heard that some other studio was considering the subject for a film. Admiral Rickover said he did not want to discuss the matter and told Mr. Lipsner that no other studio was considering the subject for a film…

Admiral Rickover further advised Mr. Lipsner that he would consider this matter when he, Admiral Rickover, had passed away, and to contact him at that time.

April 1958

Hearings before the Select Committee on Astronautics and Space Exploration, "Astronautics and Space Exploration"

Chairman John W. McCormack: We all know Admiral Rickover; it is unnecessary to refer to his broad experience, knowledge, and so forth. We are glad to hear from you, Admiral. Do you have a prepared statement?

Rickover: No, sir; I do not have a prepared statement, but I do have one observation I would like to make, if I may… I am not a candidate for the first trip to the moon, but I do have a number of suggestions of people I think should go on this trip. That concludes my observation.

Chairman: Is there some particular person you would like to see get up there?

Rickover: Yes, but I should discuss that in executive session. Perhaps your own list is even larger than mine.

Mr. Fulton: This is a one-way trip you have in mind, Admiral?

Rickover: Yes, sir; a one-way trip.

20 June 1958

Notes of telephone conversation between Colonel R.D. Heinl, USMC, Rm. 4216 Arlington Annex, Ext 42024 and Rear Admiral H.G. Rickover, USN, on the subject of the Department of Defense Re-Organization Bill—The President's Bill

Colonel Heinl[72] called Admiral Rickover to ask if he would make a public statement about the President's Re Organization plan—not recommending the bill. Col. Heinl mentioned the article in *The New York Times* and stated, "I have reason to believe that a piece in *The New York Times*…"

Admiral Rickover broke in to ask if he (Heinl) were a Public Relations Officer of the Air Force, would he ask Admiral Rickover, a naval officer, to make a statement; that Heinl would not like it because he pretty well knew that he would not make a public statement about the President's Re-Organization. Then Admiral Rickover asked Heinl, "What would you do? If I were in your position, what would you do?"

Heinl replied, "Strictly on the premise, I would tell him to go to hell."

Adm. Rickover then said, "I like you, and I would not tell you to go to hell." Admiral Rickover reiterated, "What would you do?"

---

72 Robert D. Heinl (d. 1979).

Heinl replied that he would not do it. But getting back to the subject of his call, he wanted "To find out whether there is even the remotest possibility of your appearing before the Senate Committee…"

Admiral Rickover then asked Heinl, "If I were for the bill, would you ask me to testify? As a Marine Corps Officer, would you ask me to testify for the bill?"

Colonel Heinl replied that he "would not ask you to testify."

Admiral Rickover then told Heinl he was "just looking for guys to support your viewpoint, but you would not be happy if you thought I did not support Heinl's views."

Heinl replied, "I am being a professional."

Admiral Rickover countered with "Professional men let the truth come out." They let the heat and light in on the subject.

Heinl replied that they needed all the heat and light, particularly the light on the bill. Then he said, "I think this Re-Organization is hot right now—making some things bigger and some things littler—" At this point, he went into the General Staff concept being made larger and the Joint Chiefs of Staff being smaller and with less influence.

Admiral Rickover then stated, "I assume this is the same as a command."

Heinl replied, "No, that it is not."

Admiral Rickover then said there was no consistency. "Change the uniforms to see if it changes the ideas" and went back to the hypothetical case of the Air Force officer calling the Marine Corps officer.

Admiral Rickover then said, "I am not volunteering to testify. If I get called up, no one knows what I will say. My private advice is not to get me up. Does that answer your question?"

Heinl, said, "Yes. I would like to meet you. I have stated out with the preconception that I am speaking as one who has been brainwashed. Fact is, we are about to be saddled with a type of decision-making in the current camp, which is going to lead to a lot of military decisions."

Admiral Rickover replied, "I am sure you have been around long enough to see what the Navy has done in the decision-making area."

Heinl said he was afraid the decision-making would be concentrated under the reorganization.

Admiral Rickover stated, "I thoroughly agree with the basic premise—not to concentrate decision-making."

Heinl stated he did not agree with all JCS decisions.

Admiral Rickover stated, "I have been around and watched decisions being made; any change would be good."

Then Admiral Rickover, going back to the original subject of the call—"I advise you to see more fertile fields."

Heinl replied, "I am grateful for the tongue lashing."

Admiral Rickover replied to Heinl, "I am not tongue lashing at you."

Heinl said, "I was grinning when I said that."

Admiral Rickover then said, "I have to deal with the goddamned clunks in personnel… All right, but advise you not to get me up."

Colonel Heinl, "Thank you, sir."

23 June 1958

Memorandum of Visit by Commander F.A. Manson on June 20, 1958

Subj: Discussion about Department of Defense Reorganization

Commander Manson[73] telephoned and asked me if he could visit me on a vital confidential matter. I agreed.

Commander Manson told me that the Navy was very much concerned about the pending reorganization bill. They thought that if this bill were enacted as passed by the House, the Air Force would be in complete control and the Navy would be relegated to a secondary position. He stated that Admiral Burke[74] was "sick" about the whole matter. In fact, he was seriously considering resigning over the issue. The Secretary of the Navy felt the same as Admiral Burke about the matter but would not come out openly and say what he really thought because he was a staunch Republican and did not want to hurt the Republican Party.

Admiral Carney also felt the same way. (It was evident from what Commander Manson was saying that Admiral Carney was actively engaged in this fight, and that Commander Manson's visit to me had the knowledge of all the top people in the Navy.) Commander Manson stated that it was the consensus of the top people in the Pentagon that Congress would listen to me more than to

---

73 Captain Frank A. Manson (1920–2005). At this time, Manson served as head of Plans and Policies Analysis for the Chief of Naval Operations.
74 Admiral Arleigh Burke (1901–1996), U.S. Naval Academy Class of 1923; served as Chief of Naval Operations (1955–1961).

anyone else in the Navy about this subject because they respected my opinion and knew that I had no axe to grind.

I told Commander Manson that I believed that he, as well as others in the Pentagon, was unduly overwrought concerning the situation; that no matter what bill Congress passed, the thing that was important was the people who ran it and not the organization itself; that I had expressed this view many times before.

Commander Manson, however, stated that it was the feeling of the Navy leaders that the Navy would be "sunk" if this bill were passed. He gave as an example the quick action the Navy was able to take in the Mediterranean and the Asiatic waters because the Navy directly controlled the naval forces. Whereas, if these forces were controlled by higher echelon, such fast action could not take place.

I stated that the president was a man who was quite familiar with military matters and consequently would not be advocating a course of action which would hurt the United States. Commander Manson replied that the president was quite ignorant of naval matters. He gave as an example that when President Eisenhower was Chairman of the Joint Chiefs of Staff, he had decided the question of whether or not there should be four additional carriers simply on the basis that General Bradley and General Vandenberg happened to be on a golf course on a Saturday morning that Admiral Carney had raised the issue. It was on the basis that these two officers were not at work Saturday morning that Eisenhower had decided to let the Navy have four additional aircraft carriers. The president was quite unfamiliar with naval matters. He had always been so, even during the war. Also, the president apparently intended to install an Admiral Anderson as Chief of Naval Operations in place of Admiral Burke. Admiral Anderson had served with the president on his staff in Europe. This would be very bad for the Navy because Anderson would carry out the president's policies.

Admiral Carney was also very much concerned about this matter but did not know what to do.

Commander Manson also added that the president decided that no individual below the Department of Defense level could talk to Congress about various matters. This meant that no naval people could have direct access to Congress to tell them what the Navy's problems and needs were. I replied to Commander Manson in this connection that as he well knew, and as I had frequently stated in Congress, I believed that Congress should have full and complete access to all information. This was necessary for them to be able to do their job properly. If called upon to testify, I would state my views in this connection. However, I added that I firmly believed, as did the president, about the reorganization. Consequently, if I were called upon to testify and was asked my opinion on the reorganization, I would necessarily have to agree with the president.

I noted that Admiral Radford was for the president's reorganization bill, and did the Navy people think that Admiral Radford was against them. The reply was that Admiral Radford had now become a politician and was doing whatever was politically expedient.

During the conversation, I mentioned the fact that apparently the Navy was not going to do anything for me with regard to my promotion, and I wondered why the Navy leaders were coming to me to ask that I speak up for them in this fight. Commander Manson replied that I must consider this matter as a broad national policy and not confuse it with personal issues; that the matter of reorganization was far more important than my promotion.

The discussion ended with Commander Manson apparently being quite disappointed. However, I did get him to understand that if I were called by the Senate that I would testify but I would do so only in the way I actually felt. I would not testify in a manner dictated by anyone.

20 March 1959

Hearings before a Subcommittee on Government Operations, House of Representatives, "Organization and Management of Missile Program," Subcommittee on Military Operations

Subcommittee Chair Chet Holifield[75]: "We know from past experience that you are a frank and outspoken witness. You have always recognized the fact that Congress has a special duty to perform in representing the people of the Nation, and one of the things that all of us have always admired about you has been your responsiveness to questions from Congressmen when you are before us. We have not always had witnesses with the quality of frankness that you have. I wish we could expect the quality of frankness that you usually give in your appearances before committees from some other members of the executive department.

14 April 1959

Letter to Senator Saltonstall marked "Personal"

Dear Senator Saltonstall[76]

I am enclosing herewith some suggestions for consideration by you for possible inclusion in the Report of Board of Visitors of the Naval Academy. I realize that the very short time available to board members to survey a situation as complex as the Naval Academy is inadequate; for this reason, the board must inevitably depend on advice from Naval Academy Officers in formulating its recommendations. I have studied a number of past board reports and find that in general there is a tendency to acquiesce in existing procedures at the Naval Academy.

---

75 Chester E. Holifield (1903–1995) served as a member of Congress 1943–1974.
76 Leverett Saltonstall (1892–1979) served as a U.S. Senator 1945–1967.

As you know, my work in nuclear power has definitely shown me that the present course of instruction at our military academies is inadequate for the needs of the Army, Navy, and Air Force in this rapid spiraling scientific and technological age. I have interviewed hundreds of officers of many branches of the Navy, and I find that by and large they are technicians and not professional men. Officers with far greater professional competence are required. This includes a thorough grounding in liberal arts subjects. I thoroughly believe that no man today in a position of responsibility can perform his duties properly without such a liberal arts background. I have spent considerable time considering the present situation at the Naval Academy, and I believe that beneficial changes must be made now.

As a U.S. Senator, you have a unique opportunity to help because the words of congressional leaders are not disregarded by the Navy. I hope the enclosed remarks will be of assistance to you in this regard.

- Age limits 17–22
- Scholastic requirements college boards
- Physical requirements—consideration be given to reducing certain physical standards in light of the shifting emphasis of modern warfare away from physical activity and toward mental ability.
- Curriculum—balance between practical and theoretical work; increase optional courses.
- Academic staff—make greater use of professional civilian educators and exchange professors from leading engineering colleges.
- ECA and military burdens on midshipmen.

18 May 1959

"Scientific Manpower and Education," Hearings before the Committee on Science and Astronautics, House of Representatives

Mr. Miller: May I pay my respects to Admiral Rickover and say that in the history of the Navy, you have had people who have sponsored and fought through those major changes that continuously broke with the past. You had a Dahlgren who insisted on rifling guns, and completely changed naval warfare. You had a Mahan who designed new types of attack, and now you have a Rickover, who will go down in history as a man whose sheer force of character and ability has completely changed naval warfare.

Rickover: From that standpoint [of my background] and the judgment of the National Education Association, I am completely unqualified to talk about education to your committee, sir.

Chairman: Well, I want to say this: I don't believe the members of the committee share that viewpoint.

Rickover: Well, the members of this committee aren't qualified either.

Chairman: I will advise the members of the committee not to file their applications to teach in the District of Columbia.

19 November 1959

Speech "The Role of the Critic." Thomas Alva Edison Foundation, New York

I am pleased to be here today since this year's meeting of the Edison Foundation coincides with the end of my first decade of involvement in American education. It is an honor to inaugurate my second decade by addressing this distinguished audience. May I put in a petition to the Foundation for a place on its agenda ten and twenty years from now, God willing?

You may think me unduly pessimistic. Why should I expect that twenty years hence it will still be necessary to advocate reform of our schools? Are not the American people beginning to see that such reforms are essential if we are to survive as a free nation? However, if there is anything I have learned in the last ten years, it is the overwhelming power of resistance to reform possessed by organized groups with a vested interest in the status quo. Educational officialdom is such a group. It has been so successful in resisting needed reforms that we are today in grave danger of being overtaken in science and technology by a nation with a more efficient and rigorous educational system…

Most of the pedagogic errors and monstrosities that infest our schools originate in administrative directives coming from persons high in the hierarchy of educational officialdom who have themselves rarely had any classroom experience. Seldom is the real expert—the teacher—consulted in the matter of curriculum planning, pedagogic methods, and selection of textbooks. He is simply handed the newest products of progressive theory based on the very latest so-called "psychological research" and told to apply them in class.…

I dislike getting personal, but what I say has been so thoroughly misrepresented that I should like to go on record on a few points. I speak about education as a private citizen; my official duties give me no access to secret information—everything I saw is in the public domain and can be found by anyone taking the trouble to look for it. Nor does anyone order or pay me to talk about education. Sometimes fees are offered; I have made it a rule to ask that these and royalties from my book be turned over directly to specified charities. My concern with education is a wholly private and volunteer activity. I carry it on late at night after having put in a long day at work; rarely is this less than seventy hours a week, fifty-two weeks a year. I find recent accusations that I am preparing speeches on government time insulting; of course they are wholly untrue. They show to what astonishing lengths people will go to hit out at a social critic.

Angry educationists are forever demanding that I stop meddling in matters of no concern to me and that I stick to my trade of building reactors. Such reasoning shows a profound misconception of the rights and duties of democratic citizenship. It would have us all become what the Greeks called *idiotes*—private persons who take no interest in civic matters. Our educational bureaucracy is in this respect no different from other bureaucracies and pressure groups who seek escape from all criticism by branding the inside critic as a disloyal traitor to the organization, and the outside critic as a troublemaker without qualification to judge what the bureaucracy does. Unless we stop this attempt to make of criticism a modern kind of *lese majeste*, we shall assuredly lose control over the powerful organizations that increasingly control our life. These organizations tend to forget they were set up to do a specific job and that when they fail to do it satisfactorily, they must expect to be criticized. In particular, no public agency can conduct itself indefinitely in a manner which harms the nation as a whole without being castigated in public.

Having called the critic's motives into question, educationists invariably proceed to declare his facts are wrong or at least suspect because he has not documented each of them…they claim he cannot really say anything worth listening to about education unless he has personally inspected every school in the country, or sat in every classroom of every school…

When I find a statement of mine, based on official sources and subjected to a careful check by experts—such as my remarks on Dutch education—being airily dismissed as wholly erroneous by some educationist who claims to know all about Dutch education but who does not bother to support this accusation, I am sorely tempted to draw up a bill of indictment on factual errors committed by educationists. So far, I have not yielded to so ignoble an impulse, and I hope I shall continue to resist the temptation.

But I cannot let the third attack on the person of the critic go by unanswered; this is the educationist argument that, unless he is part of the public school system, a critic is not qualified to speak on education.

In "The House of the Intellect," Jacques Barzun calls this viewpoint a "superstition that understanding is identical with professional skill," which he brands as denials of intellect, and so it is. The attitude of educationists that they alone possess knowledge and wisdom in all things concerned with the learning process is not convincing, coming as it does from people whose own education—general and professional—is rarely impressive.

To carry on my assigned task in nuclear propulsion, I need intelligence and well-educated men. Though a great many of our best college graduates and officers apply, only a small percentage show enough promise to be accepted...

Angry educationists often threaten to tell me how to build nuclear submarines. My reply is that if they have as thoroughly studied nuclear physics and engineering as I have education, if they can devise better ways to build these ships, we in the naval reactor group would gladly welcome their advice. We are deeply appreciative when people take enough interest in our work to think up new ideas. So far, we have not received any from educators...

In truth, the critic's lot is not a happy one. Yet he has a useful role to play in a democratic society; he is an important part of the democratic process. He finds the facts we need but rarely have the time to discover for ourselves, and on which we base our decisions on national issues. He alerts us when the bureaucracies now dominating life start marching ponderously down a dead-end street of error, and so gives us a chance to put them back on the right road before it is too late. One hopes that present warnings of educational critics will be heeded before it is too late for us to catch up in those areas where Russia has forged ahead of us because of her greater wealth in trained professional people.

It should never be forgotten that it was the critics who first called attention to the Russian educational menace; educationists didn't get around to checking on Russian schooling until last summer, but scientists and engineers reported what was happening in Russia in 1953, and in that year, I myself began to speak of this danger. I never thought that by calling attention to this ominous development, I would become an "enemy of American education"; or that comparing Russian schools with ours would make me the favorite *bete noir* of educationists who see fit to call me hysterical, a lover of Russia, a warmonger, and a jackass. At that I consider myself fortunate, since I have not yet been put in a class with Dillinger and other professional murderers. This has happened to another critic whose sincerity and scholarship I admire.

Comparisons with foreign school systems are painful to American educationists, and one regrets that. But it cannot be maintained that they are not relevant.

It is through comparisons that critics try to demonstrate our deficiencies to the American people so they can do something about them. Fifty years ago, medical and legal schools in this country were a disgrace and a scandal. Two famous studies comparing them to similar schools abroad were written under the auspices of the Carnegie Foundation. They created a furor and inspired such drastic reforms that we soon got professional schools as good as those of Europe. Today's critics hope that by comparing general education here and abroad, they will bring about a similar upgrading of our public schools.

Educationists will doubtless continue to fight reform and hold it up as long as they can. As I said at the beginning of this speech: I anticipate that the campaign will go on for many, many years. As long as I am able to stand up and express my views, I shall keep on fighting for schools that will really "educate" our children—all of them.

1960s

3 February 1960

"Missiles, Space, and Other Major Defense Matters," Hearings before the Preparedness Investigating Subcommittee of the Senate Armed Services Committee

Sen John Stennis:[77] You can be frank with us. Do we call you to the Hill too often?[78]

Rickover: No, sir.

Stennis: Or take too much of your time here, or for reports?

Rickover: No, sir, that is not my problem. I don't mind coming up to the Hill. I don't mind getting a chance to talk with congressional committees because I think I do some good. I have never been unduly bothered by Congress or by requests from Congress. A lot of people complain about Congress, that Congress asks for too much. Maybe they are asking too much of Congress. Maybe that is why Congress is questioning them so much. They may not be

---

77 John C. Stennis (1901–1995), U.S. Senator 1947–1989.
78 Editor's note: Rickover would testify more than 200 times before various congressional committees in his career.

completely straightforward with Congress. I have no complaint so far as Congress is concerned. I would like to wash that one up. My problems are with the executive branch...

8 January 1961

"Intellect in a Democracy," Anniversary Dinner of the American Nobel Anniversary Committee, Waldorf Astoria, New York City

In casting about for a suitable subject to discuss with you, it occurred to me that I might examine the perennial problem of intellect in a democracy from the specific point of view of its bearing on modern weaponry. There is no need to dwell on the fact that today, unfortunately, we depend for our very survival upon the ability to come up with new ideas and to cut short the lead time between idea and finished military item. Intellect is the key factor in developing new weapons systems, as it is in all large-scale engineering projects designed to move us ahead technologically. National attitudes toward the man of intellect are therefore of crucial importance to the future of this country.

From de Tocqueville onward, thoughtful observers of the American scene have been struck with the paradox of anti-intellectualism in a nation which is the embodiment of pure 18th century rationalist thought. The Founding Fathers produced a Constitution suffused with the light of reason; the nation they called into being incorporates the best thought of the most illustrious political theorists of the Age of Reason; democracy itself, as the term indicates, means rule (*kratein*) of the people (*demos*), hence presupposes the ability of all men to exercise state-craft, that is to be intelligent enough to decide who is to govern them and how they are to be governed. There is no inherent antithesis between intellect and democracy; respect for the one is inherent in belief in the other.

Apart from the exclusion of unfree members of the community who by reason of bondage cannot bring their intellect to bear on public issues, the real or alleged reason for excluding any citizen or group of citizens from participation in self-government has always been absence of intellect. It justifies the permanent exclusion of the mentally deficient; the temporary exclusion of the immature—that is the minor. Women's "alleged" intellectual inferiority has traditionally been a favorite argument for denying them the vote.

Far from being antagonistic to intellect, democracy depends upon it. Moreover, as civilization advances and life and government become more complex, native intelligence will no longer suffice, and educated intellect becomes the sine qua non for responsible discharge of duties of democratic citizenship. All modern democracies have therefore made education free and compulsory for increasingly longer periods of time...

My own concern is not with anti-intellectualism in politics but with the effect which hostility to superior intellect has on our technological progress. I believe we can no longer afford to squander our intellectual resources, nor continue to commit errors that result in overlong lead times in weaponry and other important new developments. It is no longer true that "no other state threatens us." My thesis is that hostility to superior intellect is a national idiosyncrasy rather than a necessary consequence of our devotion to the democratic ideal. To alter our attitude toward men of high intellect does not run counter to democratic principles; it would, in fact, merely re-establish the respect for learning that existed here when this nation came into being...

Our admiration for so-called "practical" men and dislike for "eggheads" incline us to overvalue the manipulator of men, money and words—the administrator; and to undervalue the man of superior intellect, the creative innovator—the professional man. Whatever the original purpose of an organization, be it private or public, be it commercial, spiritual, cultural, or educational, it inevitably becomes a bureaucracy unless we clearly define the activities of those who administer and those who create and produce. Progress is hampered by unintelligent administrative meddling, by insistence on routine. Clear definition is most important when an organization must combine novel developmental projects alongside routine activities.

The military is such an organization. Its main activity is operational and emergency in nature, requiring clear channels of command and spelled-out routines. But to carry out its operational task, the military must also be capable of continuous innovation in weapons and in ways to use these weapons effectively. Such innovations do not flow from command channels or routines. They are brought forth through the efforts of men of high intellect and professional competence. Technology is relentlessly shifting the criterion of military strength from the operational to the material side; the best military qualities avail naught unless equipment is up-to-date.

This change is not yet reflected in our military structure. We still operate on the principle that officers are interchangeable men; that they can perform any task assigned them. Included among such "military" tasks is the direction of complex technical projects for new weapons systems. Here the actual productive work is performed by qualified technical experts, but the direction is by officers who rarely possess the necessary technical knowledge to understand the work. Moreover, they are rotated in and out of assignments for short periods of duty, usually two to three years. Officers thus exercise management control without having the requisite technical competence, which today can only be acquired by a long and arduous professional education. Their term of office is so brief they do not have time to become familiar with the work they direct. We could not have devised a more ineffectual system had we deliberately set out to do so.

The military establishment is our national life insurance. Respect for tradition must yield where the country's survival is involved. We must not continue practices resulting in ever longer lead times while the Russians keep on cutting theirs. Were I asked to identify the principal cause of this dangerous state of affairs, I should unhesitatingly give it as the unwillingness of the military to make room for the men who alone can produce new weapons—the technical professionals. We shall continue to lose the few capable men of this kind we now have, and certainly fail to attract others, unless we reverse present practices which hamstring them and rend them unproductive. Parenthetically, I may say that another bureaucratic weakness—excessive loyalty to one's own organization—runs a close second. A recent LIFE article states that "debilitating, inclusive rivalry between all three services was among the factors that blinded both military and civilian officialdom to the importance of space development before the Russians enlightened the world with their Sputniks."

In this country, large-scale development projects of military significance—such as missiles, space vehicles, and nuclear propulsion—all suffer grievously from over-administration. Technically unqualified officers do not hesitate to decide complex scientific and engineering problems; to overrule their technical subordinates; to meddle in their day-to-day activities. In my own group, at least two-thirds of my own time and that of the top scientists and engineers is wasted by administrative fiat. Time and again everyone must stop regular work and exhaust his energies in combatting administrative errors. Thousands of hours are lost dealing with the avalanche of memoranda descending from higher administrative levels. A short while ago, every senior technical man in the group was doing paperwork ordered from above; we had difficultly releasing one of them from his writing chores to deal with an urgent technical problem. We were scribbling instead of building nuclear ships; the Russians were forging ahead with new weapons, widening the lead times between the two countries.

Russia carries complicated technical projects through more efficiently than we, chiefly because she does not subscribe to our quaint notion that top-management of projects is a part-time chore for technical amateurs! Her long-range development projects proceed on schedule, while ours flounder in a tangle of red tape produced by legions of committees and layers of supervisory administrators—all with great power but little personal responsibility for the ultimate success of the work. Even when we ostensibly vest responsibility in a "Czar," he will long since have moved on to a new assignment by the time the smoke screen of organizational "public relations" has been dissipated and the truth about his performance has become public.

Let me repeat: Today, a nation's strength depends more on the scientific and technical competence of those who conceive, design, and build military equipment and who devise new strategies for their optimum use than on the men who operate these new weapons. Technical experts ought not, in their professional fields, be subjugated to officers unless these are technically competent and stay in their managerial posts long enough to acquire understanding of the work they direct. Our present system, appropriate in a simpler age when weapons were uncomplicated and change was slow, is unsuitable to an age of rapidly spiraling technological progress. Progress now depends on men of superior intellect. Democracies cannot survive unless such men are properly fitted into the huge organizations now dominating life, most particularly into the military bureaucracy.

To speed military technology and reduce lead times, I suggest the following simple reforms—in order of importance:

First: Make power coincide with competence; recognize that "pure" administrative ability alone does not fit a man to direct complex technical work performed by highly trained professionals; that even a technically trained manager needs time to familiarize himself with the work; short assignments must therefore be avoided.

Second: Make power coincide with responsibilities; hold men all along the line responsible for the directions they give; keep managers of technical projects in office long enough so they can be judged by their success or failure.

Third: Recognize that routines do not give rise to new ideas and technical developments; therefore, creative workers should be freed from unnecessary routines; recognize that such freedom is essential if they are to do their work and does not constitute a pampering of eggheads.

Fourth: Change the administrative structure to permit technical experts the right to their own professional judgment; unless this professional right is preserved, such men are degraded to the status of mere technicians, and technicians will not win us the race with the Russians.

Above all, in this period of danger to our country, let not devotion to the "ways of the organization" hold back capable professional men with creative ability. Superior intellect is essential to all organizations, none more than to a democratic state.

9 February 1963

Telephone Discussion with Admiral George W. Anderson, USN

I told Admiral Anderson[79] I was to see the president on Monday, February 11, 1963. I added that I assumed the subject was multilateral manning of Polaris ships. Admiral Anderson stated that as of now, he believes the president favors surface ships rather than submarines.

I told Admiral Anderson of the 9 February 1963 request I had received from Admiral Lee in which he asked for considerable detailed information on multilateral manning. I told Admiral Anderson I had discussed this with Admiral Sharp, who had advised me that this information had already been supplied by the CNO to Admiral Lee and that Admiral Sharp considered that such requests for information should properly be addressed to CNO and not to me. Admiral Anderson replied that this was correct. He considered it improper for Lee to deliver such requests to me. I told Admiral Anderson that Admiral Lee had advised me today that the concept of multilateral manning was a Navy Department policy; that I had asked Admiral Lee who in the Navy Department had set this policy.

---

79 Chief of Naval Operations, 1961–1963.

Admiral Lee could not name anyone, but stated he was operating under a Navy Department statement issued several months ago. Admiral Anderson stated this was not a Navy Department policy and so advised Admiral Lee. I advised Admiral Sharp of the above.

16 April 1963

"Education for Naval Leadership," Address at the United States Naval Academy

Admiral Kirkpatrick was good enough to ask me to speak with you today. He thought you might be interested in my views on some aspects of the education of naval officers. I hope what I saw will have pertinence to the problems you face throughout your naval career.

First, I will explain why education is indispensable to leadership. Then I will tell you what I consider to be weaknesses in the education of officers—weaknesses which are inimical to the development of the military leadership our nation requires. Finally, I will urge you as individuals to take specific steps which can assist you in developing your own potential for military leadership. I limit myself to the Navy because of my greater familiarity with the service in which I have been on active duty for 45 years.

Science and technology are rapidly and radically changing the world and forcing mankind to face up to two alternatives: adopt new ways of thinking or risk extermination. I need not belabor this point; no thoughtful person can help but be aware of the grave problems confronting us and of the inadequacies of traditional ways of dealing with them. Some of the concepts that we have long been taught and accepted are no longer relevant; others are no longer adequate; still others have now become profoundly dangerous. As Magnus Pike[80] has said: "There have been many well-run societies, and there have been well-run armies, too. The danger arises when big changes take place. When this happens, a system designed for a particular

---

80 Magnus A. Pyke (1908–1992), British scientist.

purpose needs to be changed to meet the changed circumstances. If the system has become rigid, however, and people are not willing to change it, then it begins to impose itself on them."

We cannot cope with this new world if our minds are like attics stored with abandoned and useless furniture. What this new world demands of us is that we learn and that we think. Only those who have been taught to think with their own minds can discover and remedy their own deficiencies...

Like other colleges, the Naval Academy has been attempting to improve its curriculum. Some improvements have been made; others are currently being considered. Independent of these attempts, however, each of you should acquire an awareness of the importance of grasping the basic fundamentals of mathematics, science, engineering, and the humanities. There is evidence you are not doing this. I know some of you feel that because the Academy is a military institution, it need not compete with other colleges on an intellectual level; that perhaps military leadership is not in any significant way dependent on intellectual development. Nothing could be further from the truth, as I hope to show you.

Let us examine closely and critically just what military leadership consists of in the changing world in which your naval careers will be spent. The significance of military leadership has reached unprecedented importance, not only because of the obvious military threat to our country but also because of the increasing role of the military in our foreign relations and in our national economy.

Certain attributes of military leadership have always been important to success in warfare; among these is knowledge. History warns us to recognize the importance of this attribute; it supplies us with many examples where failure to do so has led to defeat...

The consequences of error in today's world of nuclear warfare are far more ominous than they were in 1870. The destiny of our country and of all free peoples is now at stake. Today, it is too dangerous to harbor illusions... Illusions are a form of excess baggage which prevent a man or a nation from facing squarely up to the issues and solving problems properly. How we fare will be determined in large measure by the relative capabilities of enlightened leadership in all areas, including the military. By enlightened leadership, I mean leadership that sets new standards for itself as dictated by the dynamic developments of the times; leadership that is not bound by tradition; and that is not based on frozen concepts, which may have been important yesterday, but are no longer very important today…

What then are the main characteristics of military leadership in today's world of guided and ballistic missiles, supersonic aircraft, high-powered sonar and radar, deep-diving nuclear submarines, and other complex weapons? In such a world, military power depends upon technology, and technology depends on educated brain power. Therefore, today the keystone of military leadership clearly is an educated mind. Indeed, the motto of the Naval Academy itself is truly prophetic. For it says: "From Knowledge, Sea Power."

The educated man has knowledge that makes the world around him intelligible; his mind has been sharpened so that he can use it effectively; he is receptive to ideas; he thinks about them; he imparts something of himself to them and comes forth with something new. Because he has broad general knowledge, the educated man is able to see things in perspective, as well as in relation to other things…

Many studies have sought to find a definition of "leader." To most people, the answer is simple: a leader is an active, forceful, outgoing person, the kind others look up to; the type that gets elected class president or football captain—the "Big Man on Campus."

But there is another point of view that holds that the true leader makes no effort to impress his personality on others; he has no obvious "following." But because of him—because of the quiet influence of his ideas or his example—other people change their thinking and act in new ways.

About all that can be said for sure about a leader is that his actions influence others. Qualities which contribute to this ability to exert such influence are above-average intelligence; originality and constructive imagination; practical knowledge relative to the situation; speed and accuracy in thought and decision; and intensity of application and industry...

Convinced as I am of the importance of intelligence and education to military leadership, I have in the past proposed certain changes at the Naval Academy. I have for instance recommended decreased emphasis in nonacademic areas like organized athletics and extracurricular activities. These too often tend to become ends in themselves and thereby detract from academic effort, which should receive foremost attention. The retort invariably is the old chestnut attributed to the Duke of Wellington: "The Battle of Waterloo was won on the playing fields of Eton." This implies that the qualities required for success in warfare are acquired on the playing field rather than in the classroom. If it ever was true of any wars, it is certainly not true of modern wars. There is no clear evidence that the Duke ever made this statement. The Headmaster at Eton incidentally believes the Duke said something to the effect that he had learned the spirit of adventure by jumping over a ditch. The Duke, you may be interested in knowing, liked to toboggan around the corridors on a tea tray drawn by a team of young women.

Athletics are of course essential to the physical fitness of young men. But not over-organized athletics. They become a drain on time and energy which should be devoted to the more important aspects of education. The time one has during his life for uninterrupted devotion to intellectual development is too brief even under the best of circumstances. Long ago, a Greek physician said, "The life so short, the art so long to learn." I commend this sentiment to all of you. It is unwise to devote too much of your time to nonessentials, athletic department and alumni pressures notwithstanding.

It is not really the function of the Naval Academy to engage in large scale competitive spectacles for the benefit of the public. Of course, it will be said that this sort of competition develops leadership. But for many years, the Naval Academy did not in fact engage in such activities. Was its leadership, then, deficient in the years prior to the advent of organized intercollegiate contests? I doubt this. The American economic and industrial system is also based on competition, yet the better colleges from which business recruits its leaders are now de-emphasizing organized athletics. Knowledge now doubles every ten years, hence the demands on the intellectual qualities of leaders are therefore growing apace. Can we then afford to devote precious time—time that can never be regained—to anything that is not essential?

You know that much of college athletics today is big business. Professional coaches are hired at considerable expense to win some sort of status for the college where they happen to be working that year. But do the methods used by most coaches really develop leadership in the student player? The coaches call the "shots"; they manipulate the players in accordance with schemes developed by professional staffs. If it is initiative, team spirit, and the like which is intended to be stressed, then it would seem logical to let the students call their own "shots." In this manner, individualism, originality of thought, and pride in accomplishment would be inculcated in the player and not remain with the coldly calculating professional athletic organization.

Take the case of intramural sports. It so happens they were started here when I was a midshipman. The idea was good. It was to get as many midshipmen as possible to learn to play various games—to extend such an opportunity to more than varsity squads. The organization and schedules were left up to the midshipmen themselves. While important to the individuals involved, the outcome did not count for the company competition. Today, however, it seems that intramural sports are in danger of becoming over-organized, like varsity athletics. The important role they now have in intercompany competition may induce midshipmen to give them too much emphasis. Is the excess emphasis worth it? Does it really contribute to developing good officers?

Another problem in developing qualities of military leadership has to do with instilling a proper understanding of the relationship between authority and independent thought. This always has been a problem, but it is particularly acute today...

Any formula followed unthinkingly may lead to disaster.

Take the traditional concept of morale. I often ask young officers which destroyer they would prefer to take to sea in war: the dirtiest one in the force, the one that had low morale, yet stood first in gunnery; or the smartest one, with high morale, but which stood last in gunnery. The answer almost invariably was the smart ship with the high morale. Now I admit this is a loaded question, because it is unlikely the dirty ship would have stood highest in gunnery. Yet in terms of my question, wasn't it the better ship? Isn't the real purpose of a naval ship to hit the enemy? Is morale an end in itself, or is it only a means to an end? Should we judge the value of a ship by its morale, or by its ability to sink an enemy?...

I have made recommendations for the improvement of education at the Academy. But I do not intend to discuss these today. Rather I will show you weaknesses that you yourselves can do something about. I believe I can best do this by telling you about my observations of a large number of midshipmen and naval officers.

Over the past 14 years, I have interviewed more than 3,300 naval officers and prospective naval officers. I have done this in order to be able to recommend those whom I considered to have the requisite qualifications for duty involving operation of nuclear-powered ships. Over 1,000 of these have been midshipmen fresh from the Naval Academy and from civilian colleges. These interviews confirm my conviction that the Naval Academy midshipmen are not acquiring as good an education as do the midshipmen from civilian colleges. This conviction is supported by my observations of the remaining 2,300 officers who had varying amounts of experience in the Navy; most of these officers reflect the same shortcoming in education I saw in the young midshipmen.

Whenever one attempts to compare graduates of the Naval Academy with those from civilian colleges, he is told that the need to develop leadership at the Academy gives it a unique mission requiring special time-consuming efforts. It is said that the Academy is a military institution preparing men dedicated to a loyal career in the service and, hence, cannot be like other colleges. It is also said that midshipmen are assigned military and administrative duties so that they may learn, by doing, to be followers and leaders; that regimentation is essential to the development of a fighting man and therefore, a necessary part of the experience of a midshipman...

The central deficiency in the education of Naval Academy midshipmen is that they do not learn principles and therefore do not learn to reason from principles. The extent of this deficiency is perhaps best understood by those who have themselves been educated at the Academy and then at a civilian college of the first rank. The contrast is marked in favor of the civilian college. That this weakness in Academy education exists is real enough. Where the difficulty lies is in conveying a comprehension of this weakness to those who need to know about it...

Deficiencies in Naval Academy education show up clearly in our nuclear power schools. We find that the NROTC graduates, on the average, do better than Naval Academy graduates, the principal reasons being that they have, as a group, a better educational foundation than have officers from the Academy. For example, in one nuclear power school group, the top 11 students are all non-Academy graduates. These 11, again as a group, were B-minus students at college, yet they stand higher than ten Academy graduates, four of whom stood in the top 100 of their class. These are unpleasant facts. But it is better that you know them now than that you keep on deluding yourselves about your educational development...

Many Academy graduates also believe that the academic phase of their education ends with graduation and that thereafter they merely apply in a routine manner what they learned at the Academy of the trade of naval officer. I seldom find an officer who devotes a significant amount of free time to continuing his general and professional studies. Perhaps there is too little reward or encouragement offered for this type of self-development. Most officers devote their energy to routine and perfunctory tasks associated with their jobs. Few maintain intellectual interests in science, engineering, history, languages, or similar academics. Without them, officers are really no more than technicians. They are stagnating intellectually. The fact that they are judged by their practical skills tends to mask this intellectual stagnation. This only reveals itself when real leadership and keen insight are needed to guide their decisions in dealing with the unforeseen problems that our rapidly changing times throw at them.

What impresses me in interviews is the greater maturity of the NROTC students compared to Academy students. I attribute this to the fact that the generally superior academic education and the open life at civilian colleges tend to foster maturity. Or perhaps some practices at the Academy, such as hazing, tend to foster continuance of an adolescent attitude through and beyond the age when one should reach maturity...

A misconception I find prevalent among midshipmen and younger officers is the feeling that during their years at the Academy and as young officers, they are so far down the ladder that nothing they do can have real importance. This is exactly the opposite of the truth. Generally, the first 10 to 15 years of a man's career are the truly creative ones. Therefore, you cannot ever postpone doing the very best you know how. On the contrary, you must use your years at the Academy and as a young officer to work and study your very hardest. It is in these years that the foundations of your career are laid. Otherwise, you will find to your sorrow later in life that you have lost an opportunity which cannot be recovered...

The question for each of you is this: What can I do personally? No one can answer it for you. If you have listened to what I have said, it should be clear that each of you must find his own answer...

Is broad and continuing intellectual development my foremost objective here at the Naval Academy? Or am I content merely to get by?

Am I striving to acquire a real understanding of the fundamentals of science, engineering, and the humanities? Or am I resorting to techniques whose purpose it is to get the best possible grade for the least effort?

Do I choose electives which are difficult and intellectually stimulating? Or do I choose easy ones which may improve my class standing, yet contribute little to further my educational development?

Am I taking advantage of every available opportunity to broaden my knowledge? Or am I devoting time to meaningless activities which have little relevance to my development as a human being and as a professional naval officer?

Am I developing the habit of independent thought and inquiry, which requires me to question doctrinaire and traditional approaches to problems? Or do I blindly accept everything that is cloaked with the mantle of authority?

In attempting to answer these self-imposed questions, you may discover that you are discontented with what you have accomplished. You may find that a strong effort on your part is needed to wrench your mind from intellectual stagnation. While positive corrective action in your environment may be difficult to acquire, remember it is your responsibility to do what you can to overcome such difficulties. Ignorance is a voluntary misfortune...

The Navy can offer unlimited opportunity to anyone who is willing to study and work hard—to anyone who is willing to exercise his brain and who is not afraid to question outworn shibboleths. The Navy is also a place where an officer can, for a while, coast; where he can get by with a minimum of effort and with perfunctory work.

Take your choice. When the time comes for you to contemplate your life and you ask yourself, "What have I accomplished?" will you have something to show; will you have had an impact on your environment, or will you have become nothing but a statistic?

10 July 1963

Handwritten note from Chief of Naval Operations Admiral George Anderson, Jr.

Dear Rick,

I will shortly be leaving active duty after forty years of service and two years as CNO. I leave with deep regret because there is so much to be done. While we have the greatest Navy in the world and the finest people I know anywhere, we still have many problems. Some of our problems appear to have no ready solutions—others are susceptible to actions within our own capabilities.

I would like to suggest to you something that I think you might do on your own initiative that I believe would greatly help the Navy as a whole and probably also help the recruitment programs to which you and your people have contributed so much. That is simply to drop the "interview" procedure in the selection process for nuclear power training.

I would retain the process of carefully screening records by your people with [the Bureau of Naval Personnel]. I would order people directly to training based on this selection procedure. I would give a strong motivation talk (by you or by one you designate) at the opening of each class. I would closely monitor progress and would not relax standards below acceptable levels. Certainly I would require conformance with standards on completion of training.

Would you please think this over and talk to me about it when we can get together because I sincerely believe that you have a great opportunity.

All the best,
George.

16 July 1965

Speech at the University of Birmingham, England, "The Meaning of University"

I am grateful for the honor you have bestowed upon me and happy to share in your graduation exercises.

To witness the ceremony is a moving experience. Each roll of parchment put into the hand of a young man or woman represents a promise fulfilled—the promise of the mind potentially able to reach the level of learning that earns an academic degree. The young people here assembled have made good on the promise.

Being born bright is pure luck, but to complete the long and tough course of studies that brings the special gift to fruition is a personal achievement kind of victory in which everyone can rejoice, for it is one on individual resources alone, with no aid from social, material, or technical props. The diploma you received today is a just and fair assessment of a proven competence. Rarely will any prize won in later life so precisely measure personal merit, pure and simple.

The traditional solemnities of the ceremony remind us forcefully of the continuity and unity of higher learning in Western education socialization. Today's graduates are only a small contingent in the long procession stretching back some 800 years; time so remote from our daily lives that it seems extraordinary any of its institutions have survived should have survived. Yet, as the late Charles Homer Haskins of Harvard remarked, much of the institutional framework of the medieval University lives on: its character as "an Association of masters and scholars leading the common life of learning"; its corporate organization with faculties and deans and rector; the notion of a curriculum of study, definitively laid down as regards to time in subjects, tested by an examination leading to a degree, as well as many of the degrees themselves. Plato's Academy in the Greek and Roman

professional schools of medicine and law may be considered fore-
runners, but the University itself is an invention of the European
Middle Ages, arising as part of, and in response to the revival of
learning of the 12th century—the first Renaissance.

One can but horribly litter society rigidly divided into he-
reditary classes, each performing a designated practical function,
should have tolerated associations of scholars cutting across
class lines; corporate bodies into which one entered of one's own
volition-if one had the requisite intelligence-and not because his
father had been a member. I find it amazing to that medieval
society, which produced only a small surplus above the minimum
that sustains life, set aside some of the surplus to support intellectual activities that must've seemed of little practical value to
most people. Yet, universities obviously stood highly in public
popular esteem, as witness the saying of the time: "Three nations
are more fortunate than all others: the Germans because they have
the Emperor, the Italians because they have the Pope, the French
because they have the University of Paris." Informally, thinking
of medieval man, these three organisms stood, respectively, for
power, faith, and wisdom.

It was early recognized that there could be no disinterested
pursuit of knowledge unless the University was protected against
political and dogmatic interference. Therefore, from its inception,
the University sought to establish itself as an entity separate from,
and perhaps equal to, state and church—as a Republic of letters.
This was the only way then possible to achieve independence in
the management of its own affairs.

I have dwelt on these ancient matters because I want to emphasize what has remained constant throughout the University's
long history. In the present age of rapid and drastic change,
brought on by the scientific and technological revolution, we
are inclined to look askance at anything old, assuming that technology has rendered it obsolete. This assumption, whatever its
validity for changes in the material aspects of life, does not apply

to human beings, to their intellectual and spiritual growth, their ethical commitments, their relations with one another—to the very matters that concern education in general and the University in particular. Before we seek to alter the character of core functions of an institution, which has so excellently served man over so long a span of time, I suggest we ponder most carefully the possible consequences of any proposed change.

Straightforward meddling by government or by religious bodies does not often occur in civilized modern democracies. Similar, but other, newer, possibly more dangerous pressures are beginning to bear down on the University—not to the same extent in every country, but to some extent nearly everywhere. They threaten University's unique task, which is to hold in trust the highest level of knowledge attained by contemporary men; to re-examine, reformulate, and enlarge this knowledge to pass it on to young scholars. The University can perform this task only if it remains what it has always been, an association of scholars; and if it is allowed to pursue, without outside interference, its disinterested concern with knowledge of the highest intellectual level.

I should like in the remainder of my remarks to discuss briefly some of the new pressures currently threatening the essential function and character of universities.

Like other organizations which provide valuable non-materialistic benefits—for example, top-level music or art—universities cannot earn their way. This means they must depend upon patrons; consequently, upon the capacity of patrons to understand and value the particular work the University does. In modern democracies, the principal patron is the electorate. Even when universities have large private endowments, they usually require some financial help from the taxpayer. Moreover, the tax exemption of their endowments depends on the goodwill of the electorate. As a patron, the electoral majority in most countries has a somewhat uneven record. Nearly everywhere it is in favor of education and reasonably generous in voting education funds, but at times it meddles unwisely, evincing less respect for University autonomy and certain royal autocrats… This is to be explained by the tendency of the public, even in the most civilized and politically mature countries, of viewing universities through spectacles ground in utilitarian and egalitarian notions about education.

For most people, it is difficult to overcome a deep conviction that something so costly to the taxpayer as higher education ought to have immediately discernible practical uses—"practical" having the connotation of amenities, comforts, material things; also, services to the adult community in the handling of problems that require expertise. Exactly the sort of things the University is not able to supply if it is to meet fully its basic responsibilities. Indirectly of course, the University's activities to yield the results desired by the public. From some of its most esoteric researchers have come eminently practical products, but these have been developed outside the University. Rarely does the public at large grasp this necessary two-step procedure. Instead, it would like to order University research as one orders lamb chops from the butcher, not realizing that the most productive use society can make of a scholar is to leave him free to pursue ideas that interest him, whether they appear to lead to useful ends or not.

Let me quote to Americans who commented perceptively on popular concepts of higher education. They describe American attitudes, but I note that similar attitudes are beginning to be discernible in Europe as well.

According to Richard Hofstadter,[81] the public looks on education as "instrumentality rather than one of the goals of life," and feels that education "ought to be its way." Harvard's president, Nathan M. Pusey, warns of the threat to the University of "demanding, dominant forces and concerns—largely economic—that now run rampant." He calls these the "mundane world…the world without spirit, the world of the ordinary—the

---

81 American historian (1916–1970).

un-circumscribed, narrowly material world of men, which drains most of our energies into its service and will not, unless it is made to do so, find meaning beyond its own superficial self." Universities, he declares, "were not put into the world to play the servile role administering exclusively to ordinary, mundane means."

Should the University be used as a reservoir upon which the adult world may call whenever it encounters difficult problems? If as an institution is drawn into handling such problems as urban congestion, unemployment, social inequalities, or if individual professors are lured away-often in the middle of class-to act as consultants to government or industry, the purpose of the University is subverted. This purpose is not to deal directly with such matters, but to train professionals who will then be equipped to handle them. Again, the two-step procedure. Not the least of these being education of professionals who have become the one wholly indispensable part of a modern workforce; without whom, indeed, modern society cannot function at all.

Most technically advanced countries are hardcoded to meet the demand for these people. Under the circumstances, it would seem to be as unwise, as it is ungenerous, to divert the University from its basic responsibilities: ungenerous, because we rob you of the full attention they must have from the University; unwise because we are eating our own seed corn.

It would also appear the better part of wisdom to refrain from attempting to change the essential character of the University. The ability of the University to do a special kind of work is predicated on its being an association of scholars. This, perforce, makes it a minority institution, as our opera companies, symphony orchestras, ballet ensembles, Olympic teams, or any other organization operating at the summit of human capabilities. Most people can sing a little or play instruments of some kind, or dance, ski, swim, or run. But only if you qualify for admission to the elite institutions where tough performance in these fields is expected.

Every normal child, properly taught, is able to complete an education that makes them literate and numerate and gives them mastery of the elements of learning he needs to function on his own in today's complex society. But not all can absorb enough post-elementary education and specialized training to become skilled workers, technicians, or significant professionals. Only a minority of young people have the requisite intelligence for academic studies. Nearly half of those who start out on a University preparatory program can complete it. If every bright child to be discovered induced to develop his mind to the fullest, perhaps as many as 10% of a given age group might complete a University education. Countries now boasting of larger University enrollments simply equate a much lower type of education with that pursuit in a true University.

What makes University is the caliber of its human constituents. Lower the quality of the students or of the professoriate and you have something other than University. It may be an institution surrounding itself with the most splendid paraphernalia of higher learning—buildings, libraries, laboratories, playing fields; it may hand out beautifully engraved degrees, but all this is debased academic coin. A story about Abraham Lincoln comes to mind. He asked, "If you call a dog's tail leg, how many legs has he?" The answer being five; calling a tail a leg doesn't make it so.

To boost University enrollment figures by mislabeling inferior institutions is futile; sooner or later, the truth will out. Yet, it appeals to a public more concerned with the names of schools on degrees than with the content of the education these represent.

Nothing so becomes modern man as his determination that every child must have an equal chance to become educated out of the state. Out of this determination has come the modern trend toward shifting financial responsibility for education children from parent to taxpayer.

But removing the price tag is at the curious and perhaps unexpected result that in popular thinking, education has become a consumer good. By this I mean that the public regards it one of the many desirable consumer items modern societies offer all their citizens cost to the individual recipient, or at greatly reduced cost. They expect higher education to be mass-produced and issues out equally. Any demand that one must qualify for it strikes them as undemocratic.

Education differs from other consumer items; there can never be more than the offer of an opportunity which the individual must earn by making the necessary effort. It was so when parents paid school fees, and it cannot be otherwise even when fees are abolished. Socializing cost of education clearly eliminates ability to pay as a prerequisite. It merely equalizes children as far as the financial resources of the parents are concerned. It does not equalize human intellect or the motivating power that drive some great children through the tough preparatory program and into the University, while others, equally bright, drop out on the way society is prepared to do without the benefits that flow directly or indirectly from the work that universities alone are able to do.

May 2, 1966

Memorandum of Telephone Conversation with Secretary Nitze last night:

1. Secretary Nitze[82] called me at 11:00 p.m. last night to discuss my impending appearance before the House Armed Services Committee Monday morning at 10:00. The Secretary told me that the Navy had originally asked for one DLGN[83] and two DDG's in the FY'67 shipbuilding program. The DOD had approved only the two DDG's. He said that two DDG's in the FY'67 program was now the position of the U.S. Navy. I said that the Committee had asked me to testify and to give

---

82 Paul Nitze (1907–2004), Secretary of the Navy 1963–1967.
83 Nuclear-powered guided missile destroyer.

my opinion of nuclear versus conventional escort vessels, and he well knew that I firmly believed nuclear escorts to be superior to conventional escorts, and so I would have to testify to that effect. I added that I would recommend that the Armed Services Committee authorize two DLGN's and two DDG's in Fiscal '67, but that the two DLGN's should be given priority.

2. I said that the present basis for aircraft carriers was that they are floating air fields with self-contained facilities, and so were to a great extent independent of logistic support. Therefore, I could not understand why the Navy did not see the same logic for reducing logistic requirements for the carrier task force, by making not only the carrier nuclear-powered but the escorts as well. I pointed out that the recent study on escorts forwarded to him by Admiral McDonald stated that of the fuel required by a conventional carrier task group, 1/3 was to supply the carrier herself, 1/3 was for the escorts, and 1/3 for aircraft.

3. Mr. Nitze said that the Navy desired to have five nuclear frigates and 15 conventional ones over the next five years. I repeated that I considered a nuclear frigate definitely superior to a conventional one, and I would so state to the House Armed Services Committee. I said I would also recommend that if any escorts were to be cut out, it should be the DDG's and not the DLGN's. This was so because I was afraid that if Congress voted for all four (2 nuclear and 2 conventional) the DOD would cut out the nuclear ones. I couldn't blame the Navy for asking for conventional escorts because the Navy had always been turned down by DOD when they had asked for nuclear ones.

4. Mr. Nitze said that he was the Secretary of the Navy and was responsible for the welfare of the Navy, and I should not take it upon myself to mastermind what the Navy or the Secretary of Defense should do. I replied that I was being asked to testify

as to my own opinions and not the Navy's or DOD's. I added that if I had never voiced my own opinions to Congress, if it had been left to the Navy itself, it is doubtful the Navy would today have any nuclear ships. We would not now have the Polaris system, which is the best protection the U.S. has today against nuclear attack or nuclear attack submarines, or nuclear surface ships. Mr. Nitze said I had a point.

5. I repeated that I would recommend that the House Armed Services Committee vote for two nuclear and two conventional escort vessels but that the nuclear escorts be given priority; otherwise, they would probably never be authorized for building by the DOD, as has been the experience to date.

2 June 1966

Speech "Summary of Liberty, Science, and Law" at the Athens Meeting of the Royal National Foundation

Two and a half millennia ago, Athens found a way to reconcile the inner conflict between civilization and liberty, thus solving man's most difficult political, social, and economic problem. The principles and procedures she developed to provide the political framework for a society of free men retain their validity to this day. They are the precious heritage Greece gave to the nations of the free world.

Liberty, never gained without enormous effort and sacrifice, is all too easily lost. Each generation must win it anew. Each must defend it against new perils. These perils arise because men, being endowed with free will, continually alter the conditions of life. Countless decisions made in pursuit of private objectives may so transform society that institutional safeguards once adequately protecting human liberty become ineffective. It is then necessary to return to first principles and to adapt them to altered circumstances.

Certain developments in modern democracies have an adverse effect upon the liberties of the individual and the social and moral values cherished by free men. The causative factor of this new threat to liberty is science and its offspring, science-based technology. It is my convictions that unless certain practices in the technological exploitation of scientific knowledge are restrained by law, they will cost us liberties.

How in future to make wiser use of technology is perhaps the most vital public issue facing the electorates of industrial countries. It will tax their mental resources and challenge their political acumen.

I offer certain suggestions; others may have better ones. What is important is that we never for a moment forget that a free society centers on man. It gives paramount consideration to human rights, interests, and needs. Society ceases to be free if a pattern of life develops where technology, not man, becomes central to its purpose. We must not permit this to happen lest the human liberties for which mankind has fought, at so great a cost, will be extinguished.

9 July 1966

Letter from Secretary of the Navy Paul Nitze

Please provide me with a copy of any communications you may have had with the Committee of Conference of the Senate and House... on the Fiscal Year 1967 Defense Procurement Authorization Bill.

28 July 1966

Memorandum for File

Subj: Meeting with Secretary of the Navy Paul H. Nitze and members of the Joint Committee on Atomic Energy

1. In accordance with a telephone request from Senator Jackson, I met with him in his office on July 26, 1966. Senator

Jackson told me that on July 25, 1966, Secretary Nitze had met with him in connection with the notes I had written to individual members of Congress about the nuclear frigate.

2. Senator Jackson said that Mr. Nitze was doing this on orders from the Secretary of Defense, and that the real issue was the fact that Republic members of Congress were using my testimony to embarrass the administration. I told Senator Jackson that my testimony had been cleared through the Department of Defense and that it had been made public, and consequently there was nothing I could see that was wrong about this. Senator Jackson said that the statement I had given to individual members of Congress was embarrassing to the administration because Republican members were using it. I replied that to my knowledge no Republican members had used it and that no public use had been made of it by anyone, either Republican or Democrat. All that had been used by Republicans and others was my testimony, which had been given public release.

3. Senator Jackson said that Secretary Nitze had asked me to furnish him with a copy of the notes and that I had refused. I replied to Senator Jackson that this was not the case. One of Mr. Nitze's assistants (A commander who is his Special Counsel) had at first telephoned Mr. Leighton[84] saying he had heard a rumor that I had written a memorandum to the Senate-House Conference and, if so, he would like a copy. Mr. Leighton told him he didn't know of a memorandum sent from me to the Conference. The assistant then called me about the "rumor." I told him I made it a policy not to respond to rumors, that I was frequently misquoted. He said it was one of the Navy congressional liaison officers. I asked him if he was speaking for himself or for the secretary. He said he was speaking for the secretary. I was annoyed that

---

84 David Trent Leighton (1925–2017), U.S. Naval Academy Class of 1946. Nuclear engineer who worked for Rickover for more than two decades.

the Secretary of the Navy would use this means of inquiring into my activities, so I suggested to his assistant that he obtain an official statement from the officer who had told him the rumor and send me an official request for me to submit my comments and I would, of course, do so.

4. Senator Jackson added that Mr. Nitze was a very shy man, that he was doing a number of things which were personally disagreeable to him.

5. Senator Jackson said that Mr. Nitze himself was on the spot from his superiors (Mr. McNamara and Mr. Vance[85]) and would have to demonstrate to them that he had taken action in my case. Therefore, the senator had made arrangements for a meeting to be held among myself and Senators Anderson, Jackson, Pastore, and Congressmen Holifield and Price. On July 28, 1966, I received a telephone call from Senator Jackson stating this meeting would be held at 1600, Wednesday, August 3, 1966, and that I would meet with him ahead of time in his office at 1500 on the same day.

6. I told Senator Jackson that I could not be placed in a position where I would guarantee never to contact members of Congress until and unless I had notified and obtained permission from anyone in the Department of Defense. Furthermore, I did not think it was proper that every time such a request was made of me, I would inform the Department of Defense of what had transpired during personal meetings with members of Congress. Senator Jackson said the issue would all probably be straightened out during the ensuing meeting. He reminded me that he had assured me last week that he would take care of the situation and that nothing would happen to me. I told him that I did not care of the situation and that nothing would happen to me. I told him that I did not care what happened to me, but that Mr.

---

85 Secretary of Defense Robert McNamara and Deputy Secretary of Defense Cyrus Vance.

Nitze and others in the Department of Defense should be fully aware of the harm that they could do to the nuclear program by forcing this issue. I also told Senator Jackson that the crux of the problem was that the Department of Defense had made a wrong technical decision; their insistence on following this wrong decision had carried them into this mess. If the Department of Defense did what was right and what knowledgeable members of Congress believed in, they would not be in this mess today.

7. I told Senator Jackson it would be a good idea if at some time there were to be a private meeting between myself and Mr. Nitze to discuss this problem. He said he would suggest such a meeting to Mr. Nitze.

8. I told him that at all meetings Mr. Nitze had held with me since he became Secretary of the Navy, he had always had someone present either to take notes or to listen in, even though on several occasions I had requested a private meeting with him. Under these circumstances, it was not possible to have a free and meaningful conversation with anyone. I asked the senator how he would like to conduct his business on the basis that a third party was always present.

12 October 1967

Memorandum of Telephone Conversation with Paul R. Ignatius, Secretary of the Navy

1. The Secretary of the Navy called me about 1630. He said he had been thinking about my staying on, and he thought it would be a good idea if I were to stay on for another two years starting January 1968. I told him this was agreeable to me but that it should be on the same basis as the two previous extensions; that is, "as long as I am willing and able." The secretary said it would be this way.

2. I then told the secretary I had seen a newspaper article that said a successor was to be appointed, and I was to train him. I told him this would not work, and I could not continue on the job on that basis. The secretary said this would be the subject of discussion at some future time.

12 October 1967

Memorandum of Telephone Conversation with Paul R. Ignatius, Secretary of the Navy

1. I called the Secretary of the Navy at 1720 and suggested that the press release should include the following words:

   "I believe Admiral Rickover's contributions to the Navy and the nation will be needed for so long as he is willing and able to serve."

2. I told Mr. Ignatius that there had been comments in the press about a successor being appointed to replace me and that I was to train him; that this would create an impossible situation. Therefore, the press release he proposed to issue should use the same words which had been used in Secretary Nitze's letter of 30 September 1965, and which had been included in the press release issued at that time:

   "I believe your contributions to the Navy and the nation will be needed for so long as you are willing and able to serve your country."

3. Mr. Ignatius asked why I wanted this sentence in. I told him that I understood the letter he was to send me was to be the same as the one Mr. Nitze had sent to me on 30 September 1965, and that letter contained this statement. Mr. Ignatius

asked why I understood that the letter he sends will have that statement in it since I didn't have the letter yet. Mr. Ignatius said, "I am appointing you for two years." I said, "Do you mean that is the end of it?" Mr. Ignatius said, "I didn't say that. I said I am appointing you for two years." I then asked him if that meant that I am to be on pins and needles for the next two years. Mr. Ignatius asked why should I be on pins and needles? I replied that I had been on pins and needles for the last six months. I told him that I felt I had been shabbily treated in this matter; that the issue of my staying was raised six months ago in an official letter from the Chairman of the AEC (acting on the request of the JCAE[86]) to Mr. Nitze, and not one word came to me from the Navy.

4. Mr. Ignatius replied, "Since I got into this matter, I have discussed it with the Chief of Naval Operations, and he and I agree you should be reappointed." I told Mr. Ignatius I was not blaming him as I understood "that he had not been a free agent in this matter." Mr. Ignatius asked, "Why do you think I have not been a free agent?" I said that I had known for quite some time from congressional sources that Mr. Nitze has been opposed to my reappointment, and that if Senator Pastore and others had not gone to the president on this matter, I would not have been reappointed. I then said, "You and I both know that this has been handled on higher levels in the Department of Defense, so let us not shadow box with each other." I then said that the leading people in Naval Reactors know what has been going on, and they are not going to be content to stay on with this indeterminate situation. Therefore, the sentence, "for as long as I was willing and able" should be inserted to assure them of continuity.

---

86 The Joint Committee on Atomic Energy existed from 1946 until 1977.

5. I told Mr. Ignatius I would be glad to send him a copy of Mr. Nitze's letter sent me two years ago so that he could see what it said. Mr. Ignatius said he was thoroughly familiar with what that letter said, but that he (Mr. Ignatius) was appointing me for two years, and he had not told me what his letter would say. I said that if this was not to be the same arrangement as before, I was not sure that I wanted the appointment. I said that it would not matter much as far as I was concerned since I had already made up my mind that I would not be reappointed, but there are many very fine people in Naval Reactors, and I want to do everything possible to keep them working for the Navy. Secretary Ignatius said he understood I have some fine people. I then told him that I could not run this job if I could not keep the organization intact.

4 November 1967

Memorandum of Discussion between Mr. L. Mendel Rivers, Chairman of the House Armed Services Committee, and VADM H.G. Rickover, USN (Mr. David T. Leighton was present)

Subject: Mr. McNamara's desire to take disciplinary action against me

1. In a discussion this morning, Mr. Rivers told me that some time ago Mr. McNamara had visited him and said he intended to take disciplinary action against me. Mr. Rivers said he asked "Why?" Mr. McNamara replied, "Because Rickover comes up on the hill." Mr. Rivers told Mr. McNamara that Admiral Rickover never came to see him except when he had been sent for.
2. Mr. Rivers asked Mr. McNamara what disciplinary action he intended to take. Did he intend to give Admiral Rickover

a court-martial? He told Mr. McNamara that if he wanted to give Admiral Rickover a court-martial that was fine, but that he would then run into Mr. Rivers, Mr. Bates, Mr. Philbin, Mr. Hasmer, Senator Anderson, Mr. Hollifield, the Speaker of the House, the entire House of Representatives, the entire Senate, the Jews, the Catholics, the Protestants, and anyone else you wanted to name. He told Mr. McNamara if he wanted to do it, to go ahead and do it, but he couldn't imagine why he wanted to do it.

3. At that point, Mr. McNamara said, "Thank you," and departed.

1 November 1968

Memorandum for the Record

Secretary of Defense Clark M. Clifford requested that I visit him. We met from 1700 to 1915 on October 21, 1968, and the following is a memorandum of the subjects covered during the meeting

1. The electric drive submarine will become a classic case of indecision and delay by the Department of Defense. The Navy was notified on May 29, 1968 that no additional construction funds were to be expended on that project. Since May 29, there have been numerable memoranda, letters, meetings, sessions of Congress, etc., and no final decision has been forthcoming. This is a grave reflection on the way the Department of Defense is doing business.
2. During the latest exchange of memoranda, Dr. Frosch was told not to let anyone in the Navy assist him with preparation of the memoranda. Then, after Dr. Frosch submits his memorandum, Dr. Foster calls in Dr. Fubini to study this memorandum in order to rebut it, and no one in the Navy is ever told what the technical arguments are against the electric drive submarine.

3. All nuclear submarine designs starting with the Navy have been opposed by the Department of Defense, yet every one of them ultimately was undertaken, generally through the efforts of Congress in overriding the Department of Defense. Also, every one of these projects has contributed significantly and been of great use to the furtherance of submarine design, development, construction, and military value. Even the SEAWOLF, the sodium-cooled ship which was ultimately scrapped, gave us a great deal of information and was instrumental in preventing us from subsequently spending large sums of money, which would otherwise have been spent...

4. ...

5. With the turning down of the electric drive submarine, the Department of Defense will have achieved a 100% negative rating. That is, it will have been wrong 100% of the time in its decisions relative to nuclear-powered ships, submarine and surface, starting with the NAUTILUS in 1947.

6. Reduction of noise is an art; it is not a science. It has not yet reached the point where it is possible on a standard scientific and engineering basis to predict just what should be done to make a submarine quiet. No amount of talk and meetings by experts will change this.

7. I have personally talked with the commanding officers of our nuclear submarines who, at the risk of their lives and their ships, have observed Russian submarines. They all back the electric drive submarine particularly in view of the many and significant improvements the Russians are making and which is causing the latter to outdistance us in submarines not only in number but in quality. The difference in their attitude compared with ours is one of reality versus studies.

8. I am being asked to justify explicitly and in exact detail what the electric drive submarine will do when it starts operating, and what its value relative to other submarines will be 10

years from now. The electric drive submarine is a developmental project. Therefore, no one can today prognosticate what it will do 10 years from now. If it was possible to so prognosticate it would not be a developmental project. Those who ask questions of this type have no proper understanding of research and development...

11. Every development Naval Reactors has undertaken has opened up new vistas. The human mind is not capable of seeing too far ahead. It is limited by its own experiences. Therefore, if everyone who wants to do something must convince one man for everything (Dr. Foster), we are drastically limiting ourselves to his one mind and the limited time he has to think about the problem. On the other hand, when a number of knowledgeable and experienced people recommend the development, their experiences and vision is integrated. Furthermore, when the development starts, the experiences, vision, and ability of many other scientists and engineers are added. This nearly always leads to a product which is superior to the one originally anticipated...

12. The fact that the United States now has an excellent reactor design capability is due to the decisions made a number of years ago. Nearly everything we are now able to do is based on these decisions, but today we are being effectively stopped by the Department of Defense from making any progress...

13. I told Dr. Foster that historically he will go down as the individual who during his tour of duty in the Pentagon succeeded in reducing the speed of our submarines by three knots.

14. Personnel policies in the Navy... I told him that we currently had 50% annual turnover in enlisted personnel in our nuclear ships, and it was not possible to operate such complex ships with such a turnover. He agreed...

I explained the difference between the Navy, the Army, and the Air Force, and I pointed out that a modern naval ship such as the Polaris submarine and a nuclear-powered aircraft carrier were the most complex devices ever made by man. We could not continue to operate these ships properly except if we changed our personnel policies and made sure no matter what the considerations and the rate of pay that people were suitable for the jobs required, and stayed in these ships long enough to learn to operate them. The rapid turnover was also resulting in poor condition of machinery, frequent and expensive repairs, and frequent and expensive and possibly unnecessary use of spare parts...

18. I told him of the problems of the Ad Hoc Committee which had been set up by CNO on 8 March 1968. I told him it was my idea, and I had envisioned its primary function would be to decide what different types of submarines we should have. I elaborated on this concept by giving the example of the first battleship. When it appeared, it was "Queen of the Seas"—nothing could oppose it. Then the other side built similar battleships, making it necessary for both sides then to build cruisers, destroyers, etc., the same sequence of events that happened on the aircraft carriers. At first, they could be operated independently, and then they had to be protected so that today we have carrier task forces. Exactly the same was happening with the Polaris submarines. When they first appeared, they could operate independently. Now the Soviets have their own Polaris submarines, making it necessary to provide screens for them. It would also be necessary for us to build submarines specifically designed to sink enemy Polaris submarines. It was my concept that the Ad Hoc Board, being composed of experienced submarine line officers, should study and recommend on the different kinds of submarines the U.S. Navy should build. At the present time, we only had one type of submarine. I called it the

"omnibus" type. Since we only had this type it was expensive and we could not afford to have a sufficient number.

19. I then talked about the fast submarine, that this also had taken about four years to receive approval in the Department of Defense. In fact, it now generally required about four years to obtain approval for a new project—just about the length of time it took to build it. I reminded him that on 1 July 1968, he had approved proceeding with the fast submarine. Nevertheless, systems analysts had in the last few days recommended killing it in one of their DPNs. Furthermore, all that has been accomplished since 1 July were studies in organization—how the fast submarine project was to be organized, how many organizations were to be involved in it, how many additional officers were to be assigned to each of these organizations. So complex a system of organizations was being set up as to overshadow the entire project. Practically no thought was being given to how to design and build it. Apparently, everyone in the Department of Defense today is concerned with organization—not with items....

28. I told Mr. Clifford from what I had observed about the way the Department of Defense was being operated and the kinds of decisions that were being made, I was convinced we would lose the next major war...

37. The secretary then asked me how I managed to get along so well with Congress. I told him this was easy. I just told them the truth. Further, whenever I promised something to a Congressional Committee, I always kept my promises; I never asked for more money than I needed. He should realize that Congress judged people by what they accomplished, not by what some system said about them, as was the case in the Pentagon. I recommended to him that he follow this

practice of Congress, and that he also judge people by their accomplishments and not by what his inexperienced advisers told him. The latter frequently had little or no experience in the matters they discussed and made decisions on.

38. I told him that most of the submarine admirals I had known for the last 15 or 20 years were not as good as other admirals. One reason for this is they live a secluded life; in essence they ran a tight club to which no outsiders had access. I told him that we could not depend on the submarine forces themselves to inspect the ship properly. They had large staffs but used them for unimportant trivia, such as wives' clubs, athletics, etc., and did not require their staffs to get down into the ships and inspect them and to observe whether they were being operated properly. I also told him that in my opinion, casualties such as the loss of the THRESHER and the SCORPION were caused by improper operation and not by direct material failures. There were enough safety factors in any submarine to prevent loss in peacetime if operation was properly conducted.

39. I suggested that he talk to some of the young submarine captains who had risked their lives operating near enemy coasts to obtain information. Such submariners when faced with the actual prospect of being discovered were all in favor of the quiet electric drive submarine. It was only those who sat at their desks in the Pentagon and who were inexperienced in submarine warfare and in details of machinery design, who took so positive a stand that a quiet submarine was not essential...

44. I then told him there was an anomaly in my situation in the Department of Defense. Apparently, everybody approved of what I did but did not approve of my methods. I knew that I was being called names by some of his assistants, and I did

not mind being called an SOB, but the thing I did mind was if they called me a simple SOB, and I assumed that he himself did not mind being called an SOB but not a simple SOB.

8 April 1969

Memorandum of Discussion with Naval Academy Superintendent Admiral Calvert about the Naval Academy Curriculum

1. I asked Admiral Calvert if he had read "The Brass Factories" by J. Arthur Heise. He said he had. I told him that although I did not agree with all of the author's conclusions, I did feel he had plenty of facts that should be given careful consideration by the three Service Academies.
2. I said I recommended the following:
   a. I would completely abolish the entire plebe system. Admiral Calvert said he was getting recommendations from a group of plebes as to what this system should be, and would incorporate it into the Naval Academy "rules." I told Admiral Calvert this would not stop the plebe nonsense. The only way to stop it is to abolish it completely. Admiral Calvert disagreed. He said it was necessary to teach the young men discipline, and, in fact, he was getting a large amount of mail from parents of plebes who approved of the system when they saw the beneficial effects it had on their sons.
   b. I told Admiral Calvert that it was wrong for senior military officers with little or no academic experience, as was the case at the three Service Academies, to set academic policies. It would be best to leave this to the faculty. For this reason, he should consider giving the faculty authority in such matters and not himself dominate the policies; this was the system being used at the Military Academy, but not at the Naval or Air Force Academies.

I said that when the civilian dean system was set up at the Naval Academy several years ago, it was the intent of the Secretary of the Navy that this be done. But it has not been done. For this reason, the Naval Academy cannot attract good people to its faculty.

c. I told Admiral Calvert that the Naval Academy had far too many courses. As a result, midshipmen were getting a smattering of knowledge in many subjects, but they did not really understand any of them. It would be better to reduce the number of courses considerably and make sure that the midshipmen really understood them. He agreed there were too many courses and said that he was taking some steps along this line. He said he had come to the conclusion that each midshipman should have a major; he considered that about 75% of the majors should be in engineering and about 25% in the humanities. I told Admiral Calvert that he would not solve this problem until he reduced not only the number of courses but also the military requirements on the midshipmen, which were taking a considerable portion of their time. I suggested that he review the need for these military items in view of the present-day technological character of the Navy. He replied that the Naval Academy was, after all, a military school. I said that he must make up his mind which is more important, the military or the academic. Admiral Calvert replied he was getting a large volume of correspondence from alumni stating that the military part must be emphasized. I told him that no matter what he did, he would be criticized. Admiral Calvert said the alumni were pointing out that those midshipmen who were good in engineering were being offered positions by industry; therefore, they should not be taught too much engineering. Admiral Calvert agreed with me that this was no reason to stop teaching engineering—which

was needed by present-day naval officers—their retention should be taken care of by the Navy and not by the
Naval Academy.

7 May 1969

*Speech "A Humanistic Technology," St. Albans School, Washington,
DC, Convocation on Ecology and the Human Environment*

The matter that concerns us tonight is of utmost importance and
great urgency—nothing less than keeping our small, crowded planet
habitable. If I may use a legal expression, the "last clear chance" to
avert catastrophe may soon be upon us. We have been brought to
this critical situation by the scientific-technological revolution, and
can extricate ourselves only by a change of direction in thought and
action so drastic it would rate the term counterrevolutionary.

To the historian, this is a familiar sequence of events. During
revolutions—social, political, technical—long established patterns
of living are swiftly and radically altered by concentration on the attainment of a single objective without regard to cost. Eventually the
cost is revealed, and if it is too high there is a counter-revolution.
But this takes time, perhaps more than is available to us. Few lay-
men as yet have any conception of the true price we pay for the
marvels of technology, although the mass media are now full of
stories of poisoned water, air, and soil, of depleted resources and of
over-crowding—all clearly among its adverse effects, all crying out
for remedial action.

What chiefly delays public recognition of the costs of the scientific-technological revolution is, I submit, the universal popularity
of its objective: material abundance and an easing of man's earthly
lot through mastery of nature, the "empire of man over nature,"
of which Francis Bacon dreamed three and a half centuries ago.
Modern technology, solidly based on accurate scientific knowledge,
comes remarkably close to this goal. Even the poorest in technically

advanced countries are better fed, housed, and clothed, work in safer, more comfortable surroundings, enjoy greater leisure and more varied entertainments, live longer and healthier lives than they could ever hope for in the vast backward regions of the earth; this accounts for what W.H. Ferry calls the "stupid love affair," he said, "does not mean abandoning technology, but replacing infatuation with an understanding of its toxic qualities, and finding ways to direct it to humane ends."

Fortunately, we have a means to such an understanding in ecology—a science conterminous with modern technology.

Derived from the Greek oikos, meaning household or living place, ecology deals with the interrelationships of plants and animals (including man) and their environment. Ecology, until recently a modest academic discipline chiefly serving agriculture and medicine, is destined to become the key science for correctly assessing the negative aspects of technology. If I may, I should like to make two suggestions: First, limit the study to plant and animal ecology, which is a fully developed branch of the exact sciences, omitting for the time being what goes under the name of social ecology. We tend in this country to try to do two or more things simultaneously; in consequence we do neither of them as well as we might. Second, consider the possibility of beginning the study at an earlier age. During a visit to Switzerland for the purpose of familiarizing myself with their educational system, I was much impressed by the way ecology was taught in a one-room village schoolhouse. It was part of the curriculum throughout the primary grades, being presented at first very simply—but always graphically; later, on a more complex level; and always alongside the three R's and history and government, so that the children absorb it as part of their general education.

What needs to be developed at the earliest opportunity is a habit of thinking ecologically, of being thoroughly familiar with the balance of nature which Barry Commoner, the biologist, recently defined in simple words comprehensible to the non-scientist, old or young. All living things, he said, "are dependent on the great inter-woven cyclical processes, followed by the four elements that make up the major portion of living things and the environment: carbon, oxygen, hydrogen, and nitrogen. All of these cycles are driven by the action of living things."...

I wonder, too, whether ecology, properly presented at the higher secondary school levels, might not help dissipate the ten-dency in contemporary thinking of regarding technology as an irresistible force with a momentum of its own that puts it beyond human direction and restraint. Mere awareness of all the adverse effects of technology may not suffice to mobilize public support for countervailing measures. What is additionally needed is a change of attitude on the part of the public and of its leaders, that is, of the prevailing concepts of what technology is and what purpose it should serve. Only when viewed humanistically—in other words, as a means to human ends—can technology be made to produce maximum benefit and do minimum harm to human beings and to the values that make for civilized living. It may even enable man to become more truly human than it has ever been possible for him to be. Of technology it can rightly be said that it is not "either good or bad, but thinking makes it so."

23 May 1969

[Editor's note: Throughout his tenure at Naval Reactors, Rickover conducted interviews of applicants for the nuclear power program. These interviews became legendary for his testing of their knowledge on issues other than the Navy and placing them in uncomfortable situations to test their reactions. See earlier 10 July 1963 letter from the Chief of Naval Operations. The names of these interviewees have been removed by the editor. The collection includes many transcripts of the interviews. Most are more harsh than the following.]

Interview of Ensign _____

Rickover: I see you have studied major British writers.
Ensign: Yes, sir.
Rickover: Who are they?
Ensign: Keats, Coleridge, Yates, Wordsworth, Arnold.
Rickover: What have you read by Keats?
Ensign: I can't remember.
Rickover: Have you heard of "Ode on a Grecian Urn?"
Ensign: Yes.
Rickover: When did Keats live?
Ensign: I can't remember.
Rickover: When did Wordsworth live?
Ensign: I can't remember.
Rickover: 15th or 16th Century?
Ensign: 17th.
Rickover: What did he write?
Ensign: I can't remember.
Rickover: When did Coleridge live?
Ensign: I can't remember.

Interview of a Catholic midshipman:

Rickover: You mean you would do that which violates the laws of your church if it conflicted with your beliefs?
Candidate: I think so.
Rickover: You aren't a very good Catholic.
Candidate: I think I am.
Rickover: You disobey its laws, and you are?
Candidate: Yes, I think I am.
Rickover: How do you know there is a God?
Candidate: I believe there is.
Rickover: How do you know there is a God?
Candidate: I have faith in it.

Rickover: Well, how do you know there is one?
Candidate: I don't know.
Rickover: Then you don't know there is a God.
Candidate: Yes, sir. I don't know if there is a God, but I believe there is one.

1970s

January 1971

Speech "What are Schools For?" (Delivered on multiple occasions.)

As I see it, our educational philosophy and practice suffer from two fundamental defects.

I would rank first that we rush in all directions, pouring out vast sums of tax money for new research and experimentation concerning one of the oldest Western activities—transmitting knowledge and intellectual skills accumulated past the young—without asking ourselves why exactly schools are needed and what exactly they must do that no one else could do, so that it becomes necessary to ask the American people to the tune of some $60 billion annually to support formal schooling.

Second, I would list our failure to think through how we can combine our commitment to equal educational opportunity for all with the sad but indisputable fact that of all the species on Earth, human beings are the most unequally developed by formal schooling. As I have suggested in numerous speeches—which unfortunately have had no effect—we would be well advised to examine the most successful European school systems where ability to pay less for some generations has been wholly removed as a factor in educational advancement, but where ability to learn is recognized as the single most important factor upon which any educational program must build.

In this country, very little research money has gone into possible remedies for these two defects—chiefly because they are not admitted to by those who dominate educational officialdom. The principal reason, I think, being that for half a century, educational thinking has been swamped by the social scientists who have completely replaced the humanism that formally permeated the best education everywhere in the West. It is sociology that produced what I consider the error of progressive education.

Humanism in public education centers on the individual child and seeks to develop diverse sequential programs to accommodate differences in learning capacity and educational objectives—some European countries have as many as seven parallel but qualitatively differing secondary school programs, each open to those meeting specific standards and—what we too often forget—all tuition free. Social scientists concern themselves chiefly with group behavior, group needs, and are therefore singularly susceptible to doctrinaire egalitarianism. They tend to treat children—in the name of equality and democracy—as an undifferentiated mass that must be kept together in class, whatever the cost may be to the children. Not because this would best enable each child to advance as fast as his ability and efforts allow, but for purely political reasons. Constant admirable dogma that no man should be made the instrument of another's purposes is daily violated throughout our schools—for man in the context of Kant's comparative surely includes children. Whenever we experiment with the schools, do we ask ourselves, is this "innovation" good for our children?

We will not face up to the fact that beyond the most elementary level, children simply vary greatly in their capacity to absorb a given body of knowledge and to learn to think analytically and logically on the basis of whatever knowledge they've acquired—but keeping them in the same class short-changes every ability group...Starting with Dewey's "learning by doing" philosophy, through group adjustment theories to the current experimental school where each child chooses what to do, there's been a desperate search for some activity that all children could be engaged in simultaneously. Some of the reports of the press of the new free or experimental schools raise the question of why they could not be replaced by a community playground with a few mothers recruited to provide toys, gadgets, and meals.

Other reports, depicting classrooms where each child operates his own "teaching machine," with the teacher at the center switchboard on call when crises arise, remind one of nothing so much as industrial assembly lines with each individual isolated with his particular gadget, and no learning going on through the interplay of words and ideas between students and teachers—to me the very essence of good education. And all this costly nonsense just so that children might not separate when their educational paths are taken naturally into different directions. Does anyone really believe that such comprehensive education will, in adult life, find a rich man, poor man, beggar man, thief, doctor, lawyer, and Indian chief into a warm togetherness of shared educational experience?

The kind of dogmatic ego terrorism that goes beyond security and equality before the law, equality vis-à-vis the government and equality of opportunity, ultimately leads to a reversion of primitivism. In preliterate societies, children learn by doing with the adult community around us—parents, relatives, and neighbors give a hand, so do other older children. Learning and play are intermingled. Such casual education by untrained older members of the community suffices when to succeed in life one needs only modest competences involving no great intellectual training. But as society moves up the ladder of civilization, the competencies people need shift more from the physical and manual to the intellectual. New occupations arise which require more intensive, more theoretical, more sequential programming education than can be obtained through apprenticeship to the adult world alone.

This is the need that formal schooling should supply. This is what schools are for.

15 May 1970

Letter to Secretary of the Navy John Warner[87]

My position in the Navy has given me an unusual opportunity to observe at close hand the interaction between technology, machines, and people.

Our Navy consists of 748 ships and 710,000 people. Many of our ships, especially those that are nuclear-powered, are the most technologically advanced and complex creations of man.

Take a Polaris submarine: it is capable of remaining submerged for months at a time; it is completely independent of the Earth's atmosphere; it needs no air for the nuclear reactor; it generates its own oxygen for the crew. It carries 29,000 different items of spare parts, the total number being 180,000. No civilian experts or technicians are on board to make repairs or to advise the crew on how to make them. The ships are completely self-sustaining.

In order to have these ships operate in this manner, you must have officers and men with the highest order of training. Their safety and that of the ship depends on each man doing his duty conscientiously, with knowledge, and with precision. Such men are hard to find and difficult to train. Because of our recruiting problem, we must depend on young men. Division Officers average 27 years of age, and there is a turnover of 40% per year; the enlisted men average 24 years of age, and their turnover is 42% per year.

Faced with this personnel problem, most administrators would tend to set up a system expected to be self-executing. But our experience has shown that such a complex task cannot be accomplished

---

87 John Warner (1997–1921), Secretary of the Navy 1972–1974, U.S. Senator 1979–2009.

by means of any routine system. So, we train these young men not in the manner of:

> "...Theirs not to reason why,
> Theirs but to do and die..."[88]

Instead, we teach them the principles on which the machinery operates; we teach them the elements of design; we teach them maintenance.

Each of the men who have to do such responsible and exacting work must be treated as an individual human being—not as a cog in a machine or as a statistic.

22 July 1970

Memorandum of discussion with Senator Pastore[89]

Subject: My retention in the Navy

1. During a conversation on nuclear matters, Senator Pastore told me privately that when the renewal of my tour came up the last time, Secretary of the Navy Chaffee visited him and said he had decided to make this extension for one year only. He said he had discussed it with me, and I desired a two-year period.
2. Senator Pastore told him that if the only condition under which I would stay on would be for a two-year tour, he had better do this. Otherwise, there would be serious repercussions from Congress.

---

88 From Rudyard Kipling's "The Charge of the Light Brigade."
89 John Pastore (1907–2000), U.S. Senator 1950–1976.

6 October 1970

[Editor's note: Captain Murray B. Frazee90 wrote on 30 September 1970 to Rickover, which in part read: "I frequently had the feeling that I was getting a lot more help and advice from you than I needed or wanted. In retrospect, I can only say that you knew then, and seem to know now, the right answers to a lot of our country's problems."]

Response to Captain Murray B. Frazee, Jr USN (Ret)

Thank you for your kind letter. It is quite difficult to accomplish anything in this world, particularly in the Defense Department. Modern military technology imposes requirements in training and operation, which only those intimately and personally involved in the details can understand. Opposition is not based on ill-will but on a lack of imagination and of detailed familiarity with the inexorable requirements.

17 November 1971

Speech "An Effective National Defense—Why?" The General Leslie R. Groves Gold Medal Award from the American Ordnance Association, New York

I have been asked to give you an estimate as to where we are and where we are going and what needs to be done in a military way in these times of turmoil and peril. There is, as you know, a division of opinion among the American people regarding the necessity of reinforcing our military strength.

The first point I would like to make is that in judging between conflicting views on this matter, the deciding factor must be their relevance to the world as it is, not as we would wish it to be. Granted the hideousness of modern war, can we deduce therefrom that mankind is now wise enough to forego recourse to arms? A look at

---

90 Captain Murray B. Frazee, Jr. (1916–1007), U.S. Naval Academy Class of 1939.

history should put us on guard against those who claim that humanity has now reached a state where, in formulating national policy, the possibility of armed aggression can be safely disregarded.

I am reminded of the intense opposition to the Navy's 15-cruiser bill in 1929. It was argued by many that with the signing of the Kellogg Peace Pact the year before, it was no longer necessary to build new warships. And this in light of the lessons of World War I, which erupted despite the various Hague peace treaties. These ships were of inestimable value in helping us win World War II. The war itself was prolonged because Congress—heeding the "merchants of death" argument—in 1939 prohibited shipment of war materials to Britain and France.

Then, too, weight must be given to the credentials of those propounding opposite views. Are they public servants charged with the awesome responsibility to secure our country against foreign conquest, or are they private individuals not accountable to anyone for the consequences of their opinions; are they private individuals who feel free to express their personal abhorrence of war and to agitate, within the screen of rhetoric, for a reduction of the financial burden that military preparedness imposes on the taxpayer? Would the majority of the electorate accept their argument that, given our unmet domestic needs, we cannot afford an effective defense position vis-à-vis our potential adversaries? Or that war is so horrible that it is better to suffer defeat than to fight?

There can surely be no doubt that the overwhelming majority of the American people are opposed to relinquishment of our defense capability, recognizing full well that there will then be no one left to prevent the takeover by Communist power. Whether one takes the optimistic view that a permanent East-West détente can be negotiated, or the pessimistic view that ultimately we shall have to fight for our liberties, this Nation has no future if it allows itself to be outmatched militarily.

As for the high cost of preparedness, the approximately 70 billion dollars allocated to defense for fiscal year 1971 was the smallest percentage of our Gross National Product in 20 years—just seven percent. Defense expenditures in that fiscal year represented about 35 percent of our total Federal budget outlays, compared to 44 percent in FY69. Omitting the costs of the Vietnam war and allowing for inflation, our Armed Forces have less buying power today than they had two decades ago. In the Soviet Union, on the other hand, resources have been diverted from the farm sector to defense, and there appears to be increasing preoccupation with national security. And you must bear in mind that actual war costs absorb but a small portion of their expenditures while we are spending many billions of dollars a year in Vietnam. As for myself, I would rather be alive at ten percent than dead at seven percent.

If history teaches anything, it is surely that weakness invites attack; that it takes but one aggressor to plunge the world into war against the wishes of dozens of peace-loving nations, if the former is militarily strong, and the latter are not. Yet, there are those who deprecate the need to maintain military supremacy or at least parity with the Communist empires, on the grounds that other nations have accepted a decline from first to second or third rank and that we ourselves for most of our history were militarily a second-rate power yet secure enough within our borders. They forget that we then profited from the Pax Britannica, even as the former great powers of Europe who have lost their defense capability enjoy political freedom today only because we are strong enough to defend them and ready to do so. What it means to be weak and without American protection should be evident to all who observed the tragic drama of Czechoslovakia "negotiating" with Russia the continuing subjugation of her people.

The concept that a "weapons race" is the cause of war was a widely held theory prior to World War I. Many historical studies of the causes of that war have disproved this fallacy. And certainly it cannot be claimed that World War II was caused by an armaments race. In fact, that war might well have been prevented had Britain, France, and the United States been better prepared. It was for this very reason that at the end of World Wars I and II, we vowed never again to be caught unprepared. Whether or not to use our military forces is decided by our civilian leaders, not by the military. The military is asked for advice, but the decision is that of the civilian leadership.

Our Navy is not a direct threat to any country. Its strength lies in its ability to be deployed rapidly at distances from the United States. Its very existence as a "fleet in being" serves to deter those who might otherwise think lightly about starting hostilities.

Many valuable lessons for today can be drawn from our experiences in past wars. For example, when Germany decided to invade Russia in 1941, their staff studies showed that the Soviet Union would be defeated in eight weeks, ten weeks at most. Our military attaché in Moscow advised the War Department that the war would be over in three months. I well remember that the German estimate for the length of World War I was also three months.

These estimates should place us on guard against those who believe that long, worldwide wars are no longer possible. Even the present "minor" Vietnamese war has endured for longer than the foremost defense civilians and our military leaders predicted. Having served in both World Wars, I may perhaps be forgiven for not being as optimistic about permanent peace, the beneficence of unilateral disarmament, and the current belief held by many—especially by our "intellectuals"—that the sheer horror of a long war will compel its avoidance...

Few people study history which accounts for the truism that history repeats itself in fact many of our people understand the devastation wrought by World War II that war ended the quarter of a century ago. Half the people in the United States were alive then; they, as well as people in their early teens, had no direct connection with the war. It is not too far-fetched to say that 75% of the American people have a vivid memory of what a world war really means. The lesson of the war, its page of history, is worth the book of logic.

You may remember Blackstone's statement that security of the person is the first, and liberty of the individual the second "absolute right inherent in every Englishman." Just so, the first right of every American is to be protected against foreign attack; the first duty of government is to keep our nation alive. Given the world situation, this calls for maintenance of a defense capability adequate to discourage potential aggressors. Pres. Nixon has said "it is essential to avoid putting an American president, either this president or the next president, in the position where the United States would be second rather than first, or at least equal to any potential enemy." He has also said, in discussing the Cuban missile crisis, "I do not want to see an American president in the future, in the event of any crisis, have diplomatic credibility compomised because the United States was in a second-class or inferior position. We saw what it meant to the Soviets when they were second."

Turning back to the present, you may ask what needs to be done in these times of turmoil and peril. The blunt situation facing us is that Soviet Russia is doing all things a nation would do if it wanted to be the number one military power with clear unequivocal superiority. The U.S. Navy has not taken any further steps to increase its strategic offensive force. There has not been an arms race; the Soviets have been running at full speed all by themselves.

However, as I am most familiar with the threat posed by the Soviets to our naval power, I would like to confine myself to this area, specifically to submarines. The logic of what I say is valid for land policy, and airpower as well.

The Soviets are embarking on a program which reveals a singular awareness of the importance of seapower and an unmistakable resolve to become the most powerful maritime force in the world. They demonstrate a thorough understanding of the basic elements of seapower: knowledge of the seas; strong, modern merchant Marines; and a powerful Navy. They are surging forward with a naval and maritime program that is a technological marvel.

Starting with 200 diesel-powered submarines at the end of World War II, most of which were obsolete, the Soviet Union embarked on the largest peacetime submarine construction program in history, producing over 580 modern submarines in 25 years—most designed for long-range operations. During the same trip, the United States built 113 submarines. In two years alone, in 1955 in 1956, the Soviets completed 150 submarines, almost 1/2 times the total number of submarines this country's produced in the past 26 years.

The Soviets applied tremendous national resources to the expansion and modernization of their submarine construction yards. They have the largest and most modern submarine building yards in the world, giving them several times the nuclear submarine construction capacity as that possessed by the United States.

They are credited with a nuclear submarine production capability of 20 ships a year on a single shift basis. They have the facilities to increase this rate of production considerably. At present, while Poseidon conversions are going on, the maximum U.S. capacity to build nuclear submarines is less than half of the Soviets. Upon completion of these conversions—about 1977—the best we could do would still be well below their capacity.

One of the most important steps they have taken has been the development of a large reservoir of trained engineers to support their submarine design building program. They graduate 10 times as many naval architects and marine engineers per year as we. While we cannot specifically count the number of Soviet scientists and engineers devoted to naval work, it is apparent that they have created a broad technological base. They have committed extensive resources to support development of their naval forces.

According to the latest unclassified data, the Soviets now have a total of about 40 submarines, all built since World War II. About 100 of these are nuclear-powered. The total U.S. force is 137 submarines, nine of 95 of which are nuclear-powered, the remainder are diesel-powered, and most of the diesel units were built during World War II.

Today, as a result of the Soviet large-scale construction program, our lead in nuclear submarines has disappeared. They are nearly out-producing us in nuclear submarines by three or four to one. Even if we should decide it wants to reverse this trend, our efforts could not begin to bear fruit for several years; in the interim, the Russian fleet will grow substantially. By 1975, it is estimated they will have something like 50% more nuclear submarines in the United States.

Of even greater concern in total numbers is the fact that since 1968, the Soviets introduced several new designs besides converting older designs to improve their capabilities. They have introduced significantly improved second generation versions of. the first-generation attack submarine.

While the extent of their submarine design and construction effort is alarming, this is not the only area of concern. We have long relied on superior quality in our submarines to compensate for lack of numbers. But recent evidence indicates that the Soviets are making considerable progress in all aspects of submarine building, thus markedly reducing whatever qualitative advantage we had. Weapon systems, speed, detection devices, and quietness of operation will make a significant contribution to the effectiveness of the submarine force. From what we have been able to learn, they retain equality in a number of these characteristics, and superiority also.

Soviet submarine forces, like the entire Soviet Navy, has become capable of sustained open ocean operations and is being used to support foreign policy areas of the world. Last year, the temple one submarine operation was at an all-time high. During the 1970 large-scale naval maneuvers that included over 200 ships in the Atlantic and Pacific oceans and nine adjoining seas, they deployed a large number of nuclear submarines away from their home bases.

Because of their expanding range of operations, the Soviet Navy could now deploy long-range missiles and submarines hidden underwater along the entire length of our Atlantic and Pacific coasts in the Gulf of Mexico...

The Russians are in the Mediterranean. They operate regularly and continually in the north Atlantic communal Regency. Russian neighborhoods are now being seen with regularity along coasts of Africa. There in the Pacific, the Arctic, and the Antarctic. Their Russian bear is not yet 10 feet tall that is 5'8" and growing rapidly. If we are not alert, we may find tomorrow that our strength is been checkmated at sea.

Throughout our history, the waters that wash our shores have been friendly. They have given us geographical protection, making it practically impossible for anyone to attack us. They've also given us time to build up her strength when danger threatened.

But the temple of modern technology has changed all this, as it has changed so many things. The Atlantic and the Pacific are no longer "friendly"; they have become broad highways from which attacks can be launched against us.

It has affected our country, previously invulnerable. It has now become vulnerable, and this must sink into the public consciousness.

Today it is fashionable to advocate a reduction in defense and to use the money saved for domestic purposes. Those whose sole advocate do not test their theories or their deductions by events. While men are perishing from the eruption of a volcano, they are blissfully beating time and listening to the music of the heavenly spheres and marveling at the harmony. Meanwhile, Soviet Russia is preparing the military establishment which, by 1975, can be ahead of ours in virtually all respects.

The bearer of bad news is always punished. In ancient times, he might be put to death. Today, that person becomes controversial and unpopular. But if there is one subject on which the American people must know the truth, however unpalatable, is our military position vis-à-vis the Soviets.

"Peace and peace for our time!" declared Neville Chamberlain. And what was to follow was six years of one of the bloodiest conflicts ever experienced by mankind—conflict that nearly wrecked Western Civilization.

25 November 1970

Letter from Rep. Tim Lee Carter to President Nixon

Hyman Rickover, as we all know, was the father of development of nuclear power in the Navy. He is, in my opinion, one of the most highly respected and dedicated men in the United States Navy.

With such men as Rickover in responsible positions, Russia will never gain superiority in submarine capabilities.

For the third time, Mr. President, I recommend Vice Admiral Hyman Rickover for his fourth star.

[Editor's note: a copy of Rep. Carter's letter was sent to Rickover with this handwritten note: "If it takes an Act of Congress, I am going to see that you have it!"]

20 January 1971

Letter to Miss Jean Scroggins,[91] at sea, North Atlantic
"The Difference between Winning and Losing Battles"

Dear Jean:

We are returning from the post-refueling sea trials of USS ENTERPRISE (CVAN65), our first nuclear-powered aircraft carrier. The ship completed all tests, including full power operation, powered by her new design reactor cores, which have enough fuel to last more than ten years. The ENTERPRISE was overhauled and refueled by her builder, the Newport News Shipbuilding and Dry Dock Company of Newport News, Virginia...

Nuclear power in surface warships gives them the ability to operate continuously at high speed, which affords them protection not available to non-nuclear ships. This can mean the difference

---

91 One of Rickover's long-time secretaries.

between winning and losing battles. As the number of our advance bases decreases and the size of the Fleet shrinks, the need for ships independent of the logistic umbilical cord for propulsion fuel will continue to increase.

Next to providing the major deterrent to all-out nuclear war, I believe that the most important mission of our Navy is to ensure that our first line naval striking forces can carry out their mission against the threats the Soviets are presently developing. A significant portion of our surface warships must be nuclear-powered, or we may end up without a credible deterrent to communist encroachments which do not warrant escalation to a nuclear war. As the Soviets achieved parity in nuclear weapons strength, a credible deterrent against lower levels of aggression becomes vital. As recent developments have shown, we can no longer rely on the threat of nuclear war to stop communist aggression unless the issue is so vital to us that we are willing to risk destroying ourselves to resolve it.

To structure our defenses on Vietnam-type wars and let our capability to hold our own in a larger, non-nuclear war go by default is to invite disaster. It is widely understood that American nuclear superiority over the past 25 years has deterred nuclear war; it is not as widely understood that our naval superiority over this period has deterred lesser wars. If we do not maintain the capability to operate our first line naval striking forces in all areas our national interests dictate, we will have given up the ability to carry out sustained military operations away from our shores, not only by the Navy but by the other services as well.

For the foreseeable future, the aircraft carrier will be the principal offensive striking arm of the Navy in a non-nuclear war. No other weapon system under development can replace the long-range, sustained, concentrated firepower of the carrier air wing. Torpedo-firing nuclear submarines, cruise missile-firing nuclear submarines, nuclear frigates with antiair and antisubmarine capabilities, are all needed to supplement and augment the capabilities of the nuclear carrier.

Our carriers are vulnerable to attack by Soviet cruise missiles—as are all surface ships. However, the first line of defense our surface ships have against such missiles and their launchers is carrier-based aircraft. Without carriers and their aircraft, other surface warships, replenishment ships, and amphibious forces, would all be much more vulnerable. The nuclear carrier task force with its capability of unlimited operation at high speed is the most powerful, least vulnerable surface ship force in the history of naval warfare.

Nuclear-powered carrier task forces can steam at high speeds without concern for fuel consideration or slowing to refuel. When necessary, nuclear ships can steam at high speeds to areas of low threat for replenishment of combat consumables, such as weapons and aircraft fuel. These options are not available to conventionally powered ships.

Oil-fired warships must be refueled every few days; their operations will be restricted if the tankers they need are sunk or diverted by the presence of enemy ships. The U.S. lost over 130 tankers in the World War II Atlantic Campaign, mostly due to German submarines an order of magnitude slower and less capable than the submarines the Soviets have today. The Germans started World War II with 57 submarines. The Soviets today have some 350 submarines; at least 85 being nuclear-powered.

Some have objected to nuclear warships on the basis of higher initial investment cost. These ships are often compared in cost with cheaper conventional ships of much lesser military capability, the argument being that we should build more of the cheaper conventional ships rather than fewer of the nuclear ships. Yet study after study has shown that when all costs are considered, nuclear warships cost little more than conventional warships having the same weapons systems—and the nuclear warships are far superior militarily.

Further, the cost of war itself far exceeds any cost needed to be prepared to prevent a war. The best warships we can build, hence the cheapest, are those which are never used in combat because they have served to prevent war.

With the heavy military and non-military demands on the budget, the United States must only spend where it is necessary and where the value received is clear. But the real value of having a Navy capable of countering the Soviet threat cannot be measured in dollars alone; our survival may depend on it.

The Soviets recognize the importance of becoming the world's strongest sea power. We have now chosen not to challenge them with numbers of ships. It is, therefore, essential that the ships we do build are the most powerful and effective weapons we know how to build. This means nuclear propulsion for major warships. The penalty for any other approach is the steady erosion of our conventional military forces; a consequent reduction in our influence and in our "options" in world affairs; and the reliance for our security on a nuclear weapons force which, if used, could mark the supreme failure of mankind.

11 June 1971

Letter from Jeffrey Cook, Associate Professor, Arizona State University, Regarding Rickover's Aspen Design Conference of 1965 speech

I am wondering whether your remarks have been published anywhere in their entirety. If not, would you be so kind as to provide me with a copy for review and consideration for reprinting?

16 June 1971

Response to Jeffrey Cook

As I have never considered having you publish any of my material, I do not understand why I should submit it to you for "your review and consideration for reprinting."

12 July 1971

[Editor's note: This a personal note by Francis Duncan, Rickover's eventual official biographer, upon showing a biography of Admiral Arleigh Burke to Rickover.]

He is wondering how a person could have such material written about [Burke]. I said that I understood Burke was not over impressed with the biography and wanted another...

His opinion of Burke is not high. Burke is the one who had Mrs. Rickover scratched from the sponsor of the Triton. (I think in an earlier note I mentioned to you that Burke was a close friend of Mumma.[92]")

[His] problem with biographies is that they didn't teach anything.

3 February 1972

Letter to Queen Mother of Greece (Queen Frederica, from Mary C. Carolou, Lady in Waiting)

Your Majesty:

Thank you for the gracious gift of your book, "A Measure of Understanding," which I read with great pleasure. I am honored to have been included in the report of Your Majesty's visit to Shippingport. The helicopter ride remains a vivid memory, though somehow not as dramatic as our mad rush from Boston to New London to get to the Nautilus on time, with the Massachusetts police escort, sirens screaming, clearing your way.

May I tell you what touched me most in this charming portrait of your life? It was the difficulty of adjusting to the fact that doors no longer open automatically upon your approach. For all of us, life proceeds on an ascending curve for a while and then loses altitude.

---

92 Rear Admiral Albert G. Mumma (1906–1997), U.S. Naval Academy Class of 1926 who was deeply involved with the development of nuclear propulsion in the Navy.

Every busy person wonders occasionally how he will cope when he must finally let go of the reins he wields during his active life. In a small way, this is not unlike the doors you spoke of which no longer spring open. One hopes he will be able to accept this as gracefully as does Your Majesty.

With my best wishes for your continued well-being and contentment, and my warmest regards to your children.

20 June 1973

Letter to Captain Henri H. Smith-Hutton[93]

Dear Smith-Hutton,

As you know, Ruth died about a year ago. It was more than a loss for me because we had been close together for nearly 40 years, and no one has been as helpful to me as she was. I attribute whatever I may have been able to do to her inspiration and constant help. A great void has now been left in my life.

I have often thought of our friendship, not only during our Naval Academy days, but also later on when you were the only one I could turn to for help when you were on the AUGUSTA. So, I have always been grateful to you. It is not easy for me to make friends, and it meant a great deal to me to know you. I well remember our midshipmen's cruise when you and I used to sleep on coal scuttles...

Please give my best wishes to Jane. I remember her as a young, beautiful, lively, gracious, and charming young woman. I am sure that the passing years have merely accentuated her fine qualities.

25 August 1972

[Note typed by Francis Duncan. Ruth Masters Rickover had passed away on 25 May 1972]

---

93 Captain Henri Smith-Hutton (1901–1977), U.S. Naval Academy Class of 1922.

The admiral remarked yesterday that he has never had any trouble in getting along with women. They seem to like to talk to him even if he is, he says, funny looking.

His wife didn't have to marry him. She had other offers, and also some money, and her parents were reasonably well off.

He asked her once why she had married him. She replied that she sensed that he was unusual and would do things.

He felt that mature women do feel this way about men who achieve things. He feels it is a deep instinct, and may be connected with a feeling of preserving the race. He says many girls marry so fast they don't know what they are doing, but mature women are very careful and choose carefully.

6 October 1972

[Note typed by Francis Duncan regarding the history book he was hired to write for the nuclear submarine program]

Yesterday was a long and exhausting day… Wegner[94] and Leighton are opposed to publication, arguing that it can hurt the program…

Re: chapter on congressional relations…[Rickover] recognizes that it may be better for the book to come after his retirement.

7 February 1973

Letter from Secretary of the Navy John Warner

I believe your contributions to the Navy and the nation will be needed for so long as you are willing and able to serve your country.

---

94 Commander William Wegner (1926–2014), U.S. Naval Academy Class of 1948. He served for 16 years as Rickover's deputy at Naval Reactors.

22 February 1973

(Note typed by Francis Duncan)

The admiral asked me again to come in. He is very determined that we get into the book the essence of management. He sees this upon the highest ethical plane, the importance of allowing a human being to fulfill himself, and this can only be done by giving him a job and letting him do it—and holding him accountable if he does not...

16 April 1973

(Note typed by Francis Duncan)

The admiral called about the engineering center at Annapolis. He said he had nothing to do with this. The JCAE members went to Ebert of the Armed Services Committee who passed a resolution. (Wegner told me this was true. It was [Secretary John] Warner's idea.)

20 June 1973

Letter to George T. Boldizsar[95]

Dear Boldy:

Thank you for your kind letter. I have been out of the hospital for the past two weeks and back to my usual 70-hour work week.

You need not concern yourself with all the "brickbats" thrown at me. This has been the case for almost 50 years, and I have developed a hard skull. Few people throw stones at trees that bear no fruit.

---

95 Captain George Thomas Boldizsar (1898–1976), U.S. Naval Academy Class of 1922.

19 October 1973

Letter from Governor Carter

I thoroughly enjoyed my visit with you and have read most of the materials you gave me. The House Appropriations Comm testimony was extraordinarily interesting.

Enclosed is my statement re the Corps of Engineers and the Georgia dam project.

Please send me additional information on defense and national affairs, which you think I may use in preparing for 1974 and 1976 as it becomes available.

Sincerely, Jimmy

16 November 1973

Letter to Congressman Carl Vinson[96]

During my more than half century of government service, I have had the privilege of knowing many fine men who, by their patriotism and devotion, have done much to uphold our government and its institutions. I consider you one of the finest of these men.

Many will praise you today, but few will know as well as I do the significant part you played when, as Chairman of the House Armed Services Committee, you enunciated the principle in 1961 that all new construction naval warships over 8,000 tons should be nuclear powered. Your advice was not heeded by the Defense Department then; and it is still being disregarded by some, despite the lessons of the recent Middle East war.

---

96 Carl Vinson (1883–1981) served in the U.S. House of Representatives from 1914 to 1965. Rickover was referring to the naming of the aircraft carrier (CVN-70). On November 18, President Richard Nixon announced the carrier would be named USS CARL VINSON.

It is easy to learn after the event; it is far more difficult to foresee events and prepare for them.

May I extend my best wishes for your continued health, as well as my gratitude that the United States had a man with great wisdom in a position of responsibility at a time when vision was essential to our future.

25 January 1974

Letter from Chief of Naval Operations Admiral Elmo Zumwalt[97]

Dear Rick,

Your recent testimony before the House Armed Services Committee Seapower Subcommittee at Norfolk was simply outstanding, and I want you to know of my personal appreciation for your contribution and support.

I have already heard a number of good comments from the Hill as a result of the time we spent in Norfolk, and I believe that, with your excellent presentation and the new insights gained by the Committee members, we will be off to a running start for this year's hearings on the Navy budget.

25 February 1974

"Naval Nuclear Propulsion Program," Hearing before the Joint Committee on Atomic Energy [On the advantages of long-life reactor cores]

Sen. Pastore: Let me phrase my question in another way: Maybe I am out of my ballpark on this.

---

97 Admiral Elmo Russell Zumwalt, Jr. (1920-2000), U.S. Naval Academy Class of 1942.

Admiral Rickover: I think you are, sir.

Sen. Pastore: You are an expert. Don't rule me out too fast. I was being gracious to myself.

23 October 1974

Letter from Jimmy Carter

I wanted you to know that I have decided to run for President. Although the difficulties and obstacles to victory are obvious, I do not intend to lose. Although it would be presumptuous of me to expect your support, knowing of your friendship for Sen. Jackson, nevertheless I would like to have your advice and counsel in developing a clear concept of what our defense establishment should be. Later, with your permission, I would like to discuss this with you personally. In the meantime, I would like to study any suggestions you might send to me.

You have had a great and beneficial effect on my life—more than you could know. That is why I want you to know my plans well before any public announcement is made.

Jimmy

26 November 1974

Letter to Jimmy Carter

Dear Governor Carter,

In accordance with our telephone conversation, I am enclosing extracts from testimony I have given to Congress; also, a recent address, "The Role of Engineering in the Navy." In addition, testimony I gave in 1972 on the energy situation. I hope they may be of some use to you.

I believe that from your naval experience as well as that as Governor of Georgia, you are aware that all organizations tend to become bloated, thereby reducing their efficiency. Soon they no longer operate in accordance with the purpose for which they were set up. The only way to correct this situation is to reduce the size of the organization. This will lead not only to reduction in cost but also to increased efficiency. (Enclosures: Defense Department Bureaucracy and Excess Number of Senior Officers.)

25 March 1975

Letter to Governor Jimmy Carter

Some time ago you asked me for information about our defense posture. I mailed you some of my testimony at that time.

There was recently issued additional testimony on naval ship-building and shipbuilding claims. I testified that I did not believe these were being handled properly by the Navy, resulting in additional cost to the government.

I am enclosing my testimony, together with the Committee report, which I believe generally supports my views.

25 April 1975

Letter from Don Winters (freelance writer)

In his public appearances around the country, and in conversations with me, Gov. Carter has made several statements containing references to you. In the interest of accuracy, I would appreciate your confirming them, where possible. The references, and my questions, are:

1. Gov. Carter's campaign slogan is, "For America's third century, why not our best?" He traces the genesis of this slogan

to the time he had applied to become a nuclear submarine officer. At the end of his interview with you, Carter says, you asked him if he had always done his best, he answered no, and you asked him, Why not? Then and now, he says, he has no answer. Does this agree with your recollection of the interview?

2. Gov. Carter told me that had he remained in the Navy instead of resigning in 1953, "I think I would have had a fighting chance to be CNO. Nobody was ahead of me; in my whole class (Annapolis, 1947) I was out in front." Do you remember Carter's performance as being good enough to support, not his assessment of himself, but the ambition it contained?

3. Gov. Carter told me that you did not want him to resign from the Navy, and that he was able to resign partly because of good officers rendered by the late Sen. Richard B. Russell. Were you at any time opposed to his resignation? Do you recall any intervention by Sen. Russell?

30 April 1975

Dear Mr. Winter

This letter is in reply to yours of April 24, 1975 concerning Governor Carter:

1. The genesis of the slogan you mention is correct. Your first paragraph agrees with my recollection of this interview.

2. In connection with paragraph two, Lieutenant Carter did an excellent job in his assignment. I am aware that Lieutenant Carter was an ambitious person, but, obviously, I cannot judge whether his ambition together with his future performance would have guaranteed him the ultimate aim, many years hence, of becoming Chief of Naval Operations.

3. Relative to paragraph three, it is correct that I did not want
   him to resign from the Navy because he was doing an excellent job, and I needed his services. I do not remember
   whether or not Senator Russell intervened with the Navy in
   his behalf.

26 April 1975

Letter from Jimmy Carter

I really appreciate the information you send me concerning
your own work and your testimony on Navy contractors and the
defense department. I study it carefully.

Sometime when I'm in Washington and it is convenient with
you, I would like to visit for a while with you. My campaign is going well. I am working at it every day and do not intend to lose.
Your advice about military matters is very valuable to me, both as a
candidate and especially if I am elected.

– Jimmy

(*Note from Rickover's staff*: Monday May 12, 1975–2000 hours.
You are to meet with Governor Carter and his Assistant Mr. Jody
Powell at the home of Dr. and Mrs. Peter Bourne)

8 July 1975

*"Department of Defense Appropriations for 1976," Hearings
before a subcommittee of the Committee on Appropriations,
House of Representatives (George Mahon, Texas, Chair)*

Chair Mahon: How would you like to proceed, Admiral Rickover?

Rickover: First, Mr. Chairman, thank you for your kind words.
You permitted me to make some preliminary statements, and I

would like to tell the members of this committee that recently I was honored to talk in Midland, Tex., which is in the heart of the chairman's district, and if they could have voted that night, they would have voted him in for life, which is unconstitutional, but they would have done it anyway.

Mr. Sykes: Is that because of your visit?

Rickover: No; that is because I elucidated on the chairman's qualities, and once I did, they saw the true light. I would like to say that the same thing happened some time ago when I talked in Mr. Sikes' district. Had there been an election that night, he would have been voted in for life, too.

Mr. Sykes: That was because of your visit.

Rickover: Well, you mentioned about the new strike cruiser, and both of you would like to know---

Mr. Giaimo: When did you come back to the United States, Admiral?

Rickover: Really, I am not fully back yet. I was going to say that the designation of the new strike cruiser is CSGB. The CS stands for Confederate States. The CS was deliberately chosen so we could get the Southern vote. [Laughter from the senators...]

I would like to express my gratitude for the way I am always treated by all the members of this committee. It is personally very gratifying to be able to talk to you because I am free to express my personal opinions. I appreciate your listening to me, and your consideration of what I say.

9 September 1975

Memorandum of Meeting with Secretary of the Navy J. William Middendorf at 1100 this morning at the Pentagon

1. Earlier today, the secretary telephoned me and said he would like me to meet with him at 1100. He said that Admiral Holloway[98] had just seen him and had related to him the discussion he (Admiral Holloway) had yesterday with Mr. Leighton and Mr. Wegner. He said that he and I knew each other well enough to discuss frankly a misunderstanding that had come up. A few minutes later, Captain D.F. Mow, Executive Assistant to Secretary Middendorf, telephoned and said that my meeting with the secretary would be with me alone—I was to bring no one with me. During my meeting with the secretary, Captain Mow was present most of the time and took notes. I took no notes.

2. Mr. Middendorf said the misunderstanding was about the part I had played in congressional action concerning building the first Aegis ships as a nuclear-powered ship. He said that Secretary Schlesinger and Admiral Holloway had decided that the first Aegis should be installed on a variant of a DD 963 Class destroyer. Nevertheless, I had gone to the Hill and told Members of Congress that the first Aegis ship should be nuclear-powered.

3. I replied that I had been asked by Members of Congress for my views on the matter and had given them these views— namely that the first Aegis should be nuclear powered. I said that I was required by law to answer questions put to me by Congressmen, and I had always done so. I added that I had known Congressman Bates, author of the law, well and he had explained to me the reasons for its enactment—that Defense Department officials were preventing Members of

---

98 Admiral James Holloway III (1922–2019), Chief of Naval Operations.

Congress from getting facts they needed to perform their duties from individual military members. Further, what I had recommended to Congress was in accordance with Title VIII, the law which provided that all major warships should be nuclear powered. Therefore, I did not understand what could be wrong with my support of a nuclear-powered strike cruiser. The law also provided that Title VIII could be waived at the request of the president. To the contrary, the president had supported Title VIII and recommended that the strike cruiser be nuclear powered. I said I would continue to support the law if again asked by Members of Congress about this matter.

4. As the meeting appeared to be drawing to a close, I asked the secretary if there was any other matter he wished to take up with me. He said no.

5. I then asked him about my retention in the Navy....

Record Note:

1. This meeting was the first time the Secretary of the Navy had communicated with me in any way concerning my continuation. It appeared to me that his reason for calling me over was to give me the message that my advocacy to Members of Congress that the Aegis ship be nuclear powered, after the Secretary of Defense had decided otherwise, was being used as an argument against my continuation. After our discussion of this particular issue, he was prepared to stop the meeting. It was I who raised the subsequent discussion concerning my continuation, as recorded in this memorandum.

2. Several hours after this meeting, Mr. Leighton, in a telephone conversation with Captain Carter, Executive Assistant to Admiral Holloway, was informed that Captain Mow, Executive Assistant to Secretary Middendorf, had told him that in the telephone conversation between Secretary Middendorf and Mr. Thomas Corcoran, a Washington representative

of Tenneco, mentioned previously, Mr. Corcoran had expressed at length complaints about me. According to Captain Mow, Mr. Corcoran had told Secretary Middendorf in effect that he had to choose between me and Newport News; that he could not have both. This confirmed the information I had previously heard from other sources that Secretary Middendorf had been told by Tenneco that if the Navy reappointed me, Newport News would not continue to take Navy contracts.

14 October 1975

Memorandum of Discussion with Mr. Thomas Corcoran, Washington Lobbyist for Tenneco

1. I met Mr. Corcoran at the Newport News reception following the launching of the EISENHOWER and the keel-laying of the VINSON on 11 October.
2. I told Mr. Corcoran that he probably did not realize it, but he had been on the verge of being called by a congressional committee to testify under oath about actions he had taken and statements he had made to Members of Congress and to officials in the Navy about my retention. He said that what he did was for "the purpose of frightening me."
3. He also said that he would have no objection to appearing before a committee and testifying under oath.

3 February 1976

Letter to Editor, Yale Alumni Magazine

I found your series of articles on "The Writing Group" in the January issue to be a cogent statement of the generally poor condition of student writing today. Good writing is inherently difficult;

Joseph Conrad compared writing to carrying heavy bales under a low rope on a hot day. Unfortunately, parents and schools alike have tried to cater to student desires by allowing students to eschew writing in junior and senior high schools, with predictable results.

It is particularly disturbing to me that there are some college students—even at Yale—who do not care if they cannot write well. It is one of the truths of life that, if you want to influence others, it is not enough to know a subject; you must also be able to express what you know.

Further, I do not understand why Yale—one of our most outstanding colleges—should spend its endowments and the energies of its faculty on those who are unable or unwilling to learn. There are many other "colleges" such students can attend.

17 February 1976

Memorandum for Commander, Naval Sea Systems Command
Subj: 1976 Naval Sea Systems Command Queen Contest

1. Your memorandum of 30 January 1976 requests nomination for Queen of the Naval Sea Systems Command.
2. To comply with your request places me in the most difficult of situations. The girls in Naval Reactors are all uniformly beautiful. To choose from among them would be tantamount to choosing the most chaste from a bevy of virgins.
3. You may remember that the three goddesses—Athena, Hera, and Aphrodite—chose Paris to be judge in their dispute over the Apple of Discord, inscribed "for the fairest." Athena offered him victory in war, Hera royal power, and Aphrodite the most beautiful woman in the world. Paris gave Aphrodite the award. He then traveled to Sparta, where he met and eloped with Helen of Troy. This caused the Trojan War and the many misfortunes that ensued.

4. Although I deeply appreciate the opportunity you have offered me, I do not desire to create the dissension within Naval Reactors that would inevitably follow. Therefore, I am submitting no nominations.

[Editor's note: In July 2023, I interviewed a retired employee who worked at Naval Sea Systems Command in the 1960s, 1970s, and 1980s. She confirmed that there was a "Queen of the Naval Sea Systems Command," which was an annual contest. After nominations, a formal dinner-dance was held to crown the queen.]

14 May 1976

Letter to Dennis Brezina

In accordance with our conversation, I am enclosing a copy of "Some Thoughts of the Future of the U.S. Government."

15 May 1976 phone 0955 hours.

Dennis Brezina[99]—Jimmy Carter Campaign—would like to talk to you about the task force on government reorganization. He would like your advice on this topic.

6 June 1976

Memorandum for HGR from CAPT Charles Smith (office of Chief of Naval Operations)

---

99 Dennis Brezina, (1937-), U.S. Naval Academy Class of 1959. He served as a staff member on the Senate Government Operations Committee and then on the personal staff of Senator Gaylord Nelson before working on Governor Carter's presidential campaign.

Subj: Information conversation with the Chief Editor of Morsky Sbornik

1. RADM V.A. Dygalo, Soviet Navy, talked with me at some length about you and your achievements during a reception at the U.S. Naval Attache's residence in Moscow on 27 May 1976. He was very well informed about your professional life and also expressed great admiration for the range and depth of your knowledge of the arts and letters. As you may know, RADM Dygalo was designated a Hero of the Soviets at the age of seventeen for his participation in the defense of Crimea during WWII. He is presently the Chief Editor of Morsky Sbornik. From his own statements, and from his presence at this particular gathering, I judge that he is very highly trusted by Admiral Gorshkov. He met you during your visit to Russia and was apparently close at hand during your entire visit.

2. I gained the distinct impression that his meeting with you is frequently used by him as a conversation piece. He refers to you as a man of destiny, a man of history, and uses other such terms of high praise voiced with rising inflections, which carry clearly to the entire assemblage....

3. It is possible that FADM Smirnov came for the specific purpose of discussing the advantages and disadvantages of nuclear-powered warships, large carriers vs. small, etc. You might be interested in talking with VADM Train about his conversations with FADM Smirnov. From my conversation with RADM Dygalo and other Soviet officers, I gained the impression that they are no better settled than ourselves on policy within their Navy regarding nuclear-powered surface ships.

28 June 1976, USS Los Angeles, at sea off Newport News

Letter to Eleanore Rickover

Dearest,

It is now 10 p.m. We have just completed all our trials. I just get up at 5 a.m. to get on a tug, which will take me to a small island, and from there by helicopter to Norfolk Airport.

Saturday afternoon I walked to the airport; then I walked 2 miles from the Newport News airport—the last 2 miles before reaching the Shipyard. So, I was 3 miles ahead on my walking for Sunday.

We left the pier for trials at 6:30 p.m. instead of at sunrise Sunday. This turned out to be a good idea because many unanticipated things accrued; these required extra time to investigate and correct.

This is to be expected on the trials of the first ship of a class, especially since much of the machinery cannot be fully tested before the ship is actually at sea.

Many things had already gone wrong during the previous week, but we had been able to correct them. At sea, it is far more difficult to do so. Further, each item causes a delay.

Finally, there were difficulties with the alignment of the turbine and reduction gear shaft and bearing. They ran hot, and there appeared to be some rubbing of the shaft. The experts on board recommend that about the trial, go back to the yard and have the items investigated. This could have delayed the trials for at least a week or more.

When I turned in late Sunday night, I lay awake and thought the matter over. If I did as they suggested, we would not find out at sea what was wrong. Also, much of the machinery would have had to be disassembled, it would cost a lot, and besides we would not really know of what we learned at the yard and corrected would be valid at sea.

So, I called the leading people together early Sunday morning, and we devised a plan to find out what was wrong. Then we started running the turbines and building up the speed slowly—taking many measurements all the time. Finally, following this procedure, we almost reached the full power speed. Then another major difficulty accrued, and we had to start all over again. I guess I was in the engine room most of the time. At one time I was there from 4 p.m. Monday until 2 a.m. Tuesday. We were keeping detailed records and charts all the time.

At about 3 a.m., I decided we had all better stop and get a few hours' sleep. We started going again at 7 a.m. today, and fortunately everything started working. [....]10 a.m. I started the submerged full power run. It worked fine. The ship was steady, and everything was perfect.

This sort of thing should be expected, I suppose, but we have never, in the entire history of the program, had so many serious difficulties. However, it is good it all happened, because we now know how to correct the other 26 fast submarines while they are in the yard.

Had anything gone wrong by my permitting the full power run to take place under these conditions, it would have been my responsibility. Nearly everyone else, I supposed, would have returned to port. Finally, late this evening we ran the surface full power—and again it was fine.

So, you can see I have been fully accepted. There is a small passageway adjacent to the central room. I took my walking there, so I am caught up on my exercise, including the 80 or so bends.

I hope you have enjoyed your visit. It is good for you to be with your mother at Virgnia, and others who like you.

I love you precisely for those ways which distinguish you from others—for your youth and your infinite touching [promise]; your transparency, impulsive variety, your elasticity, innocence, good intentions, friends, everything.

In you I see nothing but love, ever more full, richer, and more profound. People who do not experience love, can have little understanding of human beings.

One's feelings are complicated toward anyone we love, whether it is our parents, wife, children, or friends. What we feel toward others gives them some power over us. Our feelings render us vulnerable, subject to injury. And so, sometimes we are afraid, not only of the danger to our own feelings, but of our own power to inflict wounds.

As for what I think of you:

> May the Lord bless you and keep you.
> May the Lord make his countenance shine upon you
> and give you peace
> For evermore, and to all eternity.
>   –Numbers, 6:24-26

This is how I feel about you evermore! With all my love…

29 July 1976

Letter from Herman Wouk[100]

Dear Admiral,

Raymond Peet[101] said to me, when we were both Stan Turner's[102] guests at the Villa Nike, that you and I should meet. I write novels for a living. Two of them that concern the Navy are THE CAINE MUTINY and THE WINDS OF WAR. You've probably been too busy to read much modern fiction, but I think your associates will give my work a satisfactory rating.

---

100 Herman Wouk (1915–2019), author of historical fiction about World War 2, including the Pulitzer Prize-winning "The Caine Mutiny" and a book made into the television series "The Winds of War."
101 Vice Admiral Raymond Peet (1921–2021), U.S. Naval Academy Class of 1943.
102 Admiral Stansfield Turner (1923–2018), U.S. Naval Academy Class of 1947. At the time of this letter, Turner was serving as Supreme Allied Commander NATO Southern Europe. He later served as Director of the Central Intelligence Agency.

Long ago Eli Reich said I ought to meet you. Eli has been my submarine consulting expert for "The Winds of War" and its sequel.

Ray said he'd try to bring me to your office next time he comes to Washington. I'd like that, and this letter is to let you know that if he does, nothing we say to each other will appear in fiction or journalism. My interest would be, I guess, talking to a man who has changed the age. I have no interest in writing about you. I avoid being written about myself.

16 October 1976

Memorandum for File
Subject: Private meeting with a naval officer

1. This morning I met with a naval officer and told him I would present some facts in connection with the CGN 41 option. I said I desired no comments from him but that he just listen to a few points. These points are included in the attached memoranda.
2. I read the memoranda to him while he took notes. When I finished reading, and when he was ready to leave, I said I would like to make some philosophical statements to him. These were:
    a. I knew he was an honest and religious individual.
    b. As for myself, I had made up my mind a long time ago to live with myself.
    c. I suggested that in taking any action, he bears in mind Emmanuel Kant's philosophy that the proper way for a decent and responsible human being to act in any situation was to consider that his action would be the last one he would ever take on Earth and to act accordingly.

21 December 1976

Letter to Vice Admiral Edwin Hooper[103]

Although I said goodbye to you when you retired, I feel I must express in writing my deep thanks for the many years we have known a man as intelligent, kind, sincere, competent, and helpful as you. Therefore, it is difficult for me to accept the fact of your retirement.

I have enjoyed our work together. I shall remember often the many occasions when we have discussed and exchanged ideas. You are a valued friend, and I am grateful for all you have done for me officially and personally…

19 January 1977

Memorandum of Discussion with President Gerald R. Ford at the White House

1. At 1400 today, I visited President Ford. After expressing our mutual regard, we reminisced about the time he was in Congress on the House Appropriations Committee and how much he had helped me with the Navy's nuclear propulsion program during all those years. He said he had always been glad to do so and said I was a great American who had accomplished a great deal in the defense of the United States.
2. The president then asked me what part of the Navy I considered most important. I replied that probably the Polaris submarine represented the best means the United States had to deter war. Better than any other weapon, it could remain undetected; if necessary, we could operate them under the polar ice. The president agreed.

---

103 Vice Admiral Edwin Hooper (1909–1986). Hooper and Rickover likely met when the former was assigned to the Atomic Energy Commission in 1947.

3. He asked my opinion on the cruise missile and where it should go. I said that the best means of using the cruise missile for the defense of the United States is in submarines. He agreed.

4. He then asked me what I thought about using the cruise missile in the B1 bomber. I said I had no objections, provided its use in submarines was given priority.

5. At the conclusion of my visit, I asked the president if he would be so good as to convey my thoughts on the cruise missile to President Carter tomorrow. He said he would.

6. The meeting lasted about fifteen minutes.

6 February 1977

Memorandum for the Record

These are my impressions from lunching with President Carter on Saturday, 5 February 1977:

He brings a spiritual and practical philosophy to the awesome burden that is his alone. He recognizes the complexities of the issues, both domestic and foreign, which confront us. He knows that all virtue and justice do not belong only to one party or to one group. Deeply conscious of the essence of human character, he believes we must all accept responsibility, we must all work to restore unity and quiet to the country, so that together we can all resolve these issues, for ourselves and those who come after us.

He considers the president—as did the Founding Fathers—to be the Chief Magistrate of our country. To this office he brings intelligence and patience, courage and compassion, leadership and service. He sees the president as the first servant of the nation.

President Carter is fully aware of the grave issues, foreign and domestic, which we face today: He knows that all of virtue and justice are not embodied in one party and none in the other; rather that we must all accept responsibility and work for the restoration to the country of quiet and harmony, without which these issues cannot be resolved.

He considers himself as a Chief Magistrate of our country. He speaks as a man of the people—a man for whom the deepest spiritual truth is approachable only through the heart and can be grasped only when embodied in the realities of the world.

He is a patient, laborious, and intelligent man at his tasks. He has the gift of instantly seeing the main point at issue, no matter how much it is covered up with a mass of details, and the courage to speak his mind. He has the tremendous sense of the essence of human character. To me, his greatest characteristic has been his courage to lead—an essential quality for any man who is in a position where leadership is the primary requisite...

17 February 1977

Letter from Aubrey Brown, Editor, The Presbyterian Outlook

For a book—in 50 words how do you respond: If you could say one thing to students facing the unrepeatable opportunity of four years in college, what word of guidance, encouragement, admonition, or experience would you offer?

24 February 1977 (St. Matthias Day)

Response to Aubrey Brown

From a cursory check of the King James Version of the Bible, I estimate it contains about 773,700 words. The succinct Ten Commandments and Sermon on the Mount have 156 and 2,442 words.

To give advice in 50 words is a feat no one, including the Father or the Son, was apparently able to perform. However, since you ask for my mere mortal attempt, here it is—in exactly 50 words:

The supreme object of education is to develop man by teaching the meaning and purpose of life. This requires hard work—a form of prayer—and is the highest type of human endeavor. Man then knows his ignorance; he has acquired the pearl of knowledge and becomes like unto God.

24 February 1977

Letter from Mrs. Constance Hutchinson

Dear Rick, you have the ear of the president, the citizen hasn't. Please, it seems a small worry, but I am distressed about the exploitation of the child, Amy, and I am sure that I'm not alone. "Midshipman Carter" must realize that he's ruining a child…

2 March 1977

Dear Constance,

Thanks for your note of February 24th. It was nice to hear from you, and I hope you are getting along well.

With regard to your suggestion on raising children, I regret I cannot be of help. It is trouble enough to raise one's own; it is presumptuous to advise others. With your experience on raising children, perhaps you should write a book.

9 March 1977

From: H.G. Rickover
To: S. Claus, North Pole

1. I know you are preparing your Christmas gift list, so I am writing you early in the year before you become too busy.

2. There are some deserving cases I recommend you consider. These are:

Donna, Victory, and Bird, Chiefess, Aardvark, and Bivouac[104]

3. I am enclosing a list of the gifts I believe they would like to have but, because of their innate modesty, are reluctant to tell you so themselves. These gifts are marked in the fashion section of *The New York Times* Magazine, a copy of which is enclosed. Each item indicates the size and color befitting their individual form and beauty. Knowing you, I am sure you will give this request the consideration it merits.

4. The weight of gifts mentioned should be within the capacity of one load that can be carried on your sleigh. You can also count on my help with the transportation should one of our submarines be near your Christmas workshop on December 24...

Cordially, ho, ho, ho,

H.G. Rickover

9 March 1977

MEMORANDUM FOR THE PRESIDENT

Subj: Cruise Aboard the USS LOS ANGELES (SSN 688)

1. I recommend a one-day cruise aboard the USS LOS ANGELES (SSN 688), our latest and fastest submarine.
2. To properly understand and "feel" the capabilities of this ship, it is necessary to operate at full power submerged, in water deeper than 100 fathoms.

---

104 Likely the nicknames for his staff since "Chiefess" often appears in his papers.

3. The best date, in view of the ship's operating schedule, is Wednesday, 20 April. Alternate dates are Friday, the 6th, 20th, or 27th of May.

4. The recommended schedule for your visit is to depart Washington at 0800 and return at 2315 the same day. Passengers would embark and debark at Port Canaveral, Florida.

5. Should the above dates not be satisfactory, please let me know other dates that can be used.

Respectfully,

H.G. Rickover

20 May 1977

(Note by Francis Duncan)

He telephoned today the captain of the ship that the president will be going out on. He wanted no special touches—no side boys—just the usual menu. He thought the president would probably eat with the crew. He did want the fat slobs of officers in sight. He asked what had been done in cutting down the weight of these men. He warned that nothing should be said—the White House would release the news. Apparently, the captain had told his division heads, so he was warned to get them together and warn them to keep quiet...

*President embarked 27 May.

Press: How was it?
Carter: It was good.
Hi, everybody.
I think the best thing to say when I come off this nine-hour trip on one of the latest nuclear submarines is that it strengthens my own confidence in the superb quality of the people who man our very crucial

defense mechanisms. It also strengthens my confidence in those who design them and keep them operating in such a superb way.

Admiral Rickover's involvement in this program has insured literally thousands of years of cumulative operation of nuclear power plants under the most stringent conditions and in the earliest phases of research and development with never a mishap.

I believe this is a credit to him and our own country's technical capabilities and to the men and women who serve in the Navy...

Question: Admiral, how did he handle the ship, please...

Rickover: It shows that any sailor or officer in the Navy can become President...

Question: Does the president still have his sea legs, Admiral?

Rickover: Sea legs? It shows that you are not familiar with submarines because no sea legs are required for a submarine.

Baltimore Evening Sun, Saturday, May 28, 1977, "'Fat,' Banished Seaman May Sue"

A 250-pound sailor, one of five ordered from a submarine because they weren't "smart-looking" enough to be seen by President Carter, says he's angry, insulted, and ready to sue... Captain Austin Scott,[105] commodore of Submarine Squadron 6, told 11 sailors during an inspection Thursday that they could not be aboard during the president's visit because they were overweight.

15 March 1977

Notes for Discussion with Chief Justice [Warren] Burger

---

105 Rear Admiral Austin Scott (d. 2018).

1. The judicial process, as a forum for discovering truth, is breaking down.

2. In the field of government contracts, litigation has become a lucrative industry for law firms and their clients. Companies, particularly large corporations, have found that litigation, or the threat of litigation, may yield a greater return than actually performing their contract.

3. Regardless of the merits of their cases, many large corporations, spurred by claims-oriented law firms, are pressuring the government to bail them out on contracts that turn out to be less profitable than they planned. The magnitude of the problem is evidenced by the $2.3 billion backlog of claims that three large shipbuilders have submitted against the Navy.

4. The stigma that once discouraged contractors from threatening customers with litigation is disappearing. One reason is that claims have proven to be profitable. Another reason, however, is that claims lawyers have been promoting the claims approach as a respectable means of doing business, by appearing frequently at symposiums and seminars to explain how to prosecute contract claims against the government.

5. These claims firms are also active and well-represented in the American Bar Association, especially in the Public Contract Law Section. Their influence is seen in positions taken by the ABA....

6. With increasing frequency, contractor attorneys tend to broaden and obfuscate issues, thus stretching out the judicial process and frustrating the search for the actual facts. Massive interrogatories and requests for depositions as well as other forms of legal maneuvering are commonplace when large sums are involved.

7. The Navy is confronted with vague and general claims based on "imaginative" legal theories and priced out based on estimates and judgements which are difficult to disprove.

Frequently the amount claimed is grossly inflated. Evaluating the claims and responding to the ensuing depositions and interrogatories prevents the government from preparing an effective defense. This tactic also ties up government people to the point they must neglect their regular duties...

...

21. What I have said about shipbuilding claims is merely a gross example of what is happening in our whole society. We have become a litigious society. You have said this in your speeches. Every phase of life is now open to the machination of the high number of lawyers.

22. Legal precedents are being set by new, "innovative" legal theories, which leads to further complexities.

23. Some Federal judges are rendering decisions which appear to be based on local considerations, rather than on protecting the public. Decisions of doubtful legality then become precedents for future decisions.

Recommended that:

1. In commercial litigation, require litigants and their attorneys to disclose at the outset, all facts, whether favorable or unfavorable, relating to their lawsuit. In filing a case before the courts, the plaintiff and his attorneys should be required to sign a stringent certificate that the information submitted in support thereof is current, complete, and accurate. Criminal penalties and disbarment proceedings should be invoked for false certifications.

2. But far more important, our entire judicial system needs to be modernized. Wherever possible, we should adopt codes of laws, along the line of the Napoleonic Code. We should adopt the Western European system of having trained judges—and without juries—decide most civil cases.

3. My recommendation is to establish by Act or Resolution of Congress a panel to conduct a study for the modernization

of our legal system. This panel should consist of the Nation's top jurists, include the Supreme Court, federal and state judges, Department of Justice, and other government lawyers, members of the Senate and House, and legal scholars. They should be charged with recommending changes in Federal statutes for the purpose of eliminating abuses which are impeding the proper administration of justice.

28 March 1977

Memorandum of Discussion with Earl Mountbatten of Burma and Sir Peter Ramsbotham, the British Ambassador, at a luncheon on Sunday, 27 March at the British Embassy

1. Present at this luncheon were the ambassador and his wife, Earl Mountbatten,[106] Mrs. Rickover, and myself.
2. The ambassador said that he was the head of a group of ambassadors in Washington who meet regularly. He also said that there was a meeting every two months between Mr. Dobrynin, the Russian ambassador, and himself, at which they had frank personal discussions which they did not repeat.
3. One of the items discussed at their last meeting was the president's policy toward dissidents in Russia. He and the Russian ambassador had agreed that the president's actions relative to individuals in Russia and his meeting with them were contrary to international consonance.
4. I said my understanding, in accordance with the basic principles of international law, was that before a nation could be admitted to the international community, it had to agree to act in accordance with "comity" between States. This required an agreement on certain basic principles of international relations as laid down by Grotius. I pointed out the case of the "War of Jenkins' Ear" where the British had gone to war with

---

106 Louis Mountbatten, 1st Earl Mountbatten of Burma (1900–1979).

Spain because a British subject had been mistreated and his ear cut off. Contrary to this was the relationship of Idi Amin of Uganda with other countries, including Britain. Not too long ago, for example, Mr. Amin had four Englishmen carry his palanquin in public and threatened to kill them. This merely elicited a visit from a senior British official to Uganda, who politely asked Mr. Amin not to carry out his threat. From the above two examples, it was clearly evident that a new situation had developed in relation to the principles of international law. I also pointed out that the Soviet Constitution, as well as the recent Helsinki Agreement, had provided for freedom of speech. Therefore, I could see no impropriety in Mr. Carter's attitude.

5. The ambassador said he agreed with Mr. Dobrynin that the president should not interfere in the international affairs of foreign States. He had discussed this action with the British Prime Minister, Mr. Callaghan, who had agreed with him. He added that Mr. Dobrynin had not objected in public to Mr. Carter's statement because he felt this would not lead to good relations between their two countries.

6. He said that Mr. Dobrynin had said the Soviet definition of equality was a broader one than that of the United States. It included welfare, health care, equal opportunity, and equal educational opportunity; whereas the U.S. position was limited to freedom of speech. For this reason, the American definition of freedom was a narrow one…

9 April 1977

Dear Mr. President:

Yesterday you requested that I send you, for your consideration, some "energy principles" to be in your hands by Monday.

As I am leaving Washington this afternoon for previously planned sea trials of a new submarine, I have had but a short time to prepare these notes; therefore, none of this material may be new to you. I will not be back in my office until Tuesday.

It is questionable to me that, in a democratic society, it is possible to face the energy problem with the urgency it requires. Humanity has never before been faced with such a situation; people in previous times lived in areas suitable for all their needs. Today, industry and the use of irreplaceable raw materials permit us to live in areas where we would not normally live.

I hope the enclosed material will be of assistance to you.

Very respectfully,

4 May 1977

[Rickover note to "Chiefess," one of his aides: Read this to Captain Poindexter,[107] aide to Admiral Holloway]

There are times when it appears that some naval officers consider themselves to be members of and owe allegiance to a special corps or group. For example, there are the expressions: "Surface Ship Navy," "Surface Navy," "Black Shoe Navy," "Aviation Navy," and "Submarine Navy."

It is proper for every officer to be proud of his particular branch of the Navy. But, above all, he must understand that each group has the sole purpose of serving the Navy as a whole. We must direct our actions accordingly if we are all to serve the Navy's common purpose.

The accompanying document, which is excerpted from my Memorandum to Flag Officers of 17 February 1977, explains the

---

107 Rear Admiral John Poindexter (b. 1936), U.S. Naval Academy Class of 1958 where he graduated first in his class.

purpose of our Navy and how each officer can best serve his primary obligation to support its mission.

5 May 1977

[Notes typed by Francis Duncan]

The admiral said that he has been working very hard these last few days on energy legislation, doing things that no one in ERDA or the DOD knows.

The problem is getting provision into the law so that naval reactors cannot be transferred to the DOD at the action of the Secretary of the Department of Energy.

He thought he had it all fixed up in the House Committee on Government Operations, but this turned out not to be the case. The language he wanted inserted was omitted "forgotten" according to a staff member.

He tried to see Brooks, who was out of his office. So then he went to see Horton, ranking Republican member, who favors the idea. He also saw Jones, the staff director.

The Senate was all set anyhow—that had been taken care of earlier although here, too, he had to be careful of the relations between Jackson and Ribbicoff...

As this conversation took place, a telephone call came from [Knowles Atomic Power Laboratory]. He found out that KAPL had hired some illiterate workmen in the laboratory. He felt this was terribly dangerous, for they could not read the radiation signs.

20 May 1977

Letter to Rear Admiral Bertam Korn, Chaplain Corps, USNR-R

Admiral Rickover has asked me to acknowledge receipt of your letter of May 10, 1977. I am sorry, but he cannot meet with you.

Throughout his career, he has never discussed religion because he feels that it is a personal and private matter, resting upon an individual's conviction. Therefore, he has never sought the religious opinions of others or expressed his own.

– J[ean] Scroggins, Secretary to Rickover

1 June 1977

Handwritten note from President Carter

To Admiral Hyman Rickover,

Your nuclear submarines are, I believe, the finest exhibition of superb engineering ever created by man. Our country owes you a great debt. As President, my cruise with you on the Los Angeles strengthened my faith in the nuclear Navy. Well done!

I expect you to keep all of our nuclear plants safe and operating properly.

6 June 1977

Letter to President Gerald

Dear Mr. President:

Thank you for the gift of Fostoria Crystal.

It was extremely thoughtful of you to remember me in this way. During my more than half century of government service, I have had the privilege of knowing many fine men who, by their patriotism and devotion, have done much to uphold our government and its institutions. I consider you one of these men.

May I extend my best wishes for your continued health, as well as my gratitude that the United States had a man with your wisdom in a position of responsibility when vision was essential to our future.

16 September 1977

MEMORANDUM FOR M.E. MILES and BRODSKY
Subject: Entry Permission for Radioactive Spaces

1. All four-star admirals on active duty in the United States
   Navy who are over 77 years of age are hereby permitted to
   enter all radioactive areas in Navy or [Energy Research &
   Development Administration] nuclear facilities without
   wearing a film badge.
2. It has been determined that such visitations will have no
   effect on the population potential of the United States.

*[Editor's note: This was written in response to Rickover having
been denied entry without an appropriate badge.]*

19 September 1977

Letter to Mr. Benjamin Hooks, Executive Director, NAACP

Thank you for meeting with Mr. Foster of my staff on 9 September to discuss the need for National Scholastic Standards proposed
by me to Senator Pell's Subcommittee on Education [of the Committee on Human Resources].

Mr. [T.L.] Foster told me his discussion with you was encouraging. He said that while you did not necessarily agree with all in
my statement, you did support establishment of a national panel to
set standards—providing minorities were represented. He also said
you endorsed testing students against these standards at frequent
intervals, provided the test questions were not phrased in a manner
that presumed a white, upper-middle class background.

According to Mr. Foster, you then asked your educational specialist to draft a letter of endorsement along the lines you indicated
and sign it for you since you had to leave. What happened thereafter

largely nullified the benefit of his meeting with you. Attached is Mr. Foster's report.

The letter prepared and signed for you by your educational specialist is of no use to me. It is written in "educationese" and makes little sense to me or to others who have read it. Mr. Foster's report states that despite his repeated efforts, your educational specialist was unwilling to simplify the language, insisting that the letter was clear, that it reflected NAACP policy, and that it was consistent with your comments during the morning meeting with Mr. Foster.

In my experience, I have found that unclear and complicated writing is generally an indication of unclear thinking. Therefore, I did not use her letter during my testimony before the House Subcommittee on Education for fear it could reflect adversely upon you and your organization.

The development of National Scholastic Standards such as those I proposed would be of great help to all children. This is especially true of black children, of whom a disproportionate number are shunted into so-called "special education" or remedial classes, according to the NAACP Report on Testing. As I am sure you are aware, I consider all children to merit the best education we can possibly give them; that this is the primary function of parents and legislatures as well as schools.

Should you still be willing to support this concept, I would be most appreciative of receiving a simple letter from you to this effect.

11 October 1977

Letter from President Jimmy Carter

I just want to say "thanks" for your many kindnesses to me and my family.

Rosalynn and I are still talking about the enjoyable time we had aboard the USS LOS ANGELES. We are proud of our personalized jackets—as is Amy of hers and her own personalized cap. The dolphin candleholders, handcrafted aboard the USS SPEAR, are most unique. A real sailor's delight!

I also want to thank you for continuing to send me the commemorative cachets, and Rosalynn has asked me to tell you how much she appreciated receiving an inscribed copy of Ruth's Pepper, Rice, and Elephants.

All in all, we are much in your debt.

Sincerely,

Jimmy

9 November 1977

PRIVATE
Memorandum of Discussion with the new French Ambassador, His Excellency Francois De Laboulaye, and Mr. Andre Giraud, General Administrator for Nuclear Energy in France, at a dinner hosted by Ambassador Gerard Smith on 8 November 1977

Subject: (1) Visit of American Nuclear-Powered Ships to French Ports (2) Information on French Liquid Metal Breeder Reactor

1. I described both the importance to the United States and to the NATO Alliance of nuclear ship visits to French ports. The French Ambassador responded that discussions were currently underway with our State Department about such visits. I also discussed the French law which prohibited such visits and provided for bilateral agreements. I described the impracticability of bilateral agreements. After much discussion, the ambassador said he would look into the matter and attempt to help.

2. In my discussion with Mr. Giraud, he first said he had no influence in the above matter. I told him I did not believe such a statement because of his control of atomic energy in France. He finally admitted that he did have influence and would help where he could.

3. In further discussion with Mr. Giraud, I asked him why the French had shifted to water-cooled reactors and whether they had been dissatisfied with their gas-cooled reactors. He replied that the gas-cooled reactors had operated well, but the French desired to have a type of reactor which would be suitable and agreeable for sales to foreign countries. For this reason, they had shifted to water-cooled reactors.

4. The next item I discussed with Mr. Giraud was obtaining information concerning the French liquid-metal breeder reactor. I said there was an impression in the United States that the French had not been entirely forthcoming in giving information on the performance of the reactor. I discussed with him the breeding ratio of 1.16, which was claimed for this reactor. I asked him to provide, and he said he would, the complete calculations on which the 1.16 ratio was based.

5. He said that the French did not place too much weight on the specific breeding ratio. They had made a firm decision that their future energy supply would come from breeder reactors and were willing to wait for the outcome—they were willing to devote great effort and money toward achieving this end. The breeder reactor was especially important because ultimately, they believed they could get sufficient energy from breeders by using the quantities of uranium and thorium they could obtain.

6. He invited Mrs. Rickover and myself to visit France and said he would see to it that we stayed in General DeGaulle's house and slept in his bed. He said he would arrange for me to visit their breeder reactor and to obtain any information I asked for and would so instruct the people there. I made

no comment. He also invited me to visit a French nuclear submarine. I declined this invitation.

7. We then discussed the beginnings of the French nuclear submarine program. I asked him why they had started with a graphite reactor. He said this was because there was no available supply of enriched uranium. He added that the person who had developed the water-cooled submarine reactor for the French had also recommended that the same type be used for central station plants, and that it was a mistake not to have followed his advice.

8. I told him that early in the 1950s, a French admiral had written in one of their naval magazines that it was better for France not to have an atomic submarine if the way they had to get it was to have a person like me head the project. I asked if he would be so kind as to find the article and send me a copy.

9. We discussed in general the advantages and disadvantages of gas-cooled, water-cooled, and liquid-metal reactors. He said that the French had had no significant problems with the gas and liquid-metal reactors. I told him that I had investigated gas, liquid-metal, and water-cooled reactors at the beginning of our submarine program. He knew about the SEA WOLF with its liquid-metal reactor. I told him I had come to the conclusion that water was the best coolant for submarine propulsion. We did not discuss the Shippingport breeder reactor except that I told him it was now in the testing period. He asked no questions about it, and I volunteered none.

10. He appeared very anxious to please me in anything I desired. I made no suggestion or offer about exchange of nuclear information with the French. I told him that the main reason we had not desired, in the early days, to exchange information with the French, Dutch, or the Italians was because of the possibility of this information leaking to the Russians

due to the prevalence of Communist parties in these countries. He replied that no Communists were employed in the
French atomic programs. I said this was unusual because
of the strength of the Communist Party in France and the
fact that they were so powerful they had nearly won the last
French election.

11. He said he would have his aide telephone me and make
arrangements for obtaining the information I requested
concerning the French liquid-metal breeder reactor.

1 February 1978

Memorandum of Telephone Conversation with President Carter

1. The president called me this morning answering my telephone call of yesterday.
2. I told him the subject of my discussion was comments on
his TV speaking. I made the following suggestions to him:
   a. When he reads from a prompter, the audience can tell
   his is not talking to them. He should face the camera as
   if he were looking at the people. This cannot be done by
   looking at a prompter.
   b. He should be himself completely. He must be oblivious
   to the camera and have fire in his belly. Any attempt at
   artificiality in this manner is readily discernable by the
   audience.
   c. Sometimes it appears he is searching for what to say next.
   d. He is a warm, decent, loving human being. Therefore,
   he should not be concerned that he will make a mistake.
   The people can tell if he is honest with them and will
   forgive the error. He can be too apprehensive about
   making a mistake.
   e. He is a teacher, not a salesman.

I added I did not want him to consider me as presumptuous in giving him the above information. As he knew, I was deeply concerned that he do the very best possible.
3. He said he thoroughly understood and thanked me.

28 April 1978

Letter to Richard Nixon

Dear Mr. President:

I want to express my appreciation for the time and assistance you gave Mr. Duncan in his work on a history of the naval nuclear propulsion program. He has told me that your recollections and insights gave him a new understanding of the importance of your visit to the Soviet Union in 1959.

I remember the trip clearly. One incident I particularly recall was the time in Leningrad when I asked your permission to remain on board the Lenin and argue with the Russians to keep their promise to let me see the nuclear spaces. I knew you recognized the importance of looking at an example of Russian nuclear engineering and would back me.

With this letter I am sending a copy of "How the Battleship Maine was Destroyed." It is almost certain the ship was destroyed by an interior explosion and not by the Spaniards. As you said to Mr. Duncan, the 1898 war led to vast consequences, many of which were not to the best interests of the United States. You may be interested in reading my comments on pages 105 and 106.

With my best wishes to Mrs. Nixon and to Julie

[Rickover's book inscription:]

With appreciation for your complete backing during your 1959 visit to Russia and Poland. Few men are capable of delegating responsibility in the way you permitted me to act. Only in this way can one do his best.

This results in the self-imposed responsibility to merit the trust placed in him; it also causes one to develop himself. In this manner you contributed to my life's work.

4 May 1978

Memorandum of Telephone Conversation with Secretary of Defense Harold Brown on 1 May 1978

1. I told Secretary Brown that, in continuation of our conversation of last Friday evening, I had additional comments concerning the efficiency of the Department of Defense. I asked if he was interested in hearing them; he said he was. I therefore made the following points:

   a. Many organizations in the Department of Defense are unilaterally creating functions for themselves, in addition to the specific duties for which they were set up. This is made possible by the frequent changing of officials, civilian and military, at all levels, particularly because there is no reasonable overlapping within echelons or with echelons above and below.

   b. Each time a new official is appointed, the permanent members of an echelon have another opportunity to promote their ideas for increasing the scope of the work and the number of people. There is never an idea for decreasing the scope and the people. Examples of this are:

1) Naval War College
2) Naval Material Command
3) Postgraduate Schools

2. Naval War College. Its original and primary function was the study of game plans for naval battles. Its faculty consisted of a small number of very senior line officers. The students were, or expected to become, admirals who would command the Fleet in wartime. Today, the Naval War College has been vastly expanded into an organization with many young students who are being taught international relations, systems analysis, business administration, etc. It essentially duplicates the functions of other existing schools. The present incumbent of the War College, Vice Admiral James B. Stockdale, is well known because he was a war prisoner in Hanoi for several years. He is undoubtedly a fine and brave officer. Recently, in an interview, he told about his experiences in the prison camp. He said that the classical reading he had done while at postgraduate school at Stanford had helped him stand up to the North Vietnamese. For this reason, he was now inaugurating in the War College curriculum studies of Thucydides, Aristotle, and various other historians and philosophers.

The questions that occurred to me was, "What does all this have to do with the primary function of the Naval War College?" I therefore called Admiral Stockdale and raised this issue. He became quite angry and said the reason I asked such a question was because I had never been in an actual war situation and couldn't understand—I have been in "actual war situations," but this does not affect my thoughts on the issue. Admiral Stockdale said such study was essential training for command. In reading the classics, he had learned fortitude and other characteristics which made a man more human.

I then asked him just why would an admiral in command of a fleet waging a naval battle against the enemy, have need of this ability? Would he permit thoughts of compassion and sympathy to influence him in his actions? I reiterated that I did not understand why teaching the classics was a function of the Naval War College. He replied that every officer would benefit by knowing the classics. I agreed, but repeated that I could not understand why they should be taught at the War College.

31 May 1978

Francis Duncan conversation with Admiral Rickover recounting a meeting of the Joint Committee on Atomic Energy in the 1950s on board NAUTILUS

Subj: Joint Committee Trip on the NAUTILUS

1. The admiral said that he had not realized the importance of taking the Joint Committee out on the NAUTILUS. He said that they understood the implications of nuclear propulsion at once. What he had not realized is how important these figures were in Congress and that by having convinced them he had won a very high position in Congress. He said he was a novice in these affairs.

2. He said that this paid off at the time the Department of Defense was trying to give a submarine to the French. He wanted to talk to Senator Anderson, who was on the floor of the Senate. Anderson came out, and they talked in the cloakroom. Rickover explained the problem and Anderson said, "Lyndon owes me one." And this was a factor—but how I don't know—in defeating the plans to sell a submarine to the French…

31 May 1978

[Francis Duncan - Brief notes on Conversation with Admiral Rickover]
Subj: Design Philosophy

1. [Rickover] said that he conscientiously designed and built with a future in mind. That was why he took such pains with the prototype hull in Idaho for the NAUTILUS. He said that he put the Shippingport plant underground and only recently have some people begun to recognize the wisdom of this decision.
2. He stationed his own representatives at Shippingport with authority to close the plant down if necessary.

8 May 1978

Letter from Richard Nixon

Dear Admiral,

I appreciated your letter of April 28 and will read your book on the "Maine" with great interest.

It was a pleasure to talk to Mr. Duncan. I hope he gets across the point that the State Department bureaucrats raised hell because they thought you had been too tough on the Russians when they tried to give you a "snow job" when you insisted on inspecting the "Lenin"! It was one of the best decisions I made on the trip, and I am glad you were there to do the job that needed to be done.

Keep fighting!
Sincerely,
Richard Nixon

7 June 1978

President Carter addressing the graduating USNA Class of 1978

I invited my old boss, Admiral Hyman Rickover, to come and join us. He sent word back he would, of course, comply with my orders as Commander-in-Chief, but he thought that his work for the Navy in Washington was more important than listening to my speech and...I was not surprised.

7 July 1978

[Conversation by Rickover and recorded by Francis Duncan]

You can never do something without taking a point of view. To be vague is of no value.

I am not interested in copies of myself. I do not want to look in a mirror all the time. I try to look for people who can object to what I do, in a positive way, and propose something else.

You cannot express new ideas with old material. History shows that constantly. When you desire to accomplish something new, you must pick a man who has a new thought corresponding to the new material.

19 July 1978

(Private copy to ADM Watkins[108] regarding United States [Naval] Institute Proceedings)

---

108 Admiral James Watkins (1927–2012), U.S. Naval Academy Class of 1949. Chief of Naval Operations 1982–1986. At the time of this letter, Watkins was serving as Chief of Naval Personnel but would leave three days later to serve as Commander, Sixth Fleet.

Until June 1975, applicants for membership in the United States Naval Institute were informed that the mission of the organization was "the advancement of professional, literary, and scientific knowledge in the Navy." In Jun 1975, applicants were told the mission of the Institute was "the advancement of professional, literary, and scientific knowledge in the naval and maritime services, and the advancement of the knowledge of seapower." The change was made to broaden the program of service to provide professionally oriented publications for members of the Navy, Marine Corps, Coast Guard, and others concerned with seapower.

The following questions might be asked about the Institute and *Proceedings*.

1. The change of purpose was an acknowledgement of a trend of several years. Has broadening the mission led to the dilution of the professional purpose for which the Institute was founded and *Proceedings* was published?

    The June 1935 issue, for example, had ten articles, among them Rear Admiral Yates Stirling, Jr., on "Sea Power," Admiral William S. Sims on "Service Opinion Upon Promotion by Selection," Captain L.S. Border (C.C.) on "Planning and Estimating at Navy Yards," Lieutenant Commander Robert B. Carney on "Selection, Seniority, and Morale," and Rear Admiral John W. Greenslade on "Security of National Interests." Of these articles, all but three were by officers on active duty.

    The June 1978 issue contained five articles, two of which were by officers on active duty. The highest ranking officer was Captain James D. Elliot with "A Solution to Retention." The prevalence in recent issues of historical, anecdotal, and leadership articles is another indication that *Proceedings* does not have a clear mission.

2. The presence of very high-ranking officers on the Board of Control, most of whom are naval officers on active duty, gives the inevitable impression of a naval imprimatur to the

articles in *Proceedings*, despite the disclaimer that the views of the authors are not necessarily those of the Navy. If the purpose of *Proceedings* is no longer exclusively naval, should the membership of the Board of Control and its functions be reconsidered?

3. If the mission of *Proceedings* has become broadened, is it appropriate that its offices be located on the grounds of the Academy? The location of these offices, the fact that most of the annual meetings have been held at the Academy in Academy facilities, cast doubt upon the disclaimer that the Institute is "not a part of the U.S. Navy Department."

4. Does the Institute pay for the space that it occupies and the Academy facilities that it uses?

15 September 1978

[Francis Duncan conversation with the admiral]

Yesterday evening, the admiral began talking about his career and the modern practice of individuals trying to make images.

He said he did not do this. He was not concerned with developing a recognizable personality; that came naturally. He believes that if a person tries to establish a recognizable image that his real work will suffer, and he will not accomplish much.

He said that when he was in the academy, he had to repress himself because he knew that he would have a hard time to stay in. He thought that if there had been a vote taken of the midshipman most likely to make Admiral, he would have ranked very low. It was when he got out of the academy that he decided that what he would do would be to focus upon getting the job done.

2 October 1978

Letter to Helen Press Kovarsky

Dear Mrs. Kovarsky

Thank you for your letter of September 20. It is good to hear from one who was a neighbor during my early years in Chicago.

I well remember when we lived on Grenshaw Street. I worked for your father when I was 10 and 11 years old. In the earth floor basement of the house, I helped him operate a machine that was used to shape galvanized sheet metal for ornamental and other uses in the construction of buildings in that area during 1910–1912.

As I recall, there was no artificial lighting in the dark basement, and I would hold a kerosene lantern so that your father could see to operate the machine. My pay was three cents an hour. Later on, your father had a store located on the left side of 12th Street in the block between Troy and the next street east.

At one period in the years we both lived on Grenshaw Street, the street surface was replaced with asphalt. This made it necessary to remove the roadbed of wood blocks that had been laid down in their original shapes as cut from the trees.

I gathered these blocks and chopped them up into firewood for use in the kitchen stove.

It was thoughtful of you to write.

2 October 1978

Letter to Admiral Watkins

Mr. Wegner has given me a copy of your letter to the Naval Institute and Commander Bowler's reply. I agree that this issue should not be continued.

If Commander Bowler's reply is typical of the logic and acuity of top management of the Naval Institute *Proceedings*, the Navy is in a sad way as far as its "official" organ is concerned. Under the circumstances. I believe we would be better off if *Proceedings* were abolished. In actuality, it is doing harm.

With my best regards to you and your family,

13 October 1978

Portion of speech in Charleston before the Charleston Council of the Navy League

It takes a great man to stand alone in the "Arena" that is the Office of the Presidency, and President Carter is such a man. He has the patience, the courage, and the quiet authority that enables him to strive and solve the many issues and problems which confront him daily. He brings a spiritual and practical philosophy to the awesome burden that is his alone. And he has the experience, determination, and strength of character, combined with high resolve and patriotism, to perform his duties in the best interest of the United States.

23 October 1978

[Francis Duncan conversation with Rickover]
Subj: Discussion with Chief Justice Burger

1. The admiral said he had lunch with Chief Justice Burger about Constitutional Conventions. The chief justice said he would read the memorandum the admiral gave him and call the admiral back. The two men discussed the Skokie Case, the Bakke Case, European law, and lawyers, and the state of the country. The chief justice showed the admiral a picture of his grandfather who lost an arm in the Civil War.

2. The admiral said that he thought topics of this kind might be useful in the final chapter to show that anecdotes are not sufficient to explain all that goes on here.

9 November 1978

Memorandum of Discussion with President Carter at the White House on 8 November 1978

1. The meeting, although scheduled for 15 minutes, lasted about half an hour. I gave the president the material shown on the attached list.
2. In connection with the calling of a Constitutional Convention, he said it might be a good idea to limit the subjects the Convention should discuss. I replied it was doubtful this could be done. A Constitutional Convention would consist of citizens from each State. It was the purest form of democracy—the people themselves considered and recommended changes to our form of government.
   Members of the original Constitutional Convention had, in some cases, been given instructions by their States as to what issues they should consider. However, they had gone beyond this, and this had never been made an issue by the States concerned. After the Civil War, a number of Southern States held constitutional conventions. In most cases, these men had not considered themselves limited to specific issues. I said I doubted the Supreme Court would sustain a limitation on the subjects to be considered by a Constitutional Convention.
3. The president asked what I thought of the Israeli situation. I replied that, as he knew, I had never made an attempt to discuss this issue with him, nor had I done so with the Israelis, members of the executive branch, or of Congress. On a number of occasions, I had been approached by Israeli

officials visiting the local Embassy and by organizations concerned with Israelis but, because of my official position, I
had never become involved.

4. He then asked me what I thought of the solution. I replied
that I believed the major consideration of the Israelis was
security. He said he believed the acquisition of the East Bank
by Israel was a mistake because the Israelis already had a
large percentage of Arabs within their existing borders, and
the acquisition of additional territory would exacerbate this.
I told him of an article I had recently read in the New Republic about Hannah Arendt. Many Jews have been critical
of her because of her book on the Eichmann trial. In this
book she had been critical of Israel. The article pointed out
that her thesis was that the Jews in Germany had not been
assimilated into the German body politic in that they had
never become part of the political structure. She said it was
not sufficient for a minority group to acquire economic and
other rights; they would never become a true member of the
nation unless they engaged in politics and their members
were elected to office, as for example the Catholics in Germany who had become an integral part of the country.

5. I said that, in my opinion, she was wrong in this concept
because it was the Germans who had refused to admit the
Jews into the political life of the country. In the case of Israel,
the Arab population was close in number to that of the Jews.
Further, Israel was surrounded by a vast number of Arabs.
If such a small country gave complete political equality to
the Arabs, they would soon be overwhelmed by them and
would lose their identity.

6. I thought that one solution to the territorial problem would
be for Saudi Arabia to guarantee the Israeli borders. I said
that I believed the friendship between the United States and
Saudi Arabia was sufficient for him to broach the subject
with them. He replied that the United States did have a

friendly relationship with them. I said that if he thought it would be worthwhile for me to discuss the matter with Saudi officials, I would be glad to do so.

7. I then discussed a possible visit by me to China. He asked what I thought about Chinese credibility. I replied that my study of Chinese history, my experience in China, as well as their current actions gave me assurance that the Chinese were reliable people with whom we could deal. He agreed.

8. I said it would help the United States in our relationship with Russia if we became an ally of China. I considered it would be beneficial to the United States if we helped China acquire atomic submarines. This would be a great concern to the Russians. He said he would think about this.

9. I told him I considered he had made a mistake in canceling the fifth nuclear-powered carrier. I knew he was seeking economy in government to reduce inflation, but I believed he could save far more money by building up to a Navy of six nuclear carriers, and placing most of the others out of commission. In this connection, I said he should be aware that the way the Secretary of the Navy was handling shipbuilding claims would not contribute to his policy of controlling inflation.

10. I told the president that Secretary of Defense Brown had never asked to see me. He was surprised. I said this does not bother me, but I thought he might benefit in running the Defense Department by listening to some of my ideas. He said he would talk to Secretary Brown about this.

12 February 1979

[Letter from the fiancée of a midshipman. During his interviews with applicants, he would often tell them to have a family member or someone else write in defense of the applicant.]

Sir,

This letter is in reference to your request of my fiance' Midshipman _____ 1/C, who has recently applied for your Nuclear Power Program. I understand the elements of your request and am willing to make the following proposal.

In order to facilitate his study efforts, I will agree to insist that I see him only one weekend per month.

13 February 1979

Memorandum of Telephone Conversation with Mr. F.W. O'Green, President, Litton Industries Inc.

I called Mr. O'Green at Pascagoula, Mississippi to discuss Ingalls' performance on nuclear submarine work. I told him the following:

- Ingalls is the worst in schedule and cost performance of any shipyard, including Navy yards, in overhauling nuclear submarines, and this has been the situation for years.
- It is a constant aggravation to deal with Ingalls in submarine work. The Navy has written letters repeatedly for a long time pointing out the problems at Ingalls. We get good letters in reply but no results. Ingalls is the only yard that is not improving in this work.
- The situation is such that it would save money for me to go to Congress and request $50 million to give Ingalls in return for not taking submarine work over the next ten years.

I asked Mr. O'Green for his comment. He said unfortunately he could not refute what I said. I stated I intend to tell Congress about this situation the next time I testify. He said if he were I, he would do the very same thing.

360

I then asked Mr. O'Green for his solution. He said he would get back to me in a couple of days.

21 February 1979

[Note typed by Francis Duncan]

I asked [Rickover] about how he got into submarines. He did it to further his career. He had been to [Naval Post Graduate] school, and his contemporaries were getting ahead of him. He thought the chances of command were better in submarines. He remembers going to the school and being about four years older than anybody else. He had written his thesis on batteries and had written a manual chapter on the subject, but this did not excuse him from the assignments at the submarine school, and he learned quickly that they did not want him to volunteer the information that he had.

11 May 1979

[Speech] "...To Form a More Perfect Union..." by Admiral H.G. Rickover, USN

I believe we in the United States today must reassess our governmental machinery if we are to continue as a democracy. The reason for the reassessment is simple: conditions change. Political systems which worked well in one age may grow weak and falter with the passage of time. The failure may not be in the principles but in the working of the government. In the proposal I am going to make, one principle must be clearly understood. I firmly believe in a democracy that recognizes the work and dignity of the individual. Nothing in the words that follow alters that fact.

Since the end of World War II, the country has changed drastically. In 1950, the population of the United States was slightly over 151 million. In 1980, it is expected to be over 222 million, an increase of over 45 percent. Although the increase in numbers alone is serious, the demographic character of our population is also shifting. We can see the impact on the demands for social services. The flow of people into the cities, even if no longer what it was, still raises staggering problems. Our schools, transportation systems, waste collection and disposal, and forces for maintaining safety, law, and order are hard-pressed to meet the essential needs of communities. The plight of New York City is only the most striking instance of the urban financial crisis. In the economic arena, the growing power of conglomerates and the decline in the rate of increase of American productivity are very troubling phenomena—and the two are connected. Conglomerates, mass media, and the increasing use of computers for storing financial and personal information are transforming our society in ways that make the future hard to predict.

Evidence of uneasiness and frustration is on every hand. In newspaper columns, editorial pages, and letters to the editor, we read of worry over inflation and government spending. There is resentment against a proliferating and multi-layered bureaucracy that promises much and delivers little. Regulatory agencies too often seem captured and corrupted by the very segment of commerce or industry from which they are intended to protect us. The weakening of the traditional two-party political system, with its ability to compromise, is giving way to single issue groups, which are adding a new, sharp, and abrasive quality to the political scene.

Today, the growing number of references to constitutional amendments and constitutional conventions shows a questioning of our political institutions that cannot be ignored. Chief Justine Warren E. Burger, speaking in 1978 before the Seminar on Legal History, offered an interesting proposal. He suggested a series of studies over several years to see if the three major branches of the government are "faithful to the spirit of the Constitution" or whether in many instances we have not gone wrong.

My experience leads me to the firm conclusion that over the last quarter of a century, the burden of bureaucracy has become so great as to prevent the functioning of government. It is impossible for the president, the Congress, and the Supreme Court to do their jobs properly. The more specialized and intricate the government is, the more it is subjected to undermining by special interests. The less the government is able to respond to the needs of the people, the more they feel that events are beyond their control. Nothing is more fatal to the spirit of democracy than citizens who believe their lives and work no longer have meaning...

I cannot grasp the logic of the politician who congratulates the voters on their wisdom in electing him, yet asserts that constitutional matters are too complex to trust to the very same voters. I cannot grasp the logic of the columnists and editorial writers who explain to their readers the intricacies of government, but deny that they have the intelligence to understand the fundamentals of government. Another point these individuals forget: juries are an essential part of our judicial system. If we consider ordinary citizens wise enough to decide on the issue of life or death, why cannot we trust them to judge ways to improve the government?

The Constitution is not the sacrosanct preserve of the politicians, the press, or professors. It belongs to us all.

...We are no less capable than the men of Philadelphia. By providing means for changing the Constitution, they had faith in us. We can justify that faith by calling a constitutional convention as set forth by Article V.

...I believe it should, among other things, provide for a constitutional convention to meet every fifty years. A reading of our history, a survey of the problems we face today, and the shadows of the difficulties that lie ahead call for a flexibility and an opportunity to calmly and rationally assess how well the government is maintaining the rights and duties of its citizens...

Another proposal I want to offer deals with the relations between the federal government and the states. One of the greatest problems we face is the imbalance between the two. Despite efforts to return power to the states, very little has been accomplished. The federal government's activities in welfare, finances, and regulatory matters has been a centripetal force leading to an accretion of power in Washington. The Founding Fathers had to consider the relations between thirteen states, with the anticipation that additions to this number would come slowly. But now we have fifty, not thirteen...

Our government is too large to manage; the problems are too big for the states. What we need are centers of authority between the individual states and Washington. My idea is to divide the country into several groups of states, say six or seven. All functions would be removed from the Federal government, which can be performed by these groups of states. They would assume responsibility for education, welfare, transportation, postal services, and other matters. The Federal government would be confined to international affairs, military matters, and foreign trade.

The concept is practical. We already have regional undertakings which cross state lines...

Accountability in the use of power is the greatest safeguard of democracy.

American is at a true crossroads in its history, not simply at an arbitrary vantage point dictated by the calendar but by something far more serious... It is for this reason that I propose a Constitutional Convention...

13 May 1979

[Speech] "Thoughts on Man's Purpose in Life," Address at the Commencement Ceremony of Hampden-Sydney College, Virginia

Voltaire once said, "Not to be occupied, and not to exist are one and the same thing for a man." With those few words he captured the essence of a purpose in life: to work, to create, to excel, and to be concerned about the world and its affairs.

The question of what we can do to give purpose or meaning to our lives has been debated for thousands of years by philosophers and common men. Yet today we seem, if anything, further from the answer than before. Despite our great material wealth, and high standard of living, people are groping for something that money cannot buy. As Walter Lippman said, "Our life, though it is full of things, is empty of the kind of purpose and effort that gives to life its flavor and meaning."

I do not claim to have a magic answer. But I believe there are some basic principles of existence, propounded by thinkers though the ages, which can guide us toward the goal of finding a purpose in life.

Among these principles of existence, responsibility is the one which forces man to become involved. Acceptance of responsibility means that the individual takes upon himself an obligation. Responsibility is broad and continuous. None of us are ever free of it, even if our work is unsuccessful.

Responsibility implies a commitment to self which many are not willing to make; they are strongly attracted to accepting a course of action or direction for their lives, imposed by an external source. Such a relationship absolves the individual from the personal decision-making process. He wraps himself in the security blanket of inevitability or dogma, and need not invest the enormous amounts of time, effort, and above all, the thought required to make creative decisions, and meaningfully participate in the governance of his life.

The sense of responsibility for doing a job right seems to be declining. In fact, the phrase "I am not responsible" has become a standard response in our society to complaints on a job poorly done. This response is a semantic error. Generally, what a person means is, "I cannot be held legally liable." Yet, from a moral or ethical point of view, the person who disclaims responsibility is correct. By taking this way out, he is truly not responsible: he is irresponsible.

The unwillingness to act and to accept responsibility is a symptom of America's growing self-satisfaction with the status quo. The result is a paralysis of the spirit, entirely uncharacteristic of Americans during the previous stages of our history.

The task of finding a purpose in life also calls for perseverance. I have seen many young men who rush out into the world with their messages, and when they find out how deaf the world is, they withdraw, to wait and save their strength. They believe that after a while they will be able to get up on some little peak from which they can make themselves heard. Each thinks that in a few years, he will have gained a standing, and then he can use his power for good. Finally, the time comes, and with it a strange discovery: he has lost his horizon of thought. Without perseverance, ambition and a sense of responsibility have evaporated.

Another important principle of existence which gives purpose and meaning to life is excellence. Because the conviction to strive for excellence is an intensely personal one, the attainment of excellence is personally satisfying. Happiness comes from the full use of one's power to achieve excellence. Life is potentially an empty hole, and there are few more satisfying ways of filling it than by achieving and exercising excellence.

This principle of excellence is one which Americans seem to be losing, and, at a time when the nation stands in need of it. A lack of excellence implies mediocrity. And, in a society that is willing to accept a standard of mediocrity, the opportunities for personal failure are boundless. Mediocrity can destroy us, just as surely as perils far more famous.

It is important that we distinguish between what it means to fail at a task, and what it means to be mediocre. There is all the difference in the world between the life lived with dignity and style, which ends in failure, and one which achieves power and glory, yet is dull, unoriginal, unreflective, and mediocre. In a real sense, what matters is not so much whether we make a lot of money, or hold a prestigious job; what matters is that we seek out others with knowledge and enthusiasm—that we became people who can enjoy our own company.

In the end, avoiding mediocrity gives us the chance to discover that success comes in making ourselves into educated individuals, able to recognize that there is a difference between living with excellence and living with mediocrity.

Creativity is another of the basic principles of existence, which I believe help to give purpose in life. The deepest joy in life is to be creative. To find an undeveloped situation, to see the possibilities, to decide upon a course of action, and then devote the whole of one's resources to carry it out, even if it means battling against the stream of contemporary opinion, is a satisfaction in comparison with which superficial pleasures are trivial.

To create you must care. You must have the courage to speak out. The world's advances have always depended on the courage of its leaders. A certain measure of courage in the private citizen also is necessary for the good conduct of the State. Otherwise, men who have power through riches, intrigue, or office will administer the State at will, and ultimately to their private advantage.

To have courage means to pursue your goals, or to satisfy your responsibilities, even though others stand in the way, and success seems like a dream. It takes courage to stand and fight for what you believe is right. And the fight never ends. You have to start it over again each morning as the sun rises. Sir Thomas More wrote, "If evil persons cannot be quite rooted out, and if you cannot correct habitual attitudes as you wish, you must not therefore abandon the commonwealth. You must strive to guide policy indirectly, so that you make the best things, and what you cannot turn to good, you can at least make less bad."

These principles of existence—responsibility, perseverance, excellence, creativity, courage—must be wedded with intellectual growth and development if we are to find meaning and purpose in our lives. It is a device of the devil to let sloth into the world. By the age of twenty, some of us have already adopted a granite-like attitude, which we maintain throughout life. Intellectually, we must never stop growing. Our conscience should never release us from concern for the problems of the day. Our minds must be forever skeptical, yet questioning. We must strive to be singularly free from that failing so common to man, deplored by Pascal in the "Pensees," of filling our leisure with meaningless distractions, so as to preclude the necessity of thought. To be an intellectual in the fullest sense, one's mind must be in constant movement.

Aristotle believed that happiness was to be found in the use of the intellect. In other words, ignorance is not bliss; it is oblivion. The inspired prayer does not ask for health, wealth, prosperity, or anything material, but says, "God, illuminate my intellect." Man cannot find purpose in his life without expanding and using his intellectual qualities and capacities. Liberal learning is a primary source of these qualities. By liberal learning, I refer to discerning taste; wise judgment, informed and critical perspectives that transcend specialized interests and partisan passions; the capacity to understand complexity, and to grow in response to it.

A cause of many of our mistakes and problems is ignorance—an overwhelming national ignorance of the facts about the rest of the world. A nation, or an individual, cannot function unless the truth is available and understood; no amount of good on the part of the leaders or the media will offset ignorance and apathy in the common citizen. Since the United States is a democracy, the broad answer is that all of us must become better informed. Reading is one method of accomplishing this purpose. By spending a few dollars for a book, the thoughts and life's work of a great man are available to us.

As a reader, man is unique among living things. The ability to read—and more broadly, the ability to express complex ideas through language—distinguishes him from all other life forms. Without language, complex thought is inconceivable, and the mind is undeveloped. The inability to speak and write imprisons thought. In the same vein, sloppy, imprecise thinking begets sloppy, imprecise language. Language and thought are interconnected, and the written word is the vehicle which best advances both.

Therefore, I count reading, and its associated skill, writing, among the most significant of all human efforts. Good writing, after all, is simply the result of enormous reading, detailed research, and careful thought. It means studying to gain a good vocabulary, and practicing to learn how to use it. It seems to me that these kindred skills should be developed and nourished from the very first, if man is to grow intellectually. And unless he can express his thoughts well, he can exert little influence on his fellow men.

I now will discuss one final principle of existence essential to man's purpose in life: the development of standards of ethical and moral conduct. God, it is generally conceded, has made a remarkable job of the physical universe, but has, strangely, not done quite so well with the spiritual element. There is abundant evidence around us to conclude that morals and ethics are becoming less prevalent in people's lives. The standards of conduct are no longer are absolute. Many people seem unable to differentiate between physical relief and moral satisfaction; they confuse material success in life with virtue.

We are now living on the accumulated moral capital of traditional religion. It is running out, and we have no other consensus of values to take its place. This is partly so because man can now obtain on earth what previously was vouch-saved him when he reached heaven.

In our system of society, no authority exists to tell us what is good and desirable. We are free to seek what we think good in our own way. The danger is that where men compromise truth and let decency slip, they eventually end up with neither. A free society can survive only through men and women of integrity. Fortunately, there still exist human beings who remain concerned about moral and ethical values, and justice towards others. These are the individuals who provide hope of the ultimate realism that is marked by a society's capacity to survive rather than to be eventually destroyed.

It is important also to recognize that morals and ethics are not relative; they do not depend on the situation. This may be the hardest principle to follow in working to achieve goals. The ends, no matter how worthy they appear, cannot justify just any means. Louis Brandeis,[109] who was deeply convinced of the importance of

---

109 American jurist (1856–1941) who was an Associate Justice on the Supreme Court, 1916–1939.

standards, said, "One can never be sure of ends—political, social, economic. There must always be doubt and difference of opinion." But Brandeis had no doubt about means. "Fundamentals do not change; centuries of thought have established standards. Lying and sneaking are always bad, no matter what the ends."

This is a very enabling statement. Life is not meaningless for the man who considers certain actions wrong, simply because they are wrong, whether or not they violate a law. This kind of moral code gives a person a focus, a basis on which to conduct himself. Certainly, there is a temptation to let go of morals in order to do the expedient thing. But there is also a tremendous power in standing by what is right. Principle and accomplishment need not be incompatible.

A common thread moves through all the principles I have discussed: it is the desire to improve oneself and one's surroundings by actively participating in life. Too many succumb to the emotional preference of the comfortable solution, instead of the difficult one. It is easy to do nothing. And to do nothing is also an act—an act of indifference or cowardice.

A person must prepare himself intellectually and professionally, and then use his powers to their fullest extent. This view is well expressed in two extracts from I Ching, the Confucian Book of Changes:

- The superior man learns and accumulates the results of his learning; asks questions, and discriminates among those results; dwells magnanimously and unambitiously in what he has attained to; and carries it into practice with benevolence
- The superior man nerves himself to ceaseless activity

To find a purpose in life, one must be willing to act, to put excellence in one's work, and have concern for what is right ahead of personal safety. Life must be felt, not observed. But to do so means applying oneself to the task daily. Ralph Waldo Emerson said, "God offers to every mind its choice between truth and repose. Take which you please—you can never have both."

No professional man has the right to prefer his own personal peace to the happiness of mankind; his place and his duty are in the frontline of struggling men, not in the unperturbed ranks of those who keep themselves aloof from life. If a profession is to have its proper place in the further development of society, it must be increasingly dissatisfied with things as they are. If there is to be any exaltation in one's work, one must learn to reach out, not to struggle for that which is just beyond, but to grasp at results which seem almost infinite. As Robert Browning wrote, "Ah, but a man's reach should exceed his grasp, or what's a Heaven for."

Man's work begins with his job, his profession. Having a vocation is something of a miracle, like falling in love. I can understand why Luther said that a man is justified by his vocation, for it is a proof of God's favor. But having a vocation means more than punching a timeclock. It means guarding against banality, ineptitude, incompetence, and mediocrity. A man should strive to become a locus of excellence.

Most of the work in the world today is done by those who work too hard; they comprise a "nucleus of martyrs." The greater part of the remaining workers' energy goes into complaining. Employees today seldom become emotional about their organization or its output; they are only interested in making money or getting ahead. And many organizations are killing their employees with kindness, undercutting their sense of responsibility with an ever-increasing permissiveness. This is a fatal error. For where responsibility ends, performance ends also. Man has a large capacity for effort. But it is so much greater than we think it is, that few ever reach this capacity.

We should value the faculty of knowing what we ought to do, and having the will to do it. But understanding is easy. It is the doing that is difficult. The critical issue is not what we know, but what we do with what we know. The great end of life is not knowledge, but action. Theodore Roosevelt expressed this concept well in his "Man in the Arena" statement:

"It is not the critic who counts, not the one who points out how the strong man stumbled, or how the doer of deeds might have done them better. The credit belongs to the man who is actually in the arena, whose face is marred with sweat, and dust, and blood; who strives valiantly; who errs and comes short again and again; who knows the great enthusiasms, the great devotions, and spends himself in a worthy cause; who, if he wins, knows the triumph of high achievement; and who, if he fails, at least fails while daring greatly, so that his place shall never be with those cold and timid souls who know neither victory nor defeat."

The man in the arena has found a purpose in life. He daily experiences Emerson's declaration that nothing is achieved without enthusiasm. He knows that men seldom come within shouting distance of their hopes for themselves. Yet he does not quit in resignation, as have those who have taken trouble with nothing except to be born. In his work he is buffeted from two sides: challenged by his own ideas, which revolt at the compromises of reality, and assaulted by reality, which fights the ideas. He spends himself in that struggle, and he wins by a constant renewal of effort in which he refuses to sink either into placid acceptance of the situation or into self-satisfaction.

I believe it is the duty of each of us to act as if the fate of the world depended on him. Admittedly, one man by himself cannot do the job. However, one man can make a difference. Each of us is obligated to bring his individual and independent capacities to bear upon a wide range of human concerns. It is with this conviction that we squarely confront our duty to posterity. We must live for the future, not for our own comfort or success.

For anyone seeking meaning for his life, a figure from Greek mythology comes to mind. It is that of Atlas, bearing with endless perseverance the weight of the heavens on his back—Atlas, resolutely bearing his burden and accepting his responsibility, gives us the example we seek.

For a more modern source, I will refer to St. Matthew, Chapter 6, verses 14–15: "For if ye forgive men their trespasses, your heavenly Father will also forgive you: But if ye forgive not men their trespasses, neither will your Father forgive your trespasses." And then from St. Luke, Chapter 6, verse 37: "Judge not, and ye shall not be judged: condemn not, and ye shall not be condemned: forgive, and ye shall be forgiven."

To seek out and accept responsibility; to persevere; to be committed to excellence; to be creative and courageous; to be unrelenting in the pursuit of intellectual development; to maintain high standards of ethics and morality; and to bring these basic principles of existence to bear, through active participation in life—these are some of my ideas on the goals which must be met to achieve meaning and purpose in life.

1 June 1979

Memorandum of Conversation with President Carter at my Apartment on 31 May 1979

1. Unbeknownst to me, my wife had invited the president, Mrs. Carter, and Amy to have dinner with us on 31 May. She had told me the dinner was for a friend who belonged to a religious group and would be coming over with her husband, a lieutenant colonel in the Air Force, and their young 10-year-old daughter.
2. While awaiting the arrival of the lieutenant colonel and his family, there was a knock on the door. When I opened the door, in walked President Carter, Rosalynn, and Amy.
3. I later learned that the genesis for this visit was the airplane trip to Groton for the keel-laying ceremony of the GEORGIA by Mrs. Carter. My wife and I had been on the same plane

with Mrs. Carter and, on the return trip to Washington, my wife had discussed (without my knowledge) the possibility of having them to dinner. It seems that for the past week many arrangements had been made—telephone calls, security checks by Secret Service personnel, etc., of which I had not been aware.

4. The president and his family were with us for about three hours. This gave me an opportunity to have lengthy discussions on a number of subjects. I will mention these as I remember them, though not necessarily in the order of their occurrence.

- Black Leadership. I said I was distressed with the attitude of the black leadership in the United States. It appeared to me they were more interested in their own self-advancement than in the advancement of the black people. I said I would appreciate his not making any comments on what I was saying in this matter, so that it could never be construed he agreed or disagreed with me. The president said he would make no comments.

I said I had dealt with Benjamin Hooks and Vernon Jordan. I had also met Coretta King on a plane trip two years ago from Washington to Atlanta. I sat next to her and had heard her talking to a companion. When I asked her if she was the wife of Martin Luther King, she said she was. Thereupon I said, "You don't look as good as your pictures." For some reason, she seemed surprised and distressed at this comment. That was the only opportunity I had to speak with her. She turned away and thereafter talked only with her companion.

I told the president that my impression on all the occasions I have spoken with black leaders was that they were more interested in advancing their own personal interests than in pushing for the needs and welfare of blacks in general. I contrasted this with the attitude years ago when wealthy Jewish leaders often took responsibility on themselves to improve the condition of the Jewish people in the United States. I recounted how I had tried to interest Mr. Hooks at a meeting in New York on 9 September 1977, in improving the education of black youth. (Enclosure 1)

As far as the government's attitude and actions relating to minorities was concerned, I told him there had been a letter recently from a black leader to *The New York Times* stating that the time had come for blacks not to ask for special treatment. I said I would send him a copy of the letter and replies to it. (Enclosure 2)

The president said that Reverend Jesse Jackson was trying to help black youth. I agreed, and said I had once talked to him on the telephone and asked that he arrange for us to meet in order to discuss the matter. I had never heard from him. The president replied that he would telephone Jesse Jackson and discuss with him a meeting with me.

- Political Action Committees. Next, I discussed the vast power being acquired in the United States by large conglomerates through their lobbyists in Congress. It appeared to me that they were, in essence, running the United States. As a student of history, I knew of no period in the history of the United States, including the 1880s after the Civil War, when lobbying was so prevalent. In those times it was for land, railroads, and mining rights. But today this has extended into all aspects of politics, business, and industry. The president agreed.
  - o I told the president that, as far as I could determine, there was considerable suborning of Congress by large campaign contributions from industry to Members of Congress and to State officials from

375

funds that the law permits them to obtain from their officials. I had personally witnessed this in connection with the Renegotiation Board.

o The president said he fully supported the Renegotiation Act but was not able to get it through Congress. I told him about the time Congressman McCloskey of California had obtained the signatures of a majority of House Members to a petition to kill the Act. Later I learned that many of the signers did not know what they were signing.

o I said it would be a fine thing for the United States if Congress enacted the bill, which would give $75,000 to each Member of Congress toward financing his campaign. The president said he did not think the bill would get through Congress this session.

- The Party System. We then had a lengthy discussion on Congress. I said that the party system had gone by the board. The president was once the leader of his party, but today Congress was largely fragmented with committees, subcommittees, and their large staffs. These bloated staffs were, for example, keeping Energy Department officials busy testifying and answering questions, so that it was almost impossible to get any work done.

o I recalled Clarence Cannon's attitude on staffs. I said I had been very close to him when he was Chairman of the House Appropriations Committee. In fact, he had invited me to his home where he played the piano for me. Time and again the members of his committee had urged him to increase the staff. He had invariably refused to do so. I said I considered this an excellent example to follow in view of the great proliferation of congressional staffs in recent years. For example, the Energy Department must now deal with about 38 committees and subcommittees. This means that all Energy Department officials have most of their time taken up testifying. The president agreed.

- o The president mentioned that he received considerable help from Senator Byrd, the Majority Leader of the Senate, but he did not get as much help from Congressman O'Neil, the Speaker of the House.

- o I mentioned that Mussolini had set up a corporate state in Italy in 1921. He had organized the government on the basis that there would be equal representation in the Italian Parliament among government, industry, and the public. However, as this fascist system actually worked out, the representatives from government and industry actually controlled the government; the representatives of the people had little power.

- <u>SALT Talks</u>. I told the president I thought it would be a good idea to consummate the SALT talks quickly in order to reduce tension between the United States and Russia. I once more recommended that upon consummation of the SALT Treaty, he should initiate naval disarmament talks to reduce the cost of military forces throughout the world. He made no comment.

- <u>Fast Russian Submarine</u>. The president asked about the Russian 40-knot submarine. I said that our 688-Class, by taking certain measures, could probably make about four knots more than its present speed and we would therefore be close to the Russian's speed. I said the Russian submarine was a test vehicle and not a complete combat submarine, as was the 688.

  - o I said that while issues were being made that we were behind the Russians in speed and numbers of ships, the Navy civilian sector was recommending at the very same time that we reduce the speed of our

submarines. I said the 688-Class was a fine submarine and should be continued.

- The Naval Nuclear Program. I told the president that I had
never spoken out against any administration stand on the
Navy or any other matter. He agreed with this. However,
in connection with the aircraft carrier, I said I considered
him to be in error in advocating a 53,000-ton carrier, which
could only carry a small number of planes. I said if there was
to be an additional carrier, it should be nuclear powered for
reasons he well knew—particularly with the oil crisis becoming more severe. I could see no purpose in spending money
to build a 53,000-ton carrier or even a Kennedy Class carrier
if his objective was to save money. I recommended that he
cancel his request for any carrier other than a nuclear one.
I said I knew it was not my decision to make—whether we
should have an additional carrier or how many carriers were
to be in operation—but if there were to be another carrier, it
should be nuclear powered.
  - o I mentioned there were now 12 carriers in opera-
    tion. How that number had been decided I did not
    know, and suggested this should be looked into. I
    said that possibly the National Security Council had
    decided the number.
- Shipbuilding Claims. I told the president that at the present
time two grand juries were investigating the Newport News
Shipbuilding and Dry Dock Company and the Electric Boat
Division of General Dynamics on potential fraud.
- DC 10. I said that it may be worthwhile having the FAA
investigate whether there were requirements for routine
inspections of this aircraft. Also, whether records were kept,
and whether these were listed in detail and whether those
persons conducting the inspections signed for each item
inspected. Also, whether the basic design of the plane had

even been checked by an agency other than the company that designed and manufactured it.

- o I said that in the Navy's nuclear program, we had kept records from the beginning of each item to see that it had met all inspections. In fact, we had records of each weld in the ship, as well as for the equipment installed going back to when it was being manufactured. We could go back years later and consult the record of the welding rod used, who made the weld, who inspected it, and the signatures of those who certified the work.

- o I suggested it might be worthwhile to see what similar standards were used in the aviation industry.

- Interviews for Entry into the Navy's Nuclear Program. I mentioned earlier that day I had interviewed 25 candidates for entry into the nuclear propulsion program. He of course, knew that I had three or more people interview each candidate before I conducted the final interview. I recalled two interviews that were particularly interesting.

  - o The first was with a student who did well in his class but had studied little. During my questioning, it developed that his father was paying the student's expenses through college. I asked the student whether he was playing fair with his father by using the latter's money and not studying. The student finally agreed that he was not fair. Thereupon I asked him to write to his father and tell him what I had said about his conduct in this matter, and to send me a copy of his father's reply. I happened to have this letter (Enclosure 3) close at hand, and I let the president read it.

  - o The other candidate was a Dartmouth student who had been interviewed by five leading people at Naval Reactors, all of whom had recommended that he not be selected. After two discussions, I decided that he was intelligent, worked hard, and probably would get through our school. I had therefore accepted him contrary to the advice of my people.

o   I told the president of a recent case where I had interviewed a black student from a small Southern black college. I believed he was familiar with the caliber of these colleges. This student had a SAT score of 800, the lowest I had ever seen for an applicant for the nuclear program. To put this in perspective, the minimum SAT score required by the Naval Academy was 1200. I had decided to accept this man over the advice of the interviewers. In my discussions with this black applicant, it developed that he came from a very poor farming family and had little chance for education. I considered that with his apparent intelligence, and the fact he had worked hard in school to overcome his educational shortcomings, I was willing to take a chance on him, and so I accepted him for our school. This was the first time I had ever accepted anyone with a SAT score lower than 1050.

- The Media. The president talked about the many inaccuracies attributed to him by the press, and gave a number of examples by newspaper reporters. Even after he had advised them of the errors, they still did not print proper retractions. He said that Mr. Reston of *The New York Times* quoted him correctly.

o   I asked the president whether he liked his job. He said he was quite comfortable with it and did not mind the criticism too much. He would keep on doing what he thought was best regardless of what the press and others said about him.

o   I brought up the subject of the articles in the *Atlantic Monthly* by Jim Fallows who had been on the White

House staff; these articles had been critical of the president's conduct in office. He said that Fallows had been a relatively minor member of the staff and had no direct dealings with him.

o I then said there had been considerable criticism in the press concerning the members of this staff from Georgia. He replied that these were good men; in fact, nearly all members of his staff from Georgia had been with him for over eight years and that he had personally chosen them. I said I had observed that his staff members were no longer avid for publicity, as had been the case at the beginning of his term when their private affairs and other personal matters had been openly discussed in the press. I said I believed it was an excellent move that now kept his staff as anonymous as possible.

- Reorganization of the Defense Department. I told the president about the recent discussion I had with Peter Szanton of the Office of Management and Budget concerning the reorganization of the Defense Department; a study initiated by the president himself. He replied he knew nothing of this, and would look into the matter. Mr. Szanton had visited me to get my views about the Defense Department. In a conversation several days later, he said he had taken the matter up with the Head of the Office of Management and Budget and was told that nothing could be done because the time was now too close to the national election. The president said this was not true. I also said I had telephoned Mr. Eizenstat twice to tell him this, but had never received a reply.

- Organizations. In connection with eliminating useless jobs in the Federal government, I said I had found over many years that it is not enough just to reduce the number of people in an organization. The organization must be completely eliminated. In other words, the only permanent way is to extirpate it entirely.

- <u>General Robert E. Lee</u>. I expressed my opinion that General Lee, in view of his position in the Confederacy, should have told the Southern leaders after Gettysburg and Vicksburg that he could no longer hope to win the war. Thus, the ultimate loss of life and wealth to the Confederacy would have been lessened. In view of his position in the Confederacy, his advice would probably have been heeded. The president was not certain he could agree.

- <u>Visit with the Pope</u>. Mrs. Carter mentioned her recent visit with Pope John Paul II, at which Amy was also present. Amy had a number of items she wished the Pope to bless. Every time she placed the items in front of him, he had other thoughts and would change the subject. This happened several times. I never did find out whether the Pope blessed the items.

    o I told the president and Mrs. Carter about the time in 1957 when I had visited the Vatican. I had been taken by the curator through a long corridor containing many ancient works of art. I asked Mrs. Carter if she had seen these. She said she had and was quite impressed.

    o I asked if she had also visited the room in the Vatican which contained the four frescoes painted by Raphael. She did not remember it at first but, as I recounted the details, she said she did see it. I mentioned my visit to the Vatican when the frescoes were being renovated. Mrs. Carter was quite interested in this story.

4 June 1979

[Editor's note: Letter to Amy Carter giving her his book on his investigation of the explosion on the USS Maine. This letter was one of the rare handwritten letters sent by Rickover.]

Dear Amy,

Someday, I hope you will read this book. I had high school students in mind when I wrote it and arranged with my friends in the Government Printing Office to publish it as a paperback and sold for $1.25, so all students could afford to buy it.

I attempted, to the best of my ability, to use good English, so that the book could also serve the purpose of teaching how to write well.

If it helps you to learn history and to write clearly, it will have served its purpose.

You are fortunate to have parents as gifted, intelligent, and warm-hearted as your mother and father. I know you are learning from them that one must depend on one's self to achieve a full and worthy life.

Reading is one of the best aids in doing this.

With love,
HG Rickover

15 September 1979

Letter from Francis Duncan

On Friday evening, September 14, Chief Justice Burger held a reception at the Supreme Court for some government historians in connection with the Supreme Court's history program. From his remarks, it is clear that he has a deep interest in American history and the court's role in it.

I mentioned to him that I worked for you.

At once his face lit up, and he said instantaneously, "What a wonderful man! What a wonderful mind!"

1980s

18 January 1980

Letter to Chief of Naval Operations
Subj: U.S. Naval Institute

Thank you for your memorandum of 9 January 1980 in which you assured me the Naval Institute will not participate "in the publication of any book concerning a distinguished member of the naval service which that member finds personally offensive."

As I pointed out in my 2 January 1980 memorandum, I do not desire to get involved with writers and publishers who would exploit my life for their profit. Assuming that, for the purpose of applying the above stated policy, I qualified as "a distinguished member of the Naval service," I find the proposed biography of me by Messrs. Polmar and Allen "personally offensive." I refer you to the authors' prospectus, which I enclosed with my original memorandum. My view, however, would be the same if the authors proposed to portray me in a favorable light. Therefore, I trust that the Naval Institute will neither publish nor promote the proposed book.

2 January 1980

Letter to Chief of Naval Operations regarding U.S. Naval Institute Involvement in a Proposed Book about Me

I have, for some years, felt uneasy about the thin, often indistinguishable line between the Naval Institute and the Navy Department. In its widely distributed monthly magazine United States Naval Institute *Proceedings*, the Institute explains in fine print that it is "not part of the Navy Department." Despite this disclaimer, the Institute fosters the popular perception that it speaks for the Navy's senior officer corps. For example:

a. The words "United States" in the title "United States Naval Institute" connote Government sanction.

b. The Chief of Naval Operations is traditionally the President of the Institute; the Directors are primarily senior active-duty Naval Officers.

c. The Institute operates out of offices at the U.S. Naval Academy.

20 February 1980

Memorandum of Conversation between Admiral Rickover and Secretary of the Navy Hidalgo

The Secretary of the Navy telephoned me to ask if I would speak at the ceremony for the decommissioning of the NAUTILUS at Mare Island. I replied that I had a lot of work to do and did not have time to attend decommissionings. The secretary continued to press me, and I repeated that I had a lot of work to do. I said I thought Mr. Hidalgo would rather have me at work than making speeches.

I then suggested that Mr. Hidalgo himself make the speech. I added that not only did I have a lot of work to do but that Mr. Hidalgo was a good speaker. I referred to speeches of this type as "nutty stuff" and said that this was the sort of thing the secretary could do.

The secretary implied he would make the speech at Mare Island. The conversation throughout was amicable.

25 February 1980

Telephone conversation between Rickover and President Carter summarized by Francis Duncan

In your telephone call to the president, you are suggesting that you believe the nation needs a series of speeches from him that deal with the basic issues confronting us. These speeches should be non-partisan and above the campaign. More than anything else they are a report on the state of the union—not to Congress—but to the citizens. One might be on foreign affairs. It should be factual and state the position of the country, its strengths and limitations.

Another might be on economics. Again, the emphasis should be factual.

The type of thing you have in mind is similar to the fireside chats of Roosevelt or, an even better example, the Federalist Papers.

From these issues he would be able to go on to talk about re-defining the concept of citizenship and responsibility. Considering the concern over foreign affairs, inflation, the decline in educational standards, productivity, standards among the professions, the growth of special interest groups, and the increasing complexity of government, a call to reconsider the obligations—not the rights—of citizenship is important.

You are not suggesting that he is calling for a program such as Wilson did with his New Freedom, Roosevelt did with the New Deal, or Eisenhower did with his Great Crusade. These were largely campaign platforms. What you are proposing is something fundamental that perhaps has not been done before.

It may be that he has no one around him who is prepared to take this approach. In this case you might want to suggest Daniel Boorstin. You are proposing an historian because you believe he needs someone who understands and has studied the American experience. There have been precedents: Kennedy had Schlesinger, and Johnson had Goldman (although the latter was not a happy or fruitful relationship). Perhaps Doris Kearns might be a possibility.

You believe a series of such speeches would be welcome. He would be speaking from what Theodore Roosevelt called a "bully pulpit" in a way no other candidate could do.

11 March 1980

Conversation with Cyrus Vance, Secretary of State

1. I told Mr. Vance I had been thinking at length about the Afghanistan situation.
2. I recommended that we send a small body of American troops, possibly a battalion, into the country to show the Russians they could not do anything they wished and with no consequences. These troops would not confront the Russians, but it would be evident to the Russians and to the American people that we would not take anything lying down that the Russians do.
3. Mr. Vance said this might result in armed conflict with the Russians.
4. I replied I did not believe so, because if the Russians started an armed confrontation, they must know it would inevitably lead to war with the United States; I did not believe the Russians would conceive of going this far.
5. I said the Russians have announced they would withdraw their troops. We could tell them after the event, that when they withdraw their troops, we would withdraw our troops.

6. Mr. Vance said he would give the matter further consideration.

12 April 1980

Telephone Conversation with Virgil Pinkley

I told Mr. Pinkley, in reply to a recent letter from him, that I did not desire a biography of me by anyone.

I said that a Mr. Polmar, who is connected with the U.S. Naval Institute, is presently writing a biography of me. He had approached me, and I told him that I would under no circumstances cooperate or give information, since I did not wish a biography written. I understand that Mr. Polmar's biography will be published this year. Should he send me a proof, I would not read or comment on it.

I told Mr. Pinkley that his biography of Dwight D. Eisenhower is a masterpiece, and I would be proud, did I ever desire a biography of me written, to have him undertake it. I added that I doubted any man, alive or dead, could ever be perfectly honest in talking about himself. I believe this was also true of Samuel Peeps and his diary.

Mr. Pinkley thanked me for my consideration and said that he understood.

18 August 1980

Letter to Norman Polmar

This letter is to advise that in the event you are considering having the book you are writing about me used as a motion picture, I am as unalterably opposed to such a venture, as I am about the book you are writing about me.

This letter will further advise that should you, your agent, or any other person or agency engage in the writing or publication of the book, or in the production of a motion picture about me, I will aggressively pursue whatever rights I have.

Enclosed is a copy of my letter dated 31 October 1979 concerning your book, which I sent to Simon and Schuster.

24 April 1980

[Editor's note: In this memo, Rickover shows his humorous side with his staff.]

MEMORANDUM FOR GOVERNMENT SECRETARIES ORGANIZATION

1. It is with deep sorry and regret I am compelled to report that this morning, during Secretary Week, I arrived at my office three minutes before 8 o'clock and found three of the secretaries actually engaged in work. This is the grossest violation of secretary rules I have ever seen in my many years of government service.

2. I, therefore, request you take immediate action to expel these non-conformists from your organization. Otherwise, this practice may spread. When questioned about their dereliction of duty they said, "We are compelled to give an honest day's work for a day's pay."

3. I cannot cope with such a situation. Please give me names of secretaries to replace these disloyal members of your organization. Also, I would like to know what disciplinary action you plan to take in these cases.

4. It may also interest you to know that they kept on working before 8 o'clock despite my effort to have them live up to their moral obligation—particularly during Secretary Week!

[Undated] May 1980

Duncan conversations with the admiral

[Rickover] said that sometimes you have to offend people to get them to realize how stupid they are. He said this after having been to Charleston, where he was very hard on some of the officers (his own people say too hard).

He said that often people give him credit for getting things done, but say that he does them the wrong way. The fact that he gets things done well may mean that he is doing things the wrong way.

4 June 1980

Remarks by Admiral H.G. Rickover before the Congressional Research Service, Defense Breakfast Seminar

I appreciate the opportunity to discuss some of my views on current topics affecting our defense posture and the future of our country. The views I will express are my own from my perspective after 50 years as a naval officer, engineer, and student of history.

I will not dwell on the specifics of the naval nuclear propulsion program I am responsible for because I have testified on that subject before several congressional committees. I would like to share with you thoughts on the importance of the Soviet naval threat as compared to our naval strength.

The Soviet Naval Threat

Recent Soviet aggression in Afghanistan has brought renewed realization of Soviet intentions for world power and concern for the adequacy of our own defense. What many may not realize is that the Soviet threat in naval power, as in other areas, has been growing more ominous. Past warnings by many in the military have been greeted with some indifference. However, today we are faced with a naval threat more serious than any since World War II.

Twenty-four years ago, Admiral Gorshkov, Commander-in-Chief of the Soviet Navy, headed a Navy which was little more than a defense-oriented extension of the Soviet Army. Under him, the Soviet Navy has been transformed. Since 1958, the Soviets have built over 1800 new ships and combatant craft, a program of naval expansion that surpasses the efforts of any other naval power. From a defensive fleet in World War II, it has evolved into a major blue-water that challenges the U.S. for control almost everywhere in the world. The Soviet momentum for superiority in naval warfare continues while U.S. naval plans fluctuate every year. Never in peacetime has there been anything comparable to the growth of the Russian naval power. This certainly raises concern over the Soviet desire to maintain the peace.

Here are some comparative examples to illustrate these concerns.

- In the past 10 years, the Soviets have built over 900 major and minor surface combatants, mine warfare, and amphibious ships, while the U.S. has built 100, or just over 10 percent as many.
- The Soviets have more major surface combatants than we, and are introducing new ships at a greater rate. These include 4 new classes of cruisers, one of which will likely be nuclear powered. At about 22,000 tons, it would be the world's largest nuclear-powered cruiser and will carry a formidable array of weapons.
- The Soviets have almost 3 times as many submarines and one-third more nuclear submarines.
- They have 5 submarine construction yards; we have two. All U.S. submarine construction capacity could fit into one Soviet submarine yard.
- Since 1970, they have introduced 10 new submarine designs; the U.S., two. During this period, the Soviets have put to sea

more new design submarines than any other country during a comparable period in all of naval history.

- Their program has strong support and virtually unlimited funding. They are striving for qualitative superiority. They already have numerical superiority. Our program is uncertain and does not get strong support from the Defense Department.

Any comparison of the Soviet and the U.S. Navy must be viewed from the context that we are a maritime power dependent upon being able to maintain sea lanes of communication necessary to conduct military operations overseas and to support our allies. The mission of our Navy is a far more difficult one than that of the Soviets of denying us free use of the seas.

We have given up any chance of matching the Soviet Navy in numbers of ships. Therefore, the quality of our ships must be superior. It is axiomatic that a nation dependent on the quality of its weapons must design its forces around an offensive strategy if it is to prevail over a numerically superior foe. It cannot afford to fight a defensive war of attrition.

Need for Flexible and Capable Ships

A few years ago, few people gave much thought to deploying naval forces to the Indian Ocean to protect our interests. Today, that has become a reality. Few appreciate how difficult it is to maintain a significant naval force halfway around the world. The supply line, particularly for oil-fired ships, is tenuous. There may be a new realization that a war of attrition at sea is a real possibility. In these circumstances, our naval forces must be able to defend the sea lanes and carry the battle to the enemy as well. In a global wartime situation, we will not have the time to build the complex ships we need the way we did in the last World War. The ships we build in peacetime are those we will have to rely upon in the event of hostilities.

If we miscalculate or succumb to the easy economic choice of putting off decisions, and do not build ships adequate to face the threat, our choice will be to either give in to our enemies or resort to nuclear war. The cost of adequate strength to ensure peace is small compared to the cost of war...

[Editor's note: At this point in the speech, Admiral Rickover goes into some depth on four issues—the attack submarine, the Trident submarine program, the need for nuclear-powered AEGIS cruisers, and the retention of experienced naval personnel.]

Closing Comments

I have shared with you my thoughts from my vantage point of being involved in our nation's defense for a long time and in charge of the nuclear propulsion program since its inception over 25 years ago. From that perspective, I am particularly sensitive to the role that the Congress has played. Without congressional actions and help throughout the years, we simply would not, today, have the strong nuclear fleet we have, now representing over 40% of the Navy's major combatants. You have the constitutional responsibility to maintain this nation's ability to defend itself. Indeed, no other national issue is more critical than national defense. If we are not able to prevail against our enemies, all other issues, however significant, become irrelevant. It is to the Congress that we all must look for a defense posture strong enough to assure our survival as a nation.

25 November 1980

Letter from Lieutenant _____

After completing my Engineer's Exam on 18 November 1980, you called me in to talk to me. You asked me if I told my priest that

I did not know who Peter was. When I replied that I had not, you directed me to inform my priest that an infidel had to tell me who Peter was and to tell you by letter what he said.

On 23 November 1980, I told Father Edwin Bohula Cdr,[110] CHC, USN that an infidel told me who Peter was. He asked me who the infidel was, and I replied, "Admiral RICKOVER." He said to tell Admiral RICKOVER that Peter, too, was an apostate, and that there is hope for Admiral RICKOVER.

10 December 1980

Some points discussed with President Carter, 10 December 1980

1. Electoral defeat does not mean personal defeat. As a still young Former Chief Magistrate of the Nation, he has an important responsibility to fulfill and a service to offer. Few individuals have accumulated his experience.

2. This service can take many forms. Examples are: Thomas Jefferson helping to found the University of Virginia; John Quincy Adams serving 17 years in the House of Representatives; William Howard Taft spending 9 years as Chief Justice of the United States; Herbert Hoover heading a commission to reorganize the Federal Government.

3. In recent years, ex-presidents have taken to writing. This is important, though often the books have been written too soon after leaving office and are often regarded as defensive and partisan.

4. He should not withdraw from public life. In addition to writing, he might wish to take up speaking before public interest groups and on behalf of his party's candidates. He could make an important contribution by using his experience to bring out the fundamental problems the government faces today. Theodore Roosevelt called the presidency

---

110 Rev. Edwin Bohula (1930–2007).

a "bully pulpit." The experience of an ex-president is also the subject for a "bully pulpit." Because he is no longer in office, he can focus upon principles.

5. While I cannot presume to suggest what he should take up, I believe that one of the greatest issues the nation faces is whether we can maintain our 18th Century heritage of personal liberty against the demands of the 20th Century energy crisis.

30 December 1980

Letter to President Richard Nixon

Dear Mr. Nixon,

As usual, it was a pleasure and privilege to talk with you. You are always so kind and good to me.

Enclosed is the paper, "Some Thoughts on the Presidency," of which I spoke with you today. I would very much appreciate any comments you may have.

A president will never hear the truth again. Everybody in high places stands in a room full of mirrors and sees himself multiplied by servile reflection. The Oval Office can easily become such a room...

The Staff

In the inner councils of the White House, the presence of the president alters other men's words. Some wait to hear what he says, then agree. Others are intimidated and do not say what is on their minds. Subordinates are needed who are committed to goals rather than to the process, and who are not afraid to criticize when they no longer agree with the goals...

It is essential to have an alternative to the official version of things—a rival account of reality, a measure by which to judge the efficacy of officials.

Those outside the inner circle who have your ear but who seldom see fit to question your judgment should also be listened to.

Their judgment is what is needed to balance the parochial judgment of your immediate staff, and they should be given a hearing…

Private Lives

I have always made known to those who worked with me that I would not pry into their private lives, nor require social relationships with them; whatever they did in their private lives was entirely their affair, provided this did not reflect unfavorably on the organization.

The President

The president should try for a place in history rather than for a second term. Those who are ambitious to make a place and name for themselves are nearly always despised and laughed at by lesser souls, and what they do is construed as wrong. History has the tendency to overlook the faults of men who mattered, just as contemporaries overlook the contributions of men who fail while daring greatly. Few rulers we now account great, were great or popular in the eyes of contemporaries; the few who were, were admired for reasons which are not ours.

A president has been assigned much authority, yet little power. Power is something acquired, something earned, something developed by an individual's personality and accomplishments. Authority is no match for it. The most influential leaders are askers of questions, like Socrates and Jesus…

To adhere to one's first principles is not always correct. Principles change with maturity. It is only the ignorant who attribute the doings of the government to the person of its Head—like the yokel who believed that the Crimean War was ended only when the English Queen captured the Russian Czar. People do not notice the existence of the best leaders. When such a leader's work is done, they say, "We did it ourselves."

It is a mistake to attempt to appear as the sort of person one thinks should be the leader, rather than being himself. It is sometimes necessary at the top of authority to bear with disloyal colleagues, to remain calm when others panic, and to withstand misguided popular outcries. It is not a credit to have been right when others have been wrong; but this has always been the consolation of dedicated men. The willingness to reassess and move beyond an earlier formulation is precisely what makes one's actions a model. This testifies to the ability to outgrow parochialism, to move beyond the starting point, to give up the comfort of having a fixed position...

If you are called a kind president, your rule is a failure...

26 January 1981

Jacksonville (SSN 699) Precommissioning Unit, at Sea North Atlantic Letter to Eleanore Rickover

As usual, as soon as I am away from you, I begin to re-understand what a most unusual person you are, and how blessed I am to have your love. In all the world there is nothing more wonderful than a truly compassionate and truly beautiful woman. Where does a woman's beauty lie? Is it in her eyes, her nose, her mouth, her mind, her hair, her body? Some hold that Truth is Beauty, and Beauty is Truth. It is difficult, if not impossible to say which is the primary aspect. But a choice is not necessary when I consider you, because you combine beauty and truth.

Perhaps what I have written contains a measure of the love you induce in me.

18 February 1981

Note to President Carter

Dear Mr. President:

I enjoyed talking with you, and I am happy you are just about back to being yourself.

No man can be properly judged by his own generation; only the future can truly discern and evaluate his worth.

30 March 1981

[Rickover's reflections to Duncan]

Friday night, 27 March 1981, I was at the Mare Island Naval Shipyard, at the conclusion of a week's visit by ten leading naval reactors engineers to conduct the biannual nuclear inspection of the yard. Upon conclusion of this inspection, I addressed about thirty senior shipyard officials, about twenty-five were the leading civilians in the yard; the others were officers. I told them what the team had found and the lessons to be learned. When I was finished, I thought it would be appropriate to tell them the following story. None had heard of the incident—it happened before any of them had begun working at Mare Island.

In the summer of 1923, the Navy decided to try out a new way of rebricking boilers. The standard way was to use a special kind of heat resistant brick able to withstand the high temperatures in the boiler firebox, as well as the flames of the burning oil.

The USS LAVALLETTE, of which I was Engineer Officer at the time, was sent from her homeport, San Diego, to Mare Island for a one-month period to make the change to our boilers. Since there was a scarcity of repair money at the time, the work had to be done by the ship's force—which meant the fireroom gang.

I had never been to Mare Island Naval Shipyard, so I took this opportunity to become acquainted with the leading people who ran the Yard. I soon learned that the most important of these were two civilians, the Gee brothers, who had worked in the yard for many years. One headed the Production Department; the other headed the Planning Department. The two essentially ran the yard; they were among those I visited. I used this acquaintanceship to help me get work done in the engineering department—work not connected with the change to the ship's boilers, and for which no yard funds were available. I found this "friendship" invaluable at that time and at the annual overhaul of the ship the following year.

One day, in walking about the yard to learn about the work in progress in each shop, I noted from a distance two workmen standing in front of the machine shop. Several moments later as I passed the shop, they were still there. I walked a while farther, then turned and went back. The men were still there. I continued this several times. Finally, I stopped and stood silently staring at them. At this point, the two picked up a large, heavy 2x4 and walked away. This would have indicated to a casual observer that they were engaged in doing "useful" work. I followed them. They kept on looking back and saw me still following. After half a mile, they stopped, threw the board to the ground, and said, "We give up."

June 6, 1981

Remarks on the Completion of USS OHIO First Sea Trials

The first sea trials of the OHIO have now been completed. The officers and men operated this new type of submarine in an exemplary manner—like veterans. I say this from experience in submarines going back more than half a century—from O-Boats, S-Boats, to this one of 19,000 tons. I can remember when, in a 500-ton submerged boat (we called them "boats" at the time)—two men going from the bow to the stern would make a difference. As diving officer, I would have to shift 300 lbs of water from the after to the forward tank—we then figured 150 pounds per man.

Also, we then had what was called the "periscope trim." The balance was so fine that when we raised or lowered the periscope, we had to take in or pump out a few pounds of water. I also remember the time I was assigned to an 800-ton S-Boat—at Coco Solo. We often shifted our operations from the Atlantic to the Pacific. After transiting the Panama Canal, we had to take in seven tons of water on reaching the Pacific side because of the difference in the salinity of the sea water in the two oceans.

There was no air-conditioning then. When we went on a 9-day patrol, we were constantly hot—we developed rashes. When we turned in and tried to sleep, we were so tired that we didn't bother fighting off the bedbugs, and in the upper bunk, the dripping of water that had condensed on the over-head interfered with sleep—and dreams. When we occasionally surfaced after sunset, we brought a bucket of fresh water top-side and took a fresh water bath. Sometimes we jumped into the sea to cool off, but the salt water caused the skin to be sticky.

So, you young noblemen in the OHIO do not know how fortunate you are: fresh, not canned food; all the fresh water you want; a shower that can be run, not just enough to wet your body and then turned off until you rinse the soap off.

I could tell you more about the early days of submarines, but I won't. When you get to my time of life, I can envision all of you sitting at your fireside telling your grandchildren about that ancient ship, the OHIO, of which you were a "plank-owner." So I will stop and let you youngsters carry the torch.

I wish you the best of luck. I hope you will make full use of the opportunity the Navy has given you to lead a worthwhile, therefore a happy life. And just imagine—the Navy is even paying you for the opportunity of engaging in this interesting work! I am sure there are many ashore who would give much to enjoy the experience that has just been your privilege.

You will remember this day—the day the first Trident submarine, one of our most powerful deterrents to war, returned from successful sea trials.

It should remind you of St. Crispian's Day, also an eventful day. As Shakespeare said then in Henry IV:

> This day is called the feast of Crispian:
> He that outlives this day, and comes safe home,

Will stand a-tiptoe when this day is named.
And rouse him at the name of Crispian.

My thanks and the Navy's thanks for a job well done.

14 August 1981

Telephone Conversation between Mr. William Wegner and Admiral Rickover

1. I asked Mr. Wegner what had caused the trouble between Zumwalt and me. He gave the following points:
    a. The time I interviewed him.
    b. He was on a group of System Analysts when the question of nuclear-powered ships came up.
    c. Mr. Nitze chose him as executive assistant.
    d. Nitze apparently "adopted" Zumwalt, and the latter, for a while, lived in Nitze's home.
    e. Zumwalt became an admiral ahead of his time and was assigned the Riverine Fleet in Vietnam.
    f. Very early in Zumwalt's life and rank, Nitze made him CNO.
    g. Zumwalt wanted surface-controlled ships.
    h. Admiral Shear wanted to give away our submarine technology to the Italians. (This is contained in the NR records.)
    i. The issue of Captain Swanson in charge of Pearl Harbor. (Rogers knows about this.)
    j. TRIDENT program, which Zumwalt and I both backed. This was finally won by one or two votes. I was responsible for lobbying senators and obtaining three votes for it.

19 August 1981

[Rickover notes to himself]

Why is it that in business the high officials are those who have had successful financial or manufacturing experience—that they had been chosen not because they were "leaders," but because of their practical abilities? But in the Navy, high officials are chosen because they are "leaders" by superiors who had also been chosen for this same reason.

Why do I never choose a "leader" for command of a nuclear ship or other important position? Only those who have demonstrated the ability to operate nuclear power plants successfully are assigned to command.

I also require this at the civilian Shippingport Atomic Power Station. But I do not believe this is the case at some other nuclear stations, where those in charge were chosen because of their seniority.

In the Navy, those at the top generally were chosen because of their "form"—by superiors who likewise were selected for this reason. This is why, when a war starts, we have always had to replace the "leaders" in office at the time. The new officers were chosen, not because they had demonstrated peacetime "form," but because they had shown tough practicality. For example, Admiral Ernie King had been passed over for high command during peace because he was a "tough" and disagreeable person. But when war broke out, he was made Commander-in-Chief of the U.S. Fleet.

Charisma (leadership) is proper in religion, but not in worldly affairs. To do a job properly, solid knowledge, practical experience, and a disciplined organization are required.

In baseball, when a player does his job well, we study his "form." In the Navy, in peacetime, the "form" (leadership) has become the important attribute factor. The baseball coach is judged by the number of games he wins, not by his "form."

Friday 13 November 1981 0740

> *[Editor's note: Rickover's official schedule shows only one meeting scheduled. This was the meeting at which Rickover was formally told he would not be reappointed to his position and that he would be forced to retire.]*

Secretary of Defense and Secretary of the Navy
Room 3E880—Pentagon
"HGR went"

> *[Editor's note from another document: Immediately following that meeting at the Pentagon, Rickover met with Senators Jackson, Stratton, Thurmond, Warner, and Congressmen Horton and Price.]*

17 November 1981

Subj: My Relief

1. The Secretary of the Navy has asked me to train, for a period of several months, the person he will assign to replace me. Obviously, since he is dissatisfied with my manner of operating Naval Reactors, he must desire that my replacement conduct affairs in a manner different than mine.
2. I see no logic in this request for me to train my relief, as this could only result in his continuing my bad methods.
3. No superior, over a period of more than 30 years, has ever told me that anything was wrong with the way I have run my job. Both Presidents Carter and Nixon have telephoned me and asked why I was being relieved. I replied that no one—the Secretary of the Navy, Secretary of Defense, or the president—had ever said a word to me about my job. In fact, only one of the three, the Secretary of the Navy, has ever spoken with me during this administration, and the

secretary has only done so twice for a few moments. Therefore, I do not know why I am being replaced.

4. Obviously, the Secretary of the Navy considers me incapable of running the job. It would appear illogical that I should train my relief. Therefore, my relief should not come into Naval Reactors until I leave. My key people are fully capable of advising him of the nature of the work in this organization.

24 November 1981

Telephone Conversation with Admiral Waller, Superintendent of the Naval Academy

1. About two months ago I had a telephone discussion with Admiral Waller on the subject of whether the time of midshipmen was being used properly at the Naval Academy. That is, were they being required to engage in functions which did not contribute to their becoming the best naval officers possible. This issue was important, because much more must now be learned by a midshipman to enable him to do his job properly on board ship when he graduates.

2. Admiral Waller replied that indeed he had looked into the matter. He had gone into it thoroughly and found a number of areas which should be eliminated. He had also found some activities which did not contribute to their training as naval officers.

3. I had asked him specifically to look into the area of intercollegiate sports. He said he found these to be over-emphasized and was taking some actions. He had also looked into the curriculum and found areas where the time of midshipmen was not devoted to the major purpose of the Naval Academy. He had not yet completed his studies, but improvements would result from his investigations.

4. I told him that as I was to interview several hundred midshipmen in a few days for entry into the nuclear program, I would note whether his actions had led to perceptible improvements. He replied he would be glad to get my comments.

5. Admiral Waller also stated that many more midshipmen were now interested in the nuclear program and were volunteering. Their duty in nuclear-powered ships during the summer had had an exemplary effect. They now realize that in the nuclear program they could learn more than in other programs and could become professional naval officers.

27 November 1981

Memorandum of Meeting with Chief of Naval Operations
Subj: My Retention on Duty

1. The CNO told me Admiral McKee[111] will probably be the one who relieves me. I replied that my job was essentially a technical one, and that the person who relieves me should be technically qualified. I also told him that I had previously recommended my deputy, Mr. Vaughan, as my relief, that I had trained him for the position. He replied that the top man must be a military person.

2. I then discussed the action of the Secretary of the Navy in having my "firing" announced on TV, without my having been notified. I had returned from sea trials late the night of the announcement and was told by my wife that it had been on TV. He replied that he also had not been consulted.

3. I reminded him that the Secretary of the Navy had told the press he was letting me go because of "actuarial" reasons— which means I am decrepit and may die soon. I told CNO that my latest formal physical exam by the Navy stated that

---

111 Admiral Kinnaird McKee (1929–2013), U.S. Naval Academy Class of 1951.

I was "fit for active duty," and suggested he tell SecNav that an official Navy document on this point had been available when he made this statement to the press.

4. I then informed the CNO of the recent visit of Polmar and Allen, who have written a book about me, to the Naval Academy. They had discussed me with the first-class midshipmen. I said this was the first time in naval history where the authors of a book about a four-star admiral, without his knowledge or permission, or on any other naval officer on active duty, were permitted to have formal discussions with midshipmen on a book before it was even published. Further, I was to interview, in a few days, many of these very same midshipmen for entry into the nuclear program. His remarks will surely have a bad effect on them. Also, to give special permission to these authors to "sell" their new book to the midshipmen has created a precedent for other authors. They likewise will want to have this captive audience to make a "pitch" for their books. The CNO said he would look into the matter and let me know.

30 November 1981

Telephone Conversation between Admiral Rickover and Martin Peretz, Editor-in-Chief and President of The New Republic

1. I called Mr. Peretz and asked him if he read the article printed in his magazine, *The New Republic*, regarding me. He said that he had.
2. I objected to the writer stating my "career seemed to be a continuous struggle against some inner self-doubt, at least in the early years." I asked in what way he had come to know about my "inner self-doubt." I also asked him how he knew about my parents, as I have never spoken about either of them in public. Apparently, the writer assumed

that because I spoke but little of my father and not at all of my mother in public, that within the "authorized snippets of family background, there were signs of a harsh, disciplined, unsupportive family."

3. The writer also stated I was a "small, frail, and sickly child, who quickly tired under the pressure of work and was an in-different student who had few friends." If I was so sickly, how could I work 72 hours a week in addition to going to school?

4. The writer also refers to my being a Jew. This has nothing to do with anything.

5. Mr. Peretz asked if I desired a retraction in the magazine. I told him I did not want a retraction to the article, but I did want to bring this to his attention. He said he would take the matter up with the one who had written the article.

4 December 1981

Memorandum of Telephone Conversation with Senator Jackson, Subject: Extension of Service for Rickover

Senator Jackson called at 1529 and said they had discussed extending Admiral Rickover's service indefinitely as a turnover period. This would be done in order to give Congress time to return from recess and set up a definite role and duties for Admiral Rickover as a National Security Advisor. He would remain on active duty and retain his four-star status. Congress would have to approve another four-star admiral slot in order to take care of the admiral who would take over Naval Reactors.

Admiral Rickover would have an office and staff (possibly at the Navy Yard).

7 December 1981

Notes for Call to Secretary of the Navy John Lehman

I have read your letter carefully, and it merely reiterates that I will not be retained beyond January 31 and asks me to take the job of science advisor to the president. I have already turned this job down. What I thought would be in the letter was what we discussed in the meeting today. Namely, I would be:

1. Special Assistant to the CNO and SecNav
2. Remain on Active Duty
3. Have an office at the Navy Yard
4. Have a full-time secretary
5. Have a driver and car
6. Have travel money.

This is the position I am interested in. If you are willing to consider it, I suggest you draft a letter along these lines and let me see if before you send it formally.

15 December 1981

Letter to Senator Henry "Scoop" Jackson

Dear Scoop:

As we discussed by phone last week, I obtained the agreement of the Secretary of the Navy to give him a draft letter outlining an arrangement for me to serve as Special Navy Advisor after January 31, 1982.

Before I send him the draft, I would appreciate your advice as to the acceptability of what I propose. A copy of the draft letter is enclosed...

25 January 1982

Letter from Secretary of the Navy John Lehman

Dear Admiral Rickover,

Subsequent to our previous discussions concerning your continuing on active duty beyond 31 January 1982, I have considered the matter carefully and have decided not to recall you to active duty beyond that date. However, in recognition of your long and distinguished service, I have advised the Chief of Naval Operations that he may extend to you courtesies, for a period of three to six months, similar to those provided a retiring Chief of Naval Operations. These courtesies consist of the use of an office, together with administrative assistance, to include a Navy-enlisted person who can serve in the dual capacity of Flag Writer and driver. You may be provided with the use of a government car for local transportation needs.

Admiral, I continue to believe your advice and counsel can be of great benefit to the Navy and the Nation. I would hope that you will permit me from time to time to seek your counsel on appropriate matters.

29 January 1982

Remarks by Admiral H.G. Rickover on the occasion of his leaving Naval Reactors

I leave in full confidence that the spirit of Naval Reactors will remain, that the lessons learned in the past will be taken to heart, and that the mutual respect and understanding among all who serve in Naval Reactors will be maintained and fostered for the safety and honor of our country.

In efficiency, in smartness, and in good spirit you have shown an example to the rest of the Navy of what an expert technical group should and can do.

You must remember that the period in front of you will be different; new features appear, new difficulties arise, all of which have got to be overcome. But I am confident that in the future, as in the past, you will live up to the reputation you have made. It is a great one; it will be difficult. But you can do it because the spirit will remain.

I thank all of you for your loyal and whole-hearted support during the years past. Without that support, my task would have been much more difficult, if not impossible.

I have been grateful for representing Naval Reactors. But the honor is to you as much as it is to me. I was the one responsible. I therefore had to deal with Congress and the public. But you are truly the recipients of what honor is due just as much as I am.

It is good for you to know that the feeling about Naval Reactors is what it is. Sometimes we may believe that because we are out of sight, we are out of mind. That is not so. Therefore, I would remind you that the public feeling entails obligations upon us. You must continue to hold yourselves worthy of the trust—that unfailing trust which the United States has in the Navy and the Energy Department, which we all have the honor to serve.

I now say goodbye to you. This to me is a sad day, because it brings to an end my service in the Navy and the Energy Department. But I remain a servant of the United States, and so long as I can, I will help that great Service to which I belong body and soul.

What the future holds I cannot say; I will not prophesy. I thank you, and please remember that, although I have gone, I still remain a comrade and a friend. Goodbye.

1 February 1982

Call from former Senator George McGovern [notes taken by staff]

[McGovern] said that he felt that a critical examination of the defense structure is long overdue.

You said that the defense structure is a sacred cow. That you speak with experience—know more about the structure than anyone else.

He said that there is a lot of common sense in what you said. That he has had many favorable comments about it—from businessmen riding to an airport to coal operators in West Virginia. They say defense has gotten out of hand—Rickover is right.

He said you should speak out more.

You said that the basis of a democracy is to speak out.

He said that people think they can't fight city hall. Whatever they think, the coal miners are a significant part of society. They should bring it out in the open.

You said that the statement does not mean you are forsaking what you stood for. That you changed the Navy around against its will. But just how much overkill do we need?

He said Herblock[112] is with you. You said that doesn't help you.

You said you don't know what the reaction is in the Defense Department. Military men are really technicians.

He said he has a suggestion/favor:

- Public interest group—Americans for Common Sense
- Develop thoughts on the economy, foreign policy, national defense
- Has draft rough statement on nuclear war problem
- Something's wrong with the drift in nuclear policy
- Will send out a mailing list of people to help in this effort
- It is a tax-exempt organization—can he send it over to you

---

112 Herbert Block, popularly known as Herblock (1909–2001), a nationally syndicated Pulitzer Prize-winning editorial cartoonist.

You said he may be sizing you up wrong—that you can do his cause more good by just being yourself rather than by joining his organization. The minute one connects with any organization, he gets accused of being a pacifist. The Military Industrial Complex is far more potent than anyone knows. You said he ought to get the things you have already said.

You said Nader wants you now, too. You reiterated that you can do more good for his cause by being yourself than by joining any group.

2 February 1982

> *Letter from Chairman Henry Reuss and Vice-Chairman William Proxmire of Joint Economic Committee*

We understand that the Navy is allowing you to maintain an office at the Navy Yard for a period of three to six months. We believe that your talents and capacity for making continued contributions to public policy warrant a longer-term arrangement. We, therefore, would like to make available to you an office and administrative services at the Joint Economic Committee. This arrangement can commence either before or after your present arrangement with the Navy terminates, at your discretion.

The purpose of this arrangement would be to make you available to the Committee as a senior policy adviser on a wide range of issues of interest to the Committee. These issues include arms control and disarmament, government contracting, defense procurement and financial management, the relationship between government and private contractors, nuclear energy policy, independent research and development…and the problems of waste, inefficiency, and corruption in government programs.

8 February 1982

Letter from Jeffrey Hayden[113]

We met about ten years ago at the home of my cousin, Herman Wouk, in Georgetown. My wife, Eva Marie Saint,[114] and I were at the Kennedy Center… I think your life story is important and meaningful and would make for an exciting film. I would like to have the rights to dramatize it for a television special. If you will forgive the presumption, I see the form as follows: first act—acceptance at Annapolis, second act—nuclear power and the Nautilus, third act—forced retirement, and a strong case against it…

12 February 1982

Memo of telephone conversation with Dr. [Alvin] Weinberg, Oak Ridge National Laboratory

He said he has been reading about you in all the newspapers. Says you have defeated the U.S. Navy singlehandedly—congratulations!

You replied that it is an achievement to do anything in the military—usually you have a continual revolving door, a rotation every two years…

You said that we have overkill in defense. History has shown that any weapon in existence is always used when it is needed. You said that in the event of a war, atomic weapons would be used. You mentioned that in your last testimony, you told Congress that there is too much overkill. That both the U.S. and the Soviets could blow each other off the Earth.

He said that the main thing you did was take on the whole U.S. Navy.

---

113 American television producer/director (1926–2016).
114 American actress (b. 1924).

You said that they now want to go back to building conventional carriers. Now—when the reactor cores are so advanced that they will last 30 years. That is a service that is very feasible from a logistics standpoint, and the Navy doesn't give any recognition.

He asked if you ever thought of making public the safety record of nuclear reactors (Navy). He said the public doesn't realize that…

18 February 1982

Letter from HGR to Rear Admiral Edgar Batcheller[115]

Dear Batcheller,

As you can imagine, I was more than pleased to get your kind letter.

You and I have known each other for many years, going back to the junior officer days in the Navy. I believe you, as much as anyone else, are aware that I have always tried to play the Navy game honestly. I actually have. In my opinion, the real reason for being kicked out is the influence of the two major shipbuilding contractors—General Dynamics, which operates Electric Boat, and Tenneco, which operates Newport News. Between the two of them, they had made claims for about a billion dollars against the government. I was the one who for many years had been refuting these claims, pointing out that they were incorrect. The Navy was willing to give them this money; it was my objection that managed to stop this. Now that I am gone, I believe these claims will be prosecuted and probably will be paid by the government in full—or at least a considerable portion.

---

115 Rear Admiral Edgar Hadley Batcheller (1910-2003), U.S. Naval Academy Class of 1934. They served together on the battleship USS NEW MEXICO when Batcheller reported on board as an ensign.

19 February 1982

Memorandum for the Record after receiving a call from Ron Crawford, NASA Headquarters

[Crawford] wanted to ask you to meet with Gen. Abramson and several others from NASA on improving productivity. These people intend to leave the agency with a record of saving the taxpayers lots of money.

You stated that new people in an agency are not able to meet with the group and advise them. You said no—that there are hundreds of these groups.

He said they are looking at the F-16 program. You stated that in the POLARIS program they asked for twice as much money as they needed so they could look like they were saving money.

Further, Bath shipyards look good because they always overestimate the contracts.

You said you think these groups are bullshit. If a guy is running an outfit, he is either able to do the work or he is fired. You said you had never seen one of these groups amount to anything. That it would be a nice vacation. They meet, they sound good, they will even put out a report. But, nobody listens and nothing happens.

You said that your method was to take experts from a particular lab and send them to another lab for a week or so, let them observe the operations of that particular lab and learn from each other. Each lab would benefit from that week.

He asked you if you would do the same thing if you had to do it over again.

You said that in your organization, HQ maintained control of the field. That it is not always so in other organizations, but that you feel it is necessary that HQ maintain control and that frequent reports come in from the field activities. You said that the problem in other organizations is that the people don't know their jobs.

He restated that he would like to get you together with Gen. Abramson and 3–4 others for about 1 hour. You said no.

He then asked if you would be available for consultation. If they could put you on contract.

You said, well, you could try it—take one of these groups—but that you would recognize bullshit when you saw it.

He said he would call again.

23 February 1982

Summary by Rickover's staff of call from Jim Woolsey[116]

[Woolsey] called on behalf of the Council on Foreign Relations. They want you to speak—you said you had turned them down.

You said that you don't want to go and make a spectacle of yourself; that all you want to do is speak to the college kids—tell them to study—that this is the most critical time of their lives—that they shouldn't waste their time.

You said further that you were kicked out of the Navy on account of shipbuilding claims—that you personally were holding up the payment of over $1 billion in claims, and that this is why you were kicked out.

You went on to say that the Navy is not facing up to the issue of the next war. You said that they are still pushing aircraft carriers and that they will last about two days in a war.

He said that he agreed and that is why he is interested in getting more submarines.

You said that you are not parochial in that aspect. That we are matching the Russians now, and if they should double their numbers, you don't feel we should have to double ours. You asked how many it takes to sink everything in the ocean. You said you have

---

116 James Woolsey (b. 1941), later Director of the Central Intelligence Agency (1993–1995).

seen what submarines can do—that you know more than most what they can do.

He said he thinks you can have too many submarines, but that we are presently far from having too many.

You asked what the big issue is—if the two of you had to decide what the Navy should do, what would it be.

He said submarines, cruise missiles, that's probably the best we have.

But he wanted to know if the new submarines aren't reasonably loud. He said he knew the new Soviet subs are really fast.

You said you weren't able to build them because the money is all going to aircraft carriers—the Navy is controlled by aviators, and they are the least qualified. Their average time aboard ship is 2–3 years. You saw that year after year when you did interviews. We would never allow them to command submarines with so little experience. All they had to know was to point that thing into the wind to land the planes. I have seen this more clearly, but there is no one who will listen when I say this.

12 April 1982

Letter to Lord Solly Zuckerman,117 Cabinet Office, 70 Whitehall

Dear Solly,

In connection with our conversation of today, I believe you will be interested in reading the enclosed. It shows the steps that had to be taken in the United States to make it legally possible to give atomic submarine information and equipment to the British—as well as to train British Navy people in this country.

---

117 Solomon "Solly" Zuckerman, Baron Zuckerman (1904–1993), a scientific and political advisor in the United Kingdom, a close friend of Mountbatten and who maintained a friendship with Rickover.

Had it not been for my espousal of the cause, the Atomic Energy Commission and the Congress would not have amended the U.S. Atomic Energy Act to permit transfer of the necessary information to England.

I believe it to be harmful to Britain to have senior government officials take credit for work that was done elsewhere. It is self-defeating to an organization not to show its shortcomings.

The fact that Nature—a scientific magazine with a reputation for accuracy—prints such an article arouses my curiosity. I remember the famous statement of an Oxford don. When asked for advice by a graduating student, he said, "Check your source." Perhaps Nature needs to heed the don's advice.

My best wishes to you and Lady Zuckerman; I look forward to seeing you soon.

2 May 1982

Notes for Meeting with President Carter

After discussion with Dr. Duncan, who at one time had several hour-long meetings with former President Carter, we came up with the following points:

1. He tried to run the presidency as the Navy Nuclear Program was run.
2. We saw together on the ship-building program, but the pressures were too great for him to do anything.
3. There was a lack of ability on the part of government agencies to master the technology they were working on.
4. Nuclear ships always work.
5. President Carter was not well served by his subordinates during the Iranian hostage crisis.
6. The discipline is still not being used in the civilian nuclear program.

7. Our educational system is a national disgrace. At one time, when he was Governor of Georgia, he put into effect some of my ideas on technology.
8. Military programs are probably being better run than the Energy Department and large civilian nuclear plants.

2 May 1982

Memorandum for the Record
Subj: Matters of discussion with President Carter over breakfast

The following items were discussed with President Carter:

a. A book about his experiences. (He intends to write one.)
b. I told him of my ideas about a constitutional convention.
c. We discussed the need to unify the Armed Forces.
d. I pointed out the top-heaviness and bureaucracy in the military and civilian parts of government.
e. I also indicated that top levels in government are alienated from the people they supervise.

Undated (estimated May 1982 based on collection)

Subject: My last observations of the Energy Department

During my last few days in the Energy Department, I was at Headquarters a number of times for discussions with top officials. My impression was that no real work was going on in the organization. They were like a group of theoretical academics or religious communities who, from on high, were deciding the fate of the world—like a group engaged in finding out how many angels could stand on the point of a needle.

Had they known they were about to be eliminated, I doubt they would have made a decision. They would have delayed settling the matter for some time.

The Energy Department is the perfect example of what can happen when academics and purists are placed into a working job. Had it not been for prodding by the Congress, they would not have done anything at all.

They were soul-searching over each step they took, such as selection of nuclear sites.

Imagine how far the Naval Reactors Program would have gotten with such an attitude by those in charge! That is why, over the years, I told the AEC very little about what I did, and then only what I had to, to get funding for my projects.

Also, there were many incompetents in the AEC organization. It is remarkable that anything got done at all. I was able to do so because I told them little about what was being done in the Naval Program.

The main objective of the AEC staff was to get along and draw their pay. Further, physicists were placed in charge of some areas. It was remarkable that so much actually got done.

1530hrs 10 May 1982

Memorandum for the Record
Subj: Telephone Conversation with Ken Emerson, Articles Editor,
The New York Times Magazine

Emerson: Would be interested and intrigued by writing a series of articles on the military strategies over the Falklands islands.

Rickover: I do not wish to speak out about this issue. I do have some thoughts about the matter, but they are not for quotation and are to be treated confidentially.

The British seem faced with proving the necessity of maintaining colonialism. Are colonies worthwhile anymore? This is the issue. Is their prestige worth the trouble? As far as economics—there is no net surplus. Each nation should look cold-bloodedly at themselves, and I believe this is what the British are now doing. The British are probably saying to themselves, "What is in it for us other than prestige?"

Emerson: The world free press (and the U.S. in particular) cheered the British on and encouraged them on Falklands.

Rickover: We have more in common with the British than the Argentines. Sympathy goes to Britain. It is a matter of prestige. Argentina cannot win. It would be a loss of nothing to Britain.

Emerson: Britain has something to lose—that is, Thatcher does. Her political future is in the balance. I wish you would see fit to write articles.

Rickover: I have read extensively on history. Very little in modern warfare has changed the outcome or course of history.

Emerson: I wish you would write some articles on the obsolescence of war.

Rickover: People who engage in war cannot see the obsolescence of war. Each generation must make its own mistakes—we never profit from lessons of history.

Emerson: You seem relatively disinterested.

Rickover: I am not disinterested—should I come out publicly? No. I get most of my information from *The New York Times*. That is my source.

24 May 1982

Letter to President James Carter

Dear President Carter,

I am presently engaged in setting up the "Rickover Foundation." Its purpose is to encourage excellence in education, science, and business.

I am giving all money from speeches and articles to further the Foundation. This, of course, is not a large sum.

In order to assist in the Foundation's purpose, I am asking Presidents Nixon, Ford, and you to serve as Honorary Members of the Board. David Rubenstein may already have mentioned this to you. It would be extremely helpful and a great honor if you were to permit your name to be used in this way.

A benefit for the Foundation is planned in Washington for late January or early February 1983. I will deeply appreciate you considering being present on this occasion.

23 June 1982

Letter from Joseph Wershba, "60 Minutes" producer

Here are some photos you may want for your scrapbook. We received about 400 letters after we ran your testimony on "60 Minutes." About 395 wanted to run you for President. The others were unsure.

Give me a sign that you live and breathe.

July 12, 1982

Rickover makes a telephone call to Mr. Stuart Speiser, an attorney with Speiser & Krause of New York City, whose secretary wrote to

Rickover on 29 June asking that he "send me a statement which I could quote for the book my boss is writing on nuclear weapons."

Since the proposed book is so important, perhaps you should spend more time in your office writing your book and turn your law cases over to your secretary to handle rather than having her write the book for you. I receive requests like this from high school sophomores and perhaps college freshmen, but never from a graduate person in law with fancy embossed letterhead stationery. Since your secretary's signature appeared on your letterhead stationary, I can only assume that the letter to me was approved or directed by you.

There was no mention of financial reward for my time and effort if I would have provided the desired chapter, so I am assuming that your requested input from me was going to be free of charge. Is that a little presumptuous? I assume that all profits from your book will be given to charity—as I have done for all books and articles I have written.

If your secretary initiated the letter on her own responsibility, I suggest that it takes more than a little gall to generate such a request. It may also be worthwhile for a secretary in a prestigious organization such as yours to learn actual specific titles of persons they are addressing. If my name were not quoted on the address, there is no possibility that her letter would have reached me with the title she had indicated.

The reason I am taking this time is to impress upon you that by delving into these matters, you may actually find out what goes on in your own office.

2 August 1982

Letter to Solly Zuckerman

Dear Solly,

I have read your "Judgement and Control in Modern Warfare." It is thoughtful and illuminating and demonstrates your ability as a military thinker. However, I doubt your ideas will be adopted by present-day military leaders: First, they are not the best brains in a country. Second, they have been accustomed, all their adult lives, to operate in the formal chain of military command; this is probably necessary during peace since the primary needs of any large organization are routine in nature—hence their work generally requires conventional thinking.

After years of such experiences, it becomes difficult for most people to perceive issues in a novel manner.

Is there a solution? I believe this lies in defining the characteristics of the position, and having in readiness a few leaders in a country—military or civilian—who have demonstrated the abilities to develop solutions to novel problems.

From what you write—based on your considerable experience—it is obvious that future technologies, therefore future wars, will be more complex than ever before. Further, we must assume from past experience that wars will, if necessary, be fought with all weapons available.

If our national leaders do believe the above, then they must observe Clemenceau's dictum that wars are too important to be left to the soldiers alone.

From the above, it should be clear that, in my opinion, we can no longer trust the decision-making process to the military alone. And you may be able to understand why I have been considered an "iconoclast" by the U.S. Navy, and why I necessarily eschewed, in many cases, the standard methods used in military developmental work. Development "does not know" whether it is civilian or military.

It would be worthwhile for you to get a well-known and respected writer to comment on these thoughts in light of the unprecedented technological advancements being made in armaments.

30 August 1982

ADM Rickover's Conversation with Commander Bruce Valley, speechwriter for Secretary of the Navy John Lehman. Transcript of telephone conversation in reply to Valley's letter of 25 August 1982.

R: I do not give interviews to anyone. Go to Lehman to find out about me. He is the top guy and knows more about the Navy than anyone else. You should know that; you work for him. He has the best interests of the Navy in mind.

V: I am not looking for an interview. I just want to exchange views with you.

R: Why should I exchange views with you? You are no different than anyone else.

V: I hope someday you will change your mind and see me.

R: I doubt that very much.

31 August 1982

Letter to Ariel Sharon, Israeli Minister of Defence, following Rickover's trip

I wish to thank you for your courtesy in permitting me to discuss defense matters. I was particularly impressed and appreciative of your devoting time to me during a period when critical events required all of your time.

I was impressed by your broad national view of your position; your total dedication to your work; and your views of what must be done by officials responsible for their country's defense. This is particularly important for Israel because of its lack of natural resources and its limited manpower as compared with that of its neighbors.

1 September 1982

Letter to General Israel Tal, Assistant Minister of Defence

Thank you for devoting so much of your busy time to educate me about your tank forces and the development of Merkava Tank.

I now understand the "Triangle" (Firepower plus Protection equals Mobility) which you so vividly explained.

It was most thoughtful of you to permit me to see your tank factory and the new tank Israel has developed. It is excellently designed and built.

With my best wishes to you and to the Israeli Tank Force.

15 October 1982

Memorandum for the Record

I telephone Mr. [David] Ariel[118] this date in response to his request of 4 October 1982 and told him his letter was completely unsatisfactory. It constituted an imposition and what he wanted was for me to bare my "id" to an audience; to talk about the intimacies of my life. I told him I doubted he would get anyone to accept his invitation on the basis of his letter unless he was an "exhibitionist."

He asked me if I would still consider attending during the specified time period. My reply was "no."

---

118 President of the Cleveland College of Jewish Studies who wrote to Rickover to give a talk as a "Jew living in contemporary civilization."

25 October 1982

Letter to Coach Jerry Faust, Head Football Coach, University of Notre Dame

Dear Coach Faust,

I learned more about the game of football from watching the Notre Dame players practice than ever before in my life. Not having witnessed football since 1921, you may perhaps appreciate why, for one of the few times in my life, I was not able to give you any advice.

I felt humble the way I saw the fine young men train. But I was discouraged to learn that the average weight of a player was 260 lbs. I would be hesitant to attempt such a venture as playing on the Notre Dame team, since my weight is 130 pounds. Also, to accommodate a player of my size would require changing the rules to allow two 130-pounders in lieu of one 260-pounder...

I will be silently cheering for you for the rest of the season.

30 October 1982

Letter to Richard Nixon

Dear President Nixon,

I deeply appreciate your thoughtfulness in sending me "Leaders." Further, I am most grateful to you for autographing it. I have read reviews of "Leaders"; they are uniformly enthusiastic.

I am an avid reader and have read many books on government. There is no question that "Leaders" will become a "classic" for all who are interested in the workings of government and gaining insight into how men can influence their environment.

I look forward to receiving word from your office of an appropriate date when I may visit with you to discuss my impending trip to China; also, the publication of a book I am considering writing.

With great respect, and with my regards to Mrs. Nixon.

16 November 1982

Memorandum for the Record, telephone conversation with Archbishop James A. Hickey, Washington, DC
Subj: Nuclear Arms Policies; Church involvement

Rickover: I am calling you because of the number of recent newspaper articles concerning the Catholic Church's official position on nuclear arms. I am concerned about your stance and have put my thoughts in writing so I may state them clearly to you...

Hickey: Admiral, as citizens of the U.S., it is our (I speak for my group) moral duty and responsibility to speak out. Particularly since our modern-day weapons are not limited to their impact on combatants, but affect the general populace as well.

Rickover: I agree definitely that you should address the moral issues involved. But are you not thereby taking part in the political process—in the area of our military and national security strategy?

Hickey: We feel that we, as citizens, must get involved in this issue.

Rickover: Yes, I understand that. However, you cannot get beyond your own boundaries—you must leave that to the political arm of government. History has amply demonstrated that the involvement of Church and State in each other's affairs does not work well. This was well understood in Europe hundreds of years ago, and suitable changes were made to prevent recurrence. What

I am discussing is the use of your position (Catholic Bishops have tremendous influence). Yet you have no political obligations or responsibility. In doing so you are "hiding" within the shelter of the Church.

Hickey: We feel the Church must take a position, and it must be known.

Rickover: I do not disagree with your taking of positions based on moral principles. I do believe, however, you are improperly using the Church as a vehicle for exerting political influence. The Church thereby interferes with the functions of the State.

Hickey: Admiral, I have to go to a meeting. I did enjoy our conversation very much, and I would very much like the opportunity to meet you.

16 November 1982

Letter to Mr. Uzi Eilam, Director, Science Administration, State of Israel, c/o Diplomatic Pouch

During my visit to Israel, I visited with you and your colleagues. You will remember I discussed the availability of operating manuals for commercial nuclear power plants. I mentioned at the time that I would attempt to obtain this information from one of our nuclear utilities.

I am enclosing one set of these manuals. You will note that I have omitted the name of the specific plant and the utility involved at their specific request. I have permission to give you a copy with the provision that no reference is to be made, at any time, of the company whose instructions are being provided.

I must have your written assurance to that effect. Mention, direct or indirect, of which specific company or plant is involved or identified, should be deleted in their entirety. I obtained these documents on the basis of confidentiality and anonymity. In order that the spirit of this intent is fully honored, I request your written assurance.

It is extremely important for you to note the following:

The "For information only" stamp on the procedures is used to note that these copies are not "controlled copies." Therefore, the manual should not be used by you for actual plant operation.

You must make it absolutely clear to anyone using this material that he must make up (originate) his own instructions, as fits the case, and not use these documents other than as a general guide.

Also, these volumes are being sent to you on the condition that they be treated securely and not be disseminated, in any manner, to any individual, organization, or group outside the State of Israel. Please affirm your agreement to the above.

3 December 1982

Notes for ADM R to talk with CDR Bowler (Naval Institute)

1. Thank him for sending the calendar.
2. Tell him you have read the article "Diesel Boats Forever" by John Byron. You talked to Byron and told him you thought it was a good article.
3. Tell him you do not desire to take part in their Oral History program at the Naval Institute
   (Admiral talked to CDR Bowler).

In addition to the above, ADM R. told CDR Bowler that he should contact the admiral in 50 years, and then he would consider taking part in his Oral History program.

Reply of 13 December 1982 from Uzi Eilam (see 16 November 1982)

Ambassador M. Arens[119] forwarded, via diplomatic pouch, one set of manuals that is already being studied by our staff. I would like to state most categorically that no reference will be made at any time of the company whose manuals we have received. The books will be handled only by the professional staff actually involved in the study and planning of nuclear reactors, and will not be disseminated in any manner, to any individual, organization, or group outside the state of Israel...

3 December 1982

Letter to Richard Nixon

Dear Mr. President,

I cannot adequately express how much I enjoyed our visit and lunch in New York, Tuesday.

First, permit me to say that you are so gracious that no one could have believed that you occupied the highest position in the United States and are a leading and most knowledgeable citizen.

Also, it was most generous of you to accept the invitation to attend the Tribute, which will be given in my honor on February 28, 1983. I am most grateful. I do appreciate your asking Mr. Ruwe to assist Ms. DiGennaro with the political aspects which may arise in connection with the Foundation and Tribute.

It is hard for me to express my thanks properly. However, your attitude is one I should have expected, having known you intimately during our 1958 visit to Russia. You remain a most courteous person.

---

119 Moshe Arens (1925–2019).

Please express my thanks to your daughter for her kindness. I must say, however, that Christopher will make a better-looking candidate than his grandfather.

With my best regards to Mrs. Nixon.

21 January 1983

[Telephone Conversation] Admiral Rickover/Admiral Watkins 10:15 a.m.

Subj: Leadership Articles in [Naval] Institute Proceedings

Rickover: When the hell is the Institute going to wise up and stop publishing these nonsensical articles on leadership?
Watkins: I am in full agreement with you. I have fired some of those on active duty in the Institute and am going to put a stop to this drill. [Lieutenant junior grades] writing knowledgeable articles on principles, practices, and the art of leadership is ludicrous. How was your trip to China?
Rickover: I was well received there. Don't kid yourself about their Navy. They are first rate, and anyone who thinks otherwise should beware. Their ships are among the cleanest I have ever seen.
Watkins: Absolutely. Although their ships are predominantly old, their sailors are superb. They are outstanding seafarers, and I agree that anyone who puts their Navy down does not know the facts. We are improving rapidly. I just returned from visiting the USS MISSISSIPPI (nuclear cruiser), and it was the cleanest ship I have ever been on board. No water in the bilges; engineering spaces were great; quiet and immaculate. I was most impressed. For the first time, engineering in the Navy overshadows

weapons in the state of the art. Engineering is outstanding; weapons systems are in a terrible state.

Rickover: The key is reporting responsibilities. They should visit other ships that they see and use the good things they see. They learn something.

Watkins: Absolutely. I have been influenced by you for the past 25 years, and I see the results of your work in the fleet. It has paid off handsomely. Engineering is outstanding.

Rickover: I appreciate your saying that.

Watkins: I am calling a meeting of the Institute (I am President) and am going to stop this nonsense of the ever-continuing articles on leadership.

Rickover: Can I help?

Watkins: I will let you know, Admiral. Thanks for calling me.

21 January 1983

Letter to Huaqing Liu, Commander-in-Chief, People's Republic of China Navy

Thank you for sponsoring my recent visit to China. It was as interesting and illuminating a visit as any I have made in my naval career. Above all, the visit made plain to me the great progress your nation has made in industry, in education, and in military matters. I have always considered the Chinese people to be fine examples of the human race; my visit confirmed this. I also appreciate your courtesy in arranging the formal dinner in the Great Hall for me and my party, as well as the gifts presented to us.

It was gracious of you to arrange my visit to the Wuhan shipyard and to a submarine. I was impressed with the methods used and construction of the ship. I congratulate you for the competence of those who design and build your ships. I enjoyed our personal conversation as well as your frankness.

I wish you continued success in your work and, above all, continued good health.

24 January 1983

Letter to Clayton Barrow, Editor, U.S. Naval Institute Proceedings

I am herewith submitting an item for possible publication in the Naval Institute *Proceedings* entitled "Leadership."

Should you accept this item for publication, I desire no remuneration.

The Institute *Proceedings* frequently publishes articles on Leadership; most written by young, inexperienced junior officers.

The thought occurs: "Why is it one finds no such leadership articles in business or industry periodicals?" Yet, the Navy constantly claims it tries to emulate business methods.

Another question arises: Many naval officers, especially senior ones, have left the Navy to obtain employment in private industry. I do not recollect any of them ever writing an article on how to improve the leadership within their company or industry.

31 January 1983

Letter to Clayton Barrow, Jr., Editor, U.S. Naval Institute Proceedings

Dear Mr. Barrow,

Having been a reader of the Naval Institute *Proceedings* continuously since 1922, a thought just occurred to me:

"Has the Naval Institute been of value in improving the United States Navy?"

In thinking over this matter, I have come to the conclusion that I have witnessed no such evidence during my naval career.

I consider it desirable to answer this question by polling your readership.

Would you be so kind as to advise me of the comments of your readers? I assume you will publish this letter in the Institute *Proceedings*.

2 February 1983

[Editor's note: Rickover received thousands of letters and cards of fan mail. In a letter dated 28 January 1983, a resident of Washington, DC sent a birthday card to Rickover because "we share the same birthdate." Rickover directed his assistant, R.W. Oldenburg, to send the following letter.]

Admiral Rickover is in receipt of your birthday greeting. Your letter also states that your birthdate is January 27.

Since there are 365 days in a year, and the population of this country is nearly 230,000,000, Admiral Rickover has determined that 630,000 Americans share the same birthdate.

Therefore, to be consistent, he suggests that you send a birthday greeting to each of the approximately remaining 629,998. (This figure may change by the time you receive this letter.)

He congratulates you on your birthday and trusts you will have many, many more of them, and on each such occasion, he suggests you read this letter.

15 February 1983

Note to General John Vessey, Chairman, Joint Chiefs of Staff

I believe you will be interested in the enclosed document. This statement was solicited by the Honorable Ike Skelton (D-MO).

(Handwritten 17 February: I talked with Cong Skelton today. I think I convinced him to leave the [Joint Chiefs of Staff] alone.

15 February 1983

Memorandum for Congressman [Ike] Skelton

Subj: Organization of the Joint Chiefs of Staff

1. You have asked for my opinions on our Joint Chiefs of Staff.
2. I was on duty in Washington at the end of World War II when discussions were going on as to the organization of the military. Naturally, one of the big issues was the top direction of the three services because of the lessons learned during the war. After considerable discussion and study, the decision was made to organize the Joint Chiefs of Staff in the manner it is today. I was asked for my opinion at the time and fully agreed with the organization.
3. I have been on duty in Washington during the entire period during and since World War II and have observed the JCS ever since its inception. My opinion is that it has done an outstanding job. The reason for this happy state is that it is composed of senior members from all the services. Those chosen for this duty invariably have been of the highest level in ability, intelligence, and knowledge, not only from their own service, but from all the services. It has been my observation that in performing their functions, these officers have always acted for the ultimate good of the United States and were not partial to the parochial interests of their own service.
4. I have given a great deal of thought to the possible reorganization of the Joint Chiefs. I have also discussed this matter with many knowledgeable individuals. The unanimous opinion is that the U.S. is fortunate to have such an

organization composed of extremely competent people and which is totally responsive to its needs.

5. My definite opinion is that we not tamper with this organization. It operates extremely well just as it is and is necessary to the military needs of the United States.

2 March 1983

[Editor's note: Rickover received a letter from a boy named Hyman _____ from San Francisco who was being mocked at school for his name. He asked Admiral Rickover about his name, how he felt, and if he was ever angry about it. Rickover normally signed his name "H.G. Rickover." In this case, he used his first name.]

Dear Hyman,

The name "Hyman" is a Hebrew word; it means "life."
A person's name is not important. What is important is what sort of person he is and what he accomplishes in life; therefore, he should strive to do the best he can in everything he undertakes. You should also remember that great people talk about ideas; smart people talk about things; foolish people talk about others...

Study as hard as you can, and don't waste your time looking at too much TV.

Sincerely

HYMAN G. RICKOVER

9 May 1983

Letter from Secretary of the Navy John Lehman

I am happy to confirm that the name HYMAN G. RICKOVER has been assigned to the attack submarine, SSN 709, now being built at Groton and scheduled to be launched on August 27, 1983.

We would be honored to have Mrs. Rickover sponsor this new combatant ship and to have you be the principal speaker at the ceremony.

[*Handwritten by Rickover in large letters*: "NO!"]

30 May 1983

Address at Folder B'nai B'rith International Headquarters in accepting the Philip Klutznick Public Service Award.

I was in the Navy for more than 63 years, longer than any naval officer in our history. Nevertheless, I do not believe I have done enough for my country. I did what I wanted and was even paid well for doing it. And I obeyed all the orders I agreed with.

For those who consider me stubborn, I must tell you I started early. At the age of four, I was deathly sick. The doctor had to break my teeth to force medicine down my throat.

Throughout my life, my bluntness and plain language have made me "controversial." But I have always followed the laws of engineering and told the truth as I saw it, even if this was contrary to the views of my superiors.

I have always tried to save the taxpayer's money and acted against contractors who tried to cheat the government. My efforts were largely in vain; yet I continued.

I was reminded of the ancient philosopher who came to a city, determined to save its inhabitants from sin and wickedness. Night and day he walked the streets and haunted the marketplaces. He preached against greed and envy, against falsehood and indifference. At first, the people listened and smiled. Later, they turned away; he no longer amused them. Finally, a child asked, "Why do you go on? Do you not see it is hopeless?"

The man answered, "In the beginning, I thought I could change men. If I still shout, it is to prevent men from changing me."

I have been retired from active duty in the Navy, but I have not and will not be retired from active duty in life. Life is the pursuit of excellence. To acquiesce in mediocrity is to destroy what has made this country respected, admired, and strong. I love my country in an old-fashioned way; she has allowed an immigrant boy to realize every opportunity available to those who work hard.

I was born in Poland, then a part of Russia. I was not allowed to attend public schools because of my Jewish faith. However, starting at the age of four, I attended a religious school where we learned by rote from the Old Testament, in Hebrew. School hours were from sunrise to sunset, six days a week. On the seventh day, we attended the synagogue a good part of the day.

I remember the Russo-Japanese War of 1905. A company of Russian soldiers, wearing white trousers and carrying rifles, marched through our village looking for a place to bivouac for the night. The school served their purpose—we pupils had to leave.

I also remember the first time I ate an orange. Each year, just before the holy days, the Jewish settlers in Palestine, nearly all of whom had come from Russia or Poland, shipped boxes of oranges to the Jews in Russian and Polish towns. It was the duty of each family to buy at least one orange to help the settlers. So once each year, my mother bought an orange and shared it with my sister and me.

My father immigrated to the United States shortly before 1900 and saved enough money to send tickets for my mother, my sister, and me. My mother packed as much of our possessions as she could carry in a sheet. This included bedding and ten days' supply of kosher food.

For two days we traveled in a canvas-covered wagon to the border between Poland and Germany. At one time, a company of Cossacks on horseback rode by. They whipped the sides of our wagon and the horses. The driver had a hard time controlling them.

We came to the border at night. My mother and sister walked across the wide border; I was carried on the guide's back. We then went by wagon to the railroad station, where we boarded a train which eventually got us to Antwerp. There we stayed one night in an old hotel near the waterfront.

On board ship, we, and many other immigrants, were in steerage. The only food the ship provided was a barrel of stale bread and a barrel of salt herring. But my mother had brought her own food, because it was unlawful for us to eat anything made of any part of a pig. She feared the bread might have been baked with lard.

My sister and I ran around the lower decks while my mother sat on the steel deck the entire time, guarding the sheet with all our worldly possessions. The second-class passengers from the deck above occasionally threw us children an apple or orange, as we looked up at them from between-decks....

I started grammar school at the age of six and one-half in Brooklyn, knowing only a few words of English. Shortly thereafter, my mother, who worked at a Catholic hospital washing clothes, brought home for me a number of old St. Nicholas magazines, given to her by the nuns. It was my first gift. I read them avidly. They greatly helped me learn English. Twelve years later at the Naval academy, I finished near the top of my class in English.

I was probably as poorly prepared academically as any plebe who had ever entered the Naval Academy. Each week of the years at high school, I worked more than 70 hours, with no vacation during the entire time.

I remember those high school years vividly. Trying to study a book while delivering Western Union telegrams was difficult. It would have been wonderful to have had the opportunity for more study, for reading good books. But I did not have that opportunity.

In reviewing my past, I realize how much I have left undone—but I am still trying. Therefore, I accept this award as an encouragement to keep on. I thank you, and I pledge I will still try to get the harvest before the rains come.

1 June 1983

Telephone conversation between Admiral Rickover and Admiral Arleigh A. Burke (former Chief of Naval Operations) regarding retirement

Rickover: I find that incumbents do not care to hear what their predecessors have to say, and I wonder why. Perhaps they do not want to be bound by the past.

Burke: Those who retire have a tendency to cut themselves off from the organization: it's the way we are trained. In my case, I began consulting with Admiral Carney about a year after my retirement, because he had initiated a program I wanted to know more about. Before that, though, I made no contact.

R: Isn't there a regular conference for former CNO's?

B: There used to be. It was discontinued by Admiral Zumwalt.

R: I see. Zumwalt would do something like that. He had a lot of programs that he knew his predecessors would disagree with; so rather than have them on the record, he eliminated the conference.

B: I think the same reluctance to seek advice from a predecessor exists in civilian life. Having been on a number of boards, I know that once an individual is off a board, his advice is no longer desired (although those remaining are polite if he offers advice). The newcomers want to try things their own way. Texaco did not, for one, follow this tendency. After I left their board, they did consult me on particular issues.

R: What is your opinion about the U.S. Navy in this regard?

B: There is an annual flag officers' conference; but it is primarily a how-goes-it affair. No advice is actively sought.

R: There is no attempt on the Navy's part to get advice and opinions from the former CNO's?

B: With some exceptions. I objected to the Navy's over-reliance on computers during Admiral Holloway's tour as CNO. I told them that man's judgment skills could not be programmed into a computer and that computers could not be counted on to weigh unmeasurable variables. Admiral Holloway and his people told me I did not understand the modern Navy. So, I bought an IBM computer, to learn about how one communicates with computers. I learned that a computer is only as good as its programming. It can't think. It can't react to unprogrammed stimuli. It can't improvise. When I went back to Admiral Holloway and his people, told them that I did understand "the modern Navy," and said that I still felt that over-reliance on computers was wrong, they listened.

R: As much as I know about nuclear power, no one in the Navy has ever asked me a single question since my retirement.

B: Occasionally I have been asked for advice on a particular point; but generally, I have been left alone.

R: Perhaps that is the best system: letting each generation make its own mistakes.

B: The same thing happens with presidents.

R: If you were on the podium and had to answer the question, what is the reason for this reluctance? How would you answer?

B: In the Navy's case, I think it goes back to command of ships. The new OOD[120] has the conn: the old OOD is relieved. There is a very sharp line of demarcation.

R: True, but that is not quite the same thing. I wonder if the line of demarcation between retiree and successor is or needs to be as sharp. In the military, each man generally has a very short tenure in a particular assignment. Thus, he has only a short time to make his mark, which can lead to poor judgment. I have long advocated that each CNO should serve for seven or eight years.

B: After five years, though, a man as CNO can begin to tire. When I was CNO, I had people on my staff to tell me if I were beginning to stumble (because one can't always tell). They never did; but when I was offered another tour as CNO, I declined.

15 June 1983

Telephone conversation with Mr. Sulzberger, publisher of The New York Times *regarding article "Better Teachers Simply Aren't Coming Along," by Mr. Fred Hechinger*

Rickover: ...All I wanted is your personal commitment to this essential cause [education]. If you cannot do it, quit your job and let someone else do this. I imagine no one else speaks to you in the manner I do.

Sulzberger: Only my wife and mother talk to me as you do.

R: Have your mother give me a call; she has got to straighten you out...

---

120 Officer of the Deck.

1 July 1983

Telephone conversation with Virginia Governor Charles S. Robb

Rickover: Please remember me to your lovely wife [Lynda, daughter of the late Lyndon B. Johnson]. Tell her I am convinced that it will someday be fully appreciated how great a man her father was.

Robb: I shall be talking with her later this evening. I will pass that on to her. She will very much appreciate what you have said, I am sure.

Rickover: I shall close with the following statement: I came to this country at the age of 6½. Had I stayed where I came from, I should have been dead in World War I. This country took me in and gave me greater opportunities than I could have even dreamed. I love our country for that, and want to do everything I can to repay my great debt of gratitude.

Robb: You have gone far in your efforts to pay back that debt.

Rickover: There is always more I can do.

1 July 1983

Telephone conversation with Jean Mayer, president of Tufts University, reference to The New York Times *"Letters to the Editor" on 26 June 1983*

Rickover: I am reading here in *The New York Times* that you are not in favor of standardized curriculum for high schools.

Mayer: Yes, I am in favor of standardization.

R: Well, I am just telling you what I am reading.

M: Apparently, you cannot read.

R: I think I can read pretty good. I have written several books…

Mr. Jean Mayer at that point hung up the phone. At no time during the conversation was the admiral rude. The admiral called Mr. Mayer back and made the following statement. "Before you hang up the phone, may I make this one comment. I was going to compliment you on a fine article, you goddamn fool." The admiral immediately hung up.

6 July 1983

Memorandum for the Record. Visit with the Chief of Naval Operations, Admiral James D. Watkins

On 6 July at 1300, I visited Admiral Watkins in his office for the purpose of presenting a photograph taken during the "Salute to Admiral Rickover" on 28 February 1983.

I also gave Admiral Watkins a copy of the USDAO[121] Beijing, PRC, intelligence report, entitled "Admiral Rickover's Visit to the PRC." I specifically pointed out the following quotations:

"The fact that Hu Yaobang wanted to have a meeting with Admiral Rickover was in itself significant, as up until the Rickover visit Hu has only agreed to meet with two Americans, former President Nixon and former President Carter." During the meeting, Hu said that the PRC is more than 50 years behind the U.S. in technology and asked ADM Rickover to be his "high ranking advisor," and Admiral Rickover said he would be happy to act in that capacity.

Hu was the only Chinese leader to date the admiral met who "spoke openly and freely."

---

121 U.S. Defense Attache's Office.

Admiral Watkins asked me if Admiral McKee has ever called asking for my advice. I said, "No." Admiral Watkins said he would talk to Admiral McKee again.

7 July 1983

Letter to Melvin Price,[122] Rayburn House Office Building

PERSONAL AND PRIVATE MEMORANDUM

Dear Mr. Price

I understand that the Navy FY84 Research and Development budget for advanced attack submarine development and advanced sonar development has been reduced from the requested $218 million to $157 million by the House Armed Services Committee.

I believe it would be worthwhile that you ask the Navy to give you a personal presentation describing the impact of this reduction on U.S. military effectiveness. There has been a recent dramatic advance in Soviet submarines. I am concerned that if we now reduce our efforts in designing and developing higher performance submarines, we shall lose our technical superiority.

In particular, the reduced budget would delay important design studies and seriously delay achievement of silencing and improved sonar capabilities. Both these are essential for a modern, viable submarine force.

I believe that the impact of this budget reduction is serious enough to warrant a deep examination by your Committee.

11 July 1983

Telephone conversation with Mr. Philip Geyelin, author of an article in The *Washington Post, 7 July 1983, "Remembering the Maine"*

---

122 Melvin Price (1905–1988) served in Congress for more than four decades.

Rickover: I have just read your article in *The Washington Post* and the president is wrong. It was not the Spanish who blew up the MAINE. I have written on the subject, and it was an internal explosion. You, as a reporter, should know your history and should have done some thorough research before you wrote an article.

Geyelin: Admiral, what I was trying to say was the president should not make foreign policy on something that may not be true…

R: Have you read my book, "How the Battleship Maine was Destroyed?"

G: No, Admiral, I have not.

R: Are you aware that I have proven conclusively that it could not have been an external explosion, as had been concluded by a court of inquiry at the time?

G: No, Admiral.

R: I only fault you for one thing, and that is you need to get other people's opinion on an article before you go ahead and write it.

G: Admiral, I was only writing about what was known at that time, and the point I was trying to make was almost exactly the point you made in your book.

R: Well then, how come I couldn't read it that way? After all, I am what I consider to be a capable reader.

G: Admiral, I think you need to correct the president then. He needs correcting more than I do.

R: You think that it is every federal employee's job to correct the president or other high government officials every time they make a mistake? You think that is my job? You have the power of the paper. You are the one that should correct him through the press.

G: Admiral, if you will only write down…

R: No, that is not my job. You are the one that fucked it up. Now you have to be the one to unfuck it. I have nothing else to say about it. Goodbye.

16 July 1983

Meeting with Admiral Kinnaird R. McKee (Director, Navy Nuclear Propulsion Program) on the subject of nuclear submarines and the running of the Nuclear Navy

1. At the request of Admiral Watkins, CNO, Admiral McKee visited me this morning at 9:00 a.m. The meeting lasted one hour.
2. Admiral McKee said he wished to obtain my ideas on what I considered was the manner in which the Naval Reactors Division was being run; also, my opinion on the way the new large submarine should be designed. I discussed the latter issue first.
3. I reminded him that a submarine was a very vulnerable ship; that the larger and therefore heavier it became, the more difficult it was for it to recover from a depth emergency. Therefore, he must be very careful in making sure that theoretical people—men who did not understand the inherent danger of a submarine—would not alone decide that such a submarine be built. Above all, he must consider himself as a submarine operator and use his actual submarine operating experience as the guide.

4. I understood from what I had heard that such a large submarine was being designed, and it was for this reason I was cautioning him. I added that it would be easier, probably, to obtain funds for two good submarines, which cost more than the single huge one. Admiral McKee appeared to agree with my comments and observations.

5. I next discussed, in a general way, how the nuclear section was being operated. I said that from my experience, there were always certain leading people in an organization who attempt to actually "run" the organization. I added he must be very careful that he understands this. This is particularly so in his case, because his actual technical experience is not as great as mine—necessarily so, because he has been an "all-round" naval officer and had not put in anywhere near as much time as I had in design, manufacture, and operation of nuclear submarines and in training of men.

6. I believe this made an impression on Admiral McKee, in that he will consider more carefully the design of a very large submarine, which I understand has found favor in many eyes. I also said it was quite easy for a man in charge to become too highly involved in the day-to-day work of the organization and to depend on one or two individuals to a greater extent than others. If it were so—and it may very well be—he himself will not actually be running the organization, but in effect it will be run by others.

7. We discussed many other items relevant to what was going on.

8. Admiral McKee ended by saying that he would be happy if he could occasionally visit me and ask my opinion on some of the issues which he faced. I replied that I should be very happy to do so, provided these discussions were always considered as private and not publicized.

16 July 1983

Telephone conversation with Vice Admiral Robert R. Monroe (Director, Research and Development, Test & Evaluation [OP-098] re The Washington Post *article, "Independent Weapons Testing Voted"*

Rickover: I just read an article in *The Washington Post* which reports that the Senate has approved a bill to create an independent weapons testing office in the Department of Defense. I talked with Admiral Hays about this yesterday.

Monroe: Yes, sir. Admiral Hays asked me to call you. We appreciate your offer to help. Because this bill has passed in the Senate, we must concentrate our efforts to scuttle this bill in the House.

R: How could this bill get passed in the Senate? Who fought against it?

M: The entire Defense Department, with Delauer as the principal spokesman. Our impression is that Congress believes the military-industrial complex is trying to go into production with half-tested weapons.

R: There is no such thing as a "military-industrial complex."

M: Senators Pryor and Roth introduced the bill, and it has 20 or 30 co-sponsors, among them Kennedy and Kassebaum. This bill has been written in such a way that no one can vote against it; that is why it received a 91% approval in the Senate.

R: This country depends on the military to protect it during wartime, yet during peacetime the military leaders have the lowest respect by the government.

M: The military has always been reviled during peacetime: "Tommy this and Tommy that." [Kipling, "Tommy"]

R: Kipling was writing about cavalry and a different age. Today, the military is big business. I do not have the impression of general revulsion for the military in my dealings with the public. People in the Navy today are outstanding, and would do well in any civilian concern. You should arrange for someone from the House or the Senate to call me (I am not supposed to know about all this). My talking to Senators and Representatives is the best I can do. They know I do not do what people tell me to do, unless I agree in the first place... I can tell them what my experience is. The civilians have too strong a self-interest; they cannot see things as a military man would. I want to help. The Navy has better leadership today than ever, from Admiral Watkins on down. What committee is handling this?

M: The Senate Armed Services Committee (under Sen. Tower). But the bill was introduced in the Joint Committee on Government Affairs (under Sen. Roth and Rep. Brooks). Brooks will be a key player. Senator Proxmire is a co-sponsor.

R: I shall call Proxmire. I know him well. I also know Pryor, but he is not very strong. I shall be glad to talk with them. But you must send me the right ammunition. Have someone send me the background material as soon as possible.

17 August 1983

Sheri Venema, reporter for The Norwich Bulletin, called to ask about an article published in The Day *on 16 August.*

Venema: Admiral Rickover views the naming of the H.G. Rickover submarine after him an honor too late in coming and one that was purposefully diminished by the Navy. A source close to the

83-year-old Admiral said the admiral believes the Navy's decision was merely an attempt to circumvent a move by Congress to name a Nimitz aircraft carrier after him. He feels it is a trick, not an honor. The source said "too late in his life to be a meaningful honor."

22 September 1983

Telephone conversation with Luis R. Marcos, MD regarding his article in The New York Times

R: In your article you say that America has the obligation to teach foreigners in their mother tongue. Would you want your tax dollars to pay for this? Do you really think it is America's responsibility to teach these people who come of their own free will in their native tongue?

M: I am not sure that you read my article.

R: What country are you from?

M: That does not matter. Are you sure you read my article?

R: Yes, you said that America has the responsibility to teach immigrants in their native tongue.

M: Where did I say that in my article?

R: Here. I'll read it to you: "During this early stage, which may last up to six months, it is important for these children to have the opportunity to communicate in their mother tongue..." Do you know what? This is the stupidest thing I have read in a long time.

M: That is your opinion.

R: And I also think that you are a nitwit. (The admiral then hung up on Marcos.)

18 October 1983

Telephone conversation with Amy Green, Channel 7 News requesting an interview for a special on "The Kennedy Years" [Rickover notes that he previously published his thoughts on Kennedy]

Green: Have you had them published?

R: Yes, excepts from them were published in *The New York Times*. I tell you what, when you die and go to Heaven or Hell, you can get together with President Kennedy and have a good time. Maybe I'll meet you there, too.

G: We could get together now, right here on Earth.

R: Have you had it proved to you that there is another life?

G: No, I haven't.

R: Where do you think you are going to go?

G: I'm not saying right now, Admiral.

R: Oh! So you are going to go to purgatory. You know what purgatory is, don't you? That's in the middle, between Heaven and Hell. How old are you?

G: I'm less than 30.

R: Then you must be 29. When will you be 30?

G: In three years.

R: Do you know that after 30, people don't have any more big ideas? You only have three years left.

G: I guess this is my last chance to get a big memory for me. I would really like to get an interview with you.

R: No thanks. All the people want to see up there is a character. They don't care what I say, they only want to see a character.

G: But the character can be a philosopher while up there.

R: No, I really don't want to. Thanks. Do you know what your boss could do to improve the world? He could commit hari-kari. Do you know that television is killing the children of today? They watch too much and don't learn enough.

G: Well, Admiral, I wish you would reconsider.

R: No, but you have made my minute. Have you ever heard that before? You've made my minute. From 4:19 to 4:20, you've made my minute.

G: Well, thank you, Admiral.

R: Yeah, I'll put you in my book of memoirs. You've made my minute. Well, goodbye.

G: Goodbye, and thank you.

18 October 1983

Telephone conversation with Milton A. Loewenthal, City University of New York regarding his article in the 17 October 1983 edition of The New York Times, *"Bring Back the Rigor Colleges Practiced"*

[Editor's note: Rickover calls to tell him he does not understand the article.]

L: The people I have received feedback from have not mentioned that they could not understand it. I've gotten very good feedback on it...

R: I just did not understand any of it. Look, I do not want to make a big deal out of this, I just want to tell you that I do not understand your article.

L: Well, I thank you for letting me know.

R: Okay, goodbye.

[The admiral called back about 10 minutes later.]

R: In the military we have what is called "Estimate of the Situation." You must be logical. On one side you have fact, and then you have action. You ought to try it. It may help you in your writing.

L: Okay, but I really do not think my article is that vague that people cannot understand it.

R: Now you are making too much out of this, and I do not want to go on any further. Goodbye.

28 October 1983

Telephone conversation with Admiral Watkins, Chief of Naval Operations, regarding article "The Revolt of Navy Ship Designers," by Admiral Elmo Zumwalt in The Washington Times.

W: I have seen it.

R: Shouldn't the Navy do something about this article?

W: We are.

R: Let me look at it. I have been in this for some time.

W: I will do that, Admiral.

R: Why does Zumwalt wait until now to say something? Why didn't he do it when it was his responsibility?

W: Zumwalt has been anti-Navy since his retirement. He is the only ex-CNO to do this. He doesn't get anywhere: he sponsors this, he runs for that.

R: I have never said anything against the Navy. I am retired. I am working now to improve education, trying to develop a national standard. I think I am going to be successful. Maybe I can get you to write a letter endorsing my efforts to improve education.

W: Just sketch out a few of your thoughts, Admiral, and I'll write the letter.

R: How can I help you? You never ask my advice.

W: We are doing all right, Admiral. Most of the problems, I'll have to handle myself. I support what you are doing, because there isn't anybody else who understands the importance of having an educated youth. It is important both to the Navy and to the country. The demographic studies show that the quality of our 18-year-old recruits is going to get worse and worse. We must train them.

R: Yes, and they use that training to their advantage in civilian life. We mention that in our advertising. You ought to have me speak about this. Believe me, wherever I go, I am listened to. Send me somebody, and I will help.

W: The one thing you should understand about the Zumwalt/ Bagley article is that no one cares. Not the Congress, not the Navy.

R: This came up before Congress when I was at Naval Reactors. I told them to face facts: if you want more power, you must have a larger power plant. They were talking desires, not reality.

W: That was always Zumwalt's modus operandi. He used the Navy to get recognition.

R: Well, I don't want to take up any more of your time. Thank you for calling.

28 October 1983

Telephone conversation with Mr. John Quinn, Editor of USA Today, regarding interview conducted by Ms. Barbara Reynolds on 27 October 1983

[Editor's note: Rickover begins the call summarizing the article and noting that "black leaders have let their people down and don't care enough for quality education."]

R: What do you think about that? Do you agree with me?

Q: Admiral, I agree with your right to say that.

R: What kind of answer is that? You want me to stick my head out on education, but you won't express the opinion of the newspaper. I want to rescind my interview. I do not wish it to be published. Can I do that?

Q: Not as far as I'm concerned. You already granted us the interview.

R: Look, I'll call up a lawyer and see if I can stop it.

Q: Go ahead, if that is what you want.

R: I will never again have anything to do with your newspaper, and I will tell other people about this. What kind of editor are you that won't speak for the newspaper? I don't ever want anything to do with you or your newspaper.

Q: Admiral, I cannot agree or disagree with what you said until after I have had a chance to read your interview. I said that I would be glad to call you after I have read what you said.

R: When will you call me back? Today?

Q: Admiral, as soon as I have read it over. Probably Monday.

R: I would appreciate it if you could call me back today.

Q: I'll try, Admiral.

31 October 1983

Handwritten note to Jimmy Carter

I am sad to learn of the death of your mother. Although there is nothing one can do to lessen your sadness, I do want you to know that my thoughts are with you.

22 November 1983

Telephone conversation with Mr. Mike Wallace, Correspondent for "60 Minutes" re invitation to be on "60 Minutes"

1. Mr. Mike Wallace invited the admiral to appear on CBS "60 Minutes." The admiral declined Mr. Wallace's invitation, stating that for years he has stated his position on education in newspaper articles, books that have been published, and several speeches, but it does not do any good. The admiral also stated that as long as the American people are wealthy and no real tough times exist, they will have no interest in the problem.

2. Mr. Mike Wallace said that apparently the admiral has not been talking with the right people. "60 Minutes" reaches 50 million Americans, and Mr. Wallace believes with the admiral's special capabilities to command attention could have a tremendous impact. The admiral disagreed with the impact he would have, stating that television has become just an ordinary thing and people have grown used to it. Unconvinced by Mr. Wallace's arguments, the admiral again declined Mr. Wallace's kind invitation.

23 November 1983

Memorandum for the Record. Meeting with Vice Admiral Nils Thunman[123]

1. The following recommendations were made by the admiral to Vice Admiral Thunman:
    a. Continue to obtain the best people for entrance into the Nuclear Power School, both officers and men. The most difficult task to maintain an excellent submarine force is to get outstanding people. Offer submarine billets as choice billets for midshipmen at the academy.
    b. Continue the rigorous training program.
    c. The submarine force must continue to engage in frequent and regular inspection, as if we were at war.
    d. Submarine officers and men should start and end their careers in a single field. Officers should be judged for the jobs they do and not the number of jobs they have had during their careers.
    e. Submarines should be operated in a war atmosphere.
    f. Must have special promotional opportunities.
    g. Must get extra pay.
    h. Must have frequent briefings for congressional committees and staffs. Congress relies on their staffs for information; it is more important to deal with the staff than with members of Congress. From the admiral's dealings, members of Congress will understand and will support all of the measures. The problem is to convince the CNO and the staff.

---

123 Vice Admiral Nils Thunman (b. 1932), U.S. Naval Academy Class of 1954. At the time of this letter, he served as Deputy Chief of Naval Operations for Submarine Warfare.

28 November 1983

Letter to President Richard M. Nixon

I have read "Leaders." It should be read by all who aspire to govern in large as well as in small affairs.

It displays a knowledge of history and of mankind by one who practiced these at the highest levels. Your tenure of office was in an especially difficult and dangerous period of our history. Your acumen and ability to act surely and quickly served our country well.

I write because of my personal experience with and gratitude to you. I have never served with a man who displayed such confidence in life—a man who inspired those who worked with him to achieve his high standards.

Your position in history is assured.

2 December 1983

Telephone conversation with Rear Admiral John D. Bulkeley[124] [President, U.S. Navy Board of Inspection and Survey regarding naval ships]

1. Admiral Rickover asked Admiral Bulkeley what he thought the current condition of ships is today in the Navy. Admiral Bulkeley replied that the condition of ships is improving, and that his office now has credibility and support, whereas for many years his finding were ignored or shoved aside by top-level naval officers, particularly Zumwalt and Hayward[125] (before he became CNO).

---

124 Vice Admiral John Bulkeley (1911-1996), U.S. Naval Academy Class of 1933 who is known best as the commander of the Patrol Torpedo Boat (PT Boat) that evacuated General Douglas MacArthur from the Philippines. He was a recipient of the Medal of Honor.

125 Admiral Thomas Hayward (1924-2022), U.S. Naval Academy Class of 1947. Chief of Naval Operations 1978-1982.

2. Admiral Bulkeley compared himself to Admiral Rickover, saying that he was an independent, trying to do his job despite continuing opposition from his superiors. He said that he always told the truth, even as an ensign, and had sometimes gotten kicked in the teeth for his trouble.

3. Admiral Bulkeley said that the amphibious ships are virtually defenseless outside Beirut; the ships are poorly maintained and have no basic point defense systems. This is so because Admiral Hines would not permit his ships to undergo INSERV[sp][126] inspections. Admiral Bulkeley said that many high-level officers do not wish to report shortcomings of any kind on their ships, because to do so might affect their own promotions. Admiral Rickover said that such officers were not doing their primary job, and that they were not loyal to the Navy. Admiral Bulkeley agreed, saying that the problem lies in human nature, and that the practice of protecting one's own promotion is being passed from one generation of officers to the next.

4. Admiral Bulkeley had nothing but high praise for the Navy's nuclear ships. He said that the programs instituted by Admiral Rickover were still in effect today, and that the result is ships in top-notch condition, excellently maintained. He mentioned that the Rickover programs developed a coterie of engineers highly trained and experienced in the operation of the nuclear Navy; while during the same period, the Naval Academy has produced fewer and fewer qualified engineers.

5. Admiral Bulkeley said that if he were in charge of the Navy today, he would explain to Congress the poor materiel condition of naval ships, and ask for the funding to fix them; he would cut out all unnecessary regulations and directives; he would fire those officers who, for their own benefit, do not

---

126 Bureau of Inspection and Survey (INSURV) inspects ships and reports on their readiness.

follow orders and regulations; and he would get rid of the "people programs" that have nothing to do with the Navy.

6. Admiral Rickover asked Admiral Bulkeley to talk with Dr. Duncan, Naval Reactors historian, on this subject. Admiral Bulkeley agreed to do so.

8 December 1983

Telephone conversation with Jody Powell127 re his article in The Washington Post *(12 November 1983, "Education Crisis? Blame the Parents")*

R: The problem is that neither the parents nor their children know that the children have a stake in the marriage, that the dissolution of the marriage may have an adverse effect on the children's academic performance.

P: I freely admit that possibility.

R: The press is more to blame for this than anything else. The newspapers are filled with nonsense: sports, television, comics. This wastes the parents' time.

P: I think probably if I had to finger something in the media, it would be more the role of television. Have you read the book, "The Death of Childhood"?

R: No, but I am sure the point of that book is to show that television is not good for children. I agree, but the large networks are not going to stop showing programs. Too much money is at stake. And any legal controls enacted would be viewed as censorship.

P. Still, parents do not have to use television as a babysitter.

---

127 Jody Powell (1943–2009), former Press Secretary to President Carter.

R. Agreed. Why are parents more interested in entertainment than in their own children's welfare? That is the real question to ask.

P. I don't address that point in my article.

R: Part of the problem is that it is too easy to make a living today—even if one doesn't work. The newspapers foster the idea that increased leisure time is the ultimate end, the supreme value. That idea is false and destructive. The newspapers should recognize this and impose some kind of self-restriction.

P: I think the "feel good" generation has died out to some extent.

R: On average, parents are not very bright. Take those in Washington. Consequently, their children in particular should get the best education. But the newspapers spread the concept of the good life as the goal.

P: I agree to some extent. As a society, we get the press and media we deserve. The same goes for politicians.

R: That is easy to say. The first thing that must be done is to teach children that their first responsibility will be to their own children. This is particularly true with black people.

P: I think black people are becoming more and more aware of this problem.

R: I am surprised. The black leaders have made out, representing a silent group. The first thing the Jewish leaders did was look out for the education of Jewish children. But the blacks are not doing the same thing. The vocal and powerful blacks are simply using their position to help themselves.

As an engineer, I learned that to solve problems, one must first face the truth. A machine can't be "flattered" into working. The first thing the blacks should do is educate their people. How do you change the black leadership?

P: I don't know.

R: Then all of your articles will be pointless.

P. I am not sure this problem is subject to solution by political means.

R: The blacks don't even read the newspapers. Say that we are the two top people in the United States, recognizing that today's largest minority, the black people, will eventually be homogenized into the American culture. What do we do to make them a valuable asset for our society? Considering the evidence of history that individual races in a society eventually meld into one race, it is foolish to permit the continuing undereducation of the black people.

Black people are being duped into believing that they are equal to whites. They are not, and they should strive to become equal.

P: To the extent that laws can do so, we have made them equal.

R: Political equality is not intellectual equality. The development of the intellect depends on the individual. Giving a horse the right to be led to water does not mean that it will be led to water, or that it will drink.

We must get the black leaders to face the truth. If they can't accept the truth, they should get out of the job. When I tried several years ago to talk to black leaders about this problem, they wouldn't listen. They weren't willing to try...

P: I think the interest in this problem is growing. I don't know whether it is due to harder times, more maturity, or what.

R: A similar situation existed in Europe. Yet you can't find a sense of nationalism in the blacks. One is regrettably drawn to the conclusion that they are inferior.

P: There is an "extended family" among the blacks. Families sacrificing everything to send children to college. In the last 10–20 years, though, that attitude has been looked down upon. It was considered old-fashioned, Uncle-Tommish.

R: If the president put me in charge of solving this problem, I would get a few of the top, influential blacks together and try to discuss this issue. Discuss it with the true leaders, not the politicians. Realistically, though, I don't think such a discussion is possible. The blacks will think they are being patronized. So, what do you do?

P: The nucleus must be relatively small. I know of four or five black leaders that would participate in such a discussion.

R: Why don't you get them together, and we will talk to them.

P: Incidentally, Governor Babbitt of Arizona said I had cited a real problem, and that he was trying to deal with it in Arizona.

R: Black people represent 11% of the population. We must not ignore them. We cannot afford it. Why is it that we only had two blacks in the Navy nuclear program? All candidates were given the same chance; the blacks just couldn't do the job…

You and I have no axe to grind in this. We don't want to make a name for ourselves, or establish a power base. But since the black people will be an important part of our society, we should strive to help them improve themselves. Is this a worthwhile project?

P: Yes. Let me see what I can come up with.

20 December 1983

Telephone conversation with Mr. Mark Urman, Director of Publicity, Triumph Films, re technical authenticity of the German film Das Boot

1. Admiral Rickover explained to Mr. Urman that while *Das Boot* told a good story from a romantic standpoint, its depiction of the crew shouting orders and screaming during attack was inaccurate and misinformed the general public. The admiral said the attack scenes should have been depicted as they would be in an actual attack: i.e., with calm, quiet, and order prevailing. The admiral noted that no motion picture company wants to misinform the public.
2. Mr. Urman, agreeing that films should not misinform the public, said that he understood the admiral's point and that he would pass the admiral's comments on to the president of Triumph Films.

20 December 1983

Telephone conversation with VADM Nils R. Thunman, Deputy Chief of Naval Operations, Submarine Warfare, re technical authenticity of the German Film, "Das Boot"

Rickover: I recently saw the film, *Das Boot*. What did you think of it?

Thunman: It was good, but I felt the yelling and screaming during the attack sequences was not accurate.

R: I agree. I talked to the producer. He said he had advisers, but I don't know anyone who would advise him to put in yelling and screaming. I think this film has done a great deal of harm, because this is probably all the general public will ever know about submarine warfare. Between 80 and 100 million people have come away with this misconception. You should have your people put something in the newspapers to show that the film is not accurate.

T: The Pentagon correspondent is aboard one of our submarines now, with cameras. His report will be televised. He could address this issue in the report.

R: Have him talk to me. I am out of the Navy now. I will tell him the truth. I will tell him the film is no good, not because they have shown submarines in a bad light, but because they have created the wrong impression. How is everything else going?

T: I will soon be giving a program review of our new-design submarine.

R: What are the basic improvements in your design?

T: I can't discuss much of this information over the telephone, but the new design has better quieting, fire power, and combat systems performance.

R: How do you get the improved quieting?

T: The Improved Performance Machinery Program you advocated for years has been incorporated in this design. One of the benefits is improved quieting.

R: Have you read my translation of Admiral Bauer's[128] book, "The Submarine"? I translated the book when I was a lieutenant; that's how I learned German.

T: I am reading it now. I am quite impressed with it.

5 January 1984

Telephone conversation with Tony Kornheiser, reporter for The Washington Post, *regarding an article "Larry Speakes Speaketh His Mind"*

1. The admiral read the first sentence of Mr. Kornheiser's article. "A December frost has left a thin, sugar-cookie glaze on the White House lawn." Then the admiral asked is that the way they teach you to write at Journalist school, or are you paid by the number of words you use in an article? "Who cares about that stuff? Why don't you get to the subject and not waste my time reading crap like that?" "Obviously, you don't," was Mr. Kornheiser's response. Mr. Kornheiser further stated that he approached the story as a human-interest story not a news story and to cast the guy as always wanting the job.

2. The admiral told Mr. Kornheiser that while he was in charge of technical programs for training in the Navy, he would tell his people to get to the subject and knock off that crap. Also, the admiral stated if an average intelligent person would begin to read his article, he would not finish it because it would be wasting his time. Mr. Kornheiser's reply was, "Different courses for different horses, and that is the way I write." Mr.

---

128 Admiral Hermann Bauer (1875–1958). His book, "The Submarine: Its Importance as part of a Fleet, its Position in International Law, its Employment in War, its Future," was published in 1936.

Kornheiser concluded the conversation with an appreciation for the admiral's comments.

11 January 1984

Telephone conversation with President Jimmy Carter this date

1. The admiral called President Carter to say hello and to see how he was doing. President Carter said he was doing fine, and he had just returned from bird hunting. The admiral asked why he hunted birds if he wasn't going to eat them. President Carter replied that he liked hunting because it was an opportunity to get outdoors, train his dogs, and do some horseback riding. He also stated that he was, indeed, going to eat the birds.

2. The reason for the admiral's call was to give his impressions of the current Administration. The admiral believes that President Reagan is nothing but a public relations man. He has no ideas of his own, and he will leave no mark when he is gone. Meese is the real President. The admiral also stated that President Reagan would not have been accepted into the Naval Nuclear Power Program. President Carter agreed with the admiral and expressed a concern over Reagan's domestic, foreign, and defense policies. Due to Reagan's television image, there is the misconception that he has the public's support. President Reagan has read his philosophies from 3x5 cards for the past 30 years, and now he believes them.

3. The admiral ended the conversation by stating President Carter had done a great job as President, and he could be proud of what he did with no regrets. The admiral also said President Carter had done the best he could. After all, he is only human. President Carter thanked the admiral for calling and for having such a high opinion of President Carter and his accomplishments.

13 February 1984

Discussion with Dr. Duncan on "The Weekly Reader"

1. I was informed that Admiral McKee ordered destroyed the 30 or so articles which I had prepared ahead of time to be forwarded to members of Naval Reactors and copies which were sent to all nuclear ships and stations throughout the world. The articles had become known as "The Weekly Reader."
2. I have been told by the engineers and their wives how much they valued these articles because they covered all sorts of items, from engineering to philosophy. However, Admiral McKee, who received copies of "The Weekly Reader" while in the nuclear program, never complained. As soon as Admiral McKee took over, he was asked how many were available and had them all destroyed. Since that time, a number of engineers and their wives have called me to ask why Naval Reactors no longer publishes the articles. I advised them to ask Admiral McKee.
3. In thinking this issue over, the best expression I can use to describe his action is "cultural vandalism."

21 February 1984

Telephone conversation with Canon Charles Martin (Headmaster Emeritus, St. Alban's School)

History shows that human beings have always fought wars. Just as Nature, with her destructive storms, volcanos, and earthquakes, cannot be controlled by man, neither can man control human nature. We have learned to live with Nature and her whims; we must learn to live with human nature as well.

But people go to church every Sunday or Saturday or Thursday (whatever day their particular persuasions mandate), get their tickets punched, and then go about their business. Nothing changes.

12 March 1984

Telephone conversation with President Carter regarding prayer in schools

Admiral Rickover called President Carter at 11:00 AM, Monday, 12 March 1984, to ask him his opinion of President Reagan's political move regarding prayer in schools. The admiral said that he is very distressed over this disgraceful use of political office for personal gain.

President Carter agreed, adding that this President has done several things that no other President would try to do, and gotten away with it, and that this President has gotten more publicity than any other President.

The admiral asked President Carter what he thought Reagan was trying to do with this issue. President Carter said that what President Reagan was trying to do was to get the support of the "TV Evangelists," who are very influential throughout the country. The admiral said that they appeared to be more influential in the South. President Carter said that they were very influential throughout the country, and added that the Southern Baptist leaders were very much opposed to the issue.

The admiral asked President Carter if he thought this was helping Regan in his bid for reelection. President Carter expressed his thought that this was not hurting Reagan at all; it could well turn out to be very beneficial.

The admiral asked President Carter if he thought the Democrats were going to do anything about this and when. President Carter said that they would probably wait until the General Election before attacking this position. The admiral said that that would be too late;

they should be doing something about it now. President Carter agreed.

The admiral, again, said how terrible it was to have a President trying to involve politics and religion. He said that as an immigrant and educator, he is appalled. He asked President Carter if it would do any good for President Carter to take a stand and opposed this issue in public. President Carter told the admiral that he was in Washington about three weeks ago, and he had interviews with the wire services where he expressed his opinion on the issue of prayer in schools, but it was more important that he not be involved in a possible conflict between the current Administration and himself.

The admiral agreed and asked President Carter what he thought the admiral could do. President Carter said that the admiral may be able to take a stand against this issue: "more people listen to you than listen to me." He added that President Nixon would never have done something like this.

The admiral agreed and said he may call President Nixon to get his opinion. The admiral asked President Carter if he could repeat this conversation and President Carter's views if President Nixon asked. President Carter said absolutely.

20 March 1984

> *Telephone conversation this date with Vice Admiral William Lawrence,[129] Chief of Naval Personnel regarding enlisted performance evaluations*

1. Admiral Rickover noted that the records of enlisted personnel sent to him for interview are worthless because the performance marks are inflated. He said that in reading an enlisted man's record, one gets the impression from the evaluations that the man could do the CNO's job easily.

---

129 Vice Admiral William Lawrence (1930–2005), U.S. Naval Academy Class of 1951.

This makes it impossible to determine what the man's actual qualifications and character traits are.

2. Vice Admiral Lawrence agreed with Admiral Rickover, saying that the present system is harmful both to senior officers and to those enlisted men who truly are outstanding. Vice Admiral Lawrence said that there was much to be done to improve the present system, and that he and his people were working to do so.

3. Admiral Rickover said that the inflation of performance evaluations has been a practice of long standing, and that he did not blame Vice Admiral Lawrence for the present state of affairs.

4 April 1984

Telephone conversation with Congressman Samuel S. Stratton (D-NY), Member of the Committee on Armed Services, regarding Trident II Missile (conversation was conducted at the Rickover Foundation)

1. Congressman Stratton stated that for two days he has been listening to testimony by Admiral Grant and Mr. Schwiller concerning the Trident Submarine Missile II. From the testimony the congressman has learned the following: $42 billion have already been spent for research, development, and production to outfit the submarines; the B5 missile will not meet the original 6,000-mile range requirement without degrading the warhead; the Trident II has only a 4,000-mile range, which is the same as the Trident I; and that the Navy had never had specification for the mileage range of the missiles. The Congressman said that he cannot see why Congress should spend all the money on Trident II when it does not meet the original range specifications and

reminded them that the admiral had stated 6,000 miles in previous testimony.

2. The admiral stated that he was responsible only for the propulsion plant, but that he would speak to those responsible and get back to him...

9 April 1984

Telephone conversation with Admiral James D. Watkins, U.S. Navy Chief of Naval Operations, on 7 April, regarding Public Interest in the U.S. Navy

1. Admiral Rickover informed Admiral Watkins that he gave a speech on 5 April before the Oakton Community College. Invariably, after I deliver my speech, I am asked questions. In all cases, many of the questions are about the U.S. Navy. I find that the audience is always interested in the Navy, and it appears that they do not have much information on the subject. I take great pain and much time in answering their questions. My replies always stress the importance of the Navy for national defense and why we must support it. The responses are always favorable to the Navy.

2. The complaint is that the Navy does not seem to be telling the public of the importance of the Navy and what the Navy should do. Here we have CHINFO, a large organization, whose primary function is to advise our citizens why we should have a Navy and what the Navy should be doing. I am not sure what propaganda is putting out, but it is not getting to our citizens. Therefore, I suggest that you look into this matter because it is a great opportunity for advertising.

3. Also told Admiral Watkins that I am probably the best advertiser the Navy has, but the Navy appears that it does not desire that I become involved in its affairs. The Navy would

be surprised at the respect and attention I receive when I speak to audiences.

4. Hereafter when I am asked questions about the Navy, I shall reply that the Chief of Naval Operations, the senior naval officer, has not in the past nor does he now desire to talk with me. So, if any questions are directed to me about the Navy, they will be directed to your office.

5. Admiral Watkins stated that he would look into it.

12 April 1984

Telephone conversation with Dorothy Gilliam, reporter, The Washington Post, *regarding "the betterment of black education"*

1. The admiral called Ms. Gilliam to comment on her article in today's *Post* on blacks in television. He said he had inferred from the article that she was saying not enough black people appear on television, and asked if his inference was correct.

2. Ms. Gilliam said his inference was correct, and that she felt more blacks should appear on television, the primary means of communication in this country, because ours is a diverse society that should be reflected on television.

3. The admiral asked if black people were superior to white people, would they not get the jobs. Ms. Gilliam responded that superior black candidates would not necessarily get the jobs, because many times the people doing the hiring are not familiar with black people personally, and so are subject to the prevailing prejudices.

4. The admiral said it was his experience that there were virtually no black people qualified to work in the Naval Nuclear Propulsion Program. He said they had searched and searched, but could find only two black engineers qualified for the program—and the work of these two was inferior to that of their white counterparts.

5. Ms. Gilliam responded that she, too, as a young black reporter, had continually heard editors say that they could find no qualified black journalists. She said she had banded together with other black journalists and subsequently found hundreds of black people qualified for journalism work.

6. The admiral said that if the black journalists had been superior to the white, they would have been hired. Ms. Gilliam said she was referring not to superiority, but to equality of qualifications.

7. The admiral said he had spent considerable time and effort in trying to improve the education of black people in Washington, DC, but could get no support from black leaders. This led him to realize that black leaders today are not interested in helping their people so much as they are interested in helping themselves. Ms. Gilliam asked if the admiral would be willing to go on the record with that statement. The admiral declined, saying he was only interested in giving Ms. Gilliam a lead: she should investigate why black schools are so poor, and what those few blacks who are hired (by virtue of racial quotas) are doing for their people. The admiral said he believed those blacks who do get ahead are interested only in strengthening their own positions. He said that Booker T. Washington was probably the last black leader to work unselfishly for his race, understanding politics and getting the support of Roosevelt.

8. Ms. Gilliam said she felt that Jesse Jackson was furthering the cause of his people, because he has induced and encouraged a great number of black people to register to vote. The admiral agreed this was an accomplishment, but felt that Jesse Jackson was primarily looking out for Jesse Jackson.

9. Ms. Gilliam again said she would like to write an article on the admiral's experience in trying to improve black education. The admiral stated he would not permit the use of his name in such an article, but that Ms. Gilliam could say "a well-known expert" had spoken to her on this issue.

10. Ms. Gilliam thanked the admiral for calling, and said she would take up the cause of improving black education.

24 April 1984

Telephone conversation with Mr. Howard Simon, Managing Editor, The Washington Post

1. Mr. Howard Simon signed a contract with a division of Random House publishing company to write a book. The book will be titled "Jewish Times," and it will be an oral history of the Jewish people in America. Mr. Simon requested an interview with the admiral.
2. The admiral refused, stating that he is a private person and that he does not like to brag. The admiral apologized saying he did not want to be pitied or have people think that he was mistreated or suffered for being Jewish. Mr. Simon understood the admiral's refusal.
3. The admiral recommended that Mr. Simon contact Mr. Leonard Kaplin,[130] a graduate of the Naval Academy in 1922.

30 April 1984

Telephone conversation between Admiral Rickover and Dr. Dean C. Allard, Naval Historical Center and instructor at Georgetown University

1. Admiral Rickover called Dr. Allard and asked if it is being taught at the university level that the USS MAINE was destroyed by internal explosion.

---

130 Captain Leonard Kaplin died a month after this letter was written. He was a Jewish-American who endured anti-Semitic slurs and graduated second in his Naval Academy class. His yearbook photo was perforated to ease its removal. The yearbook's editor was Kaplin's rival and was later reprimanded for the incident.

2. Dr. Allard states that he only teaches the Spanish-American War once a year at Georgetown University and that
   he uses Admiral Rickover's book as a reference. As far as
   he is concerned, the admiral's book is fact, and his point of
   view is the MAINE was definitely destroyed by an internal
   explosion.

3. The reason as to why this is not taught throughout the educational system is because of lag time. Not all historians are
   aware of the admiral's book, which points to a low-level
   exchange of information and inefficiency in the profession.
   Many historians are very slow to change their presenta-
   tions because of traditionalism. Dr. Allard concluded the
   conversation by stating that in time, more historians will
   use his book as a reference and that he cannot excuse his
   profession.

3 May 1984

*Telephone conversation between Admiral Rickover and Mr.
Richard F. Kaufman*[131]

Admiral Rickover asked Mr. Kaufman how the investigation
against General Dynamics was going. Mr. Kaufman said that the
investigation was going slow, and what he is trying to do now
was to contact people for interviews. The admiral asked who he
was trying to get in touch with. Mr. Kaufman replied, Mr. Joe
Pierce. The admiral asked Mr. Kaufman if he thought it would
help if he would talk to Mr. Pierce and convince him to discuss
General Dynamics with Mr. Kaufman. Mr. Kaufman said yes, and
the reason he wanted to talk to Mr. Pierce was about how he was
forced out as manager of Electric Boat because he disagreed with
General Dynamics' policies.

---

131 General Counsel of the Joint Economic Committee.

4 May 1984

Telephone conversation with Congressman Sidney R. Yates[132] of Illinois

Admiral Rickover said that he held much good will for the congressman. Congressman Yates thank the admiral and told him that his new district consisted of 900,000 constituents. The admiral said that he believed the reason for the congressman's popularity was his honesty and the fact that his people did not think he was serving his own interests. Congressman Yates thanked the admiral for his call. The admiral reminded the congressman of his support for him.

May 8, 1978

Letter from Richard Nixon [handwritten]

Dear Admiral,

I appreciated your letter of April 28 and will read your book on the "Maine" with great interest.

It was a pleasure to talk to Mr. Duncan. I hope gets across the point that the State Department bureaucrats raised hell because they thought you had been too tough on the Russians when they tried give you a "snow job" when you insisted on inspecting the "Lenin"! It was one of the best decisions I made on the trip, and I am glad you were there to do the job that needed to be done.

Keep fighting!

---

132 Sidney Yates (1909-2000), Member of Congress 1945-1963 and 1965-1999.

9 May 1984

Telephone conversation with Mr. Richard Kaufman, Assistant Director and General Counsel Joint Economic Committee, re— Pork barreling/adding on to the military budget

1. Admiral Rickover stated that he thought there should be a law prohibiting Congress from adding items on to the military budget that the services do not ask for. Mr. Kaufman stated that the constitution gives Congress certain powers and that it would not be feasible to take these powers away from Congress and allow the president to keep his powers.
2. Mr. Kaufman told the admiral that in his opinion, the fundamental problem lies with over-pricing on government contracts; i.e., shipbuilding.
3. The admiral asked Mr. Kauman about the Veliotis investigation. Mr. Kaufman said that the Justice Department was talking with Veliotis now. Mr. Kaufman also stated that Senator Proxmire wants to start hearings on this matter and that the admiral should consider testifying before these hearings. The admiral agreed.
4. Mr. Kaufman asked if the admiral thought Dave Leighton would help staff the hearings. The admiral said that he would talk to Mr. Leighton about it.

11 May 1984

Telephone conversation with Mr. Payne, reporter for the McGraw-Hill Publications

1. Mr. Payne asked the admiral if he could ask a few questions about General Dynamics and Mr. Veliotis. The admiral stated he could ask all the questions he wanted, but it does not mean he will answer them.

2. Mr. Payne asked the admiral if he was asked to testify before the grand jury investigation of General Dynamics between 1979 and 1981. The admiral did not think so but reminded Mr. Payne that everything he has said or written on General Dynamics has been made public. The admiral also stated that he has not been involved for awhile, and his memory was not as accurate as it used to be. The admiral stated that he would provide Mr. Payne a copy of his testimony before the Joint Economic Committee.

3. The admiral informed Mr. Payne that he would have to find the facts of this story himself because he was not going to write the story for him. The admiral suggested that he should ask the following question: "Why didn't my superiors do something about it when they were told about it?" The admiral believed that Mr. Hidalgo may also be involved. The admiral stated that Mr. Hidalgo is now a consultant for General Dynamics and told Mr. Payne that he should look into that because it could be a "pay-off."

4. The admiral also suggested that he should look into the fact that Veliotis was a member of the board. "How could it be that other board members did not know that Veliotis was up to something illegal?" The admiral told Mr. Payne that he did not want to be quoted because he did not want to be brought into this. Mr. Payne agreed. The admiral also suggested that Mr. Payne look into Mr. Lewis' involvement.

5. The admiral stated that Mr. Payne continue his investigation into the story to its conclusion and recommended that he contact Mr. Kaufman of Senator Proxmire's staff. The admiral concluded the conversation by stating a report could make a name for himself because he believed this issue was bigger than the Teapot Dome scandal. Mr. Payne thanked the admiral for his suggestion and asked if he could quote the admiral in comparing the shipbuilding claim issue to the Teapot Dome scandal. The admiral agreed.

30 May 1984

Telephone conversation with Mr. Jack Anderson,[133] Columnist

Mr. Anderson called Admiral Rickover to solicit Admiral Rickover's support in saving government spending and money. Mr. Anderson said that he has talked with Mr. Peter Grace (Grace Commission) and Mr. William Proxmire and Mr. Bill Simon (Former Treasury Secretary and now head of our Olympic Committee). Mr. Anderson would like Admiral Rickover to join forces with him to reduce government spending. Admiral Rickover stated that he has been trying to do this all his life but has been unsuccessful in reducing government spending. Admiral Rickover has especially tried to put integrity into the shipbuilders but has been unsuccessful in this attempt. Admiral Rickover stated that there are far too many government employees. Admiral Rickover stated that instead of joining a special board, that Admiral Rickover would pass comments on along to Mr. Anderson for Mr. Anderson's personal use. Admiral Rickover stated that each government agency should only be allotted a certain amount of money, and each agency should make do with what they receive. Mr. Anderson agreed with the admiral. Mr. Anderson asked the admiral if he would be able to attend various meetings of the Board. Admiral Rickover stated that he would be willing to talk to the members of the board if the board would like to hear his comments. Mr. Anderson stated that he would get back in touch with Admiral Rickover concerning the status of the board.

25 July 1984

Telephone conversation with Mr. Jack Anderson, syndicated editorialist, in reference to Mr. Anderson's article in The Washington Post *on 25 June 1984 "Defense Firm's Shipbuilding Claims Probed"*

---

133 Jack Anderson (1922–2005), investigative journalist.

1. The admiral called Mr. Anderson complimenting him on a fine article on defense claims. The admiral felt that he did not believe it will do any good because the American public have accepted it, and the public is living well.
2. The admiral told Mr. Anderson that his editorials are the conscience of the country. The admiral compared Mr. Anderson's article to sermons. People have to go to church every week to be reminded. If Mr. Anderson prints an article on one subject, the people will read it and forget it. But if Mr. Anderson wrote several articles on the same subject, the message would eventually get through. The admiral believes that Mr. Anderson should hammer on one issue, devote himself to that one issue, instead of 365 different issues.
3. Mr. Anderson agreed with the admiral and promised that he would stick to the General Dynamics story.

13 July 1984

Telephone conversation with Mr. Clayton R. Barrow, Editor-in-Chief, Proceedings

Admiral Rickover told Mr. Barrow that the article on leadership [in the latest issue of Naval Institute *Proceedings*] is bullshit and nonsense. How did Mr. Barrow expect a Lieutenant to talk intelligently about leadership? Admiral Rickover told Mr. Barrow that the only way he learned was by learning his job. Admiral Rickover told Mr. Barrow that the Naval Institute used to write about historical items and now they are not. The admiral wanted to know why that changed. Mr. Barrow did not know. Admiral Rickover told Mr. Barrow that he used to send out articles to his people and that at the time Admiral Rickover was relieved, he had 38 prepared articles, good articles. Admiral Rickover told Mr. Barrow that his predecessor destroyed the articles. Mr. Barrow told Admiral Rickover that Admiral Moreau asked him (about the Naval Institute). Mr. Barrow said that he was writing this conversation down and he wanted to send it to Admiral Rickover, and if Admiral Rickover agreed with the article, Mr. Barrow would like to print it in the next edition of Naval Institute [Proceedings] Admiral Rickover said that this was fine.

12 September 1984

> *Letter from Captain James Barber, Publisher, U.S. Naval Institute* Proceedings

I very much enjoyed our conversation of yesterday, and have attempted to put what I understood to be your principal points into a Memorandum for the Record, a copy of which is enclosed. Unless you have an objection, I intend to present your thoughts to the meeting of the Editorial Board now scheduled for Thursday, 27 September.

Your continuing interest in the Navy and Naval Institute is very much appreciated, and your counsel is valued highly.

> *Memorandum for the Record*

The Secretary-Treasurer received a call from Admiral Rickover on Tuesday, 11 September. The admiral said that he had some comments to offer, emphasizing that his intention was to be helpful, not destructive....

1. Naval officers have stopped writing about professional naval matters.
2. *Proceedings* consists principally of anecdotes and B.S. with little professional content.
3. There is no need for a large monthly magazine filled with ads.
4. An analysis should be made of *Proceedings* for the last 15 years to see what, if anything, it has contributed to the Navy.

5. A survey of members should be conducted to determine what impact *Proceedings* has had on their professional careers.

6. If there has been no significant impact, then *Proceedings* serves no useful purpose...

10. The principal question to be asked is this: What good does the USNI do?

11. If publication of *Proceedings* ceased for 2 years, what would the impact be?...

16 October 1984

Letter to CBS "60 Minutes"

Gentlemen,

Recently Miss Diane Sawyer interviewed me for an article to be aired in December. Pursuant to my taped conversation with Miss Sawyer, I made a comment that I would like to rescind. I would also like to be put on the record officially as having notified you by this letter.

The comment, "I would sink all of them," referring to ships, was a casual and jovial remark which I made during the interview. This was a spontaneous and jovial remark and is not my official or personal feeling. As you are aware, I did not ask for or receive any compensation from this interview. I agreed to do this interview to let the public know of some events during my long tour of duty in the U.S. Navy.

Subsequently, I realized that this comment may be misconstrued by the public and that I actually meant to sink these ships.

Please advise me as soon as possible of the action you will take to correct this matter.

17 October 1984

Remarks at Center for Defense Information, New York

Peace Requires Strength

Many in our country today appear to believe that our military is an institution apart from American society—an institution that can be readily dispensed.

There is also a tendency to assume that the Soviets will refrain from employing their military strength. But one need only read the history of the Punic Wars to see what can happen to second-rate military nations in the realm of power politics. The Carthaginians, not wishing to be burdened financially with a first-class army, let that army decay. Shortly thereafter, they became the recipients of a series of ultimatums from the Romans. They gave in to these demands, until they could yield no further, then they had to fight.

The results of the Punic Wars are well known. Rome solved all the problems of the Carthaginian inner city, its ecology, and its starving population. But not in the way the Carthaginians would have liked. The people were killed or carried off as slaves; the city razed the fields sown with salt...

18 October 1984

Memorandum for the Record.

Admiral Rickover talked with Diane Sawyer. The admiral was assured by Diane Sawyer that the admiral's statement...would be removed/rescinded from the tapes of the admiral's interview. (Done at suggestion of a general lawyer at the Federal Communications Commission.)

Note: Admiral Rickover directed Chief Bishop to make a note that a legal contract will be drawn up giving the admiral reviewal rights to delete, add, or change any statement made during any such interview, with any such television company, or with any such magazine in the future.

30 October 1984

Memorandum for the Record
Subj: Telephone conversation between Admiral Rickover and Dr. Duncan regarding contract agreement for biography

1. Admiral Rickover is disturbed regarding the contract agreement between the admiral and Dr. Duncan. Admiral Rickover stated to Dr. Duncan that the agreement must be amended to reflect that the admiral will have absolute veto of any material in the book.
2. Dr. Duncan became upset with this statement of the admiral. Dr. Duncan then stated that it would be best for him to stop writing the personal biography. Conversation ended at this point.

30 October 1984

1. Admiral Rickover telephoned Mr. Ira Siegler, Admiral Rickover's attorney. Admiral Rickover stated to Mr. Siegler what Dr. Duncan had said—stop writing the personal biography.
2. Mr. Siegler recommended to the admiral to let the tension with Dr. Duncan rest for a few days. The admiral agreed, and the conversation ended.

5 November 1984 (2:30 PM)

Telephone conversation between Admiral Rickover and Mr. Truxall, Deputy Director, Naval Investigative Service

1. Mr. Truxall telephoned Admiral Rickover this morning. Mr. Truxall requested an interview with Admiral Rickover to discuss allegations made against Admiral Rickover in receiving gifts while associated with the submarine program.
2. The interview was scheduled for 1000, 7 November 1984. Admiral Rickover agreed to the interview, and the interview was to be conducted in the admiral's office. Admiral Rickover desired to have counsel present during the interview. Mr. Truxall said that would be fine.

5 November 1984 (2:45 PM)

Admiral Rickover telephoned Ms. Joann DiGennaro[134] and requested that she be present as counsel during the interview with the Naval Investigative Service. Ms. Joann DiGennaro agreed.

6 November 1984 (9:30 AM)

1. Admiral Rickover telephoned Mr. Truxall this morning to discuss the interview to be conducted on 7 November. Admiral Rickover asked Mr. Truxall two questions:
   a. Why am I being investigated?
   b. Who is my accuser?
2. Mr. Truxall responded that the Naval Investigative Service was responding to the direction of the Vice Chief of Naval Operations to conduct the interview. Mr. Truxall went on to say that no individual or party was the admiral's accuser.

---

134 DiGennaro was the individual who first suggested to Admiral Rickover that an educational foundation be established in his name and would serve as its head.

The investigation started with press coverage in various newspapers concerning the admiral's gift receiving. Mr. Truxall stated that he was aware of Admiral Rickover's previous statements admitting to receiving gifts, however, Mr. Truxall desired to interview the admiral in person.

6 November 1984 (9:45 AM)

[Call to Admiral Hays, Vice Chief of Naval Operations, with same two questions]

Admiral Hays restated what Mr. Truxall had told the admiral. Admiral Rickover stated that since he had already admitted to receiving the gifts, there was no need for an interview with the Naval Investigative Service.

6 November 1984 (10:15 AM)

Admiral Rickover telephoned Mr. Truxall, Deputy Director, Naval Investigative Service, and cancelled the interview for 7 November 1984.

6 November 1984 (11:00 AM)

Admiral Rickover telephoned Ms. Joann DiGennaro to inform her that the interview had been cancelled. Ms. DiGennaro felt that the admiral should do the interview and that the Navy was only trying to protect the admiral and that the Navy just wanted to get the whole matter of "gifts" closed. Admiral Rickover stated that the interview was still cancelled.

5 December 1984 (2:05 PM)

Telephone conversation with Mr. Foster

1. Admiral Rickover telephoned Mr. Foster to thank him for sending a copy of the Press Conference conducted by Secretary of the Navy Lehman.

2. Admiral Rickover discussed the press conference with Mr. Foster. Admiral Rickover said that he was mad about some of the things Secretary Lehman had said, especially about cleaning up the mess with Electric Boat by getting rid of Admiral Rickover and Veliotis. Admiral Rickover said that he was going to telephone Secretary Lehman and ask the secretary what Admiral Rickover had done wrong to warrant the firing. Mr. Foster advised Admiral Rickover that telephoning Secretary Lehman would be the wrong thing to do because of all the recent press coverage regarding the admiral receiving gifts from General Dynamics. Admiral Rickover agreed that telephoning Secretary Lehman would be the wrong thing to do and that the admiral has made up his mind not to say anything to anyone.

3. Admiral Rickover thanked Mr. Foster for his support and candid advice.

6 December 1984

Telephone conversation between Admiral Rickover and Mr. Mel Laird, at 1:45 PM this date

1. Mr. Laird phoned the admiral to express interest in watching the CBS program "60 Minutes" this Sunday. He commented that it would be a "tribute to the admiral." The admiral stated that the program will probably show him in a bad light because of all the recent publicity surrounding General Dynamics; i.e., Veliotis, alleged gifts.

2. Mr. Laird said the Navy should be ashamed of the way they have been treating the admiral in this matter. Mr. Laird spoke with the secretary of the Navy last week and told the

secretary of the Navy they were all nuts in what they were doing to the admiral.

3. The admiral told Mr. Laird that he first started receiving money for speeches and books in 1934. Since that time, all money was given to charities. Mr. Laird told the admiral that he was well aware of the admiral's actions. Mr. Laird respects the admiral and is fully behind the admiral. Mr. Laird further stated that if he could do anything else for the admiral that it would be a delight to do so.

4. The admiral informed Mr. Laird that he has continued to try and improve the educational system in this country. Admiral Rickover said he would not be getting involved with the press over the General Dynamics situation. Mr. Laird thought that that would be the best way to handle this type of situation.

5. The admiral thanked Mr. Laird for his interest and support in this matter.

12 December 1984

Telephone conversation with Mr. Clayton R. Barrow, Managing Director, Proceedings *at 12:45 PM this date*

1. Admiral Rickover telephoned Mr. Barrow this date to discuss the current supplemental issue of *Proceedings.*

2. The admiral told Mr. Barrow that he could do no better in publishing a magazine like *Proceedings*, but that during the last several years the magazine had nothing of real value for the young naval officers of today. The admiral told Mr. Barrow that he had just finished reading the supplement, and if someone were to ask him what he had gotten out of the magazine, the admiral would have to reply that he had gotten not one single thing out of it. That the admiral could not even remember what was in the magazine.

3. Mr. Barrow thanked the admiral for his constructive criticism that the Institute was out of touch with what was going on in today's Navy.

4. The admiral suggested that the magazine be published with a perforated page so that anyone who read it could mail in suggestions for improvement. The admiral stated that there is a place for the magazine in the Navy of today but that it should be written like it was in the '20s, '30s, and '40s. The admiral said that it was a good magazine back then. The admiral suggested that the magazine be written in a way that would introduce young naval officers into the Navy...

13 December 1984

Telephone conversation with President Jimmy Carter at 12:45 PM this date

1. President Carter phoned Admiral Rickover this date to let the admiral know that the admiral had a friend down in Plains, Georgia.

2. The admiral thanked the president for his friendship. President Carter asked the admiral if there was anything that President Carter could do for the admiral. The admiral asked the president if he would go to the newspapers and tell them what he thought of the current situation with the admiral and General Dynamics. The president told the admiral that he would be delighted to do that. President Carter stated that if any newspaper reporters should call the admiral, that the admiral was to refer them to President Carter.

3. The admiral told the president that history would probably record the admiral as a crook. President Carter stated that the vast majority of the people of this country are well aware of the admiral's contribution to this country. The admiral told the president that there was nothing that he wouldn't

do for this country. The president stated that he was well aware of this, and that the president and Rosalynn were thinking of the admiral and that their heart goes out to him. The admiral again thanked the president.

17 December 1984

Telephone conversation with Mr. Foster at 8:35 AM this date

1. Admiral Rickover telephone Mr. Foster to discuss the article in *The Washington Post* on the USS SCORPION[135] sinking.
2. Admiral Rickover explained that when the SCORPION went down, everyone was blaming it on nuclear power or on Admiral Rickover himself. Mr. Foster said that evidently there was a Board of Inquiry and that they had decided that it was from a torpedo explosion.
3. Admiral Rickover told Mr. Foster that if anything were to happen to a nuclear submarine today, that more than likely Admiral McKee would get the blame. Mr. Foster agreed with this, stating that this type of thing goes with the job.
4. The admiral further stated that contrary to the article stating that Admiral Clary and other senior Navy officials thought at the time it was a torpedo, that everyone back then, including Admiral Clary, blamed it on nuclear power. Mr. Foster agreed with this. He also was around when the Scorpion went down.

18 December 1984

Telephone conversation with Mr. O'Donnell, Associate of Mr. Peter Kahn, Mrs. Rickover's Lawyer, at 10:05 AM this date

---

135 USS Scorpion (SSN-589) lost with all hands on 22 May 1968.

1. Admiral Rickover phoned Mr. Kahn and was told he was out of town (in New York) but that Mr. O'Donnell was in. The admiral asked to speak with Mr. O'Donnell.
2. Admiral Rickover told Mr. O'Donnell that his wife had told her lawyer that Ms. DiGennaro had forced Admiral Rickover to be on a TV show in Chicago and that the admiral had said incriminating things. Mr. O'Donnell said that he did not have any information on this matter and that he would have to speak to Mr. Kahn.

24 December 1984

Telephone conversation between Admiral Rickover and staff member in President Carter's office

1. Admiral Rickover telephoned President Carter's office. President Carter was out of the office. Admiral Rickover left a message for President Carter.

   "The Presidency is the most difficult, professional, and personal office in the world. Not even Jesus Christ, if elected to the Presidency, would find much approval. All great leaders are ahead of their time. This is why it takes time for their deeds to be acknowledged. Also, many Presidents are not famous in their own time, but receive much applause years later when what they did is finally recognized. I wish him and his family the very best. There are no better human beings on this Earth."
2. The staff member Admiral Rickover spoke with assured him the admiral's message would be delivered to President Carter.

15 January 1985

Letter from Richard Nixon

Dear Admiral,

Since a rather severe case of shingles made my 72nd birthday a major media event, I wanted you to know that your thoughtful call helped to make the day a very special one for Pat and for me.

As you can imagine, we have had a lot of inquiries with regard to the state of my health and scores of recommendations as to miracle cures. My doctor tells me that none of them will work but reassures me that while shingles is extremely painful, it is never fatal. Consequently, I expect to be around for a few more birthday celebrations in the future!

[*Handwritten*] Don't let that media criticism bother you!

8 April 1985

Telephone conversation with Mr. Ron Carr, Producer for "Florence Nightingale" TV Mini-series, at 2:10 PM this date

1. Admiral Rickover telephoned Mr. Carr to offer a criticism of the TV Mini-Series "Florence Nightingale." The admiral stated that the music for the show was much too loud, that he was sure it probably ruined the show for a great many people. Admiral Rickover stated that he could not hear what the people were saying. Mr. Carr commented that the music helped set the mood for the show and that this was the standard for the film industry for today's TV shows and films.
2. The admiral made the point that in real life, music did not play when people carry on their daily work, and certainly not during a war. Again Mr. Carr stated that this was the

industry standard for film making. The admiral called Mr. Carr stupid and hung up.

10 May 1985

Telephone conversation with Mr. John Taylor, Assistant to President Nixon

1. Admiral Rickover telephoned President Nixon's office and requested to speak to President Nixon. President Nixon was out of the office and would be for the next two weeks. Mr. John Taylor, Assistant to President Nixon, spoke with Admiral Rickover.
2. Admiral Rickover asked Mr. Taylor to relay Admiral Rickover's comments concerning a recent interview the admiral watched between President Nixon and Ms. Barbara Walters. Admiral Rickover's comments were as follows:
   - President Nixon was great because his sincerity and integrity were apparent.
   - President Nixon's personality came across.
   - President Nixon should do this more often. President Nixon is thought of more highly than he may think so.
   - Admiral stated that he had never seen a President who is as direct when discussing an issue.
   - President Nixon was not treated justly.
3. Mr. Taylor stated that he had received approximately twelve responses to the President Nixon interview but that no response was as eloquently stated as Admiral Rickover's.

17 June 1985

Telephone conversation between Admiral Rickover and Admiral Watkins

1. Admiral Rickover telephoned Admiral Watkins to discuss the recent matter of gratuities.
2. Admiral Rickover stated that Secretary Lehman is a great believer in loyalty up but not down—which is characteristic of a man of his type.
3. Admiral Rickover stated his thanks and appreciation for what Admiral Watkins has said to the press and in Admiral Watkins letter to Congressman Bennett. Admiral Rickover said that he did not want Admiral Watkins to go too far. "It is essential for the good of the Navy that you remain in charge. What happens to me is now inconsequential, and I am too old and mature to be bothered by what is being said about me."
4. Admiral Watkins thanked Admiral Rickover for his telephone call, but Admiral Watkins would say and do what is necessary to preserve the symbol of Admiral Rickover. Admiral Watkins further stated that he would not allow the symbol of Admiral Rickover to be rubbed against the stone.

Undated 1980s

[From Francis Duncan notes]

Duncan: What would you like to be remembered for?

Rickover: I am not interested in being remembered.

Duncan: What would you insert into a capsule to be sent into space so that life elsewhere could understand our civilization? A book? A piece of music? An invention?

Rickover: I don't know. You are asking me how to talk to some entity, which might possibly exist, but of which I do not have the slightest conception. You are talking of things of which science fiction is made. I have found that science is much more interesting than fiction. Rather than thinking about the space capsule, I would rather think about the real problems of science, and engineering, and other fields. And these do not leave me much free time.

Editor Biographies

Claude Berube, PhD is an assistant professor of history at the U.S. Naval Academy and Director of the Museum. He is a former Hill staffer and retired Navy Commander. He also worked for the Office of Naval Research, Naval Sea Systems Command, and the Office of Naval Intelligence. He has written several non-fiction books and three novels.

Samuel Limneos, M.A. is a U.S. Army veteran, naval historian, and government archivist. His work has appeared in *Naval History*, and *The Journal of Military History*.

Disclaimer: The views expressed by the editors are not those of the U.S. Government or any part of the U.S. Navy.

As the collection was still being catalogued when this manuscript was prepared, the items in this work are only available through the date of the letter, memo, or transcript. A catalogue is available through the U.S. Naval Academy's Special Collections and Archives at the Nimitz Library in the Hyman G. Rickover Papers, 1916–2000, which are part of the U.S. Naval Academy Museum Collection.

Acknowledgements

This book would not have been possible without several individuals. Mrs. Eleonore Rickover sought a home for her husband's items and personal papers and we are grateful that she chose the U.S. Naval Academy Museum. By an agreement between the Museum and the Nimitz Library at the Academy, all personal papers were sent to the Special Collections and Archives to be properly catalogued, stored, and made available for researchers. These remain under the ownership of the Museum. For their work at the library, we note the expertise and advice provided by Dean for Information Services and Director of Nimitz Library Larry Clemens, Head of Special Collections and Archives Dr. Jennifer Bryan, and Archivist Adam Minakowski. Thank you especially to Rear Admiral Jay Cohen and Nancy Cohen for their support and encouragement for this work. Thank you also to our publisher, Dr. Stephen Phillips and Focsle LLP for bringing this work to life.